British
Political Finance
1830-1980

AEI'S AT THE POLLS STUDIES

The American Enterprise Institute
has initiated this series in order to promote
an understanding of the electoral process as it functions in
democracies around the world. The series will include studies
of at least two national elections in more than twenty countries
on five continents, by scholars from the United States and
abroad who are recognized as experts in their field.
More information on the titles in this series can
be found at the back of this book.

British
Political Finance
1830-1980

Michael Pinto-Duschinsky

American Enterprise Institute for Public Policy Research
Washington and London

Michael Pinto-Duschinsky is a lecturer in government at Brunel University and executive secretary of the International Political Science Association's research committee on political finance and political corruption.

324.78
P65b
120462
Feb.1982

Library of Congress Cataloging in Publication Data

Pinto-Duschinsky, Michael, 1943–
    British political finance, 1830–1980.

    (AEI studies ; 330)
    Bibliography: p.
    Includes index.
    1. Elections—Great Britain—Campaign funds—History.
2. Political parties—Great Britain—History.
I. Title   II. Series.
JN1039.P56   324.7'8'0941   81-7963
ISBN 0-8447-3451-9   AACR2
ISBN 0-8447-3452-7 (pbk.)

AEI Studies 330

Printed in the United States of America

To David Pinto-Duschinsky

Contents

LIST OF FIGURES

Acknowledgments

This study grew out of a paper presented at the Conference on Political Money held in December 1977 at the University of Southern California under the auspices of the International Political Science Association's Research Committee on Political Finance and Political Corruption. I am much indebted to the organizer, Larry Berg, and to other present and past members of the research committee, particularly Herb Alexander, Arnold Heidenheimer, Dick Leonard, Khayyam Paltiel, Austin Ranney, and Richard Rose.

Howard Penniman, of the American Enterprise Institute, encouraged me to write the book and has been an unfailing source of advice and help, as he has been to so many others. David Honeybone and Shelley Pinto-Duschinsky gave valuable research assistance.

It would not have been possible to write the study without the cooperation of present and former officials of the three national party organizations, who gave unstintingly of their time and expertise and who made available a considerable amount of previously unpublished information: in particular, at Labour party headquarters, John Pittaway, Lord Underhill, Ron Hayward, and members of the party's information office and library; at Conservative Central Office, George Carlyle, David Clarke, Leslie Corp, members of the organization department, and, for help at an earlier stage of research, Geoffrey Block, Stuart Newman, and Brigadier John Melsopp; at the Liberal Party Organisation, Hugh Jones, Dee Doocey, and members of the Liberal publication department, whip's office, and the party's auditors. I am especially indebted to George Carlyle for his insight and support over an extended period.

Among party officers and politicians who gave assistance were Alan Beith, Lord Chelmer, Alistair MacAlpine, Munroe Palmer, Michael Steed, David Steel, Jeremy Thorpe, and Philip Watkins. Useful information was given by Lord Chitnis and Lois Jefferson (Joseph Rowntree Social Service Trust Ltd.), Brenda Kirsch (Labour Research Department), the Certification Office for Trade Unions and Employers' Associations, the Home Office, Granada Television, and

xvii

Tom Cullen. David Butler, John Curtice, J. F. A. Mason, Persi Schroff, Leslie Seidle, William Wallace, and John Ramsden gave valuable academic aid. For help while the book was in preparation, I am grateful to Pennie Bowen, Ken Davis, Ronnie Hooberman, Ella Pembleton, and, at the American Enterprise Institute, Bill Childs, Randa Murphy, and Claudia Winkler.

I am grateful to Brunel University for leave in autumn 1978, and for research support during 1979/1980 from the Nuffield Foundation and the Social Science Research Council of Great Britain.

I am obliged to Paul Medlicott for papers relating to Liberal party finances of his father, Sir Frank Medlicott; to John Ramsden for permission to quote from his D.Phil. thesis, which has since been adapted and published as The Age of Balfour and Baldwin, 1902–1940; to Leslie Seidle for permission to quote from unpublished work; and to the following to quote copyrighted material: Mark Bonham Carter for excerpts from the Asquith Papers; Birmingham University (Special Collections) for the Neville Chamberlain Papers; the Clerk of the Records, House of Lords, for the Davidson Papers; the Beaverbrook Foundation for the Lloyd George Papers; A. D. Maclean for the Maclean Papers; Lord Salisbury for the Salisbury Papers; the Bodleian Library for the Sandars Papers; and Lady Forres for the Woolton Papers. I regret that I have been unable to trace Robert M. Sommer for permission to quote from his unpublished thesis "The Organization of the Liberal Party, 1936–1960" (Ph.D. thesis, London School of Economics, 1962).

In acknowledging the contributions of those who helped in the creation of this book, I realize that not all of them will agree with my judgments or with the facts as they are presented in the following chapters. The responsibility for errors of interpretation or fact is mine alone.

British
Political Finance
1830-1980

Introduction

In Britain, as in several other countries,[1] the existing system of financing party politics has been subjected to increasing criticism. There has been growing pressure for the introduction of cash payments to subsidize the party organizations.[2]

[1] For useful international comparisons, see Arnold J. Heidenheimer, ed., *Comparative Political Finance: The Financing of Party Organizations and Election Campaigns* (Lexington, Mass.: D.C. Heath, 1970); Herbert E. Alexander, ed., *Political Finance* (Beverly Hills, Calif.: Sage Publications, 1979); and Michael J. Malbin, ed., *Parties, Interest Groups, and Campaign Finance Laws* (Washington, D.C.: American Enterprise Institute, 1980). A valuable cross-national survey is Richard Rose and Arnold J. Heidenheimer, eds., "Comparative Political Finance: A Symposium," *Journal of Politics*, vol. 25 (1963). A useful legal survey is United States Library of Congress Law Library, *Government Financing of National Elections, Political Parties, and Campaign Spending in Various Foreign Countries* (Washington, D.C.: Library of Congress, 1979). See also Khayyam Z. Paltiel, "Campaign Finance: Contrasting Practices and Reforms," in David E. Butler, Howard R. Penniman, and Austin Ranney, eds., *Democracy at the Polls: A Comparative Study of Competitive National Elections* (Washington, D.C.: American Enterprise Institute, 1981).

[2] Two particularly influential works have been Richard Rose, *The Problem of Party Government* (New York: Free Press, 1975), and Dick (R. L.) Leonard, *Paying for Party Politics: The Case for Public Subsidies*, vol. 41, Broadsheet no. 555 (London: Political and Economic Planning, 1975). There has been a steady outflow of articles on party finance in the *Economist*. A number have been the work of Leonard, a former Labour MP and an active proponent of state subsidies. The articles, which are unsigned according to the journal's ordinary practice, include: "Who's Going to Pay for the Parties?," April 27, 1974; "Will the State Cough Up?," March 15, 1975; "Paying for Politics," September 13, 1975; and "A Stitch in Time—What Houghton Proposes," August 28, 1976. Party finance was the subject of several articles in an issue of *Political Quarterly* in 1974 (vol. 45). Newspaper articles include Dick (R. L.) Leonard, "Paying for Our Politics," *Observer*, May 13, 1973; John Pardoe, "The Penny-Pinching Which Hurts Democracy," *The Times*, October 13, 1969; John Pardoe, "A Voluntary Tax Plan to Finance Elections," *The Times*, October 14, 1969; John Pardoe, "Why a Fresh Injection of Cash Is Needed to Avoid Political Penny-Pinching," *The Times*, March 20, 1975; David McKie, "Now Is the Time?," *Guardian*, May 23, 1975; Humphry Berkeley, "Extra Money Should Go to MPs instead of the Party," *The Times*, April 21, 1975; and Norman Atkinson, "Priming the Pump," *Guardian*, August 10, 1978. For a useful survey of arguments about public subsidies made in the 1950s and 1960s, see Martin Harrison, "Britain," in Rose and Heidenheimer, "Comparative Political Finance."

In July 1974, shortly after the Labour party's return to office, the deputy Labour leader stated in the House of Commons that he supported the idea that "political parties should have part of their finance provided from public funds."[3] He announced that the Labour government was to appoint an "independent committee"[4] to study the question and to make recommendations about the allocation of the proposed payments. Lord Houghton, a former Labour cabinet minister and former chairman of the Parliamentary Labour party, was chosen as chairman of this Committee on Financial Aid to Political Parties.

In 1976, a majority of the committee (generally referred to as the Houghton Committee)[5] submitted its report, which, not unexpectedly, favored subsidies, although, of a committee of twelve, four argued strongly against their introduction and another member expressed written reservations about aspects of the proposed scheme. Further disagreements continued between and within the political parties. In general, state aid was supported by Labour and Liberal representatives and opposed by the Conservatives. But within the Labour movement itself, the National Union of Mineworkers and the engineers' union (AEUW) opposed subsidies, and the Transport and General Workers Union favored state subventions. On the Conservative side, subsidies were supported by the Confederation of British Industry and opposed by British United Industrialists and by Aims of Industry. Liberals too were divided: the English and Welsh Liberals gave evidence to the Houghton Committee on one side and the Scottish Liberals on the other. The Scottish and Welsh Nationalists and the Communists all gave evidence against state payments.[6]

After publication of the Houghton Report, the Conservatives rejected the proposed subsidies. The Labour party continued its internal discussions about the details of the Houghton scheme. In

---

[3] The statement, made on July 29, 1974, by Edward Short, the leader of the House, is quoted in Leonard, *Paying for Party Politics*, p. 30.

[4] The claim that the Committee on Financial Aid to Political Parties was "independent" of the Labour government was supported by the fact that it included Conservative, Liberal, and Scottish Nationalist representatives. Research has revealed, however, that seven of the twelve members were either actively involved in Labour party politics or held Labour party membership. See F. Leslie D. Seidle, "Electoral Law and the Limitation of Election Expenditure in Great Britain and Canada" (B.Phil. thesis, Oxford University, 1978), p. 75. Moreover, in making appointments to the committee, care appears to have been taken to ensure that a majority of those asked to serve were already disposed to favor state subsidies. See F. Leslie D. Seidle, "State Aid for Political Parties," *Parliamentarian*, vol. 61 (1980), p. 86.

[5] Committee on Financial Aid to Political Parties, *Report*, Cmnd. 6601 (London: Her Majesty's Stationery Office, 1976) (Houghton Report).

[6] Houghton Report, chap. 2.

October 1977, the annual conference of the Labour party endorsed a majority decision of the party's national executive committee "that the principal of state aid should be supported." However, in view of "varying opinions on the actual forms of aid proposed," it was agreed to "allow the national executive committee to continue to examine in greater detail the proposals of the Houghton Report."[7] When the Labour government was defeated in the general election of May 1979, it still had not introduced legislation to implement the Houghton Committee's proposals.

While the present Conservative government remains in power, there is little prospect of a system of state aid to political parties. The Labour opposition, however, abandoning its previous caution, has now declared strongly in favor of radical reforms of the law. The *Report of the Labour Party Commission of Enquiry, 1980* recommends "[t]hat state aid be included in the party's manifesto and that active campaigning for its introduction begins immediately."[8] The Labour party's proposal is for public subsidies on a far larger scale than that suggested by the Houghton Committee. The stage is set for fierce and prolonged debate on the issue.[9]

The Liberal party leader, David Steel, has meanwhile come out in favor of another reform. He has called for a ban on all political contributions by companies and by trade unions and for the substitution of the "American system of limited tax relief on the donations of individuals to the parties of their choice."[10]

---

[7] Labour Party, *Report of the National Executive Committee, 1976-77* (London: Labour Party, 1977), p. 13. For useful accounts of discussions within the Labour party about the implementation of the proposed state subsidies, see Dick (R. L.) Leonard, "Contrasts in Selected Western Democracies: Germany, Sweden, Britain," in Alexander, *Political Finance;* and Seidle, "State Aid for Political Parties."

[8] Labour Party Commission of Enquiry, *Report of the Labour Party Commission of Enquiry, 1980* (London: Labour Party, 1980), p. 16. The Commission of Enquiry was set up by the 1979 Labour party conference to examine the finances, organization, membership, and political education of the party. It condemned the "very modest" scale of the state aid recommended in the Houghton Report. It recommended "that the Houghton Formula for state aid be revised so that the sum payable at national level is increased to 10p for each vote cast for a party's candidates at the previous General Election and index-linked thereafter; and at local level the reimbursement to the candidates should be equal to the maximum legally permitted expenditure" (8.2 (ii), p. 16). In addition, it recommended an increase in state aid to opposition parties in the House of Commons to a current maximum of £500,000 a year, to be index-linked thereafter (8.3, p. 16).

[9] As this study goes to press, a committee recently set up by the Hansard Society for Parliamentary Government is studying "the financing of politics in Britain," and its report will "recommend what principles and systems of financing would be most in the public interest."

[10] *The Times*, August 24, 1978.

Arguments for State Subsidies

Proponents of state aid have generally maintained (1) that the present system of paying for British politics is unfair, (2) that it results in underfinanced (and thus ineffective) parties, (3) that subsidies would reduce the dependence of the two main parties on their institutional backers (the Conservative party on big business, the Labour party on the trade unions), and (4) that the introduction of subsidies in several Western democracies provides a precedent that Britain should follow.

Unfairness of the Present System. A desire to reduce the financial advantages of the Conservative party is a major motive of critics of the existing system. For example, Richard Rose devoted an article on "Money and Election Law" to an attack on current regulations for their failure "to assure an approximate equality of expenditure as between the parties."[11] In his article, which appeared after the British general election of 1959, he argued that the existing legal limitations on political spending are wholly inadequate because they apply only to campaign spending by parliamentary (and local government) candidates. Expenditures by local party organizations between elections and all spending by national party organizations (during general elections as well as electoral peacetime) are exempt from control. These loopholes, maintained Rose, are important because they have allowed inequalities to continue unchecked. At one end of the spectrum, the Conservatives are relatively wealthy; at the other, the Liberals are poverty stricken.

According to this view, the main advantage derived by the Tories from their comparative wealth is their ability to finance sustained national advertising campaigns during the period before a general election ("The greatest scope for influencing votes by spending money probably lies in the use of long-term public relations campaigns to affect individual values.")[12] In 1957–1959, the Tories spent an estimated £468,000 on preelection political advertising (that is £2.6 million at February 1980 prices). In 1963–1964, according to a later article by the same author, the Tories devoted £992,000 to preelection public relations (nearly £5 million at 1980 prices)—a huge sum by British standards.[13] Both in 1957–1959 and in 1963–1964, the Labour

---

[11] *Political Studies*, vol. 9 (1961), p. 2.

[12] "Money and Election Law," p. 13.

[13] Richard Rose, "Pre-Election Public Relations and Advertising," in David E. Butler and Anthony King, *The British General Election of 1964* (London: Macmillan, 1965), p. 374. See also Richard Rose, *Influencing Voters: A Study of Campaign Rationality* (London: Faber, 1967).

and Liberal parties were apparently unable to match this spending.

To make matters worse, big business has spent heavily on anti-nationalization public relations. Although such advertising is only indirectly concerned with parliamentary election campaigns (and hence is considered by the courts to be unaffected by the laws limiting campaign spending), it is "politically relevant" and harms the Labour party.

The net result is that the Conservative party and its business allies, it is argued, obtain unfair electoral benefits. Theoretically, it would be possible to reduce this imbalance by putting limits on permitted spending by national party organizations and by political pressure groups. Rose suggests that this would pose insurmountable practical difficulties. An alternative strategy is to reduce the Labour and Liberal disadvantage by a system of state grants.

The Need for Effective Parties. Another argument, stressed during recent years, is that the incomes of all the main parties have been dangerously eroded by inflation. The shortage of funds means that the political organizations are unable to function effectively.[14] They cannot afford to employ adequate research staffs or to retain sufficient numbers of full-time constituency agents. The consequence is that, at the national level, party policy is ill prepared and, at the local level, the lack of professional agents lowers public participation in politics. In the words of the Liberal party's memorandum to the Houghton Committee, "political parties . . . are currently understaffed, under-researched, undertrained and under-financed." Lord Houghton argues that state grants have in these circumstances become "a desirable, and possibly the only, way of supporting the minimum standards of political activity and efficiency required to maintain the vitality of our system of representative government."[15]

Undesirable Dependence on Interest Groups. It is suggested that the two main parties rely too heavily on institutional sources of money: the Tories on payments from business companies and the Labour party on grants and affiliation fees from trade unions.[16] The Liberals, without help from either, are left out in the cold. State aid would

[14] A typical statement was Roger Morgan's assertion in 1975 that it was an "obvious fact" that British parties were "in urgent need of additional financial aid" and that there could be "no disagreement" with the thesis "that British political parties are today in a state of financial crisis." See Leonard, *Paying for Party Politics*, pp. vi-vii.

[15] Foreword by chairman, Houghton Report, p. xii.

[16] See section titled "Dependence on Interest Groups," in Leonard, *Paying for Party Politics*, pp. 4-6.

reduce this undesirable dependence of the main parties and would be fairer to the Liberals.

The Success of Subsidies in Foreign Countries. Supporters of state payments to parties have frequently referred to their success in the many countries where they have been introduced since the 1950s. Dick Leonard has written:

> Recent years have seen the development of a worldwide crisis of political financing and the only democratic countries which seem, so far, to be in sight of a solution are those which have adopted some system of public financing of at least a proportion of the legitimate costs of party political activities.[17]

Arguments against Subsidies

Although the case for public subventions has received strong support, it has also been keenly contested. Some of the arguments against subsidies are as follows.

Fairness of the Present System. (1) The Tory advantage, it is argued, is derived entirely from small contributions from members of local constituency associations. Individual membership of the Conservative party is currently about five times larger than that of the Labour party. Were the two main parties obliged to rely on their institu-

---

[17] *Paying for Party Politics*, p. 10, and Houghton Report, chap. 8. British advocates of state subsidies have been influenced by discussions of political finance reform in the United States. A basic work on political money in the United States, which also surveys the general policy issues, is Alexander Heard, *The Costs of Democracy* (Chapel Hill: University of North Carolina Press, 1960). An important series of works on political funding in America has been sponsored in the 1960s and 1970s by the Citizens' Research Foundation under the direction of Herbert E. Alexander. See especially Herbert E. Alexander, *Money in Politics* (Washington, D.C.: Public Affairs Press, 1972), and Herbert E. Alexander, *Financing Politics: Money, Elections, and Political Reform* (Washing, D.C.: Congressional Quarterly Press, 1976). Other significant works, expressing a variety of views on the issues of campaign finance reform, include David W. Adamany, *Campaign Finance in America* (North Scituate, Mass.: Duxbury Press, 1972); David W. Adamany and George E. Agree, *Political Money: A Strategy for Campaign Financing in America* (Baltimore: Johns Hopkins University Press, 1975); Delmer D. Dunn, *Financing Presidential Elections* (Washington, D.C.: Brookings Institution, 1972); Gary C. Jacobson, *Money in Congressional Elections* (New Haven, Conn.: Yale University Press, 1980); Howard R. Penniman and Ralph K. Winter, Jr., *Campaign Finances: Two Views of the Political and Constitutional Implications* (Washington, D.C.: American Enterprise Institute, 1971); and Ralph K. Winter, Jr., *Campaign Financing and Political Freedom* (Washington, D.C.: American Enterprise Institute, 1973).

tional backers alone, Labour would now be the richer, as trade union political levy funds raised for the Labour party have since the 1970s surpassed company contributions to the Tories. (2) The disparity between the total resources available to the three national parties is greatly reduced if account is taken of the notional value of subsidies-in-kind, especially free television time for party political broadcasts.

The Need for Effective Parties. Whether state subsidies for party officials would improve what the Houghton Report calls "the vitality of our system of democratic government" is open to dispute. In fact, it can be argued that they would have the opposite effect.

If party organizations have come under financial pressure in recent years (which is itself open to debate), this has resulted—according to this view—from loss of public interest and support. Inflation is not to blame. The basic problem of party government in Britain today is that increasing numbers of electors find the established parties unresponsive, irrelevant, and boring. To give financial security to the party professionals would merely shield them from the need to respond to new political conditions and popular demands. According to this interpretation, overfinanced—and consequently overprotected—party bureaucracies become ossified and are far too slow to meet fast-changing political situations.

Undesirable Dependence on Interest Groups. To accept that Tory financial dependence on corporate contributions and Labour party dependence on trade union payments is undesirable is not necessarily to accept that state aid would be better. It has been argued that dependence on interest groups is, for all its disadvantages, preferable to dependence on the state.[18]

Moreover, if state subsidies were to be introduced along the lines proposed by the Houghton Committee, they would not replace payments from trade unions and from companies; they would merely supplement them.[19] Labour party headquarters (Transport House) received in 1976—the year in which the Houghton Report was published—89 percent of its income from the unions and about 11 percent from constituency contributions and other sources. Had the Houghton proposals been in force, 27 percent of Labour's national

[18] See Anthony Howard, "Political Parties and Public Funds," *New Statesman*, September 3, 1976, pp. 295–96. See also Douglas Hurd, "Don't Subsidise Politics," *Observer*, July 15, 1973, and Douglas Hurd, "If Politics Goes on the Welfare," *Daily Telegraph*, August 27, 1976.
[19] See Bernard Crick, "Paying for the Parties: A Review," *Political Quarterly*, vol. 46 (1975), pp. 411-17.

income would have come from the state, but no less than 65 percent would still have come from the unions.

If the elimination of the financial influence of interest groups on political parties is a major objective of state subsidies, it would be logical to link the introduction of state aid to a ban on payments to parties by companies and unions. This is a step that some senior Conservatives privately support but that the Labour party has, not surprisingly, hesitated to advocate.

The Dubious Success of Subsidies outside Britain. British supporters of subsidies have possibly oversold their success in foreign countries. It is noteworthy that several of the most experienced scholars of the subject, who had previously been keen advocates of state payments, have recently emphasized the difficulties they have caused. Khayyam Paltiel, who played a key part in the introduction of public subsidies in Canada, has written of "doubts and anxieties . . . with respect to their impact on the Canadian system in general and the party system in particular."[20] In West Germany, the huge subsidies to the main parties and to party foundations (several hundred million dollars a year) have led to the "identification of party and state," which has serious implications for democracy. In Sweden, the extreme generosity of state grants has caused "a dramatic decline in voluntary contributions." A consequence of the Austrian subsidies has been "the growing isolation and separation of the central party leadership and apparatus from sub-groups and members," while in Italy subsidies have not fulfilled their objective of eliminating corruption, nor have they led to more openness "but rather to greater bureaucratization of Italian parties."[21]

An additional point is that cash subsidies have been urged in several countries to meet problems that do not exist in Britain. Arnold Heidenheimer has pointed out that the impulse for subsidies abroad has commonly come from "increasing expenditures caused by . . . the introduction of new technologies,"[22] particularly television advertising. However, in Britain, the development of television has

[20] Khayyam Z. Paltiel, "The Impact of Election Expenses Legislation in Canada, Western Europe, and Israel," in Alexander, *Political Finance*, p. 15. See also Khayyam Z. Paltiel, "Public Financing Abroad: Contrasts and Effects," in Malbin, *Parties, Interest Groups*.

[21] Paltiel, "Impact of Election Expenses Legislation," pp. 30, 33, 35; also Paltiel, "Public Financing Abroad," pp. 363, 368.

[22] Arnold J. Heidenheimer, "Major Modes of Raising, Spending, and Controlling Political Funds during and between Election Campaigns," in Heidenheimer, *Comparative Political Finance*, p. 17.

not led to increased political spending, because British parties are banned from television advertising but are given free television time instead.

In short, opposition to subsidies is based on the view that state aid would not significantly reduce the reliance of Conservatives and Labour on their institutional backers. Rather, it would diminish the role of the individual party member. The experience of foreign countries often bears this out. It is not accepted either that public payments would improve the effectiveness of party government. If British party organizations are in difficulty, shortage of money is the consequence, not the cause. The reason is the disenchantment of their members. If state financing allows the parties to be artificially protected from the need to retain support and to encourage participation, democratic government in Britain will be damaged.

It will be seen that the cases for and against public subsidies do not solely concern the subject of political finance. They raise broader questions about the role of parties in the political system. However, it is not possible to give clear answers without much fuller factual knowledge than has so far been available. Discussions about the reform of political finance in Britain have been dogged by misinformation, shortages of information, and myths. This study attempts to fill the gap by giving an outline of the historical evolution of political finance in Britain and by analyzing the modern patterns of funding parties and elections.

Chapters 1–4 describe political finance from the nineteenth century to the Second World War. Chapters 5–7 analyze the finances of the Conservative, Labour, and Liberal parties since 1945. Chapters 8 and 9 focus on two particular features of British political finance: chapter 8 gives an account of political donations by companies and trade unions; the present regulations concerning political money in Britain and, in particular, the existing subsidies-in-kind to political parties are outlined in chapter 9. A concluding chapter assesses the arguments for and against state aid; it also discusses the problems about the financial interests of members of Parliament and about the financial links between the trade unions and the Labour party.

The study confines itself to the funds of the three principal parties. It is also limited to parliamentary election campaigns and does not investigate the cost of local government elections (although they are included insofar as they are contained in the central and constituency funds of the Conservative, Labour, and Liberal parties). The finances of political pressure groups and those of organizations connected with the parties (such as the Fabian Society and the Bow

Group) are also excluded. This book has been written as a contribution to the current debate on the reform of political money. I hope that it will also be of value to historians and political scientists who may not be primarily interested in the policy issues.

A systematic examination of party funds is revealing about several major aspects of British politics from the nineteenth century to the present time. They include the growth of mass parties and the structure of power within them, the decline of the Liberals and the rise of Labour, the development of modern electioneering, the recruitment of parliamentary candidates, and patterns of political participation.

Sources of Information

Information on party finances has been pieced together from a variety of sources. The Labour party has published the accounts of its national organization since its formation in 1900. These accounts do not seem to have been closely examined by students of Labour party politics, and they are analyzed in this book probably for the first time. Conservative Central Office accounts have been published only since 1967/1968. In addition, previously undisclosed accounts for 1950 onward have been released by the Conservative party for this study. The only national party that has not issued comprehensive balance sheets is the Liberal party. Although the routine accounts of the Liberal Party Organisation (LPO) are published, they exclude many important aspects of activity within the national party. For example, LPO accounts until 1974 excluded general election costs; until 1979 money raised and spent by the Liberal Central Association (LCA) remained secret. Some unpublished accounts were made available by Liberal party officials. However, many important financial accounts have apparently been lost or discarded by the LPO and the LCA. Besides a variety of secret funds, there seems to be no record of central Liberal spending on postwar general elections before 1970 or of LCA accounts before 1972.

Information about party finance for certain years before the Second World War have survived in the private papers of a number of leading politicians. Several important books and articles have been written on this basis. They include Robert Stewart, *The Foundation of the Conservative Party, 1830–1867;*[23] Harold J. Hanham, *Elections and Party Management: Politics in the Time of Disraeli and Gladstone,*[24] and the same author's articles on "British Party Finance,

[23] London: Longman, 1978.
[24] London: Longman, 1959; and Hassocks, Sussex: Harvester Press, 1978.

1868–1880"[25] and "The Sale of Honours in Late Victorian England";[26] Neal Blewett, *The Peers, the Parties, and the People: The General Elections of 1910;*[27] John A. Ramsden, "The Organisation of the Conservative and Unionist Party in Britain, 1910–1930";[28] and Trevor O. Lloyd, "The Whip as Paymaster: Herbert Gladstone and Party Organisation."[29]

The private papers of the following politicians have been examined: Lord Salisbury, Jack Sandars, Herbert Asquith, David Lloyd George, Sir Donald Maclean, Lord Davidson, Neville Chamberlain, Lord Woolton, and Sir Frank Medlicott.

Statistics about political levy funds of trade unions are included in the annual reports of the chief registrar of friendly societies (recently renamed the certification officer for trade unions and employers' associations). Further information is contained in the published annual reports of individual trade unions. An extremely useful study, based largely on these sources, is Martin Harrison, *Trade Unions and the Labour Party since 1945,*[30] which covers the years until 1958. However, there seems to have been no similar analysis of trade union political levy funds before the Second World War, and the gap is filled in this book.

The Companies Act of 1967 has obliged companies to declare political donations exceeding £50 in their annual reports. Information based on these reports has been regularly collected by the Labour party's research department and by a separate organization, the Labour Research Department. Material gathered by these bodies has been supplemented by examination of individual company reports.

Election expenses of parliamentary candidates have been closely controlled and published as British parliamentary papers since the general election of 1885. (Previous accounts were also published but were less complete and less reliable.)[31]

There is no convenient or dependable way of obtaining comprehensive information about local party finance, because constituency associations do not normally deposit copies of their accounts with their national organizations. It is particularly hazardous to estimate

25 *Bulletin of the Institute of Historical Research*, vol. 127 (1954) pp. 69-90.
26 *Victorian Studies*, vol. 3 (1960), pp. 277-89.
27 London: Macmillan, 1972.
28 D.Phil. thesis, Oxford University, 1974. Page references in this study are to this thesis. Similar information is given in John A. Ramsden, *The Age of Balfour and Baldwin, 1902-1940* (London: Longman, 1979).
29 *English Historical Review*, vol. 89 (1974).
30 London: Allen and Unwin, 1960.
31 See appendix C.

historical levels of constituency income and expenditure. Figures for certain postwar years have been derived from samples of constituency accounts. A particularly comprehensive survey for the years 1973 and 1974 was commissioned by the Houghton Committee and a summary of the results is included in its report.

Finally, written material has in a number of cases been supplemented by interviews with officials of the three national parties.

The use of these sources has produced a large amount of new information and has led to some radical revisions of previously accepted estimates. The figures must nevertheless be treated with some caution for several reasons. First of all, it has not been possible to examine all the relevant private papers of politicians concerned with party finance, and some significant gaps remain. Secondly, the reliability of the information varies greatly. For some years, precise accounts have survived while for others all that remains is tantalizingly brief estimates (often recalled years after the event). Thirdly, differences in accounting procedures and in party organizational structures can make balance sheets difficult to interpret.[32] To give a simple example, some national party accounts include the income and expenditure of their regional offices while others exclude them. General election expenditure is sometimes included and sometimes left out of the annual accounts of national parties. Income from dividends and interest is sometimes given net of tax, and at other times tax is shown as expenditure, and investment income is given gross (thus raising the levels of both income and expenditure). Fourthly, it is not possible on the basis of existing data to assess the amounts spent by ward branches (the subunits of constituency associations). Ward branches are often responsible for funding local government campaigns for the election of district and county councilors. These are only some of the difficulties.

The basis on which figures have been calculated is given in footnotes and in notes to the tables. It is hoped that these notes will make it easier to interpret the statistics, to locate errors, and to modify the figures as further information becomes available.

The Institutional Framework

Two features of the British political system closely affect the patterns of party organization and political finance. They are (1) the absence of nationally elected officials and (2) the variable date of parliamentary elections.

[32] See appendix E.

The Absence of Nationally Elected Officials. The only votes actually cast in a British general election are for individual candidates for the House of Commons. Unlike the American voter, who is faced with a long ballot for a multitude of both national and local offices, the British voter puts only one cross on his ballot paper—for his choice as local member of Parliament. The party leaders must themselves stand as parliamentary candidates, and this is their only legally recognized role in a general election. This electoral framework has determined the structure of British party organization. At a local level, the basic unit is the constituency association, which is responsible for one parliamentary seat. At present, there are 635 constituencies in the United Kingdom, each containing about 70,000 electors.

At the national level, the parties run extraparliamentary organizations. Unlike the constituency associations, they are not directly involved in securing the election of specific candidates. Their task is to give organizational advice and aid to constituency associations and to organize national publicity and research. The national parties have also set up regional offices, which are part of the national organizations (though in the Liberal party, the regional offices, such as they are, have a greater degree of independence from the head office).

The Variable Election Date. The prime minister may normally call for a new election at any time within the five-year term of a parliament. This affects party organization and political finance in two important ways. First, the fact that there might be a sudden election makes it necessary for parties to maintain permanent organizations nationally and locally during the periods between elections so that the framework of a campaign organization will already exist when the date of the poll is announced. Second, the uncertain date of the election means that a British election campaign (particularly at the national level) divides into two phases: a preliminary phase of indefinite length when it is expected that an election is in the offing, and the short period (usually about four weeks) between the prime minister's announcement of the impending dissolution of the House of Commons and the date of the poll. If an election is called unexpectedly early, the precampaign period is relatively short—or even absent altogether. In this case, expenditure, especially on national preelection advertising, is small. If a campaign is called unexpectedly late (as in 1964), the precampaign period is protracted, and expenditures are likely to be heavier.

	Routine *Expenditure*	*Campaign* *Expenditure*
Central		
Local		

    This institutional framework makes it convenient to distinguish between constituency and national organizations and between routine and campaign organization. The following illustration shows the divisions that will be used repeatedly to analyze party incomes and expenditures. Campaign expenditure includes precampaign expenditure, and central expenditure includes expenditure by regional offices.

1
The Aristocratic Era (to 1883)

British political finance has evolved through three stages: (1) *the aristocratic era*, which lasted until the general election of 1880; (2) *the plutocratic era*, which was established by the 1890s and continued (for the Conservative and Liberal parties) until after the First World War; and (3) *the modern era*. The patterns of this third stage were introduced by the newly formed Labour party at the beginning of the twentieth century and were adopted by the Conservatives between the 1920s and the 1940s.

The main features of the aristocratic system were bribery and high costs.[1] During the earlier part of Queen Victoria's reign, it was still possible to buy a seat in the House of Commons. In 1832, shortly before her accession, 850 out of the 1,000 voters in the constituency of Stamford were bribed.[2] In the twenty-five years following the Reform Act of 1832, 443 petitions were presented to invalidate parliamentary elections on the grounds of various electoral malpractices. Seventy-five members of Parliament lost their seats as a result.[3] Corrupt practices remained common in at least half of the borough constituencies in England after the Second Reform Act of 1867. The general election of 1880 was markedly corrupt, even by the low standards of the time: 42 election petitions followed, of which 16 in England were successful; 8 led to the appointment of Royal Commissions, and seven towns were temporarily disenfranchised.[4]

[1] See William B. Gwyn, *Democracy and the Cost of Politics in Britain, 1832-1959* (London: Athlone Press, 1962); Norman Gash, *Politics in the Age of Peel* (London: Longman, 1953; and Hassocks, Sussex: Harvester Press, 1977); Harold J. Hanham, *Elections and Party Management: Politics in the Time of Disraeli and Gladstone* (London: Longman, 1959; and Hassocks, Sussex: Harvester Press, 1978); Ivor Jennings, *Party Politics*, vol. 1, *Appeal to the People* (Cambridge: Cambridge University Press, 1960); and Cornelius O'Leary, *The Elimination of Corrupt Practices in British Elections, 1868-1911* (Oxford: Oxford University Press, 1962).

[2] Gash, *Politics in the Age of Peel*, p. 158.

[3] O'Leary, *Elimination of Corrupt Practices*, p. 234.

[4] O'Leary, *Elimination of Corrupt Practices*, chap. 5; and Trevor O. Lloyd, *The General Election of 1880* (Oxford: Oxford University Press, 1968).

The demand for corrupt payments and for entertainments made the system very costly for candidates. A candidate was obliged to pay (through his agents) to bribe voters, to fund innkeepers for refreshments on polling day, and to ingratiate himself with the electors by finding all kinds of employment for them as cabdrivers, messengers, canvassers, clerks, agents, and poll watchers. It was also the responsibility of those running for election to meet the expenses of the returning officer (the public official responsible for the poll). On top of this, candidates were expected to make heavy routine payments between elections: to give annual subscriptions to local political clubs and charities[5] and to underwrite the costs involved in registering favorable voters and objecting to the inclusion of those

[5] The routine payments expected of parliamentary candidates included both subscriptions to local party associations and "politically relevant" contributions to nonpolitical organizations. Hanham calculates the overall cost to candidates of such subscriptions as £1,750 in county constituencies and £750 in boroughs for a five-year period (*Elections and Party Management*, p. 258).

There is insufficient evidence to make reliable estimates of the total routine expenditures of the emergent local party associations in the period between 1867 and 1880 or of the amounts that parliamentary candidates were expected to subscribe to such associations. It is assumed for the purposes of table 1 that routine subscriptions by candidates to local party organizations averaged £300 over a parliamentary cycle and that the rest of the total subscriptions by candidates estimated by Hanham were for nonpolitical causes.

Donations by candidates to nonparty organizations have been excluded from table 1 and from similar tables in subsequent chapters. The reason is that it is extremely difficult to define, yet alone to calculate, such indirect routine costs. During the nineteenth century and later, candidates regularly sought to ingratiate themselves with voters by a show of nonpolitical generosity. If a candidate was a local employer or local landowner, he might give special favors to his workers, or he might support local charitable causes. Sometimes MPs and politically minded peers purchased land in areas where they had parliamentary interests. Such expenditures were not normally acknowledged as "political," and, in any case, commercial, philanthropic, and political considerations often coincided. For example, Lloyd's study of *The General Election of 1880* refers to the claim that a leading Liberal, Lord Rosebery, spent the huge sum of £50,000 on the election. Lloyd suggests that this included "the cost of property which he bought to acquire electoral influence in Midlothian" (p. 76). It is not possible to disentangle the extent (if any) of the financial sacrifice made by Lord Rosebery for such politically motivated property transactions. Similarly, millionaires, who gave huge benefactions to hospitals, libraries, and museums in the plutocratic era, often derived political advantages. Nevertheless, it would not be wholly realistic to define their charitable contributions as political payments.

To avoid such problems, political finance has been narrowly defined in this study to include only the expenses of party political organizations and of candidates standing for public office. It seems clear that subscriptions by parliamentary candidates to local good causes have greatly declined since the nineteenth century. Other forms of "politically relevant" spending by trade unions, companies, and pressure groups have possibly expanded. (See chap. 2, footnote 47; chap. 3, "Note: The Labour Party and the Labour Movement"; chap. 5, footnote 18; and chap. 8, footnote 17.)

TABLE 1

Costs of Standing for Parliament during the Aristocratic Era
(in pounds)

	Average, County Constituencies	Average, Borough Constituencies
Campaign costs		
Payments for returning officer	200	105
Cost of election campaign	3,000	1,210
Routine costs		
Registration (five years)	750	500
Political subscriptions (five years)	300[a]	300[a]
Total (five years)	4,250	2,115
Average annual cost	850	423

[a] See footnote 5.

Source: Adapted from Hanham, *Elections and Party Management*, p. 258.

likely to vote for the other side. The overall costs of standing for Parliament in the period after 1867, based on estimates by Hanham, are shown in table 1 (costs are for an entire parliamentary cycle and exclude routine charitable subscriptions to nonparty organizations).

This is equivalent to about £20,000 a year (about £100,000 for a complete parliamentary cycle) for county constituencies and half that amount for boroughs in February 1980 values.[6] Candidates elected to Parliament also had to provide their own living costs in London—MPs received no salary or expense allowance.

These high expenses meant that only the very rich (or those who could secure the support of a wealthy patron) could afford to become candidates for the House of Commons. They were generally landowners or relatives of landowners or had landowners as patrons. A minority of MPs and their backers were businessmen or professionals. The striking feature of the parliamentary scene until the late nineteenth century was the survival of aristocratic dominance. In the Conservative party, this might have been expected, but it applied also to the Liberals in Parliament. As John Vincent has pointed out, it was a long time before changes in Victorian society affected the narow social composition of the House of Commons.

[6] See appendix A, "The Cost of Living, 1830-1980." All financial statistics in this study are expressed in pounds sterling. For the foreign exchange value of sterling, see appendix B.

The two parliamentary parties "differing in so much else were yet alike in this that they were both, in a broad sense, aristocratical parties." [7] The Conservative (Tory) ranks were filled with country gentlemen, and those of the Liberals remained dominated by propertied Whigs.

One reason why men of means had traditionally been willing to pay so much to control a seat (or, in the case of some powerful aristocrats, several seats) in the House of Commons was that, under the old system, a place in Parliament could bring not only power but also some important material benefits. Control of votes in the House of Commons gave leverage over the government, and this, in turn, ensured a share in the ministerial patronage that had been lavishly available. According to a report cited by William Gwyn, 532 aristocratic families found 13,888 patronage jobs for 7,991 relatives from 1850 to 1883, worth during this period £108 million (about £3 billion in 1980 values).[8] Not only had attractive public jobs and sinecures been given by governments to those with political pull, but legislation in the House of Commons had to a great extent dealt with personal or local interests and had been the work of private bill committees.[9] In an age when decisions about docks, canals, and railways were taken by relatively small private bill committees, the heavy investment in electing a compliant MP could bring handsome dividends.[10]

Only one thing helped to limit the expense of the old system. The fact that electoral contests cost so much meant that challengers were hesitant to put themselves forward for a constituency unless they felt they had a chance of winning. Consequently, many MPs were returned unopposed.[11] The number of uncontested constituencies

[7] John R. Vincent, The Formation of the Liberal Party, 1857-1868 (London: Constable, 1966), p. xx.

[8] Gwyn, Democracy and the Cost of Politics, p. 220. See also Gash, Politics in the Age of Peel, chap. 13, "Political Patronage."

[9] Josef Redlich, The Procedure of the House of Commons (London: Constable, 1908). Private bills took up a considerable part of Parliament's time until well after 1850. It was stated in 1846 that "from the Union with Ireland to the end of last session nearly 9,200 Local and Personal Bills passed into law, and only 5,300 Public Statutes" (Select Committee on Private Bills, XII, p. 1, sess. no. 556, 1846). I am grateful to Professor Max Hartwell for letting me read a draft paper on "Committees of the House of Commons, 1800-1850." See also Ronald Butt, The Power of Parliament (London: Constable, 1969).

[10] In the nineteenth century, private bills included those relating to bridges, canals, railways, turnpikes, docks, drainage, harbors, navigation, piers, reservoirs, street tramways, sewers, and tunnels (Hartwell, "Committees of the House of Commons," p. 4).

[11] Trevor O. Lloyd, "Uncontested Seats in British General Elections, 1852-1910," Historical Journal, vol. 8 (1965), pp. 260-65. In the eighteenth century, uncon-

was also boosted by the electoral system. Many constituencies elected two MPs, and bargains were often made between Liberals and Conservatives to take one seat each without any financially consuming appeal to the greedy electors. In the four general elections preceding the Second Reform Act of 1867, between 43 percent and 60 percent of the constituencies were uncontested.

At this stage, most parliamentary candidates had party labels, but they wore them loosely. Voters usually supported the individual rather than his party. Identification with national parties, both by voters and by MPs themselves, developed gradually during the nineteenth century.[12] The growth of party organization was correspondingly slow. Consequently, little political money was raised or spent, apart from the very large sums required for parliamentary contests.

At the local level, Liberal and Conservative constituency associations had been formed from the 1830s onward. Some of them collected subscriptions, canvassed, and organized the registration of voters. By the 1860s, the existence of political clubs was already widespread in the urban boroughs. The widening of the urban electorate by the Second Reform Act of 1867 gave a further stimulus to local party organization. In some areas, constituency associations had already become active and sophisticated by the 1870s. In general, local parties were still in a primitive state. Campaign organization usually depended on the candidate's checkbook and not on the skill and party loyalty of members of the local political associations. Constituency campaigns were normally run by local lawyers who were employed as agents by the candidates. Party supporters

---

tested seats had been even more common. Jennings records that in 1761 "the electors went to the poll in only forty-eight out of 315 constituencies. Between 1768 and 1818 there were fifty-three counties in England and Wales, but on average only between six and seven went to the poll." In Scotland, "contests were as rare as the sunshine" (*Party Politics*, vol. 1, pp. 80-81).

[12] See A. Lawrence Lowell, *The Government of England* (New York: Macmillan, 1908), vol. 2, chap. 36, "Political Oscillations." This shows the considerable importance of local factors in determining votes in the nineteenth century. The growing significance of national politics in British elections during the twentieth century is demonstrated in Donald E. Stokes, "Parties and the Nationalization of Electoral Forces," in William N. Chambers and Walter D. Burnham, eds., *The American Party Systems: Stages of Development* (Oxford: Oxford University Press, 1967). The greatly diminished impact of constituency campaigning in Britain during the twentieth century has encouraged the trend toward lower campaign spending at the local level. Why spend heavily at the local level if voting choices are determined by predominantly national considerations? In the nineteenth century, the situation was different. There is evidence that money won votes. For example, of the twenty-six boroughs known to have been subsidized out of the Conservative central fund in 1859, seven were gained by the party, and only one was lost. (Robert Stewart, *The Foundation of the Conservative Party, 1830-1867* [London: Longman, 1978], p. 341).

were paid to give their services in the campaign. When the election was over, the local associations frequently lapsed into inactivity, apart from the annual task of registering voters. This, too, was in most cases the responsibility of lawyer-agents who hired helpers. The candidate or his backers footed the bills.

At the national level, elementary forms of party organization existed by the first half of the nineteenth century. When Parliament was in session, party whips helped to line up support in the two houses of Parliament. At elections, central Conservative and Liberal funds were collected, in great secrecy, to help candidates to stand for winnable seats that would otherwise have been uncontested. According to Robert Stewart, a central fund for aiding Conservative candidates already existed before 1830.[13] A fund was regularly collected for elections from the early 1830s onward.[14]

Little is known about the sums raised and spent because of the mystery that surrounded the existence of these party "war chests." The motives for secrecy were probably to avoid complaints by those who wished to receive support but were told that no money was available and also to avoid the party leaders' being implicated in scandal if it were established that money they had provided had been used to bribe voters. Another reason for hiding these payments was that politics was considered at that time an activity for gentlemen of independent means. The idea that a candidate might be beholden to a political party for money was strange and not yet accepted. Even when evidence has survived in the private papers of politicians, the problem of establishing the size of the war chests is increased by the informality with which accounts were kept, by lack of information about whether amounts raised were spent or were kept in reserve, and by the fact that more than one central fund was sometimes collected (for example, separate funds were periodically raised for Irish or Scottish constituencies). Evidence about some Conservative central funds between 1831 and 1880 is pieced together in table 2.

The most detailed surviving information about nineteenth-century Conservative central funds is contained in some ambiguous lists penciled in the 1859 election notebook of the party's principal agent, Philip Rose. The lists

> suggest that as much as £50,000 may have been paid out of the central fund to assist candidates in about three dozen English boroughs and three counties. In addition, at least

[13] Stewart, *Foundation of the Conservative Party*, p. 88.
[14] Gash, *Politics in the Age of Peel*, appendix C, "Party Election Funds."

TABLE 2

CONSERVATIVE CENTRAL FUNDS DURING SOME GENERAL ELECTIONS, 1831–1880

	"The fund existed before 1830"[a]	
1831	"The Charles Street Committee raised funds"	
	Some contributors:	
	Duke of Buccleugh	£10,000 (at least)
	Lord Bute	£ 1,000
	Lord Ellenborough	£ 1,000 (at least)
	Lord Powis	£ 2,000 (at least)[b]
1832	"The Charles Street fund was exhausted and no more money was subscribed"[c]	
1835	"a small central fund" . . . "the amounts were tiny"[d]	
1837	"A note in the Hardinge papers relating to the 1837 fund gives a list of contributions mainly from peers totaling nearly £7,000"[e]	
1841	Unlikely to have been larger than £25,000[f]	
1847	"There was . . . an election fund"[g]	
1852	A small fund[h]	
1857	£9,000 subscribed by 12 peers[i]	
1859	Probably over £50,000[j]	
1868	Disraeli hoped for £100,000 and raised £10,000 from his cabinet. There is nothing to suggest that Disraeli's target was reached[k]	
1874	"the Conservative Party Fund was as low as £20,000"[l]	
1880	£22,000 from Tory peers[m]	

SOURCES: [a] Stewart, *Foundation of the Conservative Party*, p. 88. [b] Ibid., pp. 77-78. [c] Ibid., p. 83. [d] Ibid., p. 140. [e] Gash, *Politics in the Age of Peel*, p. 435. [f] Stewart, *Foundation of the Conservative Party from Peel to Churchill*, p. 2. [g] Blake, *Conservative Party from Peel to Churchill*, p. 142. [h] Stewart, *Foundation of the Conservative Party*, p. 269. [i] Ibid., p. 330. [j] Ibid., p. 331. [k] Blake, *Conservative Party from Peel to Churchill*, p. 143. [l] Bowles, "The New Corruption," p. 52. [m] Feuchtwanger, *Disraeli, Democracy, and the Tory Party*, p. 200.

£6,000 was spent by Colonel Taylor in Ireland. There was, also, money left over after the elections.[15]

These sums were exceptionally high for Conservatives before the Second Reform Act of 1867. Harold Hanham suggests that, by the 1868–1880 period, the Conservatives "usually hoped for about £50,000, and expected to spend about £30,000 on the election itself."[16] According to an informed writer in an article published in 1914,

[15] Stewart, *Foundation of the Conservative Party*, p. 331.
[16] Hanham, *Elections and Party Management*, p. 372.

"Thirty thousand pounds was then [the nineteenth century] considered a fair sum to have in the cash-box."[17]

The funds raised by the Liberals seem usually to have been smaller. Hanham has cited lists of contributors to Liberal funds in the elections of 1868, 1874, and 1880. These survive in the Adam Papers. They indicate that the Liberal election fund totaled £15,000 in 1868, £10,000 in 1874, and £33,000 in 1880.[18] There may have been additional funds not included in these figures. According to Trevor Lloyd, Lord Cork raised an additional Liberal fund of £6,000 in 1880, bringing the total for that year to at least £39,000.[19] A disproportionately large amount of Liberal aid went to county seats and to Ireland and Scotland.

Whatever the details of these funds, it is clear that they could provide only a very small proportion of the total expenses required by parliamentary candidates. In 1880, for example, Liberal and Conservative candidates spent a total of well over £2 million. The known Liberal and Conservative funds amounted to £61,000 (£22,000 on the Conservative side and £39,000 raised by the Liberals). Assuming that undiscovered sums raised the total to £100,000, this still was less than 5 percent of candidates' expenses.

Apart from these funds collected to subsidize candidates, the party leaders raised smaller sums for the routine activities of national party organizations. The most important source of money was an annual grant of £10,000 to the government of the day from the Secret Service fund. This was intended primarily to enable the chief whip in the House of Commons to arrange properly for the business of the House. The actual expenses of the whips' office were well under £10,000, and the balance could be used for financing national party organizations outside Parliament or could be put into reserve for subsidizing candidates at the following general election. The fact that the Liberals were in government for three-quarters of the period between 1846 and 1886 meant that they benefited especially from the Secret Service money; this may help to explain why Liberal election funds were usually smaller than those of the Conservatives.[20]

National party organization outside Parliament developed first informally and later on a more regular basis. A Conservative Central

[17] T. Gibson Bowles, "The New Corruption: The Caucus and the Sale of Honours," *Candid Quarterly Review*, vol. 1 (1914), p. 52.

[18] Harold J. Hanham, "British Party Finance, 1868-1880," *Bulletin of the Institute of Historical Research*, vol. 127 (1954).

[19] Lloyd, *General Election of 1880*, p. 75.

[20] Some of the most thorough estimates of routine central party expenditure in the 1860s and 1870s are given in Hanham, *Elections and Party Management*, chap. 17, "Party Finance."

22

Office was set up in 1870 and operated jointly with the secretariat of the National Union of Conservative and Constitutional Associations. A similar extraparliamentary body had been formed on the Liberal side in 1861 and was to be called the Liberal Central Association. Party offices were later set up in Scotland and Ireland. Until 1868 a major routine function of the national party organizers, who at this early period were practicing lawyers, was to represent MPs faced with allegations of electoral malpractices. The election petition trials were originally held in London, but from 1868 onward they took place in the constituencies concerned, and the task of fighting the cases was removed from the national party agents.[21] The main functions of the emergent party headquarters were to recruit candidates, to collect political intelligence about the state of local feeling and about local organization, to stimulate local party activity, and to provide literature and speakers for meetings. These functions were carried out on a modest scale. In the early 1880s, the Conservative Central Office employed only three administrative officers and their secretaries.[22]

Hanham estimates that the Liberal and Conservative national organizations during the 1860s each spent a total of about £10,000 a year.[23] This may have included some of the costs of election petition trials. Hanham's estimates for the 1870s are about £5,000 a year for each party: £2,000 per annum for each of the whips' offices; £2,000 per annum for the routine expenses of the party headquarters in London; and £1,000 for the offices in Ireland and Scotland. This meant that only about half of the £10,000-a-year Secret Service grant was used for routine activities by the governing party and the rest "could be invested in Consols and saved up for a period in opposition."[24] During the spell of Liberal opposition between 1874 and 1880, "the annual expenditure of the Liberal Party on the work controlled by the chief whip was in the neighborhood of £3,000–£4,000."[25] The sums in table 3 are derived from the Adam Papers.

During general election campaigns, the amounts spent centrally, apart from subsidies to candidates, were negligible. The only identifiable central cost of the 1880 election is the £1,608 spent by the Con-

21 See Robert Blake, *The Conservative Party from Peel to Churchill* (London: Fontana, 1972), pp. 144-45.

22 Edgar J. Feuchtwanger, *Disraeli, Democracy, and the Tory Party: Conservative Leadership and Organization after the Second Reform Bill* (Oxford: Oxford University Press, 1968), pp. 150-51, 160-61.

23 Harold J. Hanham, "The Sale of Honours in Late Victorian England," *Victorian Studies*, vol. 3 (1960), p. 282.

24 Hanham, *Elections and Party Management*, p. 370.

25 Hanham, "British Party Finance," p. 70.

TABLE 3

ANNUAL EXPENDITURE ON WORK CONTROLLED BY THE
LIBERAL CHIEF WHIP, 1874/1875–1878/1879
(in pounds)

1874/75	4,855
1875/76	7,571
1876/77	4,764
1877/78	5,717
1878/79	1,604

SOURCE: Hanham, "British Party Finance," p. 70.

servative National Union (effectively a part of Conservative Central Office) on printing and advertising, compared with £291 for the same items the previous year.[26]

The most notable feature of the aristocratic pattern of political finance was the limited scale of expenditure by national and local party organizations compared with the large sums demanded from parliamentary candidates. This is shown in table 4, which estimates the overall amount spent by the Conservative party and by Conservative candidates during the entire parliamentary cycle leading up to and including the election of 1880. Similar tables for the plutocratic and modern periods are given in later chapters. (See tables 12, 26, 36, 45, 57, and 73 and appendix D.)

By the 1860s and 1870s this old system, whereby aristocratic nominees bribed their way into the House of Commons, was coming under pressure. Extensions of the franchise increased the size of the electorate from 440,000 before the 1832 Reform Act, to 2,230,000 after the 1867 act. This meant that there were far more electors to pay than before. The Ballot Act of 1872 introduced secret voting, thereby making payments to voters potentially less effective. Also, the growth of national party feeling led to an increase in the number of contested constituencies. In 1880 only 17 percent of constituencies were uncontested.

These developments made the "Old Corruption" less effective and more expensive. Nevertheless, the system was slow to change, and the traditional, costly abuses still survived in 1880. The enlarged electorate and the decline in uncontested seats made the general election of 1880 one of the most expensive in history. The declared expenses of candidates amounted to £1,737,000. This figure did not

[26] Lloyd, General Election of 1880, p. 77.

TABLE 4

The Aristocratic Pattern: Overall Conservative Expenditure (approximate) during the Parliamentary Cycle 1874–1880
(in pounds)

	Routine Expenditure	Campaign Expenditure
Central	Up to 50,000 ?	Negligible
Local	About ½ million[a] ?	About ½ million[b]

NOTE: Estimates of expenditure patterns are given in this and subsequent historical chapters for the Conservative party because it is the only party that has been a major partner in the British two-party system throughout the past hundred years. The table shows the level of organization at which finance is spent. Money raised centrally and transferred for local use is recorded as local expenditure (and vice versa). Local expenditure includes estimated expenditure by parliamentary candidates and by local party organizations. During the aristocratic era almost all local expenditure was by candidates and their backers. The estimated cost of election petitions is included.

[a] Mostly paid by candidates for registration.

[b] Includes declared expenses, estimated undeclared expenses, and the estimated cost of election petitions. For election expenses in 1880, see the text and table 5. For an assessment of the cost of election petitions, see O'Leary, *Elimination of Corrupt Practices*, p. 92.

SOURCES: Central routine expenditure based on Hanham's estimates in "Sale of Honours," p. 282, and *Elections and Party Management*, p. 370. For campaign expenditure (central and local), see text. Local routine expenditure based on the routine costs given in table 1.

include a substantial number of constituencies for which no returns of expenses were submitted.[27] It also did not include the heavy expenses of election petition trials. Moreover, the fact that few checks were made to establish the accuracy of the declared figures meant that actual expenditure was considerably higher than the reported sums.[28] Cornelius O'Leary has estimated the cost per vote as 93.75 pence,[29] a total expenditure for all candidates of over £3 million. Lloyd gives a somewhat lower estimate, which, however, also amounts to over £2 million.[30] (Assuming that total campaign costs for candidates were £2½ million, this is equivalent to about £60 million at 1980 values.)

Concern about these extravagant sums led to the passage, with Liberal and Conservative support, of the Corrupt and Illegal Practices (Prevention) Act, 1883. This measure proved to be a landmark in British electoral history and has provided the basis for all subsequent legislative control of political spending in Britain. The 1883 act (which is outlined in chapter 9) introduced strict limits on permitted campaign expenditure by candidates. Certain types of expenditure were banned altogether (for instance, the provision of refreshments or payments to transport voters to the polls). Moreover, it was forbidden for anyone to incur an election expense without written permission from the candidate or from his legally appointed election agent. This was intended to eliminate expenditure on a candidate's behalf but allegedly without his knowledge. Finally, tight disclosure rules set exact procedures for the presentation and the public inspection of campaign accounts.

The act was an almost unqualified success. Declared election expenses declined sharply after 1880, as shown in table 5. The actual fall was even greater than shown by the declared figures, because the tightened rules meant that there was far less scope for undeclared expenses from 1885 onward than in 1880.

Another indication that the old style of campaigning was on the wane was the drastic fall from 1885 onward in the number of petitions

[27] O'Leary, *Elimination of Corrupt Practices*, p. 156.

[28] In 1883 the rules about disclosure of campaign expenditure were tightened. In 1880 it was still possible to leave much expenditure unreported. Dozens of candidates did not even bother to make any declaration of expenses at all. See O'Leary, *Elimination of Corrupt Practices*, p. 156.

[29] Ibid., p. 206.

[30] Lloyd, *General Election of 1880*, pp. 74-75. Lloyd also gives a breakdown of declared expenses by Conservative and Liberal candidates. This indicates that Conservative candidates outspent Liberals. According to Gwyn, the lowest contemporary estimates of the cost of the 1880 election "ran from £2,200,000 to £2,500,000" (*Democracy and the Cost of Politics*, p. 51).

TABLE 5

Total Declared Expenses of Parliamentary Candidates (all parties) in General Elections, 1880–1979
(in pounds)

General Election	Current Prices	1980 Prices	General Election	Current Prices	1980 Prices
1880	1,737,300[a]	41,400,000	1931	654,105	10,900,000
1885	1,026,645	28,100,000	1935	722,093	12,400,000
1886	624,086	18,800,000	1945	1,073,216	10,400,000
1892	958,532	27,100,000	1950	1,170,124	9,000,000
1895	773,333	22,400,000	1951	946,018	6,700,000
1900	777,429	22,000,000	1955	904,677	5,700,000
1906	1,166,859	32,200,000	1959	1,051,219	5,900,000
1910	1,295,782	33,100,000	1964	1,229,205	6,100,000
1910	978,312	25,000,000	1966	1,130,882	5,100,000
1918	No published returns		1970	1,392,796	5,200,000
1922	1,018,196	13,700,000	1974	1,780,542	4,400,000
1923	982,340	13,900,000	1974	2,168,514	4,800,000
1924	921,165	12,900,000	1979	3,557,000	4,100,000
1929	1,213,507	18,200,000			

[a] The actual total, including undeclared expenses, was probably about £2½ million. That is £59,500,000 at 1980 values.

Sources: For officially declared expenses, 1880-1910, Gwyn, *Democracy and the Cost of Politics*, p. 55. For estimated actual expenditure, 1880, see text and footnotes 27-30. For officially declared expenses, 1922-1974, David E. Butler and Anne Sloman, *British Political Facts, 1900-1979* (London: Macmillan, 1980), p. 229; and for 1979, David E. Butler and Dennis Kavanagh, *The British General Election of 1979* (London: Macmillan, 1980), p. 315.

alleging a breach of the regulations and the sharp decline in the number of MPs unseated for electoral offenses. So marked was the movement toward cleaner electioneering that O'Leary justifiably entitled his book on late nineteenth-century campaigning *The Elimination of Corrupt Practices in British Elections, 1868–1911*. In modern times, electoral corruption has effectively ceased to be an issue in British political finance (see table 6).

The dramatic fall in the cost per vote following the 1883 act is shown in table 7. In 1880 each Conservative vote cost an average of £1.59 (a huge £37.80 at 1980 values). By February 1974 the cost per vote was only 6.7 pence (16.4 pence at 1980 values). In other words, the cost per vote was about 230 times greater in 1880 than in 1974. By 1979 the cost per vote for Conservative candidates was one three-hundredth in real terms of the level of 1880.

TABLE 6

THE DECLINE OF ELECTORAL BRIBERY FOLLOWING THE CORRUPT PRACTICES ACT, 1883

	Total Number of Contested Constituencies	Election Petitions Presented		Election Petitions Successful	
		No.	%	No.	%
Elections of 1865, 1868, 1874, and 1880	1,133	162	14.3	61	5.4
Elections of 1885, 1886, 1892, and 1895	2,046	30	1.5	9	0.4

SOURCES: O'Leary, *Elimination of Corrupt Practices*, p. 234; and Chris Cook and Brendan Keith, *British Historical Facts, 1830-1900* (London: Macmillan, 1975), pp. 142-43.

The success of the 1883 act is partly attributable to skillful drafting and, in particular, to the provisions about the appointment of agents. By making it an offense for anyone other than the legally appointed agent or subagent to incur expenses, the act avoided the type of situation that has existed in the United States, where expenditure limits have been evaded by the multiplication of supposedly independent campaign committees.[31]

However, the fall in campaign costs and the virtual elimination of electoral corruption owed more to the changing economic and political conditions of the nineteenth century. From the 1870s, the economic position of the landed aristocracy greatly worsened. Improvements in transportation and the development of refrigeration meant that cheap foreign corn and refrigerated meat suddenly started to flood the British market. Low agricultural prices led to the rapid depopulation of the countryside. The incomes of the landowners were seriously threatened, and this economic decline led to the end of their political ascendancy.

[31] For assessments of the 1883 act, see O'Leary, *Elimination of Corrupt Practices*, chap. 6; and F. Leslie D. Seidle, "Electoral Law and the Limitation of Election Expenditure in Great Britain and Canada" (B.Phil. thesis, Oxford University, 1978). For the limitations of the law about agency, see O'Leary, p. 203. O'Leary and Seidle also describe the laws before 1883 to regulate campaign spending; little need be said about them except that they did not work.

TABLE 7

THE FALLING COST OF CAMPAIGNING: EXPENDITURE PER VOTE BY
CONSERVATIVE CANDIDATES ON CONSTITUENCY CAMPAIGNS IN
GENERAL ELECTIONS, 1880–1974

General Election	Total Conservative Vote	Total Expenditure by Conservative Candidates (£1,000)	Cost per Vote, Current Prices (new pence)	Cost per Vote, Constant 1980 Prices (new pence)
1880	881,566[a]	1,400[b]	158.8[b]	3,780[b]
1910 (January)	3,127,887	651	20.8	532
1929	8,656,473	535	6.2	92.8
1950	12,502,567	470	3.8	29.1
1970	13,145,123	605	4.6	17.3
1974 (February)	11,872,180[a]	794	6.7	16.4

[a] Great Britain only.
[b] Estimate.
SOURCES: Cook and Keith, *British Historical Facts, 1830-1900*, p. 144; Butler and Sloman, *British Political Facts, 1900-1979*, pp. 207-10, 229; Neal Blewett, *The Peers, the Parties, and the People: The General Elections of 1910* (London: Macmillan, 1972), p. 290. See also sources for table 5.

Another development was of even more fundamental importance. During the last third of the nineteenth century, the power of the individual backbench member of Parliament was being eroded as national party loyalties and party discipline grew. The backbenchers, who in the 1860s regularly defied the party whips and defeated the government of the day almost at will, were by the 1880s and 1890s already displaying the subservience to party discipline that is the characteristic of the modern House of Commons.[32]

[32] Lowell showed in *The Government of England* that there was "a very great change" (vol. 2, p. 76) in voting in the House of Commons during the second half of the nineteenth century. The strength of party ties increased dramatically. Defiance of the party whip had been common; it now became exceptional. Party discipline tightened rapidly during the 1880s as the battlelines between the national parties became far more distinct than before. On the Conservative side, the percentages of divisions in the House of Commons defined by Lowell as "party votes" increased from 31 percent in 1860 to 61 percent in 1871, to 71 percent in 1881, and to 91 percent in 1894. On the Liberal side, the percentages were: 1860, 25 percent; 1871, 55 percent; 1881, 66 percent; and 1894, 81 percent (p. 81).

A connected trend was the decline of patronage and of "pork-barrel" politics.[33] A vote in Parliament could no longer be used as a lever to obtain patronage jobs. The extension of the merit system, culminating in the widespread introduction of competitive examinations for civil service positions from 1870 onward, severely curtailed the opportunities for jobbery.[34] The scope for private bill legislation had also narrowed. The previous system of private bill committees had been scrapped by the 1880s. Decisions about specific railways and canals were now in the hands of the ministers of the day and their civil servants, not of backbenchers in Parliament.

The growth of disciplined parties at this period explains why it became less worthwhile for individuals to stake such large sums as they had before on parliamentary contests. They could no longer look forward to independent power or material gain from being in the House of Commons. It is reasonable to speculate that, had the economic and political contexts been less favorable, the Corrupt Practices Act would have been less successful.

[33] By 1908, Lowell could write of "the absence of national grants [by Parliament] for local improvements" and that the occasions "where distinctly local interests come into play are not numerous" (*Government of England,* vol. 1, p. 499). This state of affairs would have been incomprehensible and intolerable to MPs half a century before.

[34] For developments in the British civil service, see Samuel E. Finer, "Patronage and the Public Service: Jeffersonian Bureaucracy and the British Tradition," *Public Administration,* vol. 30 (1952), passim; and Harold J. Hanham, *The Nineteenth-Century Constitution: Documents and Commentary* (Cambridge: Cambridge University Press, 1969), pt. 5.

2
The Plutocratic Era (1883-1922)

From the late nineteenth century onward, the overall cost of politics did not grow, despite the continuing increase in the size of the electorate. The development of cohesive parties, however, had the effect of increasing demands made on the central party war chests. This soon led the Liberals and, a little afterward, the Conservatives to seek these extra central funds from rich capitalists.

As politics became a battle between two national parties, both sides came under pressure to "show the flag" by putting forward candidates in nearly all constituencies, even though this involved fighting unwinnable seats, which, under the old system, had normally been uncontested. The candidates recruited to fight these hopeless seats could establish their reputations by making a creditable showing.[1] Since they had little chance of winning, they had every reason to spend as little as possible on their campaigns. Moreover, these unwinnable constituencies normally had weak party associations that could not supply the funds either. Consequently, the decision whether to put forward a candidate or not often depended on the availability of a grant from the central party fund. The demand for help from London grew fast during the 1880s. The £20,000–30,000 that had normally been given as central subsidies to candidates in elections up to 1880 grew to £60,000–80,000 by the 1890s.[2]

In comparison with the total traditionally spent by candidates and their patrons on constituency electioneering, the £60,000–80,000 needed for the central party funds of each party during the general elections of 1892, 1895, and 1900 was relatively insignificant. However, it had always been more difficult to collect money centrally than locally, and the landed aristocrats were reluctant to foot such enlarged

---

[1] Candidates for the House of Commons are not required to reside in the constituencies they wish to represent. It is therefore common for them to stand for constituencies in several different parts of the country during the course of a political career.

[2] Harold J. Hanham, "The Sale of Honours in Late Victorian England," *Victorian Studies*, vol. 3 (1960), p. 282.

central bills. The parties therefore turned to wealthy businessmen, who were only too ready to fill the gap.

Unlike the socially prominent landowners, who had purchased seats in the House of Commons in order to retain political influence in the localities where they owned property, the new men were driven by a craving for acceptance and prestige. Despite great wealth, many were still treated as tradesmen and excluded from high society. Some of them hoped that a public honor—a peerage (the hereditary title of "Lord"), a baronetcy (the hereditary title of "Sir"), or a knighthood (the nonhereditary title of "Sir")—would be an open sesame to the aristocratic drawing rooms of the land. These honors were awarded by the monarch on the recommendation of the prime minister. The prime minister was, in turn, advised by the chief whip in the House of Commons or by other party managers. The chief whip not only recommended titles, he also collected the central party fund. An obvious way to establish a claim to an honor was to contribute handsomely. Since it was also necessary to pretend that the knighthood or peerage was really being awarded for public service, businessmen frequently went through the motions of standing for Parliament or for municipal office. Sometimes "public service" took the form of contributions to charities. As time went on, the required tokens of service diminished. By the beginning of the twentieth century, titles were being marketed by the party whips like merchandise.

The Liberal party was the first to indulge in the sale of honors. Its party managers were apparently driven to this expedient because of the financial crisis they faced from 1886. In that year the party suffered a disastrous political split over the proposal by the elderly Liberal prime minister, William Gladstone, to grant Home Rule (regional autonomy) to Ireland. The idea was anathema to the leading Liberal aristocrats—the Whigs—many of whom owned property in Ireland and regarded Home Rule as a surrender to Irish terrorism. To make matters worse, Gladstone's proposal was also resisted by the leading progressive (Radical) politician in the party, Joseph Chamberlain. Chamberlain's importance stemmed largely from the fact that he had pioneered in Birmingham a new form of popular local Liberal organization and had founded the National Liberal Federation, which (from its Birmingham base) coordinated and encouraged the activities of Liberal constituency organizations all over the country.

Luckily for Gladstone, the vast majority of local Liberal officeholders remained loyal to his leadership and refused to support the rebellion by MPs. Even Francis Schnadhorst, who had worked for years as Chamberlain's famed political organizer in Birmingham, took

Gladstone's side and moved, together with the National Liberal Federation, to London, where he was put in charge of a reorganized Liberal headquarters.[3] Nevertheless, the desertion of the parliamentary Whigs and of Chamberlain's Radical supporters ensured the defeat of Gladstone's Liberal government in the House of Commons. The Liberal split transformed the political scene. Of the eight general elections held between 1847 and 1885, the Liberals had won no less than seven. Of the four elections to be held over the next fifteen years, the Liberals were to win only one (in 1892) and that by an inconclusive margin.

The split seriously damaged the Liberal finances. First, it meant that the parties were obliged in 1886 to fight an extra election, while party funds were still depleted by the election of 1885.[4] Second, the fact that Gladstone lost the 1886 election meant that he no longer had the benefit of the £10,000-a-year Secret Service money. The Conservatives, in a move that combined morality with long-term party advantage, announced after their return to power that the annual Secret Service grants were to be abolished.[5] Third, the desertion of the Whigs meant that the Liberals permanently lost their wealthiest aristocratic supporters, who went over to the Conservative side.[6] Gladstone's concern about the party's financial position is reflected by the appeal he sent in 1887 to the Pittsburgh philanthropist Andrew Carnegie: "while we have 9/10 or indeed 10/10 of the operations to carry on, all our wealth, except perhaps 1/10 has absconded."[7]

[3] Barry McGill, "Francis Schnadhorst and Liberal Party Organisation," *Journal of Modern History*, vol. 34 (1962), pp. 19-39. McGill shows that the rift between Chamberlain and Schnadhorst predated the 1886 Liberal split.

[4] John R. Vincent and Alistair B. Cooke, *The Governing Passion: Cabinet Government and Party Politics in Britain, 1885-1886* (Hassocks, Sussex: Harvester Press, 1974), esp. pp. 424-25.

[5] Harold J. Hanham, *Elections and Party Management: Politics in the Time of Disraeli and Gladstone* (London: Longman, 1959; and Hassocks, Sussex: Harvester Press, 1978), p. 371. Also Lord Chilston, "Aretas Akers-Douglas: 1st Viscount Chilston (1851-1926): A Great Whip," *Parliamentary Affairs*, vol. 15 (1961-1962), pp. 55-57; and Lord Chilston, *Chief Whip: The Political Life and Times of Aretas Akers-Douglas, 1st Viscount Chilston* (London: Routledge and Kegan Paul, 1961), pp. 90ff.

[6] A contemporary diary quoted by Cooke and Vincent refers to the "poverty of the ministerialists" (that is, Gladstone's followers) and the "unlimited funds" of the Whig rebels. A committee of Whigs under Albert Grey raised money to back anti-Home Rule candidates. By June 1886 he was reported by the *Birmingham Daily Post* to have collected £30,000. Surviving political papers suggest that he aimed at a total of £50,000 as a central "purse" for the anti-Gladstone rebels (Vincent and Cooke, *Governing Passion*, pp. 108, 110, 424-25).

[7] Quoted from the Gladstone Papers by McGill, "Francis Schnadhorst and Liberal Party Organisation," p. 32. Gladstone was possibly exaggerating. The

Carnegie responded with $25,000. Yet shortage of money appears to have continued to be a difficulty. As the term of the 1886 Parliament neared its end, and a general election was again imminent, the party faced the problem of finding a central fund to subsidize candidates. At the suggestion of Schnadhorst, the head of the party's central organization, Gladstone was persuaded to give an undertaking to two rich Liberal MPs that, in return for donations to the central fund, they would, if the party won the election, receive peerages at the end of the following Parliament. The transaction has come to light because the two men appear to have been worried during 1895 that the minority Liberal government was about to fall and that the bargains would not be honored. Lord Rosebery, who by this time had succeeded Gladstone as Liberal premier, was reluctant to authorize the peerages unless he received a written assurance from Gladstone himself that a deal had been made. It is the letters of the Liberal whips requesting Gladstone to confirm the existence of the arrangement that survive in the Gladstone Papers. The terms in which Lord Tweedmouth (the chief whip) and Arnold Morley (the ex–chief whip) wrote to Gladstone make it clear how direct the compact had been. Tweedmouth wrote of a "quid pro quo." According to Morley:

> About a year before the General Election of 1892, I came to see you with a letter addressed to me by Mr. Schnadhorst in which he dealt at some length upon the financial position of the Liberal Party, & the serious danger which we should encounter if by the time the Election came we were not in a position to give financial help in those cases where a contest could not effectively be carried out without such assistance. He then made two specific suggestions by means of which, he was in a position to state, the difficulty might be overcome. As a result of my interview with you I was enabled to make the necessary arrangements—one condition being that the obligation on our side was not to come into operation before the end of the Parliament which would commence after [the 1892 election].[8]

analysis of spending by Conservative and Liberal parliamentary candidates in the elections of 1885 and 1886, which is given in appendix C, shows that in 1886 Liberals spent an average of £659, compared with average Conservative spending of £752. The Liberal financial disadvantage is also indicated by the fact that the party allowed 117 Conservative and Liberal Unionist candidates to enter the House of Commons unopposed, whereas only 37 Liberals were unopposed. The Liberal financial disadvantage revealed by these figures, though considerable, did not amount to the poverty reported in some contemporary papers.

[8] Quoted from the Gladstone Papers by Hanham, "Sale of Honours," p. 284.

The two men duly received their peerages. They were James Williamson, the linoleum magnate, who became Lord Ashton, and Sydney Stern, who was created Lord Wandsworth. The awards were not popular.[9] Williamson was contemptuously dubbed "Lord Linoleum" and was forced by public pressure to move from his home county of Lancashire.[10]

It is possible that the Liberals had already made encouraging hints to certain businessmen before the arrangements with Williamson and Stern in 1891. A scholarly article about Schnadhorst reports the intriguing fact that, on top of his annual Liberal party salary of £1,050 (about £30,000 in 1980 values), he received £10,000 at a testimonial dinner in 1887 and a further £5,000 in November 1892, shortly before his retirement.[11] It seems extraordinary that a party that was so short of funds should have been able to afford these huge amounts (£15,000 is equivalent to over £400,000 in 1980 values). The testimonials must have included contributions from businessmen. Their admiration for the Liberal organizer may have been combined with the hope that he would use his good offices to obtain titles for them (and, on his retirement, with monetary gratitude for past services).

The Conservatives during the late 1880s were in a stronger financial position than the Liberals and were able to depend on aristocratic sources until the 1890s. In the 1890s, the situation seems to have changed. It appears that the Conservative party managers could no longer afford to ignore the overtures of plutocrats. The change is seen in the correspondence between Captain Richard Middleton, the Conservative chief agent (that is, the head official of the Central Office), and the Conservative prime minister, Lord Salisbury. In the early 1890s, Middleton felt assured of aristocratic support for the central election fund. It would not be long before he felt obliged to turn to other sources.

[9] Elie Halévy, *A History of the English People in the Nineteenth Century*, vol. 6, *The Rule of Democracy, 1905-1914*, 2d rev. ed. (London: Ernest Benn, 1952), p. 313.

[10] See Hanham, "Sale of Honours," pp. 286-87. Hanham quotes, as an example of the contemporary criticism against the peerages, which it was (correctly) suspected had been sold, the writing of H. Labouchere in *Truth*, vol. 38 (1895), p. 137: " 'It does not smell,' said Vespasian of the money that he acquired from a tax on the latrines of Rome. But the money brought in by this trafficking in hereditary legislatorships reeks of corruption. It stinks!' "

[11] McGill, "Francis Schnadhorst and Liberal Party Organisation," pp. 30, 38. The gradually changing social and political climate that led to the sale of titles is described by Hanham in "Sale of Honours" and also by Halévy, *History of the English People*, vol. 6, pp. 308ff.

Before the 1892 election, Middleton wrote confidently of the Conservative party's ability to raise £80,000 to give as aid for English and Irish seats: "with a little management this can easily be done." A marginal note to Middleton's letter by Salisbury's private secretary suggests that the money was to be raised from "the great agricultural owners." Moreover, Middleton's sense of security is seen in the fact that he did not require Salisbury to write letters asking for money: "All finance of this kind is of so delicate a nature" that Middleton did not wish Salisbury's name "connected with it *in any way* whatever."[12]

The Conservative whip in the House of Lords managed to collect £45,000 from the Tory peers in 1892. Though large by the standards of the 1870s, this was little over half the total Middleton was aiming for. Perhaps this was a reflection of the agricultural depression. In the 1895 election, contributions from Tory peers fell to £37,500.[13] Shortly after the 1892 campaign (which the Conservatives narrowly lost), Middleton started a series of letters to Salisbury asking for his help in raising money from the rajahs in India. Reversing his previous view that the party leader should not connect his name with fund raising, Middleton several times requested Salisbury to acknowledge their checks and to make personal appeals to them for money. By 1895, he was recommending to Salisbury that the party should go even further to induce "the big Rajahs" to make the donations that he was "very anxious to get": "Without doubt we might look for very material support from India if we can meet their wishes with regard to representation either in the *Lords* or Commons—the former seems to me the easier."[14] The Indian rajahs did not obtain seats in the House of Lords. Nevertheless, the unusual correspondence illustrates Middleton's anxiety to find new sources of money.

By the late 1890s, the Conservatives were receiving large sums from millionaire businessmen, who were primarily motivated by a desire for political honors. During the 1900 campaign, for instance, Middleton asked Salisbury to thank William Waldorf Astor for a "spontaneous" gift of £20,000 to the central election fund.[15] (This

[12] Hatfield House mss., Third Marquess of Salisbury, E 130, fo. 150ff. (Salisbury Papers).

[13] Quoted from the Salisbury Papers by Hanham, *Elections and Party Management*, p. 372.

[14] Middleton to Salisbury, April 22, 1895, and May 16, 1895, Salisbury Papers, E 130, fo. 303ff.

[15] Middleton to Salisbury, September 21, 1900, Salisbury Papers, E 130, fo. 543.

was a very large sum for that time—equivalent to over £½ million in 1980 values. Astor's gift was over half the amount raised in 1895 from all the Tory peers combined.) Astor, a member of the famous American dynasty, had become a British citizen the previous year.[16] He put strong pressure on the Conservatives to give him a peerage before the election of 1906,[17] but his wish for ennoblement was not granted until 1916.

Another business contributor was Ernest Terah Hooley. His donation became public knowledge when, in 1898, he went bankrupt and the official trustee asked the Conservatives for the return of the money he had given to the party.[18] Hooley was one of the most colorful self-made robber barons of the day. He made (and lost) fortunes by buying and selling companies (including Dunlop, Schweppes, Bovril, and Singer). His method of operation was itself an indication of the worsening fortunes of the aristocracy. In order to boost public confidence in his ventures, he employed titled personages (including Sir Winston Churchill's father, Lord Randolph Churchill) as figurehead directors of his companies, a role that some members of the aristocracy were now willing to play. Hooley employed a prominent Conservative politician, the former judge advocate general Sir William Marriott, as a contact man to recruit peers and to forward his personal social ambitions. Hooley appears to have bought his way into the prestigious Conservative meeting place, the Carlton Club. Through Marriott, Hooley offered £50,000 to Conservative funds. Middleton declined to accept. However, the trustees of the party's central fund had already, in 1897, accepted a sum of £10,000 from Hooley.[19] This was later returned to the official trustee for the benefit of Hooley's creditors.

These transactions indicate the growing part played by businessmen in financing the Tory party. However, there is no evidence that the contributors received titles as direct rewards for their help during the Salisbury/Middleton period.

[16] See Michael Astor, *Tribal Feeling* (London: John Murray, 1964). This book, written by his grandson, is quite open about the reasons for Astor's eventual ennoblement: "There was plenty of precedence for purchasing a title. It had been done before and was to be done many times again. William Waldorf, without showing any marked propensities for public service, acquired two titles. He was made a baron one year, and a viscount the next" (p. 19).

[17] Robert Blake, *The Unknown Prime Minister: The Life and Times of Andrew Bonar Law, 1858-1923* (London: Eyre and Spottiswoode, 1955), p. 101.

[18] There are useful references to the affair in Hanham, "Sale of Honours."

[19] Memoranda by Salisbury's private secretary, November 21 and 26, 1898, Salisbury Papers, E 130, fos. 492, 495.

In 1902, Salisbury retired as prime minister. Soon afterward Middleton retired as Conservative chief agent.[20] The political situation worsened for the Conservatives. By-election defeats and internal splits over policy made it highly likely that the Conservatives would lose the next general election. This situation encouraged the trade in titles by both parties. Plutocrats with Conservative connections were anxious to receive recognition before the party lost power (and the Tory party managers had an incentive to fill the central war chest in anticipation of a period of opposition). On the Liberal side, the hope of future honors acted as a stimulus for contributions.

The correspondence during 1905 between the Conservative chief whip, Sir Alexander Acland-Hood, and Sandars, the influential private secretary to the Conservative premier, Arthur Balfour, makes it clear that honors were sold by the Conservatives during the weeks before the resignation of the government in December 1905. The scale of the traffic does not appear to have been large in comparison with later practice, and there is some limited justification for Hood's defensive claim to Sandars that his original list of proposed resignation honors was "respectable and moderate." [21] Nevertheless, the principle of giv-

[20] It is interesting to note that Sir John Blundell Maple, who received his baronetcy in 1897, left a substantial bequest to Middleton when he died in 1904. This is reported in the *Conservative Agents' Journal* and in *The Times*. Maple was the proprietor of London's leading furniture store and was Conservative MP for the London constituency of Dulwich, which Middleton briefly represented on the London County Council. Middleton became the chief executor of Maple's will. Thus, the head official of Conservative Central Office, like his Liberal counterpart, Schnadhorst, became very comfortably off. His friendship with Maple may help to account for Middleton's refusal to accept the £50,000 offered by Hooley to Conservative party funds. Maple, who had had some unpleasant business dealings with Hooley, probably doubted his integrity. A recent study of Conservative party organization in the late nineteenth century reveals that, in addition to the later bequest from Maple, Middleton "was presented with two bulging purses of £10,000 a piece" after the general elections of 1895 and 1900. This bounty of £20,000 (over £½ million in 1980 values) compares with the £15,000 received by his Liberal counterpart, Schnadhorst. See P. T. Marsh, *The Discipline of Popular Government: Lord Salisbury's Domestic Statecraft, 1881-1902* (Atlantic Highlands, N.J.: Humanities Press, 1978), pp. 189, 212.

[21] Hood to Sandars, December 8, 1905, Sandars Papers, 750, fo. 203. A list of businessmen receiving peerages during Balfour's premiership is given by Halévy, *History of the English People*, vol. 6, p. 310. Balfour's government of 1902-1905 saw the creation of eighteen peers, including five businessmen. In Liberal eyes, the honors given by Balfour were anything but moderate. Roy Douglas writes that R. H. Davies "who was Secretary to the Liberal Chief Whip at the operative time, has written to the present author that George Whiteley [Liberal chief whip after the fall of Balfour's Conservative ministry] took stern and effective measures to suppress the touts who had evidently been active in the past—that is, under the Conservative Government down to December 1905" (Roy Douglas, *The History of the Liberal Party, 1895-1970*

ing titles in exchange for political contributions had by now been accepted by the Tories. In one letter, the chief whip wrote from Scotland (in his indecipherable handwriting): "Haig [the chief agent] comes here on Monday to talk about Scottish elections and Honours—B.———'s [?] man A.——— [?] is among names I have had on my list. He is not a bad sort and I think is a 20 [?] man—perhaps B could get a bit more out of him."[22]

One of the most controversial new peers was the powerful newspaper proprietor Alfred Harmsworth, who became Lord Northcliffe. The new lord was proprietor of the country's newspaper with the largest circulation, the *Daily Mail*. It was widely thought that he had paid handsomely for his ennoblement, a rumor that Lord Northcliffe's biographers later denied. It seems that the peerage was given largely on the recommendation of the king. However, money, or the hope of it, was also a determining factor. In Hood's words to Sandars:

> Obviously the King wishes Harmsworth to have a Peerage. If he doesn't get it now he will get it when C. B. [Campbell-Bannerman, the Liberal leader] makes his Peers on taking office. We should then lose all his money and his confidence —I very much dislike the business, but as we *can't* stop it in the future why make to the . . . [indecipherable] a present to the other side.[23]

Conservative suspicions that the Liberals were preparing to reward their largest subscribers with titles when they regained power were not without foundation. An exceptionally clear picture of Liberal funds between 1900 and 1906 can be obtained from the papers of Herbert Gladstone (the former prime minister's son), who was Liberal chief whip at the time.[24] Herbert Gladstone's description of his fundraising activities was written in the early 1920s, when the sale of honors had become a public scandal. His retrospective version was intended to demonstrate that "[i]n no single case did I hint directly or

---

[London: Sidgwick and Jackson, 1971], p. 159). This Liberal view of Tory sales of titles should be compared with the Conservative view of Liberal intentions revealed in Hood's letter to Sandars about the peerage for Harmsworth, which is quoted below. Each party used the misdeeds (or supposed actions) of the other as the excuse for selling peerages.

[22] Hood to Sandars, October 19, 1905, Sandars Papers, 749, fo. 163.

[23] Hood to Sandars, December 5, 1905, Sandars Papers, 750, fo. 147.

[24] Herbert Gladstone's papers were the basis of Sir Charles Mallet, *Herbert Gladstone: A Memoir* (London: Hutchinson, 1932), and of Trevor O. Lloyd, "The Whip as Paymaster: Herbert Gladstone and Party Organisation," *English Historical Review*, vol. 89 (1974).

TABLE 8

Donations to Central Liberal Funds Exceeding £10,000 and the Award of Titles, 1900–1906
(in pounds)

	1900 Election	1906 Election	Other Occasions, 1900–1905	Title Awarded	
Wills		20,000		Peerage	1905
Whiteley		20,000		Peerage	1908
Lever	5,000	10,000	100[a]	Baronetcy	1911
				Peerage	1917
Ashton	10,000[a]	5,000		Peerage	1895
Langman			15,000	Baronetcy	1906
Horniman	10,500	2,625		Baronetcy agreed	1906
Joicey	2,000	10,000		Peerage	1905
Robinson		10,000	10,000[b]	Baronetcy	1908
Total raised from big donations	27,500[a]	77,625	25,100[a]		

NOTE: Figures include donations to central Liberal funds for the 1900 and 1906 elections recorded in the Herbert Gladstone Papers.

[a] At least.

[b] To Lord Harcourt.

SOURCE: Adapted from Lloyd, "The Whip as Paymaster."

even indirectly at an honour."[25] Gladstone attempted to show that some men who received peerages from the Liberal government that took office in December 1905 had not subscribed (though, in these cases, he frankly admits his disappointment that they failed to do so).[26] Nevertheless, there is a high correlation between large subscriptions and titles. During Herbert Gladstone's time as Liberal chief whip, including the elections of 1900 and 1906,[27] the Liberals received donations exceeding £10,000 from eight men (table 8). Apart from one, who died before he could receive the baronetcy that had been agreed (Horniman), all received honors under Liberal administrations.

[25] Quoted by Lloyd, "The Whip as Paymaster," p. 789.

[26] Herbert Gladstone, draft of autobiography, quoted in John Wilson, *CB: A Life of Sir Henry Campbell-Bannerman* (London: Constable, 1973), p. 582.

[27] Herbert Gladsone was responsible for collecting Liberal funds before the 1906 campaign but was not chief whip during the election itself. This was because Balfour's Conservative government resigned in December 1905 and Herbert Gladstone became home secretary in the Liberal caretaker government. The general election was held at the beginning of 1906.

They included Williamson (by now Lord Ashton), whose bargain with Schnadhorst in 1891 has been described above. The total subscribed by the top eight came to at least £130,225 (over £3 million in 1980 values).

The large Liberal donors were predominantly highly successful entrepreneurs. Sir William-Henry Wills (Lord Winterstoke) was a tobacco magnate, George Whitely (Lord Marchamley) a Yorkshire brewer, William Lever (Lord Leverhulme) a noted soap manufacturer, Lord Ashton (the former J. Williamson) a Lancashire linoleum manufacturer, as previously mentioned, Frederick Horniman a leading tea merchant, Sir James Joicey (Lord Joicey) a Northern mine owner, and Joseph Robinson a South African business tycoon. Herbert Gladstone later justified the titles received by some of these men by their public and philanthropic services. It is probable that in all cases except that of Whiteley (who served briefly as Liberal chief whip) political contributions were the decisive factor.

Herbert Gladstone was later to cite these donations to show that they were modest by post-1906 standards.[28] They are, however, large compared with amounts raised by nineteenth-century Liberal whips for central election funds until the 1880s. In his capacity as chief whip, Gladstone spent £60,000 on the 1900 election. In addition, a special election fund of at least £11,000 was collected by the National Liberal Federation (NLF) (and extra money may have been collected in Scotland and Ireland for regional distribution). The arrangement between the Liberal chief whip and the NLF appears to have been that the NLF raised funds (in relatively small contributions) for giving preelection aid to needy constituencies to help voter registration and that the whip's fund concentrated on aid to candidates for campaign expenses. The total spent by the Liberals in the 1900 election was a minimum of £71,000 (if one includes unrecorded donations to the NLF central fund and possible Scottish and Irish funds, the actual total was probably £75,000–80,000). In 1906, the combined total spent from the whip's fund and from the special fund raised by the NLF rose to over £133,000.[29]

---

[28] Lloyd, "The Whip as Paymaster," p. 805.

[29] This excludes funds raised independently by the well-endowed organization of Liberal imperialists, the Liberal League. For the finances of the Liberal League, see H. Colin G. Matthew, *The Liberal Imperialists* (Oxford: Oxford University Press, 1973), p. 90; and Douglas, *History of the Liberal Party*, p. 28.

The amount raised for the 1906 election by Liberal headquarters was even larger than the amount spent: £158,000 was raised, and £10,000 more was shown in the accounts as "promised," making a total of £168,000 raised for the election. This includes the special NLF fund (Lloyd, "The Whip as Paymaster," pp. 788–89).

After the return of the Liberal government in the 1906 election, the size of the haul grew still larger. During little more than two years as chief whip, Whiteley, in addition to meeting the routine bills of the national Liberal organization, built up a reserve of over £½ million (over £15 million at 1980 values). On handing over to his successor, Whiteley reported to the new Liberal prime minister, Asquith, that he had increased the party's reserves from £20,000 after the 1906 campaign to "£519,000 less under £5000 overdrawn at the bank."[30] This was large enough to meet the central costs of no less than four election campaigns at the 1906 level of spending. But the collection of money continued as the demand for peerages continued. The two elections of 1910 provided further opportunities for a traffic in titles. Neal Blewett records that the Liberal retailer Sir Hudson Kearley intimated that while he "wasn't going to buy" a peerage, if he became a peer "he would like to voluntarily help the party by £25,000 or so." Kearley became Lord Devonport in 1910. Blewett quotes another example when the future Liberal prime minister, Lloyd George, informed the chief whip that with respect to the "general helpfulness" of "our Cardiff friend," "his prospects are distinctly good when the next ennobling list appears."[31]

The total central aid given to Liberal candidates in the two elections of 1910 is recorded in Asquith's papers as £136,185 for January 1910 and £157,849 for December 1910.[32] In order to reach the total central expenditures for these elections, it is also necessary to add some extra items. (1) It is recorded in the annual report of the National Liberal Federation that a special NLF fund was collected for the 1910 campaigns (presumably similar to the special fund of 1905), but the amount is not disclosed.[33] Assuming that the amount spent from this fund was the same for the two 1910 elections combined as the NLF fund for the election of 1906, the extra amounted to £40,000 (or £20,000 for each campaign in 1910). (2) A small sum must be added for the cost of central campaign activities (say, £5,000 for each campaign).[34] This gives a total of £161,185 for January 1910 and £182,849 for December 1910.

[30] Whiteley to Asquith, May 29, 1908, Asquith Papers, 11, fos. 139-40. Quoted in Neal Blewett, *The Peers, the Parties, and the People: The General Elections of 1910* (London: Macmillan, 1972), p. 291.

[31] Blewett, *Peers, Parties, and People*, p. 292.

[32] Asquith Papers, 141, fo. 201.

[33] *Proceedings in Connection with the Thirty-third Annual Meeting of the National Liberal Federation* (London: Liberal Publication Department, 1911), p. 47.

[34] Whereas the Asquith Papers give the totals spent by Liberal headquarters in the elections of 1922, 1923, and 1924, the figures for 1910 and 1918 include only central grants for candidates' expenses. It is assumed that other central expenditure in 1910 was at a level between that of 1906 and that of 1922.

Information about Conservative funds at this period is less complete, and there are no surviving accounts for the years before 1909.[35] Papers quoted by John Ramsden show that Conservative Central Office gave grants to candidates of £116,000 in December 1910.[36] Also, Ramsden estimates the amount spent by the Central Office on central campaign activities at £20,000, giving a total of £136,000.[37] This excludes Scotland and also excludes expenditures by the Liberal Unionists, the former Liberals who had joined the rebellion over Irish Home Rule in 1886. They were by 1910 effectively part of the Conservative party, and their organization merged with the Conservative Central Office soon after the 1910 campaign.[38]

While the Conservatives were out of office from 1906 onward, the party whips were not in a position to award titles. They could, and did, promise them as a matter of course. A memorandum from the Conservative party chairman, Sir Arthur Steel-Maitland, to the new party leader, Andrew Bonar Law, stated shortly after the 1910 elections that a "nest egg" of over £300,000 had been built up by the Conservative chief whip partly because "[a] year's peerages are hypothecated."[39] Steel-Maitland expressed confidence in the ability of the Conservatives to tap several sources of money that would not require promises of titles. He acknowledged, however, that success

---

[35] A detailed analysis of Conservative finances for 1910-1930 is included in John A. Ramsden, "The Organisation of the Conservative and Unionist Party in Britain, 1910-1930" (D.Phil Thesis, Oxford University, 1974). This chapter draws heavily on this valuable research. Lack of comprehensive statistics about Conservative central finances results from the absence of efficient accounting methods during Hood's tenure as chief whip. In the words of a memorandum on the state of the Conservative Central Office prepared after the 1910 elections for the new party leader, Bonar Law, by the new party chairman, Steel-Maitland:

> I was prepared for a lack of system but not for what I found . . . there was no annual balance sheet. They could not tell you within £10,000 what the year's expenditure had been, probably not within £20,000. There was no proper classification of expenditure, no recovery of loans (quoted in Blake, *Unknown Prime Minister*, p. 100).

[36] Boraston to Steel-Maitland, October 28, 1912, quoted from the Steel-Maitland Papers in Ramsden, "Organisation of the Conservative Party," p. 354.

[37] Ramsden, "Organisation of the Conservative Party," p. 367.

[38] The finance of the Liberal Unionist group in comparison with that of the Conservatives is indicated by constituency election expenses in the 1910 elections. The total expenses of Conservative candidates amounted to £558,822 in January 1910 and those of Liberal Unionists to £92,593. In December 1910 the totals were £454,635 and £48,120 (Blewett, *Peers, Parties, and People*, p. 290). When negotiations were proceeding in 1912 about the integration of the Conservative Central Office and the Liberal Unionist headquarters, it was agreed that the Liberal Unionists would pay one-fifth of the costs of the integrated Conservative and Unionist Central Office (Sir Austen Chamberlain, *Politics from Inside: An Epistolary Chronicle, 1906-1914* [London: Cassell, 1936], p. 419).

[39] Quoted by Blake, *Unknown Prime Minister*, p. 100.

43

in collecting a central target of £120,000 to £140,000 a year would also depend on agreements about "future honours."

The clear financial accounts left by Steel-Maitland for the five years 1909–1914 show that, during the period between 1911 and the outbreak of the First World War, the Conservatives were able to collect central funds on an unprecedented scale. The Liberals likewise seem to have kept their central coffers full. By now, the reserves of both parties were sufficient to fight several elections, even supposing that the flow of money abated, which it showed no signs of doing.

The outbreak of war led to the suspension of normal party politics and to the postponement of the general election that had been due to take place during 1914 or 1915. The trade in titles and the promises of titles appear to have continued. From December 1916 onward, when Lloyd George became premier, the volume of transactions seems to have been particularly large. In December 1916, dissatisfaction with the way in which the war was being managed led to a palace revolution and to the replacement of the Liberal prime minister, Asquith. The new prime minister, Lloyd George, was also a Liberal, but the revolt against Asquith owed its success largely to Conservative support. This led to a deep split in the Liberal party and to a deadly feud between the former premier and his successor. Most Liberal MPs and the official Liberal headquarters remained loyal to Asquith. Asquith remained the titular leader of the Liberal party and refused to accept the offer of a place in Lloyd George's cabinet. This placed Lloyd George in the unusual position of being prime minister without being also party leader. It meant that he did not have control of the large existing central party fund, which remained in the hands of the former premier. Lloyd George reacted by using the prime minister's power to create peers to obtain money to form a political machine of his own. The instability of his position led Lloyd George, in his rush to accumulate financial reserves, to sanction sales of titles even more blatantly and carelessly than had been the practice under his Liberal predecessors.[40] The Conservatives were also given a share of the honors market, since Lloyd George was dependent upon their support in the House of Commons for the survival of his Coalition government. It was the first opportunity the Tories had enjoyed since the end of 1905 to recommend supporters for titles, and they were only too pleased at the chance to clear the backlog of promises.

[40] Douglas, *History of the Liberal Party*, p. 159.

During the First World War and the four years following it, the plutocratic era was at its height. The turmoil of all-out war had the effect of accelerating and accentuating social and economic trends that had already been noticeable before the outbreak of the fighting. Men had become millionaires before 1914. Now the war economy meant that new millionaires were created more quickly. The ambition of rich men to gain social acceptance was a well-established phenomenon. Under wartime and postwar conditions, the new tycoons were intent on gaining titles and other forms of recognition without the normal waiting period. Even before the war, many men of wealth had recruited go-betweens both subtly and barefacedly to forward their claims. Now the channels through which the commercial exchange of money for title had passed became better organized, even cruder.

Some exotic, highly dubious characters acted as procurers for the plutocrats and the political parties. The most notorious of the touts was an actor-cum-Secret Service informer-cum-suspected murderer called Maundy Gregory.[41] The politicians with whom the honors brokers were in contact were themselves men of doubtful standards. In Lloyd George's team, they included Sir William Sutherland, who reportedly hawked baronetcies at West End clubs.

Conservative fund raising had, since 1911, no longer been a responsibility of the party's chief whip in the House of Commons but had been allocated to the holders of two newly created offices, the party chairman and the party treasurer. The Conservative treasurer since 1911, Lord Farquhar, was "rapidly failing in mind"[42] after the war and the Conservative leader, Bonar Law, eventually discovered that he had been putting some of the money received for political purposes into his personal account and that other donations, intended for Tory funds, had been given over to Lloyd George instead. Lloyd George rewarded Farquhar by raising him from a lord to an earl, and Bonar Law eventually dismissed him as party treasurer. One of the main questions the Conservative accountant asked Farquhar to explain was how he had disposed of a donation of £200,000 from Lord Astor (the former William Waldorf Astor).[43] The existence of such a

---

[41] Three biographies of Gregory have appeared: Gerald Macmillan, *Honours for Sale: The Strange Story of Maundy Gregory* (London: Richards Press, 1954); Donald McCormick, *Murder by Perfection: Maundy Gregory, the Man behind Two Unsolved Mysteries?* (London: Long John, 1970); and Tom Cullen, *Maundy Gregory: Purveyor of Honours* (London: Bodley Head, 1974). Macmillan and Cullen give useful bibliographical references.

[42] Robert Blake, *The Conservative Party from Peel to Churchill* (London: Fontana, 1972), p. 230.

[43] Blake, *Unknown Prime Minister*, pp. 496-98.

huge contribution (£200,000 in 1919 was equivalent to over £2 million in 1980 values) indicates how far the plutocratic system had developed since the first bargain about peerages was struck by the Liberals in 1891.

A description of this bonanza of gifts from entrepreneurs suggests, at first sight, that the amount of money being devoted to politics was growing rapidly during the plutocratic era. It needs to be stressed that the escalation of giving was confined to the central parties. Locally, there was a slight decline in levels of income and expenditure. This meant that the combined expenditure of central and local organizations remained in check. Analysis of central and local spending on general election campaigns and on routine political activity at this period demonstrates this.

Central Party Spending

General Election Campaigns. The size of central election funds increased greatly during the plutocratic era. Almost all of the money collected nationally was transferred for use by parliamentary candidates and their local organizations. As late as the 1920s, very little was spent by the national party headquarters on central campaign activities. The detailed accounts that have survived for Liberal central expenditure in 1906 show that, out of total campaign spending of over £133,000, all but £1,000 was transferred to constituency parties and to candidates. The £1,000 spent on central activities was devoted to the expenses of officials at Liberal headquarters and to centrally paid speakers.[44] The national organizations were active during campaigns in producing party literature. For instance, the Liberals sent out 42 million publications in the first election of 1910 and nearly 24 million in the second election of that year.[45] However, it appears that these items were paid for and were not a drain on central funds. In these same elections, the central Conservative organization sold 46 million and 40 million leaflets.[46] That central funds were used predominantly to aid candidates is seen in the Liberal election accounts for 1922, 1923, and 1924. In all three of these elections, about 95 percent of central expenditure was used for this purpose. This pattern is shown in table 9.

[44] Lloyd, "The Whip as Paymaster," p. 789.
[45] National Liberal Federation, annual reports, 1910, p. 17, and 1911, p. 21.
[46] Ramsden, "Organisation of the Conservative Party," p. 226.

46

TABLE 9

Liberal Central General Election Funds, 1900–1924

General Election	Total Expenditure from Central Funds[a] (pounds)	Used for Central Campaign Activities		Transferred for Use by Constituencies and Candidates	
		Amount (pounds)	Percentage of total	Amount (pounds)	Percentage of total
1900	71,000	1,000[b]	1[b]	70,000	99
1906	133,085	1,000	1[b]	132,085	99
1910	161,185	5,000[b]	3[b]	156,185	97
1910	182,849	5,000[b]	3[b]	177,849	97
1918	100,493	5,000[b]	5[b]	95,493	95
1922	126,948	6,033	5	120,915	95
1923	149,473	6,497	4	142,976	96
1924	123,479	6,524	5	116,955	95

[a] Probably underestimates, since additional funds were probably disbursed by the party organizations in Scotland, Wales, and Ireland.

[b] Based on the assumptions (1) that this item was the same in 1900 as given in the Herbert Gladstone papers for 1906 and (2) that the figures for 1910 and 1918 were slightly less than those for 1922, 1923, and 1924 shown in the Asquith Papers.

Sources: For 1900 and 1906, Lloyd, "The Whip as Paymaster"; for 1910-1924, Asquith Papers, 141, fo. 201.

The increased central grants recevied by parliamentary candidates do not seem to have affected the trend of declining costs of constituency electioneering.[47] The main consequence was to make

[47] As in chapter 1, I have not attempted to include personal expenditures by parliamentary candidates in their constituencies or money spent by politically connected pressure groups and organizations.

1. *"Charitable" expenditures by parliamentary candidates.* The legal limits on spending on constituency campaigns did not put an end to the distribution of largesse by MPs and candidates between elections. According to the *Conservative Agents' Journal*, one of the party's MPs had "afforded practical proof of his interest" in the children of his constituency at the time of King Edward VII's coronation "by presenting a bank book with a deposit of one shilling to nine thousand of them" (*Conservative Agents' Journal*, no. 3, July 1902). These gifts cost the MP in question £450, that is, about £10,000 in 1980 values. It is not possible to tell how widespread such politically motivated contributions were or to assess whether they were less widespread than during the aristocratic era.

2. *Politically connected pressure groups and organizations.* This chapter does not take account of the finances of politically connected organizations, some of which were highly active at this time. On the Liberal side, mention has already

candidates more dependent on payments from London, as shown in table 10.

Routine Central Spending. After the passage of the Corrupt Practices Act, 1883, the national offices of the two main parties grew in importance. Such central officials as Middleton and Schnadhorst were highly influential men. Nevertheless, the power of the permanent extraparliamentary headquarters did not mean that they immediately became large or costly organizations. Roy Douglas reports that in the 1890s the entire Liberal central party machine, including the Liberal Central Association, the National Liberal Federation, and the Liberal publication department (LPD), consisted of about ten employees at the most, plus a few packers of literature.[48] On the Conservative side, the organization developed somewhat earlier. Middleton established a network of district agents with offices in different regions of the country as early as 1886. This was a step the Liberals did not copy until 1908. Nevertheless, the Conservative Central Office, too, remained a compact organization until after 1911. According to Ramsden, the full-time staff of Conservative Central Office in 1911, excluding district agents, was "just six men plus typists."[49]

The relatively small size of the parties' national offices meant that the routine costs remained small. The cost of the Liberal head-

---

been made of the Liberal League. Several pro-Conservative bodies were listed in a 1908 debate about political funds that took place in the House of Commons. One MP protested about "the way in which large sums, derived from the secret funds of the Tariff Reform League and other similar societies, are spent in electoral contests without being returned in the candidates' expenses." It was alleged that "paid canvassers solicited votes nominally on behalf of the [Tariff Reform] League, but in reality on behalf of the candidate . . . these things were done under the cover and shadow of a body really acting as his agents" (House of Commons Debates, 4th series, vol. 178, February 19, 1908, cols. 917-19). Besides the Tariff Reform League, other politically connected bodies mentioned in the debate were the Primrose League, Rural Labourers' League, Brewers' League, and Protestant League (col. 923).

In a fascinating work published in 1932, a former senior Conservative official made a similar point. He wrote that, before 1918, "organisations such as the Tariff Reform League and the Free Trade Union, . . . nominally independent of any Party, actually closely associated with Party programmes and policy, poured out immense sums at every election, in fiction for a cause, actually to secure or prevent the return of the candidates with which they were really associated or to which they were opposed" (Philip G. Cambray, The Game of Politics [London: John Murray, 1932], p. 155). Some organizations connected with the Labour party are mentioned in the note at the end of chapter 3, and "politically relevant" expenditures in the modern period are briefly discussed in chapters 8 and 9 of this book.

[48] Douglas, History of the Liberal Party, p. 17.

[49] Ramsden, "Organisation of the Conservative Party," p. 272.

TABLE 10

Dependence of Liberal Candidates on Central Grants toward General Election Expenses, 1880–1923

(in pounds)

General Election	Provided by Candidates and by Constituency Parties	Received from Central Funds		Total Election Expenses of Liberal Candidates
		Amount	%	
1880	961,000[a]	39,000[a]	4.0	1,000,000[a]
1906	250,831	93,085	27.0	343,916
1910	414,049	136,185	24.8	550,234
1910	253,996	157,849	35.7	411,845
1923	215,306[a]	142,128	39.8	357,400[a]

NOTE: Column 1 equals column 4 minus column 2.

[a] Approximately.

SOURCES: Lloyd, "The Whip as Paymaster," pp. 788-90; Asquith Papers, 141, fo. 201; Trevor O. Lloyd, *The General Election of 1880* (Oxford: Oxford University Press, 1968), p. 75; Blewett, *Peers, Parties, and People*, p. 290; and David E. Butler and Anne Sloman, *British Political Facts, 1900-1979* (London: Macmillan, 1980), p. 229.

quarters, when Herbert Gladstone was chief whip (1899–1905), was about £20,000, including grants to candidates for by-elections. Income came from three funds: the Liberal Central Association (about £2,000 a year); the National Liberal Federation (about £4,000 a year); and the chief whip (about £16,000 a year).[50]

After the Liberals gained power in the election of 1906 and greatly enlarged their central funds through selling honors, the size of the party headquarters expanded. The formation of eight regional federations in 1908, each with separate offices, meant, according to Sir Charles Mallet's memoir of Herbert Gladstone, that the annual cost of the central Liberal organization "reached the astounding figure of £100,000 a year,"[51] from 1908 onward. The cost of running the central organization probably continued at this level until the outbreak of war in 1914, after which it declined because of the political truce. Mallet reports that routine central costs in 1918 amounted to £80,000.[52] This does not include the running costs of Lloyd George's

[50] Lloyd, "The Whip as Paymaster," pp. 788-89.
[51] Mallet, *Herbert Gladstone*, p. 194.
[52] Ibid.

rival political headquarters, which had been established by this time. From 1919 onward the size of the official Liberal headquarters gradually became smaller, and the cost of upkeep fell to £50,000 a year by 1922.[53]

For the Conservatives, annual accounts for the financial years 1909/1910–1913/1914 have been drawn up by Ramsden on the basis of the Steel-Maitland papers. During these years, the costs of running Central Office grew from £22,414 to £45,525. Including other items, such as the cost of the district offices and of grants to constituencies, overall annual routine expenditure of the Conservative central organization grew from £73,411 in 1909/1910 to £150,715 in 1913/1914.[54] The increase in spending during these years is explained by the expansion of activities under Steel-Maitland's chairmanship. Although no accurate party accounts were kept for years before 1909/1910, expenditure was probably comparable with that of 1909/1910. After the outbreak of the First World War, spending fell once again. The accounts in table 11, for the years 1909/1910 to 1913/1914, probably show Conservative central spending at the highest level reached during the plutocratic era. Although both Liberal and Conservative headquarters grew around 1910, the cost of their upkeep, even after their expansion, was small considering the size of the greatly enlarged incomes the central organizations were by now collecting.

Constituency Finances

Local Spending. The Corrupt Practices Act, 1883, stimulated the development of constituency organizations operating on a permanent basis between elections. The limits placed by the 1883 act on the permitted number of paid campaign helpers meant that parliamentary campaigns had henceforth to rely considerably on volunteers. However, elections under the British system could be held at short notice. It was difficult to recruit helpers in the time available unless the core of an organization already existed. The answer was to form committes that would hold social and political meetings between elections and could be transformed into campaign committees when the date of the poll had been announced.

The growth of permanent constituency associations was a feature of party politics in the 1880s and 1890s and appears to have been, to a considerable extent, a consequence of the 1883 act. The cut in

[53] Ibid.
[54] Ramsden, "Organisation of the Conservative Party," p. 331.

50

TABLE 11
CONSERVATIVE CENTRAL OFFICE ROUTINE EXPENDITURE, 1909/1910–1913/1914

	1909/10	1910/11	1911/12	1912/13	1913/14
Central Office	23,414	28,401	57,163	42,425	45,525
House of Commons office	1,281	1,232	1,134	1,247	1,217
Central Office district agents	6,150	7,590	10,580	11,450	11,414
Special campaigns	16,314	19,984	19,653	14,076	16,508
Constituency grants	10,311	13,271	12,463	20,274	25,299
Grants to outside organizations	5,192	12,381	10,492	13,158	9,675
London department	2,912	3,548	9,379	9,282	12,118
Miscellaneous	7,834	9,663	12,617	13,108	27,953
Total	73,411	96,073	133,486	126,214	150,715

NOTE: Figures exclude general election expenditure. Figures are as in source.
SOURCE: Ramsden, "Organisation of the Conservative Party," p. 331 (from the Steel-Maitland Papers).

permitted election spending thus contributed to the growth of political participation.[55] The formation of permanently active constituency parties was also encouraged by the national party organizations and, in particular, by the Conservative Central Office under Middleton.

The development of permanent local party organizations changed the role of the agent. Under the old system, the candidate's agent— usually a lawyer—had organized his campaign and had distributed the bribes. Between elections, the agent was generally responsible for the registration of voters. This, too, was essentially a legal task in view of the complex rules governing the right to vote. These duties could be carried out on a part-time basis, and the agent normally had a law practice besides his political work. With the growth of permanent constituency organizations, lawyer agents were gradually replaced by professional agents. The new agents needed some legal knowledge, since registration continued to be one of their main

[55] For assessment of the effect of the 1883 act in stimulating voluntary party activity between elections, see Edgar J. Feuchtwanger, *Disraeli, Democracy, and the Tory Party: Conservative Leadership and Organization after the Second Reform Bill* (Oxford: Oxford University Press, 1968), pp. 158-59; and Cornelius O'Leary, *The Elimination of Corrupt Practices in British Elections, 1868-1911* (Oxford: Oxford University Press, 1962), pp. 203-4.

responsibilities until 1918 (when it was largely taken over by public authorities). Unlike their predecessors, they were employed on a full-time basis by their constituency associations and made a career of working for local party associations (proceeding from one association to another). The professional agent acted in the election campaign as the candidate's election agent and, during electoral peacetime, serviced the routine activities of his local party organization.

These developments affected the structure of local political finance. Constituencies needed to find the money to pay for the agent on a full-time basis. This was normally the responsibility of the candidate or of some rich members of the local association. During this period, it was unusual for the ordinary members of a constituency association to assume responsibility for its finances. The savings to candidates from the limitations on campaign costs were partly used up by this demand to foot the routine bills of their constituency associations and of their permanently employed agents.

One of the most thoroughly prepared estimates of routine constituency expenditure during the plutocratic era is that of Ramsden. It is based on over three dozen local party accounts of Conservative constituency and city associations. Ramsden calculates that the annual expenditure of a constituency association averaged £350–400 during the period 1911–1913 and that over half this amount was contributed by the candidate or MP.[56]

The Plutocratic Pattern

The overall pattern of spending during the plutocratic era is illustrated by table 12, which shows estimated Conservative central and local spending in the parliamentary cycle preceding the election of January 1910. It is comparable to the similar table for the aristocratic era (table 4).

The main trends that emerge from a comparison between the estimates for the 1906–1910 parliamentary cycle and for an equivalent four-year period of the 1876–1880 cycle are as follows:

1. Overall central and local expenditure in current prices remained at approximately the same level between 1876–1880 and 1906–1910. (In real money terms, the overall expenditure for the two periods rose slightly.) This means that (a) the increase in national level spending was accompanied by a slight decrease in constituency level spending and (b) the decrease in spending on con-

---

[56] Ramsden, "Organisation of the Conservative Party," p. 350.

TABLE 12

(approximate) during the Parliamentary Cycle 1906–1910
(in pounds)

	Routine Expenditure	Campaign Expenditure
Central	310,000	25,000
Local	900,000	650,000

NOTE: It is assumed that routine Central Office expenditure from 1906 onward was the same as that recorded in table 11 for 1909/1910; 25 percent has been added to Central Office expenditure recorded in table 11 to cover the estimated additional expenditures of the Scottish Central Office and of Liberal Unionist headquarters.

SOURCES: For constituency campaign expenditure, Blewett, *Peers, Parties, and People*, p. 290. The other totals are derived from Ramsden, "Organisation of the Conservative Party."

stituency campaigns was largely canceled out by the increase in other types of expenditure.

2. The fact that overall expenditure remained roughly constant means that the cost per vote (including all expenses during the two parliamentary cycles) decreased significantly. The electorate was considerably enlarged between 1880 and 1910. The total Conservative cost per vote in 1876–1880 was £52 (in 1980 values), compared with £16 in 1906–1910. (This includes central and local, routine and campaign costs.)

This analysis shows that the overall level of political expenditure did not rise significantly when the explosion of donations by businessmen was happening.

Statistics of political spending do not reveal the total raised by the central Conservative and Liberal organizations from plutocratic contributions. The fact is that neither the Conservative nor the Liberal party managers could find ways of spending the sums that were coming into their coffers through the traffic in political honors. Subsidies given to parliamentary candidates were much enlarged (as shown for the Liberals in table 10); some grants were allocated to constituency associations (as shown in table 11); and the Liberal and Conservative headquarters were both expanded. Still, all these expenditures left much of the incoming money untouched. As mentioned earlier, the Liberals, who had been accustomed to a central reserve of about £20,000 until 1906, had already accumulated a huge reserve of over £500,000 by 1908, and it appears that hundreds of thousands of pounds remained unspent until after the First World War.[57] In the 1890s, the Conservatives had reckoned that a reserve of £20,000 was sufficient,[58] and after the 1900 campaign the party still lacked invested reserves.[59] The situation changed over the following years. Despite the loss of three general elections between 1906 and 1910, the Conservatives had accumulated over £300,000 by 1911. By the outbreak of war, the reserve had risen to nearly £800,000.[60]

These figures suggest that the Liberal and Conservative central organizations between them raised at least £1¼ million more than they spent during the decade before the outbreak of the First World War. This is equivalent to about £30 million in 1980 values. The proceeds of the honors sales during Lloyd George's premiership were mostly hoarded. It is ironic that the recruitment of business money, which had originally started because the Liberal party was suffering from an acute shortage of central funds, should have resulted, after a few years, in a glut of contributions that the national organizations did not need.

[57] See, for example, Douglas, *History of the Liberal Party*, p. 181; and T. Gibson Bowles, "The New Corruption: The Caucus and the Sale of Honours," *Candid Quarterly Review*, vol. 1 (1914), p. 52.

[58] This is indicated by Middleton's letter to Salisbury's private secretary about party finance, November 15, 1891, Salisbury Papers, 130, fo. 150.

[59] Steel-Maitland, in his memorandum written after the 1910 elections, writes of Hood, the former chief whip, that in 1902 "he started without any invested funds" (quoted in Blake, *Unknown Prime Minister*, p. 100).

[60] "During the three years between becoming Chairman and the outbreak of the War, Maitland doubled the invested funds to £671,000. . . . He also accumulated a special cash deposit of £120,000 in preparation for the election expected in 1914/15" (Ramsden, "Organisation of the Conservative Party," p. 330).

TABLE 13

TITLES AWARDED DURING THE PLUTOCRATIC ERA, 1875–1924

	Peers	Baronets	Knights	Total
1875–1884	36	48	448	532
1885–1894	74	116	764	954
1895–1904	52	136	1,447	1,635
1905–1914	99	203	1,794	2,096
1915–1924	129	322	2,791	3,242

SOURCE: Hanham, "Sale of Honours," p. 279.

The existence of these bountiful reserves had an important side effect. The Liberals and the Conservatives both used much of them to invest in newspapers. Lloyd George allocated the reserves of his political fund for the same purpose. This meant that, during the second decade of the twentieth century, many national and local newspapers were partly owned by political parties. Care was generally taken to make such investments through nominees in order that the political source of the money remained undisclosed.

The plutocratic system of financing politics had a number of important social and political consequences. On the social plane, it facilitated the movement of a new class of entrepreneurs into the House of Lords and transformed the British aristocracy in the process. The prospect of receiving political contributions encouraged the party whips to recommend titles more easily than before. The marked increase in the number of titles and peerages awarded during the plutocratic era is seen in table 13.

The sale of honors had significant effects on the internal structure of the political parties. It meant that central party finance had to remain strictly secret. The principal objective of businessmen in gaining public honors was to show that they were not just rich but that they were worthy of recognition by the nation. It was therefore essential both to them and to the whips who recommended titles to maintain the pretense that the peerages and knighthoods were an acknowledgment of some public service. To make public the central finances of the parties would only confirm the rumors of connections between donations and titles. Moreover, in order to protect party leaders against possible accusations of selling honors, it was the convention to keep them in the dark about the funds raised by the whips. (This was, however, a convention broken more often than prime ministers and their overprotective biographers have cared to admit.)

Because of the desire for secrecy, formal party accounts were often avoided, and contributions were held in the personal accounts of the main party fund raisers. This informality encouraged the inefficient use of central resources and, on occasion, led to suspicions that money intended for the party had been purloined by the party officials to whom the contributions had been given. Shortly after the death of Schnadhorst, the chief Liberal official, it was reported that he had received a donation of £5,000 from the South African millionaire Cecil Rhodes. The Liberal whips could not trace the money in the party's accounts and seriously suspected that he had "trousered" it (a suspicion that historical research shows probably to have been incorrect).[61] The uncertainty about the destination of money received by the Tory treasurer, Lord Farquhar, after the First World War has already been mentioned.

Under the secrecy system, fund raising remained the responsibility of a small number of people (particularly the party whips in the House of Commons). Limitations on their time made it necessary for them to concentrate on collecting a small number of large contributions.[62] Thus, the plutocratic system discouraged the collection of modest and middle-sized donations.

The reliance of the parties on business money had some far-reaching political consequences, especially for the Liberals. A feature of plutocratic political finance was that money frequently came from donors who had no ideological commitment to the party to which they were subscribing. Their desire was for the title. Usually it did not matter which side it came from. (This is the implication of the letter by Hood about Harmsworth, quoted earlier in this chapter.) The unpolitical nature of the honors trade was particularly damaging to the Liberals. From 1906, the progressive program of the Liberal government brought it into political conflict with the commercial community. The party's political future depended on its ability to establish a base of working-class support. However, the prospect of honors still induced individual entrepreneurs to increase their contributions to the Liberals long after their political sympathies for the party had disappeared.[63] The receipt of these large funds re-

[61] There is a full account of the affair in William B. Gwyn, *Democracy and the Cost of Politics in Britain, 1832-1959* (London: Athlone Press, 1962), pp. 115-20. A possible explanation of the missing £5,000 is given by McGill, "Francis Schnadhorst and Liberal Party Organisation," p. 32.

[62] Ramsden, "Organisation of the Conservative Party," pp. 326-27.

[63] Blewett quotes the judgment of the Asquithian Liberal journalist J. A. Spender about the Liberal chief whip in the December 1910 election: "He soothed the rich Liberals who were uneasy about Limehouse [where a much-quoted speech

lieved the Liberals of the need to look for new, more popular sources of finance. As soon as the Liberals lost office, the opportunist donations by title seekers came to an abrupt halt, and the party was left without alternative sources of money or of political support. For the Conservatives, the effects were less serious. Since big business was in any case becoming more Tory, political and personal motives for plutocratic contributions went hand in hand.

The existence of large central resources could have been used to enable poor but talented candidates to stand for Parliament. There is some evidence that they were occasionally used for this purpose by the Liberals. In 1910, some central grants were, according to Blewett, used to finance candidates of quality. In the words of an obituary for the Liberal chief whip of December 1910 (Lord Murray), "many unknown men without a big bank balance got their first chance in political life through Lord Murray."[64] These efforts were too little, too late. No real attempt was made by the Liberals or Conservatives[65] to use central funds to attract working-class candidates. This failure was more damaging to the Liberals because they were the party under the most direct challenge from the recently formed Labour party.

The dependence of many local constituency associations on central grants or on large payments by candidates and rich backers seems also to have had a disproportionately harmful effect on the Liberals. On the Tory side, motives of social deference made ordinary members keen to take part in local associations since this gave them a chance to mix with prominent social personalities and receive occasional invitations to gatherings in their homes. It mattered relatively little whether the local Conservative parties were financed by large contributions or not. In this era, ordinary Conservatives were content to participate in a subordinate capacity.

For potential Liberal activists, feelings of social deference were less compelling. What encouraged them to participate in

---

had been given setting forth the Liberal government's radical intentions], and got large cheques out of them to be used for their own despoiling" (*Peers, Parties, and People*, p. 292). It is unlikely that Liberal millionaires contributed because they were soothed. Many merely wanted a title and were ready to quit the party once it had been granted.

[64] Blewett, *Peers, Parties, and People*, p. 281.

[65] In late 1909 a pro-Conservative newspaper, the *Standard*, raised £6,074 to run Conservative working men as parliamentary candidates. With the benefit of this fund, four working-class candidates were put forward, but none was nominated to contest a seat normally won by the party. For December 1910 the *Standard* raised a further £7,866, and six working-class candidates were placed by Central Office, "but only two stood in seats that could be considered winnable. Neither won" (Blewett, *Peers, Parties, and People*, p. 272).

constituency politics was the chance to play a role in the affairs of the local Liberal association. The democratic structure of the famous Birmingham Caucus of the 1870s and 1880s had been a key to its success. Yet, after the 1886 split over the issue of Irish Home Rule, the main political supporter of popular Liberal organization, Joseph Chamberlain, abandoned the party, and his political organizer, Schnadhorst, left Birmingham for London, where he became more interested in collecting hefty business money than in encouraging the growth of popularly based local associations. The local Liberal organizations became pale, middle-class imitations of their Conservative counterparts. The keenness of the Birmingham Caucus was never recaptured after 1886, except possibly for brief periods between 1900 and 1905 and before the elections of 1910. In general, business money and central grants made any local Liberal participation and activity redundant. When the Liberal party was confronted with serious political problems after the First World War, its weak local associations disintegrated.

3
The Challenge of Labour (1900-1939)

The transition from an era of aristocratic dominance to a plutocratic system meant little to working-class men who wished to enter the House of Commons. Even after the reductions in permitted campaign expenditure set by the Corrupt Practices Act, 1833, the costs of fighting parliamentary elections remained prohibitive for anyone without very substantial private means or without the help of wealthy supporters. Apart from the drain of campaign expenses, a laborer or artisan elected to the House of Commons was faced with the daunting task of finding resources for food and lodgings in London, for frequent railway fares to his constituency, and for postage and stationery.[1] There was no public salary or expense allowance toward these items.

Working-class candidates received little help from the two established parties.[2] The Conservatives made active efforts to attract the votes of laboring men, but they did not feel it necessary to promote them as parliamentary candidates.[3] Limited Liberal attempts were made during the late nineteenth century to enable working-class representatives to enter Parliament. They were unproductive because, at the local level, Liberal constituency associations were hardly ever

---

[1] The financial difficulties confronting working class MPs are described by William B. Gwyn, *Democracy and the Cost of Politics in Britain, 1832-1959* (London: Athlone Press, 1962).

[2] In the 1910 elections, only 1 percent of Unionist candidates (that is, Conservatives and Liberal Unionists) were manual workers and only 2 percent of Liberal candidates (Neal Blewett, *The Peers, the Parties, and the People: The General Elections of 1910* [London: Macmillan, 1972], p. 230).

[3] The indifference of Conservative Central Office to the selection of working men as parliamentary candidates is described in Blewett, *Peers, Parties, and People*, pp. 272-73. The unwillingness of Conservative constituency associations to select working-class candidates has remained a problem to the present day. See David E. Butler and Michael Pinto-Duschinsky, "The Conservative Elite, 1918-1978: Does Unrepresentativeness Matter?," in Zig Layton-Henry, ed., *Conservative Party Politics* (London: Macmillan, 1980), pp. 186-209.

prepared to accept laboring men as candidates,[4] still less to collect the necessary election expenses for them. At central level, the task of finding funds for working-class representatives was given low priority by the Liberal hierarchy. Before the 1892 election, Francis Schnadhorst requested a lump sum from Andrew Carnegie for the campaign expenses of possible working-class Liberal candidates. When no contribution was forthcoming, the idea was dropped. Nor did the Liberal governments of 1892–1895 or 1906–1910 implement the vague plank in the Liberal "Newcastle Programme" of 1891, which called for the payment of members of Parliament from public funds.[5]

In 1900 an organization was established by some trade unions and by representatives of three small socialist societies (the Social Democratic Federation, the Independent Labour party, and the Fabian Society).[6] Its immediate aim was to secure working-class representation in Parliament. It was unclear whether the new body, which was called the Labour Representation Committee (LRC) was intended to be a separate political party or just a pressure group with Liberal connections. The position was intentionally left ambiguous for a number of years because of differences of opinion within the LRC about its ultimate objectives.[7]

[4] The father of the Labour party, Keir Hardie, had originally attempted to enter Parliament as a Liberal. In 1888 Hardie asked for the Liberal nomination for Mid-Lanark "and followed the usual course suggested by the Labour Electoral Association of promising to abide by the result of a preliminary poll of all Liberals in the constituency. The local Liberal Association would not agree to this primary, and they proceeded to select a candidate of their own, a London barrister" (Henry Pelling, *The Origins of the Labour Party, 1880-1900* [Oxford: Oxford University Press, 1966], p. 65). Pelling refers to the "unavailing pressure" before the 1892 general election "upon local Liberal caucuses in trying to induce them to accept Liberal-Labour candidates" (that is, working-class Liberals) (see Pelling, *Origins of the Labour Party*, p. 66). Ramsay MacDonald's decision to abandon the idea of becoming a Liberal candidate was a result of the refusal of the Southampton Liberal council to accept him in 1894 and his consequent view that local Liberal associations were dominated by commercial interests and that working-class candidates were repugnant to them (David Marquand, *Ramsay MacDonald* [London: Cape, 1977], pp. 34-35).

[5] The council meeting of the National Liberal Federation that met at Newcastle-upon-Tyne in October 1891 resolved "that the principle of payment of Members of Parliament should be recognised, as the only means of securing an adequate representation of Labour [that is, working-class members] in the House of Commons" (Harold J. Hanham, *The Nineteenth-Century Constitution: Documents and Commentary* [Cambridge: Cambridge University Press, 1969], p. 219).

[6] The number of members of each society for the years 1884-1901 is listed in Pelling, *Origins of the Labour Party*, p. 229.

[7] The LRC's dilemma is described by Marquand: the LRC "had been set up in order to strengthen labour's voice in the House of Commons. It had no hope

The operating costs of the Labour Representation Committee were to be met by very small fees from each affiliated body according to its membership. (Of the affiliated membership in 1900, 94 percent came from the unions.) At first the subscription was set at 10 shillings (£0.50) per thousand members. This was later raised to 15 shillings (£0.75) per thousand members. The initial affiliations paid in February 1900 amounted to £64.50 (including a total of £6 from the three socialist societies). LRC income amounted to £210 in 1900 and £229 in 1901.[8] The ability of the LRC to exist on these small amounts depended on the secretary (later to be the Labour party's first prime minister), J. Ramsay MacDonald, whose wife had the private means to support him and the LRC office at their apartment.[9]

Affiliation fees to the Labour Representation Committee were initially of symbolic rather than real importance. The main financial commitment of the trade unions and socialist societies belonging to the new body was to pay the election expenses of specified parliamentary candidates. Without such sponsorship, candidates would not be recognized by the LRC. Sponsorship was intended as a substitute for a candidate's personal wealth. In the general election of 1900, held shortly after the formation of the LRC, fifteen candidates were put forward, and two were elected. Trade unions sponsored four candidates (average election expenses: £969) and socialist societies eleven candidates (average expenses: £279).[10]

In 1903, it was agreed to set up an extra LRC fund to be called the parliamentary fund. It was financed on the basis of affiliation fees by the constituent bodies of the LRC of one penny per member (£4.17 per 1,000 members). These were to be paid in addition to the

---

of doing so unless it came to terms with the Liberals. Yet if it did come to terms with them, it risked losing its separate identity" (Marquand, *Ramsay MacDonald*, p. 83).

[8] These statistics (and most subsequent statistics about membership, affiliation rates, and central finances) are derived from the annual reports of the LRC and of the Labour party. These annual reports are an invaluable and underused source of detailed information about central Labour finances. However, the figures need to be interpreted with care, since accounting procedures varied over time and information is incomplete for some of the special funds raised periodically for particular purposes (such as general election campaigns). I have received valuable help in interpreting the accounts from David Honeybone. The adjustments made to the published figures are listed in the notes for tables 16, 21, and 23.

[9] The capital sum in Margaret MacDonald's trust fund amounted to more than £25,000 (Marquand, *Ramsay MacDonald*, p. 51). This is equivalent to more than £½ million in 1980 values.

[10] Derived from Frank Bealey and Henry Pelling, *Labour and Politics, 1900-1906* (London: Macmillan, 1968), and British Parliamentary Papers, 1901 (352) lix, p. 145.

TABLE 14

Number and Total Membership of Constituent Bodies of the Labour Representation Committee (Labour Party) and Affiliation Rates, 1900–1913

	Socialist Societies[a]	Trade Unions[a]	Basic Affiliation Rate	Parliamentary Fund
1900	3(22,861)	41(353,070)	10 shillings per 1,000 members (£0.50 per 1,000)	—
1901	2(13,861)	65(455,450)		—
1902	2(13,835)	127(847,315)		—
1903	2(13,775)	165(965,025)		1d per member (£4.17 per 1,000)
1904	2(14,730)	158(855,270)	15 shillings per 1,000 members (£0.75 per 1,000)	
1905	2(16,784)	158(204,496)		
1906	2(20,855)	176(975,182)		
1907	2(22,267)	181(1,049,673)		2d per member (£8.33 per 1,000)
1908	2(27,465)	176(1,127,035)		
1909	2(30,982)	172(1,450,648)		
1910	2(31,377)	151(1,394,403)		
1911	2(31,404)	141(1,501,783)		
1912	2(31,237)	130(1,858,178)	1d per member (£4.17 per 1,000)	—
1913	2(33,304)	n.a.		—

Note: n.a. means not available.

[a] Total number of affiliated "members" shown in parentheses.

Source: Annual reports of the Labour Representation Committee (Labour party) national executive committee, 1900-1914.

basic affiliation fee. The parliamentary fund was to provide annual salaries of £200 to each MP sponsored by the LRC (three MPs who gained seats in by-elections had by 1903 joined the two elected in the 1900 general election). The fund was also used to make token payments (a quarter of the returning officer's fees) to each LRC parliamentary candidate. The affiliation rates are shown in table 14.

In the three general elections between 1906 and 1910, the LRC (which changed its name to the "Labour party" after the 1906 election) put forward a total of 186 candidates.[11] Of these, 137 (74 percent) were sponsored by trade unions. The campaign expenses of union-sponsored candidates were on average much higher than those of the minority who were backed by socialist societies or by local

[11] Derived from Bealey and Pelling, *Labour and Politics*, p. 290-92; and Blewett, *Peers, Parties, and People*, pp. 241, 262.

TABLE 15

SPONSORSHIP AND ELECTION EXPENSES OF LABOUR (LRC) CANDIDATES IN
THE GENERAL ELECTIONS OF 1906, JANUARY 1910, AND DECEMBER 1910

	Sponsorship		
	Miners' federation	Other unions	Socialist societies
No. of candidates (1906)	—	36	14
Expenses per candidate (1906) (pounds)	—	690	490
No. of candidates (1910)	49	54	31
Expenses per candidate in contested seats (1910) (pounds)	1,255	694	467

SOURCES: Bealey and Pelling, *Labour and Politics*, pp. 290-92; British Parliamentary Papers, 1906 (302), xcvi, 19; and Blewett, *Peers, and People*, p. 296.

trade councils. Total general election expenses of Labour candidates amounted to over £31,000 in 1906.[12] This excluded the costs of candidates sponsored by the Miners' Federation of Great Britain, who ran independently of the LRC.[13] Total campaign expenses of Labour candidates were £68,000 in January 1910 and £41,000 in December 1910.[14] (By 1910, the Miners' Federation of Great Britain had affiliated with the Labour party, and the 1910 totals therefore included those of miners' candidates.) Seventy-nine percent of total expenditure in 1906 and nearly 90 percent in the 1910 campaigns were incurred by union-sponsored candidates.[15] The party's heavy reliance on union election funding is shown in table 15.

Labour (LRC) candidates won twenty-nine seats in 1906, and candidates sponsored by the Miners' Federation won thirteen more. In January 1910 forty seats were won, and the number of victories rose to forty-two in December 1910 (the 1910 totals include miners'

[12] Derived from British Parliamentary Papers, 1906 (302) xcvi, p. 19.

[13] Thirty-four candidates were sponsored by trade unions alone, two by unions in conjunction with a local trades council or local Labour Representation Committee, two by local Labour Representation Committees, and two by local trades councils. Of those elected, twenty-one were sponsored by unions, seven by the Independent Labour party, and one by a local Labour Representation Committee.

[14] Blewett, *Peers, Parties, and People*, p. 290.

[15] Sources are as for table 15. Of a total of eighty-two victories in the two 1910 general elections, all but fifteen were union sponsored.

candidates). These successes resulted largely from an electoral pact that Ramsay MacDonald had negotiated in 1903 with Herbert Gladstone, the Liberal chief whip. According to this arrangement, the Liberal whips discouraged local Liberal associations from putting forward candidates in forty-two seats (thirty of which were to be contested in 1906 by LRC candidates and twelve by miners' candidates). A significant lever used by MacDonald during the negotiations with the Liberals was the existence of the LRC's parliamentary fund and the willingness of individual unions to finance candidates.[16] Ramsay MacDonald, in one of his conversations in 1903 with the Liberal chief whip's private secretary, claimed that the LRC would "have a fighting fund of £100,000" at the coming election.[17] (This sum presumably included likely contributions by unions to their sponsored candidates. It was a somewhat optimistic estimate for purposes of negotiation, but it correctly expressed the order of magnitude of the money contributed by unions to the parliamentary fund and for election expenses.)

The party's electoral success meant that from 1906 onward the main routine item of central Labour expenditure was the cost of paying £200 a year to maintain each of its MPs. However, an increase in the affiliation rate of the parliamentary fund and the growing number of affiliated members led to sharply rising income, which more than covered the growth in spending. A central reserve of about £15,000 had been accumulated by the general election of January 1910.

The total political expenditure of trade unions (central and local, routine and campaign) in the parliamentary cycle 1906–January 1910 appears to have amounted to well over £150,000. Of this sum, campaign expenses in January 1910 accounted for nearly a third. The rest consisted of affiliation fees to the Labour party and to its parliamentary fund, independent payments by the Miners' Federation to its MPs, and payments for routine local political purposes, including by-elections.[18]

16 Bealey and Pelling, *Labour and Politics,* chap. 6.

17 Marquand, *Ramsay MacDonald,* p. 79.

18 The most valuable single boost to the Labour party during the Parliament of 1906-1910 was the decision taken by the Miners' Federation of Great Britain to affiliate. The first fees to the party by the miners were paid in 1909. The miners had a very substantial parliamentary fund of their own, with a total expenditure in 1909 of £22,567. Of this, the miners paid £4,995 to the Labour party, £7,320 for the salaries and expenses of their sponsored MPs, and £8,850 to district miners' federations for local political purposes. After these outlays, the federation still had "cash in hand of £25,661 to face a general election" (R. Page Arnot, *The Miners: A History of the Miners' Federation of Great Britain, 1889-1910* [London: Allen and Unwin, 1949], p. 368).

In finance, as in so much else, the emergent Labour party relied almost entirely on the organized support of trade unions.[19] In tapping union resources, the Labour party was establishing a pattern of political finance completely new to Britain. It was so effective that it was later to be partly imitated by the Conservatives. Previously, political money had always come from *individuals*. Now funds were collected from trade unions on an *institutional* basis. Political payments were misleadingly referred to in Labour's annual reports on a per-member basis ("1 penny per member," "15 shillings per 1,000 members," and so on). In fact, money almost never came from separate voluntary contributions from individual trade unionists. When special appeals were occasionally made on this basis, the response was invariably unproductive. The majority of trade unionists were politically apathetic, and, of those who were not, a substantial minority opposed the idea of political payments. The success of fund raising from unions depended on gathering money on some automatic basis that took advantage of the apathy of the majority of ordinary members. In practice, a contribution by a union of "2d [two pence] a member" from 100,000 members did not mean that 100,000 members had separately decided to contribute 2d each but that the union leadership had agreed to donate a block sum of $100,000 \times 2d$ (£833.33). Nor did affiliation on the basis of a particular membership mean that a union actually had this number of members, but rather that it was willing to pay a block affiliation for that number. Some unions affiliated on the basis of less than their total membership in order to limit the cost of belonging to the Labour party, and occasionally unions affiliated on the basis of a number that exceeded their total membership. A union's initial decision to make political contributions was sometimes taken by a ballot of members to set up a parliamentary fund. If successful, such a ballot permanently committed all members to contribute (including the majority of members who did not vote either way or who opposed the establishment of the fund). Alternatively, decisions to contribute out of the union's general fund could be taken by the union leadership without a ballot. Either way, the payments for Labour party purposes effectively came from the union leaders and not from individual members.

By 1900 British trade unions had a total of 2 million members— a number that was growing steadily. If leaders of unions with even half this membership affiliated to the Labour party, contributions could be raised automatically from a million members, thus yielding

---

[19] Some of the connections between the Labour party and the broader Labour movement are outlined in the note at the end of this chapter.

about £50,000 a year for each shilling per member: £200,000 for a four-year parliamentary cycle. Union levies could not yet match the contributions to the two established parties from plutocrats and were not comparable to the amounts that Conservative and Liberal candidates with private means could provide for their own campaign expenses. Nonetheless, the sums that could be raised from block payments by unions were very substantial for a party still in its infancy and enabled the Labour party to become a political force to be reckoned with.

In December 1909, the legality of union payments to the Labour party was brought into question by a decision by the law lords, which came to be known as the Osborne Judgement. W. V. Osborne, Liberal secretary of a branch of the Amalgamated Society of Railway Servants, obtained an injunction to prevent the union from raising money to elect and maintain Labour members of Parliament. Osborne's legal representatives successfully argued that a trade union's legitimate function under existing law did not extend to electing MPs whose purpose in Parliament was to support a political creed rather than forwarding the union's normal industrial objectives. Moreover, they suggested that Parliament had never intended, in passing previous trade union acts, to give power to majorities in trade unions to compel minorities—on threat of expulsion—to give financial support to political opinions to which they were opposed.

Labour leaders responded vigorously to the judgment. Osborne was portrayed as the puppet of hidden capitalist interests, which had allegedly stimulated and financed his action. An immediate change in the law to legitimate union contributions became one of Labour's top priorities.[20]

Despite the shock with which the Labour party received the news of the Osborne Judgement, it did little harm to the party since it was overturned by measures taken by the Liberal government elected in December 1910.[21] This speedy response was stimulated by the fact that the Liberal government only barely won the two 1910 elections and became dependent on Labour and Irish Nationalist support to maintain its parliamentary majority. The first new measure, announced in May 1911, provided for public salaries of £400 a year for

[20] The Osborne Judgement and the events preceding it are detailed in Gwyn, *Democracy and the Cost of Politics.*
[21] "The threat of the Judgement was primarily long-run, its short-term effects being virtually nil in the first election [of 1910], and marginal in the second" (Blewett, *Peers, Parties, and People,* p. 297). A similar conclusion is reached by Hugh A. Clegg, Alan Fox, and A. F. Thompson, *A History of British Trade Unions since 1889* (Oxford: Oxford University Press, 1964), p. 419.

members of Parliament. This relieved the Labour party of paying each of its MPs £200 a year out of the parliamentary fund, the main item of its central expenditure. The public payment of MPs meant that the Labour party's parliamentary fund could be wound up. In its place the basic affiliation fee was increased in 1912 from 15 shillings per 1,000 members to 1 penny per member (that is, an increase from £0.75 to £4.17 per 1,000 members). Relief from paying subsistence for MPs meant that the modest routine costs of Labour's head office could continue to expand despite the Osborne Judgement.[22] This pattern of undisturbed growth is shown in column 3 of table 16.

In 1913, legislation was enacted to overcome the consequences of the Osborne Judgement. The Trade Union Act, 1913, permitted unions to make political contributions provided that there were certain safeguards. First, a trade union could only make political contributions if it set up a special political levy fund, which was to be kept separate from its general funds. Second, a political fund could be established only after a successful ballot of a union's members. Third, when a political fund was in operation, those who did not wish to subscribe were entitled to "contract out" of making the political payment, and their rights as union members or officials were not to be prejudiced.

The flow of affiliation fees to the Labour party temporarily slowed in 1913 while the ballots required by the 1913 act were held. But the pattern of union payments was soon to be reestablished, and money to the Labour party from the political levy funds of unions grew steadily over the decade following the passing of the act.[23]

The stipulation of the 1913 act that a political fund could only be set up after a ballot of members was not a difficult hurdle. In many unions only a minority of members bothered to vote. If, as occasionally happened, a majority of those voting opposed the idea of a political fund, repeat ballots could be held until a majority was forthcoming. Once the setting up of a political fund was approved by a union, it could be maintained indefinitely without a need for further mandates from the members. The relatively low percentages of union

[22] The relative practical unimportance of the Osborne Judgement is seen by the fact that Labour's head office was able to spare £12,000 in 1912 and 1913 to finance the *Daily Citizen*. See the note at the end of this chapter. The judgment did, however, provide an important political issue in the 1910 campaigns.

[23] The Trade Union Act, 1913, obliged all unions with political levy funds to submit annual accounts to the chief registrar of friendly societies. The annual reports of the chief registrar are the main source of information about these funds. The statistics given in the reports for some years (particularly before 1928) are incomplete, however, and they are potentially misleading in view of frequent changes in the definition of certain categories. See table 20 note.

TABLE 16
Labour Party Central Finances, 1900–1913

		Expenditure			
	Income	Total	Head office	Central general election costs	Payments to MPs
1900*	210	154	121	33	—
1901	229	202	202	—	—
1902	606	439	439	—	—
1903	2,895	703	684	—	17
1904	5,384	1,721	921	—	800
1905	5,146	4,747	1,123	2,824[a]	800
1906*	6,195[a]	7,796	1,060	—	6,736
1907	9,939	7,101	1,327	—	5,773
1908	9,674	7,820	1,563	—	6,257
1909	15,606	9,552	2,216	—	7,336
1910*	12,576	18,102	2,175	7,196[a]	8,730
1911	9,237[a]	5,371	3,271	—	2,100
1912	6,010	9,691[b]	3,691	—	—
1913	7,544	10,585[c]	4,585	—	—

Notes: Asterisks denote general election years. This table and tables of central Labour income and expenditure for later years include special funds as well as the general fund. The following adjustments have been made, where necessary and where possible, to the published accounts: (1) The cost of literature and other trading items is given net of receipts; (2) all figures are net of income tax where possible; (3) conference expenses are net of receipts from conference fees; (4) balances brought forward are excluded; (5) profits on investments are included only if the net amount is available—that is, gross realization figures are not given; and (6) payments between different central accounts are excluded.

[a] Of the £2,824 paid out for general election purposes in 1905, £716 (net) was unused and was returned to the head office the following year. This £716 is included as income for 1906. The final central cost of the 1906 election was therefore £2,108. Similarly, in 1911, £265 (net) was repaid to the head office, making the cost of the two general elections of 1910 £6,931.

[b] Including investment of £6,000 in Labour Newspapers Ltd.

[c] Including loan of £6,000 to Labour Newspapers Ltd.

Source: Annual reports of the Labour Representation Committee (Labour party) national executive committee, 1900-1914.

members voting for the establishment of political levy funds is shown in table 17, which gives the statistics for ballots held by registered unions in the first year that the act was in operation.

Despite the low numbers voting for setting up union political levy funds, few took the trouble to contract out once they had been estab-

TABLE 17
Ballots to Establish Union Political Funds, 1913

Union	No. Supporting Establishment of a Political Fund	No. Opposing Establishment of a Political Fund	Total Union Membership	Percentage of Total Membership Supporting Establishment
Railwaymen	102,270	34,953	267,611	38.2
Engineers	20,586	12,740	143,783	14.3
Gasworkers	27,802	4,339	134,538	20.7
Carpenters	13,336	11,738	66,380	20.1
Card and blowing-room operatives	2,293	1,437	58,062	3.9
Dock laborers	4,078	501	51,755	7.9
Other ballots in 1913	128,337	59,602	485,712	26.4
Total	298,702	125,310	1,207,841	24.7

Note: Figures are for registered unions only.
Source: *Report of the Chief Registrar of Friendly Societies for the Year 1912* (London: His Majesty's Stationery Office, 1914), appendix B, pp. 91-92.

lished. Where political levy funds were not collected from members (as was sometimes the case), the reason was normally administrative inefficiency on the part of union officials or a decision to exempt certain categories of member (for example, apprentices or retired members) from paying. The small percentage of unionists contracting out was documented in a written answer to a parliamentary question in 1924 (see table 18). This suggested that on average about 80 percent of members paid political levy funds, 2 percent contracted out, and the rest did not pay because they were exempted or because of administrative failure to collect subscriptions.

The new political levy system set up in 1913 had additional advantages for Labour. The fact that subscriptions were collected on an automatic basis meant that payments continued during 1914–1918, when the First World War halted normal party politics and reduced the constituency-level incomes of the two established parties. The union political levy funds built up considerable reserves during 1914–1918, and this permitted Labour greatly to expand its activities toward the end of the war and during the postwar years.

The fast rise in the numbers joining trade unions during the 1910–1920 period also aided the political levy funds. Total union

TABLE 18
Union Members Contracting Out of Paying the Political Levy in Some Major Unions, 1924

	Number (%) Paying Political Levy	Number (%) Contracting Out	Number (%) Not Paying for Other Reasons	Total Membership
Railwaymen	326,528 (85.7)	9,217 (2.4)	45,354 (11.9)	381,099
Transport and general workers	276,938 (74.3)	6,834 (1.8)	88,788 (23.8)	372,560
General and municipal workers	323,465 (99.9)	268 (0.1)	— (0.0)	323,733
Engineers	129,606 (53.0)	11,010 (4.5)	103,857 (42.5)	244,473
Durham miners	120,000 (75.0)	763 (0.5)	39,277 (24.5)	160,040
Workers' union	146,226 (99.8)	274 (0.2)	—	146,500
Woodworkers	87,825 (78.4)	a	a	112,050
Distributive workers	89,075 (99.7)	269 (0.3)	— (0.0)	89,344
Boilermakers	52,333 (63.5)	7,632 (9.3)	22,467 (27.3)	82,432
Steelworkers	69,831 (96.6)	733 (1.0)	1,736 (2.4)	72,300
Card and blowing-room operatives	66,439 (99.9)	24 (0.04)	— (0.0)	66,463
Agricultural workers	51,144 (100.0)	— (0.0)	— (0.0)	51,144

a Separate figures for those contracting out and those not paying for other reasons are not available. The total number not paying the political levy was 24,225, 21.6 percent of the total membership.

Sources: House of Commons Debates, 5th series, vol. 188, col. 790, November 20, 1925; and *Report of the Chief Registrar of Friendly Societies for the Year 1925.*

TABLE 19
TRADE UNION MEMBERS AFFILIATED TO THE LABOUR PARTY, 1914–1920

1914	1,612,147
1915	2,093,365
1916	2,219,764
1917	2,465,131
1918	3,013,129
1919	3,511,290
1920	4,359,807

SOURCE: Labour party annual reports.

membership rose from about 2½ million in 1910 to 8¼ million in 1920. It is not possible to give accurate figures for the total numbers of union members paying the political levy. However, the increase in political levy payments that was undoubtedly occurring is reflected in the growing numbers affiliated to the Labour party. Some unions affiliated to the Labour party on the basis of a membership less than the total number paying the political levy. The total affiliated to the Labour party is therefore less than the total paying the political levy, although it gives a good indication of its rate of growth (see table 19).

Estimates derived from the annual reports of the chief registrar of friendly societies indicate that between 1914 and 1927 the political levy raised a total of about £2.5 million (about £35 million at 1980 values). As shown in table 20, expenditure came to £2.1 million. Excluding the costs of administering the funds, almost all the rest was devoted to Labour party purposes.

Toward the end of the First World War, the Labour party prepared to replace the Liberals as Britain's main left-of-center party. In the general election of 1918, 388 candidates were put forward, and nearly 2½ million votes were won. Although this result did not bring a large gain in the number of MPs elected (57), it represented a huge advance, because the Labour victories of 1918, unlike those of 1910, did not depend on electoral pacts with the Liberals. Between 1919 and 1924, there was an unstable three-cornered contest between the Conservatives, the Liberals (divided into the Lloyd George and Asquith factions), and Labour. Three general elections were held in quick succession in 1922, 1923, and 1924. Labour made a decisive breakthrough: it came second to the Tories on each occasion and, in 1923, formed a minority government that was in office for nearly a year. The party was able to withstand the financial strain of the

TABLE 20

Estimated Expenditure from Trade Union Political Levy Funds, 1914–1927

(in thousands of pounds)

	Total Expenditure	Expenditure at 1980 Values
1914	24	591
1915	43	861
1916	36	607
1917	48	673
1918*	150	1,821
1919	127	1,452
1920	208	2,059
1921	180	1,951
1922*	300	4,031
1923*	256	3,620
1924*	242	3,393
1925	159	2,229
1926	151	2,152
1927	188	2,769

Note: Asterisks denote general election years. The totals in this table include unregistered as well as registered unions. The figures for 1914-1924 are 12.5 percent above and the figures for 1925-1927 are 40 percent above those given for registered unions alone in the reports of the chief registrar of friendly societies. This represents the estimated additional sums contributed by unregistered unions (1925-1927) and unregistered components of unregistered unions (1914-1924). The changes in accounting procedures of successive reports are explained in the *Report for the Year 1927*, p. 33.

Source: Chief registrar of friendly societies, annual reports.

repeated general elections because of the support received from the trade unions, as shown in table 21.

As before, union money funded Labour centrally and at the constituency level. Enlarged union affiliation fees financed the expansion of the party's head office. The affiliation rate of 1d per member, fixed in 1912, was raised to 2d per member in 1918, and to 3d a member in 1920.

Affiliation fees to Labour's head office accounted for less than a third of the unions' political expenditures on Labour party purposes during 1914–1927. Most of the rest was directed, as before the First World War, toward the sponsorship of parliamentary candidates, the maintenance of sponsored MPs, and the support of the routine finances of local Labour parties.

TABLE 21

LABOUR PARTY CENTRAL FINANCES, 1914–1927
(in thousands of pounds)

	Income			Expenditure	
	Total	Trade union affiliation fees	Affiliation fees as % of total	Total	General election[a]
1914	4	3	92	5	—
1915	12	11	95	5	—
1916	11	11	96	6	—
1917	12	11	92	19	—
1918*	22	20	93	42	18[b]
1919	31	30	97	28	—
1920	55	48	88	38	—
1921	56	54	95	54	—
1922*	43	41	96	62	7[c]
1923*	75	48	64[d]	66	22[e]
1924*	69	36	51[d]	70	27.5[f]
1925	66	39	60	62	5[f]
1926	60	56	93	67	—
1927	47	43	91	51	—

NOTE: Asterisks denote general election years.

[a] Included in total expenditure.

[b] Grants to constituency campaigns, £15,299; publicity, £440; and a notional £2,000 for estimated extra office expenses attributable to the general election.

[c] Literature expenses of £2,480 and a notional £5,000 for estimated extra office expenses.

[d] This percentage underestimates the overall contribution of unions to the Labour headquarters because it refers only to routine union affiliation fees. Trade unions contributed additional amounts for the general election fighting funds.

[e] Grants to candidates, £16,775; and £5,000 for estimated extra office expenses.

[f] For the 1924 general election: central Labour grants to constituencies, £22,500; loss on literature, £5,000; and estimated extra office expenses, £5,000.

SOURCE: Labour party annual reports.

The expansion in the number of Labour party candidatures resulted in a considerable growth in total election expenses. The increase was limited, however, as a result of an important piece of legislation passed before the general election of 1918. The Representation of the People Act, 1918, limited the cost of constituency politics in several ways: (1) it greatly simplified and eased the qualifications needed for the right to vote; the task of registration, previously one of the main costs borne by local constituency associations, was taken over by public authorities; (2) the permitted election expenditure limits were tightened; (3) each parliamentary candidate was entitled to send without charge an item of campaign mail to each elector; and (4) returning officers' fees were no longer the responsibility of candidates.[24]

Despite the lower ceiling on campaign costs, local Labour parties did not assume much of the responsibility for raising finance for election expenses. The main burden was still shouldered by the unions. A majority of Labour MPs elected in each of the four campaigns held after the First World War were sponsored by unions. Union candidates continued to spend significantly more on average than others who did not have this backing.

As Labour was scoring its political breakthrough in the early 1920s, the income of the union levy funds was again being threatened. The severe unemployment from 1921 onward (which was an important factor in Labour's electoral success) had the effect of lowering the membership of trade unions and thus reducing the number of contributors to their political funds. Total union membership declined from a peak of over 8¼ million in 1920 to under 5 million by 1927. The decline continued until 1933, when membership was under 4½ million. Thereafter the figure climbed to over 6½ million at the outbreak of the Second World War in 1939.[25]

On top of the difficulties stemming from this decline in union membership, Labour's funds suffered a second blow when, during the tense atmosphere after the General Strike of 1926, the Conservative government of Stanley Baldwin yielded to Conservative party pressure and amended the Trade Union Act, 1913, so that political contributions were from 1927 payable only by union members who contracted in. Apathy, which had hitherto helped Labour under the contracting-out rules, became an obstacle. The new act that brought in these changes was called the Trade Disputes and Trade Unions Act, 1927.

As a symbolic expression of Tory hostility to the trade unions, the 1927 act was of major importance, but its effects on Labour party finances were limited. In the eight-year period following the 1927 act, total expenditure from union political levy funds was only about

[24] David E. Butler, *The Electoral System in Britain since 1918*, 2d ed. (Oxford: Oxford University Press, 1963), p. 9.

[25] Albert H. Halsey, ed., *Trends in British Society since 1900* (London: Macmillan, 1972), p. 123.

TABLE 22
Trade Union Political Levy Funds, 1928–1939
(in thousands of pounds)

	Union Members Paying Political Levy (%)	Total Income	Total Expenditure	Funds at End of Year	Total Expenditure in 1980 Values
1928	58.3	186[a]	201	413	2,984
1929*	59.1	174	218	369	3,262
1930	59.2	181	138	412	2,147
1931*	59.7	156	217	351	3,629
1932	58.5	166	131	386	2,237
1933	57.0	164	144	406	2,520
1934	57.7	169	143	432	2,493
1935*	56.5	175	229	378	3,942
1936	54.0	184	152	410	2,542
1937	51.5	192	172	430	2,756
1938	50.2	199	167	457	2,637
1939	49.8	196	172	481	2,634

Note: Asterisks denote general election years.
[a] Estimate.
Sources: Chief registrar of friendly societies, annual reports; and Martin Harrison, *Trade Unions and the Labour Party since 1945* (London: Allen and Unwin, 1960), pp. 32-33.

16 percent lower than in the eight-year peak period 1920–1927. This fall was less than the decline in total union membership (over 20 percent between 1920 1927 and 1928–1935) that resulted from the economic depression. The pattern of political levy funds after the 1927 act is shown in table 22 (for comparative figures for 1920–1927, see table 20).

The same pattern of moderate decline is seen in the central Labour party accounts for 1928–1939, shown in table 23.

The considerable success of the trade union movement in limiting the fall in expenditure from the political levy funds from 1928 onward (and in actually increasing expenditure in real terms) was due to four main factors. First, the bitter feeling within the trade unions aroused by the circumstances in which the 1927 act was passed stimulated intensive campaigns to contract in union members as subscribers to the political levy. In the years after 1928, nearly 60 percent of members of unions with political funds agreed to pay (see table 22). This meant that only about a quarter of those who had paid under the previous contracting-out system were lost. Second, subscription rates

TABLE 23

LABOUR PARTY CENTRAL FINANCES, 1928–1939
(in thousands of pounds)

| | Income | | | Expenditure | |
	Total	Trade union affiliation fees	Affiliation fees as % of total[a]	Total	General election[b]
1928	57[c]	33	49	52	
1929*	90[c]	26	29	93	45[d]
1930	44	35	80	45	
1931*	71	31	44	74	31[e]
1932	42	33	80	48	
1933	45	32	71	46	
1934	53	31	58	51	
1935*	73	32	44	69	25[f]
1936	48	33	68	53	1[f]
1937	61	38	62	74	
1938	57	39	69	63	
1939	67	44	66	58	

NOTE: Asterisks denote general election years. The figures are calculated on the same basis as those for table 16.

[a] These percentages considerably underestimate total union contributions because they do not take account of union payments to special central Labour funds, such as the general election funds.

[b] Included in total expenditure.

[c] It is assumed that the bid-for-power fund raised a third of its total of £49,000 in 1928 and the rest in 1929.

[d] The annual report for 1929 does not give precise or clear figures for general election spending. The total in this table includes expenditure of "about £40,000" from the special bid-for-power fund and £4,890 spent from the returning officers' deposit fund.

[e] Expenditure for general election fund, £19,345; payments to general fund from general election fund, £5,000; loss on literature, £3,381; deposit insurance fund, £3,017. Additional grants of £314 for the 1931 general election appeared in the accounts for 1932.

[f] Includes payments from general election fund, £22,220; from deposit insurance fund, £2,455; and grants in 1936, £837.

SOURCE: Labour party annual reports.

were raised by some unions to make up for some of the shortfall in the number of members. Third, advantage was taken of the fact that, before 1927, some political levy income had been regularly hoarded. Reserves were nearly £½ million when the 1927 act was passed. After 1927 expenditure slightly exceeded income. The fall in expendi-

TABLE 24

The Effects of the Trade Disputes Act, 1927:
Political Levy Funds, 1928–1935 Compared with 1920–1927

Union membership	over 20% lower
Percentage of members paying levy as a result of contracting in	about 25% lower[a]
Numbers paying the political levy[b]	over 40% lower
Amount of levy per member[b]	about 20% higher
Income of political levy funds[b]	nearly 30% lower
Expenditure of political levy funds[b]	about 16% lower
Expenditure of levy funds in real terms[b]	nearly 5% higher

[a] It is assumed that about four-fifths of members contributed until 1927 (see table 18) and three-fifths from 1928 (see table 22).
[b] Estimated.

Sources: Halsey, *Trends in British Society since 1900*, p. 123; and chief registrar of friendly societies, annual reports.

ture was consequently considerably less than the decline in income. Finally, the economic depression produced a marked fall in the cost of living. Thus the expenditure of the political levy funds, though lower in money terms, was nearly 5 percent higher in its real purchasing power. The mild effects of falling union membership and of the contracting-in law on political levy funds are summarized in table 24.

By the 1930s there was no real shortage of money for the Labour party from the trade unions.[26] The party's main difficulty stemmed from the fact that long years of reliance on union political levies meant that additional sources of funds had not been developed. In particular, the availability of easy union money had hindered the growth of Labour's constituency organizations.

The underlying conflict within the Labour movement between the unions, with their large blocks of cash, and organizations of individual socialists was not new. From the party's early days, there had been complaints that the prospect of trade union backing made constituency Labour parties lazy and that trade union nominees of little ability were frequently chosen as parliamentary candidates for safe

[26] It could be argued that contracting in nevertheless halted the previous growth in trade union political levies and limited Labour party funds at a time when Conservative central expenditures, particularly on general elections, were exceptionally high.

seats just because a union was willing and able to meet their election expenses. Gwyn cites MacDonald's condemnation in 1909 of "constituencies that had dilly-dallied and hung over for the last moment until they could set a candidate with £1,000 in his pocket [that is, a union nominee]—and not to risk local money."[27] MacDonald's worries were echoed by another of the Labour party's founding fathers, Philip Snowden: "The trade unions who found the money for the candidates naturally selected the officials of unions as their candidates. Political qualifications were not considered."[28]

While the party was still in its infancy, the rationale for union funding had nevertheless been overwhelming. From the 1920s, the case was far weaker. The fact that MPs now received public salaries meant that they no longer required union subscriptions to provide them with subsistence allowances. This had been recognized by the closing of the parliamentary fund in 1912. Campaign costs were far lower after the Representation of the People Act, 1918, and it became possible to raise the necessary amounts from small-scale individual subscriptions. By the 1920s the request by a constituency Labour party for a subvention from a union for a candidate's campaign costs was often a sign of sloth, not of need. Furthermore, Labour's emergence as a major partner in the British two-party system meant that it had to contest constituencies all over the country and not just in selected industrial strongholds (as had been the case before the First World War). If unions were to give aid to the party, it was now sensible for them to hand it over to Labour's head office so that it could be directed to the marginal seats where it would be of greatest use. Unions were, however, in McKibbin's words, "not prepared to surrender the autonomy of their political expenditure."[29] The head office did manage to persuade some unions to hand over a little cash to its special election funds from 1923 onward. It then distributed the money to needy constituencies. The bulk of union money for constituency election grants was still allocated directly by the unions to their own candidates.

The obvious alternative to union funds was to raise money from individual Labour party supporters. Before 1918 the party's constitution had not recognized individual membership. The "Labour party" had consisted of affiliated organizations—trade unions, socialist societies, trades councils, and local Labour Representation Committees.

[27] Gwyn, Democracy and the Cost of Politics, p. 171.
[28] Ibid., p. 172.
[29] Ross McKibbin, The Evolution of the Labour Party, 1910-1924 (Oxford: Oxford University Press, 1974), p. 161.

Individuals had been able to join the party only indirectly by belonging to an affiliated body. From 1918 onward, individual membership was accepted and encouraged, and constituency organizations were strengthened. The threat to trade union political funds posed by the 1927 act led to greater emphasis on direct participation by individuals in the hope that subscriptions by members of constituency parties would compensate for the expected shortfall in trade union affiliation fees. Significantly, statistics of individual party membership appeared in Labour's annual report for the first time in 1928, the year after the passage of the contracting-in act.

In the following years, the party sponsored drives to recruit members for constituency Labour parties. These efforts were only moderately successful. Total recorded membership grew from 214,970 in 1928 to a pre–Second World War maximum of 447,150 in 1937. The real problem was that the ease with which some local parties could rely on union subsidies caused resentment in other local organizations that did not get them. It was argued by constituency activists in the early 1930s that the trade unions should be made to hand over their money for stimulating activity in rural areas rather than hogging it for industrial seats, where it was wasted.

The Labour party's national executive committee realized the impracticality of requiring trade unions to hand over all their donations to the center, and a compromise scheme was accepted by the 1933 Labour party conference at Hastings. The Hastings Agreement, which was to come into force after the next general election, stipulated that a sponsoring union could contribute a maximum of 80 percent of a candidate's election expenses. The remaining 20 percent would have to be found by the local Labour organization. Moreover, if election expenses exceeded 60 percent of the maximum permitted by law, all the extra would be the responsibility of the local party. Between elections, the maximum permitted annual grant by a sponsoring union was to be £150 for borough constituencies and £200 for counties.[30]

In its statement introducing the Hastings scheme, the party's national executive committee put its finger on the main difficulty that the Hastings Agreement was intended to tackle:

> The surest and most permanent way of increasing the strength, especially the financial strength, of Constituency Parties is to build up a larger individual membership. There can be no substitute for local endeavour of this kind. The

[30] These limits have been altered from time to time to take account of inflation, but the Hastings Agreement has remained essentially unchanged.

availability of money coming from outside a Constituency Party's own endeavour frequently leads to dependence and in some cases to actual slackness.[31]

Labour had come a long way since its foundation in 1900. In the early days, union finance had given birth to the party. By the 1930s its undesirable side effects were becoming apparent. Yet the fact that Labour had not adequately developed its constituency organizations meant that, like it or not, it was unable to escape from its dependence on trade union money.

Note: The Labour Party and the Labour Movement

It is important to bear in mind that the infant Labour party belonged to a wider movement comprising trade unions, socialist societies, and cooperative societies. Some of the Labour movement's politically connected activities were as follows:

1. Socialist candidates actively contested municipal and school board elections. They were largely responsible for introducing party politics and national political issues into these elections, which had previously been the preserve of nonparty independents. By 1899 the Fabian Society and the Independent Labour party (ILP) had established a permanent local government information bureau.[32]

2. The Labour movement established and supported several educational institutions: (a) The London School of Economics and Political Science was founded by Beatrice and Sidney Webb, two leading Fabians, on the basis of a bequest left to a Fabian Society trust in 1894. The school, though nonpartisan, was intended, in Beatrice Webb's words, "to make thinking persons socialistic" and to train experts in "reforming society." [33] (b) In 1899 Ruskin Hall (afterward Ruskin College) was opened in Oxford. The object was to provide residential training for future working-class leaders.[34] A Marxist offshoot of Ruskin College, the "Plebs League," later led to the formation of the National Council of Labour Colleges. (c) The Workers' Educational Association was established in 1903 and by 1914 had 179 branches and 11,430 individual members, drawn largely from active workers in the trade unions and cooperative societies.

[31] Labour party annual report, 1933, p. 37.

[32] Pelling, *Origins of the Labour Party*, p. 186.

[33] Beatrice Webb, *Our Partnership*, ed. Barbara Drake and Margaret I. Cole (London: Longman, 1948), pp. 84ff., 132.

[34] Sir Robert C. K. Ensor, *England, 1870-1914* (Oxford: Oxford University Press, 1936), pp. 538-39.

3. By 1900, there existed a wide network of cooperative societies. These were retail shops that devoted their profits to dividends to consumers ("members") in proportion to the amount of their purchases. The cooperative societies embodied the principle of workers' self-help in the face of capitalist exploitation. By 1900 the Co-operative movement claimed a membership of 1,780,000 and share capital of £23 million. The movement was for some time hesitant to connect itself with the Labour party. However, in 1917 a Co-operative party was formed. This was, in effect, the political department of the headquarters organization of the movement, the Co-operative Union. An agreement was reached with the Labour party whereby local cooperative society parties would be encouraged to affiliate with constituency Labour parties and would run joint candidates for local government elections and for the House of Commons. Once elected, "Co-operative and Labour" MPs would join the parliamentary Labour party.[35]

4. The Labour movement sponsored newspapers: (a) In 1912 the *Daily Citizen* was launched. The Labour party provided £12,000, and much more came from the unions. By the time it ceased publication in 1915, it had consumed an estimated £200,000 in trade union funds, including £41,500 provided by the Miners' Federation.[36] (b) In 1922 the unions and the Labour party took over a previously independent left-wing newspaper, the *Daily Herald*. Once again, special party and union money was provided. In 1929 the *Daily Herald* was taken over by Odhams Press as a commercial venture, but the new management committed itself to the political policy of the Labour party and the industrial policy of the Trades Union Congress.[37]

No attempt has been made in this study to assess the finances of the broad Labour movement. However, the following points should be noted:

1. The adjuncts of Labour politics (trade unions, educational bodies, newspapers, and so on) were paralleled by equivalent institutions and interest groups supporting the established parties.

2. The fact that the Labour party was a new political force meant that the support received from sympathetic bodies was usually smaller

[35] Robert T. McKenzie, *British Political Parties: The Distribution of Power within the Conservative and Labour Parties* (London: Mercury Books, 1964), p. 529; and G. Douglas H. Cole and Raymond Postgate, *The Common People, 1746-1946* (London: Methuen, 1968), pp. 379-83, 437.
[36] R. Page Arnot, *The Miners: Years of Struggle, a History of the Miners' Federation of Great Britain (from 1910 Onwards)* (London: Allen and Unwin, 1953), p. 140-41.
[37] Francis Williams, *Dangerous Estate: The Anatomy of Newspapers* (London: Longman, 1957), p. 194.

than that enjoyed by the Conservatives and Liberals. At the same time, the links between the party and its supporting institutions was closer. The Labour party, unlike its rivals, was part of a social movement.

3. When the other parties, particularly the Tories, raised fears about the financial strength of Labour and its connections with international communism, it was the adjunct organizations and not the Labour party that they generally had in mind. This is exemplified by Sir Joseph Ball's memoranda, which are cited in chapter 4.

It should be mentioned that these Conservative fears, though exaggerated, were not without foundation. Soviet funds did reach sympathetic parts of the British Labour movement, and the Soviet trade mission that visited London shortly after the Russian Revolution took the opportunity to sell czarist diamonds for the benefit of the *Daily Herald*.[38]

[38] Christopher Andrews, "The British Secret Service and Anglo-Soviet Relations in the 1920s. Part 1: From the Trade Negotiations to the Zinoviev Letter," *Historical Journal*, vol. 20 (1977), p. 685.

4

Responses to Labour (1918-1939)

Until the First World War, the Labour party was a marginal force in British politics. From 1918 onward its fast-growing strength posed a serious threat to the two established parties and to their plutocratic methods of raising funds. The Conservatives adapted themselves to meet the challenge. The Liberals did not.

The Unchanging Liberals

After the First World War, the Liberals were politically weak, but financially extremely strong. It was a fatal combination. As a result of the intense hatred that had developed by 1918 between the Liberal prime minister, Lloyd George, and the Liberal ex–prime minister, Asquith, the Liberal party fielded two separate teams of candidates in the general election held in December 1918, a month after the Armistice. Lloyd George supporters numbered 158, and, with the benefit of an electoral pact with the Conservatives, 133 of these candidates were elected. Of the 253 candidates who put themselves forward as official (that is, Asquithian) Liberals, only 28 were elected. Lloyd George continued as prime minister but was at the mercy of his Conservative partners, who had no fewer than 335 seats in his coalition government.

Despite this poor electoral performance, both Liberal factions were flush with funds. The Asquithian Liberals still had the very large kitty built up by sales of honors until 1916, and Lloyd George was rapidly building up a hoard of his own by selling more peerages and knighthoods. The wealth of both factions made it unnecessary for them to merge their separate political organizations and thus delayed a possible reconciliation.

The official Liberal organization (the staff of the Liberal Central Association and the National Liberal Federation) was part of Asquith's team. It was slow to adapt itself to the party's new political circumstances. Men who had served in the party bureaucracy for many years were largely concerned with their own job security and their pensions. Salaries were met from investment income and from the sale of investments. The size of the official Liberal reserves provided a cushion against reality.

Asquith's fall from office prevented the Liberal whips from continuing to collect money from the sales of titles. Amazingly, virtually no effort seems to have been made to find alternative sources of central funds. The party was content to live on the riches accumulated during the salad days before 1917. The complacency of the Asquithian Liberals is reflected in the statement of Herbert Gladstone, director of the Liberal headquarters, to Asquith on August 1, 1924, that "we have had no contributions from any quarter since 1916 to our own funds and have been living on capital."[1]

This report, though not literally correct, was only a slight exaggeration. The inflow of money to Liberal headquarters from 1916 onward was pitifully small. Donations to the party's central campaign fund in the general elections of 1922, 1923, and 1924 covered only a limited proportion of expenditure and came mainly from a few rich Liberals who had participated in Asquith's government or who wished to show gratitude for titles received during his premiership.[2] According to Douglas, "The Liberal party seems to have disbursed over half a million pounds more than it received between 1916 and the 1924 General Election."[3] (This is equivalent to about £7 million in 1980 values.)

[1] Asquith Papers, 34, fo. 133. A similar view is expressed in a note in the Lloyd George Papers prepared after the 1929 general election:

> The party has been living since 1910 on Central Funds—first the Alick Murray Fund [that is, the money collected by the chief whip of 1910], then the L. G. Fund. The two elections of 1910, the elections of 1918 and 1922 and, to a certain extent the elections of 1923 and 1924 were fought with the help of the Alick Murray Fund and the Federations have lived on it. It is a mistake (as well as being unfair) to treat the system of spoon-feeding from Headquarters as if it began with the L. G. Fund. It started long ago, certainly as far back as 1910 and the Party must be emancipated from this demoralising method of financing its activities (Lloyd George Papers, LG G/86/3).

[2] For example, the accounts surviving in the Asquith Papers (box 141) indicate that, in the 1922 general election, the expenditure of the central organization amounted to £126,948. Of this total, £78,535 (62 percent) came from the realization of capital and only £48,413 from donations. Moreover, all but £7,000 of the amount donated came from a limited circle of twelve contributors. Lord Cowdray, who had received his peerage from Asquith, gave £12,000, and Sir W. Runciman, an Asquith cabinet minister, gave £10,000.

For the 1923 general election, the official Liberal organization raised a central fund of £74,187. This was supplemented by £90,000 from the Lloyd George Political Fund. In 1924 the official Liberal organization raised £40,243, and the Lloyd George Political Fund contributed £50,000.

[3] Roy Douglas, *The History of the Liberal Party, 1895-1970* (London: Sidgwick and Jackson, 1971), p. 181.

Some economies seem gradually to have been made at the Liberal headquarters, and savings appear to have been achieved by keeping salaries stable at a time when the cost of living was rising. Nevertheless, the annual routine cost of the central organization was still about £50,000 a year in 1923,[4] by which time the party's pot of gold was nearly empty.

The corrupting effects of the large funds raised before 1916 were evident at the local level of the party as well. In the words of an agonized memorandum written in July 1925 by Herbert Gladstone, "Extravagance at H.Q. from 1910 to 1918 had discouraged local expenditure and contributions."[5] This applied, in particular, to parliamentary candidates. As shown in chapter 2, Liberals standing for Parliament had come to expect ever-increasing subsidies from the chief whip. They had frequently neglected to develop local sources of financial support. The steep reductions in permitted campaign costs imposed by the Representation of the People Act of 1918 ought to have made it much easier for Liberal candidates and their constituency associations to raise funds for election expenses without outside help. But the habit of dependence on London had sapped local initiative. Many Liberal associations simply refused to put forward a candidate unless he or the chief whip footed much of the bill. Candidates became less willing than before to contribute heavily to their own expenses as the party's political fortunes and their own prospects of victory deteriorated. The fact that grants were given so readily by headquarters also encouraged candidates to claim a slice of the central cake and to decline to accept nomination until it was forthcoming. The overall result was that candidates, instead of nursing a constituency for a long period, tended to wait until the last moment before deciding whether to stand for Parliament or not. When central money was forthcoming at the eleventh hour, it was often far too late to make any impact on the voters, who had in the meantime been wooed by the Labour party and by the Tories.

By the early 1920s, most Liberal constituency associations were in a derelict condition. In Chris Cook's words, "Almost without exception, even where an active association existed, the constituency Liberals relied on a wealthy candidate and on subsidies from Head-

---

[4] Sir Charles Mallet, *Herbert Gladstone: A Memoir* (London: Hutchinson, 1932), p. 194; and Douglas, *History of the Liberal Party*, p. 134. Douglas, whose information is based on the Lloyd George Papers, states that by 1923 "annual disbursements were still estimated at £50,000 (not counting special General Election expenses—of which £30,000 went to the upkeep of Headquarters and the Federations, and £20,000 in grants to the constituencies."

[5] Maclean Papers, 468, fo. 28.

quarters."[6] Such a life-support system was fragile. Wealthy Liberal MPs were sometimes prepared to keep a local association ticking over while they remained in the House of Commons. But they almost always withdrew their backing if they lost their seats. Some Liberal MPs defected to the Labour party, and this normally led to the death of the Liberal associations in their constituencies. In Newcastle-under-Lyme, for instance, the defection to Labour of Josiah Wedgewood (a member of the pottery family) "brought about the virtual collapse of the Liberal Association."[7] Cook's research reveals that in a typical area of the country one constituency organization was "completely dormant" after 1918, another was "virtually defunct," in a third there had by the early 1920s "been a total cessation of all Liberal activities," other constituencies remained "totally unorganised," and yet others were "moribund." Nationally and locally, the subsidies that were lavishly provided during the plutocratic era contributed to Liberal disintegration from 1918 onward.

The years immediately after the First World War, which brought so much grief for the official, Asquithian Liberals, were a time of triumph for Lloyd George. As the man who had led the nation to victory against Germany, he was a hero. His personal popularity was the reason why the Conservatives wished to prolong the wartime coalition and to support him as premier. Lloyd George, without the backing of the official Liberal party organization, had a personal machine of his own. This cost £48,000 a year by the early 1920s[8] and was financed by the traffic in honors.

The postwar honeymoon with the Tories lasted for nearly three years. In 1921 Lloyd George's standing declined sharply as the brief economic boom that followed the end of the fighting was replaced by high unemployment. Many Conservative backbench MPs and constituency activists, who had previously accepted Lloyd George as a vote winner, now saw him as a liability and agitated to end the coalition. Lloyd George's personal qualities of daring and dynamism were no longer seen as virtues. There was a sudden yearning for stability, decency, calm, which Lloyd George was temperamentally incapable of providing. In October 1922, a revolt by Conservative MPs led to the breakup of the coalition and to Lloyd George's fall from office. In the subsequent general election, the Conservatives (who this time ran

[6] Chris Cook, The Age of Alignment: Electoral Politics in Britain, 1922-1929 (London: Macmillan, 1975), p. 40.

[7] Ibid., p. 34.

[8] The Lloyd George Political Fund is described more fully in the note at the end of this chapter.

independently of Lloyd George) won a convincing victory. Labour emerged as the second largest party in the House of Commons, and the divided Liberals had only 116 seats, 62 of them won by Lloyd George's "National Liberals" and 54 by Asquithian Liberals.

The Conservative backbench revolt against coalition government, which led to Lloyd George's downfall, was partly stimulated by the scandal over the honors list of June 1922. By the summer of 1922, the coalition was already under strain. It was obvious to businessmen seeking to buy titles from Lloyd George's agents that they had better clinch their deals quickly while he remained prime minister. Lloyd George's organizers were equally aware that the opportunities for building up his Political Fund would soon come to an end. In this hectic, "last chance" atmosphere, it was not surprising that a few unfortunate choices for ennoblement were made. The lack of sympathy for Lloyd George on the part of some Tories meant that the chance to attack him was used to the full.[9]

The storm centered on the peerage awarded to Sir Joseph Robinson, the South African multimillionaire. On the surface, Robinson was as qualified for membership in the House of Lords as many others who had received this honor. He had obtained a baronetcy from the Liberal prime minister, Sir Henry Campbell-Bannerman, back in 1908, an award recommended by Churchill. As indicated in table 8, he had featured in Herbert Gladstone's roll of Liberal subscribers for the 1906 election. Unfortunately, Robinson had subsequently been convicted of dishonest business dealings in South Africa and had been fined £500,000 by the South African Supreme Court. His appeal against the conviction had been dismissed by the British Privy Council in November 1921, less than a year before he was singled out for elevation to the House of Lords.

Of the others receiving high honors in the June 1922 list, one had moved his business to Argentina, allegedly to avoid British taxes, thereby throwing British employees out of work, another was condemned as a war profiteer, and a third was suspected of trading with the enemy during the First World War. One of the baronets on the list had been convicted in 1915 of trading with the enemy. The implication was that in all these dubious cases titles had been given in return for payment.

There followed motions and debates in both Houses of Parliament. Lloyd George finally agreed to appoint a royal commission. This was and still is a normal British device to head off a crisis by

[9] The honors scandal of 1922 is described fully in Gerald Macmillan, *Honours for Sale: The Strange Story of Maundy Gregory* (London: Richards Press, 1954).

setting up a prolonged, toothless investigation. By the time the royal commission issued its uninformative report, Lloyd George was no longer premier. However, the scandal of 1922 led to the passage in 1925 of the Honours (Prevention of Abuses) Act, which made it an offense to accept "any gift, money, or valuable consideration as an inducement or reward for procuring . . . the grant of a dignity or title of honour."

After the 1922 election, Lloyd George found himself, like Asquith, in the political wilderness. The quarrel between the two men had ruined them both. In 1923 their companionship in misfortune led finally to an effort to close the rift. In the general election of 1923, the Liberals ran a united slate of candidates. The Lloyd George Fund contributed £90,000 of a total of £164,187 raised for the central Liberal campaign.[10] This meant that the official Liberal organization was not obliged, as it had been in 1922, to sell shares to pay for its subsidies to candidates. The 1923 election result was somewhat better than that of the previous year. The reunited Liberals increased their seats in the House of Commons to 159, but they were still behind Labour, which formed a minority government.

The three-way division of seats in the 1923 election and the failure of any party to achieve a workable majority made it inevitable that yet another general election would be held in the near future, and this raised the question of how the next Liberal campaign would be financed. This led to a renewal of the feud between the Asquith and Lloyd George factions. The official Liberals still controlled the party organization, but they were running out of capital. Their main objective during 1924 was to persuade Lloyd George to part with money from his fund (which was reputed to have raised £1½ million during his premiership)[11] to enable them to keep the central party organization running and to subsidize a full slate of candidates in the forthcoming campaign. The Asquithians, however, were not prepared to relinquish control over their organization to Lloyd George. As far as they were concerned, Lloyd George was a rebel who had belatedly returned to the party fold and was obliged, as a sign of his good faith, not only to hand over his money but also to obey official (that is, Asquithian) party discipline.

This was too much for Lloyd George to stomach. The year 1924 was marked by a series of bitter negotiations between the supposedly reunited factions. Asquithian emissaries demanded that Lloyd George

[10] Asquith Papers, 141. See also the note at the end of this chapter.
[11] Sir Charles Mallet, *Mr. Lloyd George: A Study* (London: Ernest Benn, 1930), pp. 253-54.

hand over £30,000 a year for the routine expenses of Liberal head-quarters and undertake in writing to provide at least £100,000 for the expenses of the coming election, which, it was reckoned, would cost at least £200,000 if a sufficient number of candidates were to be put forward to make the Liberals a credible political force.[12] Lloyd George teased and prevaricated. He was understandably reluctant to obey the orders of Liberals who privately (and not so privately) declared their "detest" for his "ill gotten funds" (terms used by Herbert Glad-stone)[13] but who nonetheless wanted him to hand over the proceeds for their use.

The quarrel about Lloyd George's money dragged on throughout 1924. So acrimonious were the meetings between the two sides that, after one typical discussion in July 1924, Sir Robert Hudson, who had many years earlier succeeded Schnadhorst as head of the official Liberal organization, wrote to Herbert Gladstone (the serving head): "As to your resolution: 'D . . . L.G.,' I beg to second. Our 40 minutes talk with him was so poisonous that I took to my bed with a tempera-ture the next afternoon, & there the Dr. has kept me until this morn-ing."[14] Lloyd George's supporters were equally suspicious of the other side. In the words of one of them, "He [Lloyd George] ought not to mortgage himself and his funds in any way to the [Asquithian Liberal] organisation. They have no desire except to strangle him at the earliest possible opportunity."[15]

Not surprisingly, the protracted meetings produced no money but reaped a harvest of ill will. It was only in October 1924, when the general election poll was less than three weeks away, that Lloyd George finally agreed to give a contribution of £50,000 to the Liberal headquarters for subsidies to candidates.[16] The money was far less than the official Liberals had been demanding, and it was much too late. Only 340 Liberal candidates stood in the 1924 election, and a mere 40 won. The Liberal party had been effectively destroyed.

Arguments about Lloyd George's money continued. In a final grand effort to show that they could survive without Lloyd George,

[12] Maclean Papers, 468, fo. 38.

[13] Herbert Gladstone to Beauchamp, January 15, 1923, Maclean Papers, 467, fo. 4.

[14] Trevor G. Wilson, *The Downfall of the Liberal Party, 1914-1935* (London: Collins, 1966), p. 280. Quoted from the Herbert Gladstone Papers.

[15] Sir Edward Grigg, March 20, 1924, quoted in Wilson, *Downfall of the Liberal Party*, p. 280.

[16] Asquith Papers, 141. The entire negotiations were based on the premise of the Asquithian Liberals that it would not be possible to induce Liberals to stand as parliamentary candidates without hefty central subsidies.

the official Asquithian Liberals launched a fund-raising campaign in January 1925—less than three months after the debacle of the previous general election—to collect a million pounds for the Liberal party. The grandiose, absurd title of the campaign, the Million Fund, showed that the old school of Liberal organizers still harked back to the days when some permanent solution could be found to a party's financial problems by finding a capital sum large enough to make all future fund raising unnecessary.[17] The response to the appeal was so disappointing that the results were never announced. Toward the end of 1926, the *Liberal Magazine* indicated that only "over £80,000" had been received.[18] This was merely enough to keep the headquarters ticking over for two or three years longer.

[17] According to the *Liberal Magazine* of March 1925, the Million Fund would ensure (1) that party funds came from rank-and-file members, (2) that spending was controlled by democratically chosen Liberals, and (3) that the fund "is to be openly accounted for by published balance sheets" (p. 138). The *Liberal Magazine* of February 1925 stated that the fund aimed to provide "for a capital sum for the next election" and "for a large and sure annual income for the general purposes of the Central Organisation of the Party" (p. 76). In addition, Liberal constituency associations were to become financially self-sufficient.

Later the organizers blamed the existence of the Lloyd George Fund for the failure of the appeal to raise money in small contributions from party members. While the party was reputed to have access to this large central kitty, potential donors were deterred from contributing additional sums. As Mallet put it, "while this great fund . . . existed, it was very hard to collect much money from other sources" (Mallet, *Herbert Gladstone*, p. 285). Herbert Gladstone regarded the Lloyd George Fund "as responsible to a large extent for the demoralisation of the party" (p. 287). A similar judgment was made by John A. Spender, *Sir Robert Hudson* (London: Cassell, 1930), chap. 11, "The Liberal Party and Its Finances."

In my opinion, the experience of the Liberals in the 1920s has a direct relevance to contemporary discussions about state aid for political parties. The existence of money from the state would—like the Lloyd George Political Fund—make it far harder to raise supplementary contributions from ordinary members and would discourage party activity. This argument is put more fully in chapter 10.

It is worth noting that, ever since the 1920s, Liberals have tried to emancipate themselves from the habit of dependence on centrally raised funds and have been unsuccessful. This suggests that, were state financing of parties to be introduced, it would be difficult to revert at a later time to a system of funding by small, voluntary contributions.

[18] *Liberal Magazine*, 1926, p. 673, quoted by Douglas, *History of the Liberal Party*, p. 190. This figure is imprecise because the previous intention of the anti-Lloyd George Liberals to publish the balance sheets of the central organization does not appear to have been fulfilled. This apparent failure seems to have caused considerable confusion. It was later to be a matter of dispute, for instance, whether or not the Lloyd George Fund contributed a sum of £105,000 to the Million Fund. At first glance, it seems extraordinary that there could have been any dispute about the existence or nonexistence of such a large contribution. This is readily explained by the secrecy, chaos, and factionalism that affected the party in the 1920s and indeed until recent times.

In October 1926, Asquith finally resigned as Liberal leader. His health was failing, and he died shortly afterward. Only now did the official Liberal leadership go to Lloyd George. By this time, the prize was hardly worth winning. Nevertheless, Lloyd George at this stage poured money from his Political Fund into the party, which he at last controlled, in one last desperate fling to reestablish the Liberals—and himself as their leader—as a serious political force. The amounts spent on the central Liberal campaign leading up to the election of 1929 were among the largest (in real terms) spent by any party in any British general election. The payments given or promised by Lloyd George to the Liberal party from 1927 to 1930 included a lump sum of £300,000 for the coming general election and £32,000 a year for three years to the Liberal headquarters.[19] The Lloyd George Fund sponsored other costly activities that were part of the overall campaign. Some of the nation's leading economists, including Keynes, gathered at Lloyd George's expense to do research on the problem of unemployment. Their program, published under the title *Britain's Industrial Future* (The Yellow Book) and summarized as *We Can Conquer Unemployment* (The Little Yellow Book), was intended to prove to the country that Lloyd George was capable of solving the nation's most pressing problem. The Yellow Books were lavishly distributed.

It is not possible to give an accurate figure for the amount spent by the Liberals on the 1929 election. If the routine sums allocated to Liberal headquarters and to the production of the Yellow Books are included, the total spent by Lloyd George must have exceeded £400,000. Moreover, the distaste felt for Lloyd George by some of the old school of Asquithian Liberals and the fear that his money would be used to ensure that campaign grants would be restricted to candidates sharing his political views, led to the creation of an anti–Lloyd George Liberal Council, which raised money for campaign grants to anti–Lloyd George Liberal candidates.[20] Besides the cash given as grants for election expenses, money appears to have been spent on a very large scale on national press and poster advertising.

[19] A letter in the Maclean Papers refers to the payments given or promised before the 1929 election as £300,000 for the general election, £32,000 per annum for the National Liberal Federation, and £10,000 plus for the "Organisation Committee." Other sources give slightly different figures for the routine grants to the central Liberal organization, although the contribution of £300,000 for the 1929 election is widely accepted.

[20] Douglas, *History of the Liberal Party*, pp. 198-201. The Liberal Council existed between 1927 and 1946. In the 1929 election, the Liberal Council supported about 100 candidates and for this purpose "raised a substantial sum with the assistance of Viscount Gladstone."

In the 1929 election, there were over 500 Liberal candidates. The number of seats won increased slightly from 40 in 1924 to 59. In view of the huge outlay on the campaign, this was a miserable result and served only to confirm that the Liberals had been relegated to the status of a minor party. Lloyd George almost immediately withdrew financial support from the Liberal organization and from then on decided to preserve what remained of his Political Fund for more personal causes. From 1930 onward, the Liberal organization, which at last had no kitty, collapsed. The scale of its activities was drastically pruned and, in Douglas's words, its financial position in the 1930s was "obscure." According to a memorandum written in 1931 by a Liberal whip, the party's regular income was down to £1,000 a year, and it had the nucleus of an election fund amounting to approximately £4,500.[21]

The Liberals had suffered greatly for the treasure they had gathered through the sale of titles. For the fourteen years between 1916 and 1930, the central Liberal organization had a parasitical existence, first off the proceeds of the traffic in honors under Asquith and then off the profits of the transactions of Lloyd George. The mixture of large capital reserves and virtually no income from party members had disastrous effects: it led to extremely bitter internal quarrels about the control of the money, and it allowed the central party

[21] Harcourt Johnstone to Lord Samuel, November 30, 1931, Samuel Papers, A/84/24-42; quoted by Douglas, *History of the Liberal Party*, p. 230.

The withdrawal of aid by the Lloyd George Political Fund in 1930 certainly created a financial crisis. The central party organization was not as poor, however, as Johnstone's statement indicated. Rich Liberals still existed, and names such as that of Rothschild were to continue to be included in the party's lists of subscribers. The party's main problem was its continuing division into independent groups. The *Liberal Year Book* for 1937 (published by the Liberal publication department) reveals a plethora of organizations: (1) the headquarters at 21, Abingdon Street housed the Liberal Central Association (LCA), the Liberal publication department (LPD), and the Liberal Social Council; (2) the Liberal Party Organisation (LPO) had a separate office at 42, Parliament Street; (3) the Liberal National Organisation (that is, the organization of Liberal MPs who supported the National government established in 1931) had offices at nos. 3, 5, and 7, Old Queen Street, and the Liberal National Council operated from 15, Old Queen Street; (4) the National League of Young Liberals, the Liberal Council, and the Union of University Liberal Societies all had their own offices; and (5) Lloyd George continued to maintain his own political machine, by now almost entirely detached from Liberal party politics.

The internal conflicts within the Liberal organization in the late 1930s and during the Second World War are described in R. M. Sommer, "The Organization of the Liberal Party, 1936-1960" (Ph.D. thesis, London School of Economics, 1962). Sommer also emphasizes the weakness of the Liberals at the constituency level, characterizing the party in 1936 as "an organization with a top but no recognizable bottom. The entire organization in the country had fallen apart in the early and middle thirties" (p. 45).

bureaucracy to plod on for many years without facing up to the question of how funds could be raised now that the era of capitalistic lump sums was over.

The Conservative Response

For the Conservatives, the political confusion after the First World War brought considerable short-term advantages. Largely because of divisions on the political left, Conservative governments or Conservative-dominated coalitions ruled Britain for all but three years between 1916 and the end of the Second World War. The emergence of Labour as the main opposition party presented a formidable challenge to the Tories and caused much fear. The political battle against Labour required new techniques, which had been unnecessary during previous contests with the Liberals. This affected patterns of Conservative finance.

The challenge of Labour led the Conservative party managers to invest heavily in propaganda campaigns and professional publicity techniques. In the period between the two world wars, central Conservative spending on political advertising probably reached a level unparalleled before or since.

There were also changes in the party's fund-raising methods. Gradually, the Conservatives became less reliant on the largesse of businessmen searching for titles and adopted the patterns of fund raising that have survived to the present. At the national level, money from individual capitalists was replaced by contributions from corporations. Locally, candidates and rich backers became less important as sources of money, and funds were collected instead in relatively small amounts from ordinary members of constituency associations. These changes occurred slowly and were not completed until after the Second World War. The decline of plutocratic finance was already well advanced by the 1930s, and the Conservative success in exploring new ways of collecting money contrasted sharply with the Liberal failure.

The Pattern of Expenditure: The Development of Professional Propaganda. Until the First World War, the central party organizations had spent very little money on political advertising at the national level. Central party funds had been devoted almost entirely to routine headquarters expenses and, during general election campaigns, to the provision of grants to candidates in the constituencies. This changed completely during the 1920s and 1930s. Very large sums (by British standards) were devoted to highly professional national publicity campaigns, particularly before the elections of 1929 and 1935.

Before the First World War, British elections had involved two main parties, both of which accepted the ground rules of the parliamentary system. It was far from clear to the Conservatives after 1918 whether their new opponent—the Labour party—was willing to work within the established order of government or whether its aim was revolutionary. Tory suspicions about the emergent Labour party were intensified by the experience of the Russian Revolution, by the political instability on the European continent (where there were attempts to establish Communist regimes in several countries), and, closer to home, by the serious industrial upheavals in Britain after the end of the 1914–1918 war.

The political methods of the 1920s and 1930s were closely affected by the experience of the First World War itself. The events of 1914–1918 had led to the establishment of new, increasingly sophisticated institutions of political warfare in Britain. A secret service had been created. Governments had learned to break one another's codes.[22] Above all, the art of mass propaganda had greatly advanced.[23] In the postwar era, intelligence techniques and propaganda techniques created during the war were both adapted to peacetime politics.

[22] "The years after the First World War were the golden age of modern diplomatic codebreaking" (Christopher Andrew, "The British Secret Service and Anglo-Soviet Relations in the 1920s. Part 1: From the Trade Negotiations to the Zinoviev Letter," *Historical Journal*, vol. 20 [1977], p. 682). In particular, the interception and decoding of Russian diplomatic telegrams in the early years of the Bolshevik regime "had an important influence on the early history of Anglo-Soviet relations" (p. 679).

Some of the greatest triumphs of decoding during the First World War had been the responsibility of the director of naval intelligence, Admiral Sir Reginald Hall. Hall was later to become a Conservative MP and principal agent of Conservative Central Office.

The main significance of code breaking and other covert sources of information for a study of Conservative finance is that these sources revealed Soviet efforts to infiltrate and to finance the British left. This stimulated Conservative efforts to raise funds to combat these activities.

[23] Modern writings have tended to assume that the development of professional propaganda techniques occurred during the Second World War (for example, Richard Rose, *Influencing Voters: A Study of Campaign Rationality* [London: Faber, 1967], p. 13). It is more accurate to trace the phenomenon to the First World War. The skillful use of mass propaganda by the British government in 1914-1918 greatly impressed Adolf Hitler, who devoted a chapter of *Mein Kampf* to a discussion of the lessons to be drawn from it. As will be shown, some prominent Conservatives in the 1920s and 1930s were equally conscious of the value of "political warfare"—that is, mass propaganda.

The two men principally reponsible for the development of Conservative propaganda were John C. C. Davidson (later Lord Davidson), Conservative party chairman, 1927–1930, and Major Ball (later Sir Joseph Ball), who joined the Conservative Central Office in 1927 as director of publicity and in 1929 became director of the newly created Conservative research department. It is worthwhile to describe the backgrounds of Davidson and Ball in some detail, because their contributions to Conservative campaigning and to party finance were of the greatest importance.

Davidson had not been a serving officer of the British secret service.[24] In his capacity as private secretary and confidant to Bonar Law and Baldwin during the coalition with Lloyd George (1916–1922), however, he had acted as a liaison between the secret world and his political masters. As a member of Baldwin's governments of 1923 and 1924, Davidson acted as chief civil commissioner. This meant that, in conjunction with civil servants and the military, he superintended the secret plans prepared for the government to deal with the emergency of a general strike. These plans were brought into operation during the General Strike of 1926, when Davidson played a vital role. It is probably no accident that Davidson became chairman of the Conservative party within months of the collapse of the General Strike, when the feelings of class war and Conservative fears of Communist subversion were at their peak.

One of Davidson's early actions as party chairman was to persuade Ball to give up his commission in the army to become director of publicity at Conservative Central Office. Ball had spent his career in the police and intelligence services. According to his obituary in The Times[25] and successive entries in Who's Who, Ball had qualified as a barrister in 1913; after a spell as a civilian official at Scotland Yard, he joined the Secret Intelligence Service at the outbreak of the war and served until 1919. His activities between 1919 and 1923 are not known, but in 1923 he was once again an active British military officer and subsequently listed himself as having been on the War Office general staff in that year (this is a normal listing for intelligence officers). According to a later account by Davidson, Ball remained an officer in MI5 (counterintelligence) until he was recruited to Central Office in 1927. Davidson had first met Ball during the First World War, and it is reasonable to

[24] The main source of information about Davidson is Robert Rhodes James, *Memoirs of a Conservative: J. C. C. Davidson's Memoirs and Papers, 1910-37* (London: Weidenfeld and Nicolson, 1969).
[25] *The Times*, July 12, 1961.

assume that Ball, like Davidson, had been active in the 1920s in the task of combating Communist subversion in Britain. Ramsden indicates that "it seems quite likely" that Ball continued to work for MI5 "during the whole time that he was at Central Office."[26]

Revealing information about the attitudes of Davidson and Ball and about their work for the Conservative cause has survived in the Davidson Papers, the Neville Chamberlain Papers, and the Woolton Papers. Particularly important are four memoranda written by Ball in 1927(?), 1934, 1938, and 1946, setting out the objectives, methods, and financing of Conservative election propaganda.[27]

The Labour party was seen as the tip of an iceberg of leftist organizations. The left was so dangerous that it had to be treated as the "enemy," and Conservative organization needed to be run on the

[26] John A. Ramsden, "The Organisation of the Conservative and Unionist Party in Britain, 1910-1930" (D.Phil. thesis, Oxford University, 1974), p. 266. Ball, Davidson, and Hall all played parts in the intricate affair of the Zinoviev letter. On October 24, 1924, days before the general election, the Foreign Office released the text of a letter allegedly sent by Comintern leader Grigory Zinoviev to the British Communist party urging it to step up its infiltration of the Labour party and the armed forces. The "Red scare" intensified by this revelation is thought to have been a major cause of the Labour government's defeat.

The Labour party subsequently argued that the letter was a forgery. This view was supported in the 1960s by the *Sunday Times*, which claimed to have identified the White Russian forgers (see Lewis Chester, Stephen Fay, and Hugo Young, *The Zinoviev Letter* [London: Heinemann, 1967]). Recent academic research has found that it may have been genuine after all (see Andrew, "British Secret Service").

Through a private informant and probably through its contacts with the Secret Service and the Foreign Office, Conservative Central Office knew of the Zinoviev letter well before the official announcement. Party officials appear to have believed it genuine and wished to see it published. By leaking the story to the Tory press, they stampeded the Foreign Office into releasing the text. At an early stage of the affair, the Conservative party treasurer, Younger, offered to pay £7,500 for the letter to the informant, Conrad Donald im Thurn. This sum was intended for the mysterious agent "X" who had endangered himself by obtaining the document. The payment was not made, and it was only in 1928, when revelations were threatened and there was a parliamentary debate, that £5,000 was paid by Davidson, through Ball, to im Thurn. In 1956, when im Thurn's confidant Sir Guy Kindersley proposed to publish im Thurn's diary detailing his contacts with Central Office during the 1924 campaign, Davidson and Ball dissuaded him from doing so (see Rhodes James, *Memoirs of a Conservative*, pp. 203-4).

[27] The four memoranda are:

1. "The Present Situation," by G. J. B. (1927 ?) (Davidson Papers).
2. *Secret.* "Some Notes and Suggestions about Propaganda" (1934) (Neville Chamberlain Papers, 8/21/9).
3. *Secret.* "To the Prime Minister" (1938) (Neville Chamberlain Papers, 8/21/8).
4. "The Last General Election" (1946) (Woolton Papers, 21).

They will be referred to as memorandum no. 1, memorandum no. 2, and so on.

lines of the military campaigns of the First World War.[28] The main weapon to be employed against Labour was propaganda, "now recognised as the world's most potent weapon."[29] (An additional weapon was political espionage. Davidson and Ball set up a secret organization to spy on the Labour party, "to keep us informed of the enemy and his plans."[30] Ball referred to this private unit of party organization as the Special Information Service, whose initials —SIS—were the same as those of the Secret Intelligence Service in which he had served in the First World War.)

The need for expenditure on propaganda was argued by Ball in his first major memorandum, written in note form before the 1929 general election. Extracts are quoted below:

THE PRESENT SITUATION BY G.J.B. [George Joseph Ball]. . . .

2. Revolutionary tail wags Labour dog, e.g. General Strike, Coal Strike. . . .

3. Efforts of Opponents . . . (b) Labour educational activities. (c) Intensive propaganda by outside committees. Communists, National Minority Movement, I.L.P. [Independent Labour party], Daily Herald, Lansbury's Labour Weekly, Arcos Information Department, Sunday Worker, Young Communists' League, Labour Monthly, United Press Association of U.S.A., and many others.

4. Funds at disposal of enemy: (a) Trade Union levies. (b) Co-operative subscriptions. (c) Moscow propaganda funds. (d) Special education funds.

5. Dice at present loaded against us, e.g.: necessarily high taxation and food prices, unemployment. . . .

CONCLUSION. Our only hope at the next Election lies in an intensive propaganda campaign, carefully planned and co-ordinated on the most modern lines. . . .

Many of the advantages on the enemy's side. . . . *Our one great advantage: WEALTH* Let us use it. . . . [A] special education fund . . . should be established for an educational campaign by advertisements, posters, etc. to be run independently of the Conservative Party.

---

[28] In a memorandum prepared by Davidson in 1930 upon leaving office as party chairman, he stated, "The first job on which I set my mind was to apply the lessons of the Great War to the organisation of political warfare" (Rhodes James, *Memoirs of a Conservative*, p. 338).

[29] Ball memorandum no. 1.

[30] Ibid. For useful references to political espionage under the Davidson/Ball regime see Ramsden, "Organisation of the Conservative Party," pp. 265-67; and Rhodes James, *Memoirs of a Conservative*, p. 272.

As hinted in this memorandum, the ultimate plan was to assign the direction of mass propaganda to professional advertising agencies and to pay for it out of a fund separate from the main central party fund. It was intended that the special propaganda fund should be collected mainly from banks and business corporations. The responsibility of Central Office staff in matters of publicity was to be restricted to magazines and leaflets intended for party supporters. The motive for this arrangement was to evade what Davidson called "the dead hand of obstruction on the part of the Agents" (that is, the party organizers in the constituencies).[31]

This plan was only partly brought into operation before the 1929 election. The idea of a separate fund for national propaganda had to be abandoned for the time being.[32] Moreover, the bulk of expenditure for party publicity was devoted to the traditional leaflets, magazines, manifestoes, and posters distributed through party organizations in the constituencies.[33] Nevertheless, the 1929 campaign was innovative in several ways: the overall national expenditure on publicity (over £155,000) was exceptional by pre–First World War standards; commercial poster sites ("hoardings") were used on a relatively large scale;[34] increasing use was made of professional advertising agents to design slogans and to plan publicity strategy. The famous "Safety First" poster of 1929 was suggested and produced by S. H. Benson, a professional publicity agency.[35] In addition, Ball introduced (in the period before the campaign) the technique of direct mailing to target groups in the population.[36]

According to the Davidson Papers, Central Office spending for the 1929 election amounted to £290,475. Expenditure on candidates'

[31] Davidson Papers.

[32] As Ball wrote in memorandum no. 2 in 1934, "a plan of this kind was provisionally approved by some of the big banks in 1927 or 1928, [but] it ultimately broke down because McKenna refused to cooperate." (Reginald McKenna, a leading figure in the banking world, was a former Liberal cabinet minister.)

[33] This is shown by the detailed expenditure accounts for the 1929 campaign, which are preserved in the Davidson Papers.

[34] According to Cambray, Ball's predecessor as director of publicity at the Central Office, "at the General Election of 1929 they [the political "General Staffs"] . . . forged . . . new weapons. . . . Conservative strategists were given the special privilege of the use of the hoarding space of an advertiser of a national product" (Philip G. Cambray, *The Game of Politics* [London: John Murray, 1932], pp. 156-57).

[35] Ramsden, "Organisation of the Conservative Party," p. 263. Ramsden suggests that S. H. Benson "may well have been advertising the Party for many years before [the 1929 election]." This statement is based on the recollections of a senior former official of the publicity department at Central Office.

[36] Ball memorandum no. 2.

98

expenses was £102,547; the expenditure of the principal agents was £32,432; and, as mentioned, £155,496 was spent on publicity.[37]

Cambray points out that the use of national-level publicity "escaped legal penalties" and, in his opinion, evaded the spirit of the law limiting election expenses. This was because the law covered spending only by parliamentary candidates and did not apply to propaganda on behalf of the national party, at least in the period before the announcement of the date of the poll.[38]

The 1931 election was very sudden and there appears to have been less expenditure on advertising than in 1929. By contrast, a concerted publicity campaign was planned before the 1935 election.

After the 1931 election, the Conservatives became the dominant partners in a coalition with a few Labour MPs and some Liberals (the "National" government). This arrangement provided the pretext for Ball to organize advertising which, though to all intents and purposes Conservative, was nominally on behalf of the National government. It also enabled Ball to carry out his previous aim of conducting party publicity through a professional body independent of the regular Conservative organization.

The blueprint for this new body was put forward in April 1934 in a memorandum by Ball to Neville Chamberlain, who was then chairman of the Conservative research department.[39] The analysis was repeated in a further paper written by Ball to Chamberlain (by this time prime minister) in June 1938 in preparation for the election expected in October–November 1939.[40] (This projected election was not held because of the outbreak of war in September 1939.)

Ball suggested that Central Office and the constituency parties had "not realised the vital importance of propaganda under modern conditions."[41] Moreover, the central party organization, reliant as it was on the constituency associations, lacked the ability to conduct a professional public relations campaign and to reach the uncommitted voters. According to the memorandum of 1934:

> The really effective engines for mass propaganda today are:
> (a) The press, national and local; (b) The hoarding; (c) The B.B.C. [that is, the wireless service of the British Broadcasting Corporation]; (d) The cinema; (e) Mass distribution of special pamphlets.

[37] Rhodes James, *Memoirs of a Conservative*, p. 303.
[38] Cambray, *The Game of Politics*, pp. 154-57.
[39] Memorandum no. 2.
[40] Memorandum no. 3.
[41] Ibid.

The party machine was unable adequately to drive any of these engines. For example, an effective hoarding campaign required the advertising firm used by the party in 1929 and 1931 to plan systematically and to secure "good sites at reasonable prices."[42] A cinema campaign could not rely solely on the cinema vans run by the Central Office but demanded direct contact with the movie moguls to influence the content of films and newsreels. As Ball put it in his paper of June 1938:

> in addition to making full use of our own cinema units . . . we must devote the closest attention to the possibility of exploiting the screens of the ordinary cinema theatres throughout the country (seen by 20,000,000 people weekly). I have already paved the way for this with all the big circuits among exhibitors (including the all-powerful Cinematograph Exhibitors' Association), with Korda among the producers and with the Chairmen of the five News Reel Companies.[43]

The distribution of pamphlets also called for professional expertise. Ball's plan was for special pamphlets "written for, and sent by post to selected classes of the electorate."[44]

As a result of Ball's initiative, "a very small, very secret unofficial committee"[45] was convened in 1934. With the Conservative leader's approval, the committee set up the National Publicity Bureau, which continued to operate from an office in Westminster until after the outbreak of the Second World War.[46] It raised special funds from appeals "to the big banks . . . big joint-stock companies and big businessmen."[47] The NPB's achievements were later outlined by Ball in a memorandum written for Churchill in 1946: "This organisation was financed from a fund collected entirely from individuals and organisations who could not, or would not subscribe to ordinary Party funds. It spent approximately £300,000 during the 13 months preceding the election of November 1935 entirely on propaganda."[48]

---

[42] Memorandum no. 2.

[43] Memorandum no. 3.

[44] Ibid.

[45] Memorandum no. 2.

[46] This information has been obtained from contemporary telephone and street directories. For a fuller description of the NPB, see the note at the end of this chapter.

[47] Memorandum no. 2.

[48] Memorandum no. 4.

The £300,000 spent on central propaganda before the 1935 election is equivalent to over £5 million in 1980 values, a sum approached only by the value of Conservative advertising expenditure in 1963–1964. Moreover, additional sums were presumably spent by Central Office itself before the 1935 poll. Therefore, unless Ball's figure is greatly exaggerated, Conservative propaganda spending in 1935 was the highest, in real terms, for any party in any election in British history.[49]

National-level advertising was the most costly innovation of the interwar years but not the only one. The Conservative research department, created in 1929, required special funding, as did Ashridge, a college for the education of party workers, established by Davidson after the 1929 election.

These developments placed heavy demands on the national party's routine and campaign expenditure. They were partly offset by reductions in other types of spending. In general election campaigns, the extra money for advertising was provided largely by the significant decrease (in real terms) in Central Office grants to parliamentary candidates. As far as routine expenditure was concerned, the creation of the Conservative research department in 1929 was soon accompanied by economies at the Central Office.[50]

The trends in central expenditure are impossible to establish for the whole interwar period because the only routine Central Office accounts that have so far been discovered are those in the Davidson Papers for 1925–1929, and the only detailed general election account is that of 1929. Central Office spending in 1925–1929 is given in table 25. It excludes general election spending and the expenditure of the Scottish Central Office.

According to Ramsden's research, local Conservative associations were spending about £800 a year in the late 1920s.[51] This was very slightly more than their average *routine* expenditure before the First World War (in real terms). However, the restrictions of the Representation of the People Act, 1918, meant that candidates' *campaign* costs were lower in current prices, and far lower in real terms, than before.

[49] It seems reasonable to estimate the total cost of the Conservative party's central campaign for the 1935 election at about £450,000. This total includes spending by the National Publicity Bureau and assumes that central expenditure on grants to candidates was roughly the same in 1935 as in 1929.

[50] Ramsden cites a list of economies at Central Office at this period that survives in the Baldwin Papers (53, file 4) ("Organisation of the Conservative Party," p. 338).

[51] Ibid., p. 358. Ramsden's estimate is based on an examination of records from forty constituencies and six city parties (p. 367).

TABLE 25
Conservative Central Office Routine Expenditure, 1925–1929

	1925	1926	1927	1928	1929
Central Office	95,869	85,399	98,625	106,591	114,391
House of Commons office	138	157	128	128	1,287
Central Office district agents	24,282	25,270	26,714	30,180	29,710
Special campaigns	14,354	18,782	21,682	17,661	12,459
Constituency grants	26,941	21,574	33,174	38,048	25,789
Grants to outside organizations	675	1,024	657	1,639	922
London department	9,937	10,904	15,096	17,027	14,620
Junior Imperial League	3,335	3,547	6,658	7,950	5,460
Miscellaneous	11,255	13,541	12,734	19,199	30,231
Total	186,791	180,113	216,675	248,256	234,875

NOTE: Excludes general election expenditure. Figures are as in source.
SOURCE: John A. Ramsden, *The Age of Balfour and Baldwin, 1902-1940* (London: Longman, 1979), p. 221 (from the Davidson Papers).

The overall pattern of Conservative spending in the parliamentary cycle 1925–1929 is shown in table 26. It is labeled the "transitional pattern" because, for reasons given below, the methods of raising funds at this time were halfway between those of the plutocratic era and those of the modern period.

If the figures for 1925–1929 are compared with those for the aristocratic era (table 4) and the plutocratic era (table 12), these are the main trends:[52]

1. Overall central and local expenditure rose considerably between 1906–1910 and 1925–1929. This was largely because of inflation. In real terms, overall Conservative spending rose by 13 percent.

2. Constituency campaign expenditure fell sharply (from 34 percent of total spending in 1906–1910 to 14 percent in 1925–1929) while other types of spending rose. The most important increase was in national campaign spending (from 1 percent in 1906–1910 to 5 percent in 1925–1929). The tightened rules about candidates' election expenses thus made it possible to introduce new kinds of spending—such as national advertising campaigns—without greatly pushing up the overall cost of politics.

[52] For the purposes of this paragraph, totals of routine central and constituency spending have been adjusted to represent spending over a standard four-year parliamentary cycle. See table 73.

TABLE 26

The Transitional Pattern: Overall Conservative Expenditure
(approximate) during the Parliamentary Cycle 1925–1929
(in pounds)

	Routine Expenditure	Campaign Expenditure
Central	850,000	200,000
Local	Roughly 2½ million	535,000

Notes: The figures cover a 4½-year period to mid-1929. The totals include estimated spending by the Scottish Central Office. The figures have been calculated on the same basis as those for tables 4 and 12.
Source: Ramsden, "Organisation of the Conservative Party."

3. Largely because of the fall in constituency election expenditure, the overall trend toward national-level expenditure and toward routine expenditure continued (see table 73).

4. Although overall Conservative spending rose in real terms by about 13 percent between 1906–1910 and 1925–1929, the growth in the electorate was far greater. This was because of the enfranchisement in 1918 of many men who previously had not been able to vote and because of the grants in 1918 and 1928 of votes for women. In real terms, the overall cost per vote dropped sharply from nearly £16 (in 1980 values) in 1906–1910 to £6.4 in 1925–1929 (this includes central and local, routine and campaign costs).

5. The lack of statistics about routine Labour spending during 1925–1929 at the constituency level prevents the compilation of comparative figures for the Labour party. However, if it is assumed that two-thirds of overall Labour expenditure came from the political levy funds of the unions, then Labour spent about £1¼ million during 1925–1929. This is about a third of the overall Conservative spending.

Sources of Income. The figures in table 26 show that, despite the cost of the new publicity techniques employed to combat socialism, the level of Conservative spending rose little. There is, however, conflicting evidence about how Conservative central funds were collected in the interwar years. On the one hand, it has been argued by Davidson and by his official biographer Robert Rhodes James that the sale of titles had ended by the mid-1920s and that Central Office was obliged to find money by radically new methods; on the other hand, it has been suggested by other scholars, such as A. J. P. Taylor and Ramsden, that the changes in Conservative fund raising during Stanley Baldwin's leadership (1923–1937) were largely cosmetic and that the practices of the plutocratic era did not suddenly disappear in 1922.[53]

It is worth reviewing both interpretations. There is considerable evidence that the Conservative party stopped selling honors from 1922 onward and established alternative sources of income. During the early 1920s, the revulsion within the party against the coalition with Lloyd George was very strong. Baldwin attained the leadership of the Conservative party because he spearheaded the rebellion in 1922 against the continuation of this coalition. As part of the effort to sweep away the remnants of the Lloyd George period, Baldwin and his associates expressed their determination to end the sale of titles, which had by this stage become a public scandal. Davidson, Baldwin's closest confidante, later declared:

> The most distasteful aspect of the distribution of honours was that the Royal Prerogative was being prostituted for sordid reasons. The pretence was maintained that the grant of an honour was based on political services, whereas in fact under Lloyd George's regime there was simply a cash transaction of sale and purchase.[54]

[53] A. J. P. Taylor, *Beaverbrook* (London: Hamish Hamilton, 1972), pp. 257-58; Ramsden, "Organisation of the Conservative Party," p. 334ff.
[54] Rhodes James, *Memoirs of a Conservative*, p. 281.

In 1925 Baldwin's government passed the act that made this traffic illegal.

Moreover, Central Office worked quietly to destroy one of the intermediaries who had participated in the honors market. Extreme caution was necessary because some eminent Conservatives had previously engaged in shady dealings connected with titles and honors. They would be subject to blackmail if they donned puritanical garb and refused to respect past bargains. The main honors tout, Maundy Gregory, was in a position to reveal facts about leading Conservatives that "would have provided a *cause célèbre* of dramatic proportions."[55] In words used in 1934 by Baldwin to the Labour prime minister, MacDonald, and recorded in MacDonald's diary (the two men were by this time allies in the National government, and it was for this reason safe for Baldwin to talk), "Maundy Gregory's papers . . . [could] stir up such a filthy sewer as would poison public life. . . . all parties were involved. . . . The dunghill had to be cleared away."[56]

According to the Davidson version, given many years after the events, the problem of destroying Gregory without public revelations called for cloak-and-dagger methods. While outwardly remaining friendly with Gregory (so the story goes), Davidson, the Conservative party chairman, planted a spy in Gregory's organization to ensure that no one who was paying him money for an honor ever received one.[57]

[55] Ibid., p. 280.

[56] David Marquand, *Ramsay MacDonald* (London: Cape, 1977), p. 746.

[57] According to Rhodes James, "the task of penetrating the Gregory organization was undertaken by A. J. Bennett, appointed Assistant Treasurer of the Party in the autumn of 1927" (*Memoirs of a Conservative*, p. 280). In my opinion, it is unlikely that Bennett himself acted as an undercover agent. It was hardly a function that someone of his eminence could fulfill. Moreover, his involvement with the Gregory organization would, if publicized, cause acute embarrassment. There are at least two alternative explanations: (1) that Bennett was in charge of the operation but did not himself have direct contact with Gregory, and (2) that the spy was another man with a similar name. These are both plausible interpretations of an intriguing, unsigned memorandum in the Davidson Papers. The note is dated November 11, 1928.

> *Secret*
>
> The chairman [Davidson] has laid down that, to prevent confusion, but to preserve security, we should forthwith cease referring to A. J. B., but for his eyes only spell out the informant as either A. J. Bennett, or A. J. Bennet, taking great care that we get the spelling of the surname right according to which of the two it refers. The chairman feels this system would be less likely to arouse comment than the use of any code-name. This same method of reference is being used in communications with Balfour, Remnant and Bogovout-Kolomitzov in Paris.

If it does nothing else, this note vividly illustrates the secret service atmosphere

Rendering Gregory ineffective in securing titles would eventually lead to the loss of his millionaire custom. Gregory finally did go bankrupt in 1933.

During its final stages, the plan silently to dispose of Gregory almost came unstuck. As Gregory faced destitution, he restored to extreme measures. He is suspected of poisoning a lady who bequeathed her money to him in a will hastily prepared before her death.[58] Gregory arranged for her burial in a shallow grave by the River Thames. By the time her body was exhumed, flood water made it impossible to determine whether there had been poison in her system when she died. Gregory searched for new clients to exchange money for titles, money that he planned to pocket. In 1932 he made a clumsy approach to a retired naval officer who did not want a title but who contrived to catch Gregory. Eventually, the naval officer produced sufficient evidence for an arrest, and Gregory was charged with violating the Honours (Prevention of Abuses) Act of 1925.

Gregory's trial presented a crisis to the Conservative party managers. It threatened to bring into the open "the filthy sewer." After considerable pressure and plea bargaining, Gregory was induced to plead guilty to the charge of soliciting money from the naval officer. This plea meant that the court did not have to establish whether Gregory had ever been authorized to tout for honors, and it did not explore the existence of other clientele. While Gregory served his short prison sentence, Davidson arranged for the collection of a secret fund to provide a pension for Gregory. Its payment was conditional upon his living abroad (in Paris) and never revealing the names of those who had been ennobled through his efforts. There is evidence that the help of the diplomatic and secret services was

at the Central Office during the Davidson/Ball regime. (Bogovout-Kolomitzov was presumably an informant about Bolshevik activities directed against Britain.)

Another guess about the identity of the person responsible for infiltrating Gregory's office is that it may have been Captain R. C. Kelly. Cullen's research for his biography of Gregory indicates that it was to Kelly's home that Gregory was driven after his release from prison and that Kelly then drove Gregory on his journey to exile in Paris and thereafter "was to take Gregory in hand, install him in an apartment near the British Embassy in Paris, and to look after all of his wants, paying him frequent visits both in Paris and Dieppe." Interestingly, the detailed Central Office accounts for 1928, which survive in the Davidson Papers, show that Kelly received three payments for unspecified purposes, amounting to £750. Were these payments made to finance the operation against Gregory? Further information about Kelly's connections with the Gregory affair is given in footnote 59.

[58] See Macmillan, *Honours for Sale;* and Tom Cullen, *Maundy Gregory: Purveyor of Honours* (London: Bodley Head, 1974). A more speculative account is given in Donald McCormick, *Murder by Perfection: Maundy Gregory, the Man behind Two Unsolved Mysteries?* (London: Long John, 1970).

recruited to obtain permission for Gregory to live in France and subsequently to keep an eye on him, presumably to ensure his silence.[59] Thus, the claim is made of Davidson that he ended the sale of titles and, at the same time, prevented a huge public scandal that, it was feared, could undermine confidence in the political system.

An ironical footnote to the affair, which is not mentioned in the Davidson memoirs, is that the cash for Gregory's hush fund was provided by a man who appears himself to have been one of Gregory's customers and who now demanded a baronetcy as a reward for his £30,000 contribution. Baldwin, the Conservative leader, was obliged to pressure MacDonald, the Labour prime minister of the mainly Tory National government, into approving the honor. MacDonald regarded the donor as "one of those Honours hunters whom I detested . . . just the man whom I would not dream of honouring."[60] MacDonald nevertheless recommended the king to award the baronetcy in 1934.[61] In this way, an honor that was almost certainly

[59] Tom Cullen has kindly supplied me with information additional to that published in his interesting biography of Gregory. In his book, Cullen names the agent assigned to keep watch on the former honors tout as "Captain Phipps." This was a pseudonym for Captain A. E. Kitts, whom Cullen interviewed on several occasions before his death. Kitts revealed that he had been asked to keep an eye on Gregory by Captain R. C. Kelly. Kelly, according to Kitts, sent regular remittances to Gregory through Drummonds Bank and visited him in Paris.
Evidence of Kelly's connection with Conservative Central Office in 1928 has been given in footnote 57. He was also linked with Admiral Sir Reginald Hall. Hall was former director of naval intelligence, former principal agent at Conservative Central Office, and a Conservative MP. Kelly and Hall were both active in a brewers' lobby called the National Publicity Agency (not to be confused with the National Publicity Bureau). Kelly was to become secretary of the National Publicity Agency, a leading officer of which was Hall's former deputy director of naval intelligence, Colonel Serocold.
Whether or not Kelly's payments to Gregory were made on behalf of the National Publicity Agency (as Cullen suggests) is not known. If the bulk of the money for Gregory's pension was donated by Sir Julien Cahn, as indicated in Ramsay MacDonald's diary (see footnote 60), it is reasonable to presume that the National Publicity Agency was not directly involved.
The web of personal contacts that has been outlined is a good illustration of what can for convenience be called the "triangular relationship." In the interwar years, it linked parts of (1) the secret service, (2) Conservative Central Office, and (3) some right-wing business lobbies. They were united in their fear of left-wing or Communist influence. It was evidently felt that Gregory was in a position to reveal scandalous information that not only would harm the Conservative party and some of its business supporters but also might damage the national interest.

[60] Marquand, *Ramsay MacDonald*, p. 745.

[61] Since MacDonald was the prime minister, it was in his power to give or to deny honors. As he recorded in the privacy of his diary ("this entry is specially private"), he put up strong resistance to Baldwin's pressure to give the baronetcy. Baldwin's strongest card was that Labour politicians were among those who would be implicated if Gregory's papers ever came to light.   (continued overleaf)

illegal under the terms of the 1925 act was given to provide a pension fund to hide the past traffic in peerages and knighthoods. This action by MacDonald and Baldwin can be seen as proof of their cynical disregard for the law about the sale of titles. Alternatively, it can be interpreted as an indication of Baldwin's determination to extricate the Conservatives once and for all from the legacies of the plutocratic era.

According to Rhodes James, Davidson's new method of obtaining central funds was to appeal collectively to the business community, which felt threatened by socialism. In other words, contributions from individual businessmen seeking titles were replaced in the 1920s by subscriptions from companies that were given for reasons of ideology and commercial self-interest. Davidson described his fund-raising technique in a letter written in January 1929:

> The City has raised already something like £150,000 and are continuing to raise further funds for the Party for the

---

B. [Baldwin] replied that I must yield & when I asked why he said . . . that all parties were involved (I corrected him at once & said "No(t) ours." He smiled & said that unfortunately friends of mine were. I replied that if they were I knew nothing about it. Then I remembered that Clynes & Henderson were mentioned at an earlier stage) (ibid., p. 476).

After some delay MacDonald agreed to the baronetcy, noting in his diary "Mr. B. . . . involves me in a scandal of honour by forcing me to give an honour because a man has paid £30,000 to get Tory headquarters & some Tories living and dead out of a mess."

The incident raises the question of the extent to which the Labour party was involved in the traffic in titles. Since the Labour party funds were public, it is clear from an examination of the accounts that honors hunters did not contribute (or, at least, only in relatively modest amounts). It is possible that payments were made to Labour politicians in their individual capacities. A modern example of a personal political fund is that set up for the benefit of Sir Harold Wilson as Labour leader when the party was in opposition after 1970. See Andrew Roth, *Sir Harold Wilson: Yorkshire Walter Mitty* (London: Macdonald and Jane's, 1977). (It should be stressed, of course, that the donations received by Wilson were for his use as political leader and not for private purposes. See chap. 8, footnote 43.)

MacDonald had himself received a handsome subsidy from a manufacturer while prime minister in 1924. This had consisted of the interest during his lifetime on a capital sum of £40,000 and the use of a Daimler car. This was provided, in MacDonald's words, "so that I may not require, whilst absorbed in public duties, to worry about income." Soon afterward MacDonald awarded a baronetcy to the donor, Sir Alexander Grant. He denied that the title was linked with the subsidy. As his biographer puts it, "It is clear that Grant's public services were worthy of recognition; it is also clear that neither he nor MacDonald saw any connection between the baronetcy and the £40,000" (Marquand, *Ramsay MacDonald*, pp. 357-59). This generous interpretation is open to question. It is interesting to note that, by the election of 1929, Grant was not a Labour supporter. His name appears on the list of donors to the Conservative election fund, which survives in the Davidson Papers.

simple reason that they are thoroughly frightened at the prospect of a Socialist Government. The way the City was worked was that I went down to a private meeting and told them that only big money was any good to me. The result was that at a lunch given in November £130,000 had already been raised in £5,000 subscriptions. Stanley [Baldwin, the prime minister] made a short speech on the dangers of Socialism to finance and credit.[62]

Davidson also described plans for an appeal to "some fifty or sixty key industrialists" outside London. At this meeting, Baldwin would make "essentially an appeal to businessmen to help the only political party which possess the one national organization which is capable of fighting Socialism."

Ramsden's interpretation differs from that of Davidson and of Rhodes James. He argues that the importance of honors for Conservative party finance did not decrease in the 1920s nearly as rapidly as Davidson and Rhodes James have claimed. Citing Davidson's private papers, Ramsden quotes several instances of peerages that were given to generous donors during Baldwin's premiership of 1924–1929. In some of these cases, the expectation of an honor as the reward for a contribution was openly expressed. Ramsden concludes:

It seems clear that, apart from tidying up the residue of the Lloyd George era, Davidson did not fundamentally change his Party's attitude towards honours. It is perhaps true that no bargains were made, and in this sense honours were not "sold"; but since subscribers received honours and a high proportion of honours went to subscribers of the Party, the net result was not very different.[63]

Moreover, there remain a number of question marks about Davidson's version of how he gradually destroyed Maundy Gregory's honors-touting business. For example, if the Conservatives resolutely refused to give titles to Gregory's clients after 1922, it is curious that he was able to maintain his costly apparatus for another ten years (until 1933). To impress would-be clients, Gregory maintained a West End club, a magazine in which his customer's public virtues were extolled, and an office. An alternative explanation is that, despite later denials, the Conservatives continued an honors trade during Baldwin's

[62] Davidson to Neville Chamberlain, January 8, 1929, Davidson Papers.
[63] Ramsden, "Organisation of the Conservative Party," p. 347.

ministries of the 1920s and that Gregory went bankrupt only after a Labour premier, MacDonald, came into office in 1929.

Which of these interpretations is correct? It seems that both contain some truth. For example, an examination of Davidson's claim about his plan to destroy Gregory produces a halfway conclusion. Snippets of information in the Davidson Papers indicate that Davidson was taking steps to keep track of honors touts. There is also some external evidence. It is possible to gain an impression of the identity of some of Gregory's clients in the late 1920s by examining the guest lists of the Derby Dinner. This was held each year on the eve of the Derby horse race (a highlight of the English racing and social calendar). The host of the dinner had originally been a sporting member of Parliament, Colonel Walter Faber, who invited leading figures from all political parties and from other spheres of public life to attend. From 1925 onward, lists of the diners were printed in the social column of *The Times*.

Unknown to many of the guests, the glittering event was financed by Gregory. It enabled him to be named in *The Times* in the company of the most prominent men in the land (in the 1925 report, for example, his name appeared next to that of the Conservative party chairman, Colonel F. S. Jackson). When he obtained control of the dinner, Gregory seems to have added the names of some of his candidates for honors to the invitation list. The Derby Dinner became a bizarre mixture of cabinet ministers, celebrities, and unknowns. Some names appear year after year. A few who are first listed without a title reappear subsequently as "Sir." These recipients of titles include known associates of Gregory. One may observe, however, that the number of guests who obtained honors between 1925 and the last dinner held in 1932 was very small.

Leading Conservative party managers regularly attended the dinners (including Davidson, Ball, and Bennett, the assistant party treasurer).[64] This would indicate that the party managers did not close the door on Gregory's customers as firmly as Davidson later recalled but that they gave only a limited number of knighthoods to them. Possibly the motive was to keep Gregory in the dark about their true intentions by acceding to a few of his requests.

Apart from the efforts of the Conservative organizers to extricate themselves from the clutches of the honors touts, did they make any real attempt to abolish the trade in titles?[65] Or was their real motive

[64] Another name on the guest list was Kelly.

[65] The Conservative party's reserves stood at "something over a million pounds" at the time of the fall of the coalition with Lloyd George (Younger to Baldwin, August 27, 1927, Davidson Papers, quoted in Ramsden, "Organisation of the

to make it more subtle and respectable so that they could preserve the old system? A considerable amount of evidence survives about the identity of the main donors to Central Office in the late 1920s. There is in Davidson's papers what appears to be a complete list of fifty-six contributors to the special election fund that raised £156,000 in 1929, but a close examination of the names does not make it possible clearly to answer two important questions: (1) were the donors motivated by a desire for titles or by fear of socialism? and (2) did contributions come from businessmen in their individual capacities or from their companies and corporations?

Nevertheless, some general impressions about the pattern of payments to the Conservative central organization can be given. First, many of the donors of 1929 were industrialists who had received honors during the Lloyd George coalition. The 1929 list even includes Sir Edmund Vestey, brother and business partner of Lord Vestey, whose ennoblement by Lloyd George in 1922 had caused such a furore. This suggests that the group of rich party backers changed very slowly, but the fact that most of them had purchased their baronetcies by 1922 may indicate that they were no longer contributing for the sake of obtaining titles but to protect their business interests.[66] Second, it is clear from a broad

---

Conservative Party," p. 332). These large reserves resulted, at least in part, from Conservative honors' sales.

Between 1923 and 1927, the party lived on its capital. This suggests that it did not raise funds by selling titles during the first years of Baldwin's ministry, elected in 1924. Under Davidson's chairmanship, from 1927, the pace of fund raising increased. He later estimated that during his three years as Conservative chairman, the central party raised £1 million and an additional endowment fund of £200,000 for the Conservative college at Ashridge (memorandum by Davidson, 1930, Davidson Papers, quoted by Ramsden, "Organisation of the Conservative Party," p. 334). It was during 1927-1930 that the Conservatives were again under pressure to give titles to their benefactors.

At the end of 1928, four of the party's trusts had reserves totaling £615,774 (Sir Maxwell Hicks to Davidson, January 11, 1929, Davidson Papers). The reserves were probably higher if one takes account of other trusts not included in Hicks's note.

[66] Contributors to the 1929 Conservative election fund include the following, who had received titles during the Conservative coalition with the Lloyd George Liberals: Sir Abe Bailey (baronet 1919), Sir Leonard Brassey (baronet 1922), Sir George Bullough (baronet 1916), Sir Robert Waley-Cohen (knighted 1920), Sir Hugo Cunliffe-Owen (baronet 1920), Sir Trevor Dawson (baronet 1920), Sir John Dewrance (knighted 1920), Sir George Dolby (knighted 1920), Sir Arthur Dorman (knighted 1918), Sir William Dupree (baronet 1921), Sir William Garthwaite (baronet 1919), Sir. R. Garton (knighted 1918), Sir Ernest Jardine (baronet 1919), Sir Ernest Palmer (baronet 1916), Sir James Readhead (baronet 1922), Sir Edmund Vestey (baronet 1921), and Colonel Sir Charles Wakefield (baronet 1917). (The names of subscribers to the election fund were attached to a communication from Hicks to Davidson, January 14, 1930, Davidson Papers.)

examination of the evidence that the desire for a title featured strongly in the minds of a considerable number of contributors.[67] Although these hopefuls were now obliged to go through the motions of giving money to charity and serving the party in a voluntary capacity, it was recognized that the real objective was to create a presentable case for the award of a title or a peerage. Third, many business corporations had legal inhibitions about contributing to the funds of a political party. Such gifts had been unusual in the past and were sometimes questioned by the corporations' auditors. It appears that it was partly for this reason that some companies preferred (even in the days when all political contributions could be secret) to give money to a front organization devoted to fighting socialism—an acceptable business objective—than to give directly to the Conservative party. Moreover, personal income tax was still sufficiently low to make it possible for the directors of big businesses to contribute in their personal capacities out of their after-tax profits without undue loss.

All these considerations suggest that changes were gradual and that the plutocratic pattern did not disappear suddenly. Even at the present day, the honors list has remained a useful tool at the disposal of party managers in their quest for contributions. At the same time, it would be wrong to underestimate the significance of the changes that did take place during the 1920s and 1930s. Two factors contributed to the trend toward corporate giving. First, some major enterprises that had started as family businesses adopted a corporate structure. Second, the emergence of the Labour party presented a clear threat to business and gave an incentive for political contributions that had not existed before the First World War. The list of contributors to the election fund of 1929 includes representatives of some of the largest business enterprises and financial institutions in the country: Shell, General Electric Company, British and American Tobacco, Watney's Brewery, Vickers, Babcock and Wilcox, Dorman Long, several major steamship and shipbuilding companies, and so on.

It is reasonable to conclude that, during the interwar years, fear of the growing political power of organized labor stimulated a response from organized business. In financing the central party organizations, the clout of institutionalized capitalism was pitted

[67] In the late 1920s, the link between donation and honor was particularly close in the cases of a handful of exceptionally large donors. Two peerages were associated with donations of £100,000. In another case, a contribution of £30,000 secured a baronetcy. See Ramsden, "Organisation of the Conservative Party," pp. 341-47.

against that of the trade unions. Ramsden sums up this development with a good example:

> In 1928, the West Yorkshire Coal-Owners' and South Yorkshire Coal-Owners' Associations were both subscribing officially and liberally to Conservative Party funds; many coal-owners had no doubt supported the Conservative Party before but they had not been sufficiently unanimous in their support to subscribe collectively.[68]

The emergence of class politics also led gradually to changes in Conservative constituency finance. Over the long run these were of vital benefit to the party. During the interwar period, the ordinary members of local Conservative associations began for the first time to make significant financial contributions and to take over the burdens that had before the First World War been carried almost entirely by candidates and by a limited circle of generous subscribers.

Previously the salary of the full-time agent, the upkeep of the constituency office, and the payment of election expenses had rarely been concerns of the members of a local Conservative association. Membership subscriptions had been an insignificant component of local party income. The political climate of the 1920s seems to have resulted in enlarged membership of many Conservative associations, especially in middle-class areas.[69] The members were willing to contribute amounts that were individually moderate but were in total large. Income from membership subscriptions was supplemented by the profits of large-scale social events. The rallies and bazaars held in the interwar period had the twofold function of giving a political platform to a distinguished Conservative speaker and of raising money.

Small annual subscriptions (£1 to £5) and the proceeds of fund-raising functions gradually lessened the dependence of constituency associations on large individual donations or on heavy backing by parliamentary candidates. There were conscious moves in the 1920s and 1930s to make constituency associations financially independent of their candidates. Ramsden estimates that "about 30% of constituencies had become self-supporting by the 1930s."[70] The need for democratic local party finance was recognized in the *Handbook on Constituency Organisation* issued by Central Office in 1933: "It is now generally appreciated that each Association should be

---

[68] Ibid, p. 192.
[69] Ibid., p. 191.
[70] Ibid., p. 364.

made self-supporting. . . . The day is past when the Member of Parliament, prospective Candidate, or a few supporters, ought to provide all the necessary funds."[71]

The increasingly democratic pattern of local Conservative finance appears to have been largely a reaction to the growth of the Labour party. Middle-class concern about the Labour party's political success seems to have led to increasing local Conservative membership and activity, particularly among Tory women, who received the vote at this time. The previously technical and consuming tasks of voter registration were, after the Representation of the People Act, 1918, no longer an important concern for local Conservative associations, which devoted themselves to antisocialist propaganda and to local fund raising.

Parliamentary candidates also put pressure on local associations to assume the costs of campaigns. The gradual professionalization of politics meant that would-be candidates were often young, middle-class university graduates who did not have an assured private income and could not offer themselves for selection for constituencies where they would have to bear heavy electioneering expenses. Moreover, the Conservative leaders were very anxious—because of the emergence of Labour—to show that the party was not merely a gathering of those with independent means. As Baldwin emphasized in February 1924, shortly after the first Labour government had come into office: "no party that cannot equally offer a career to a man who has ability . . . can possibly compete with a party that does."

Ramsden additionally stresses that professional agents became reluctant to base the constituency budget on money from the candidate or from a few big backers because, though an easy source of money in the short run, they were unreliable.[72] (By contrast, when constituency Labour parties were backed by a trade union, this support was normally much more regular. The motive for building up small-scale individual contributions was therefore usually lacking.)

The old patterns of local party finance did not disappear overnight. In January 1939, Ian Harvey, a young Conservative (who later became an MP), issued a memorandum to the press complaining of the "Financial Demands Now Made upon M.P.'s and Prospective Candidates in the Conservative Party."[73] He maintained that local Conservative constituency associations still operated "A Plutocratic System." He claimed that the list of those who wished to become

[71] Ibid., p. 362.

[72] Ibid., p. 365.

[73] The memorandum is reproduced in William B. Gwyn, *Democracy and the Cost of Politics in Britain, 1832-1959* (London: Athlone Press, 1962).

114

parliamentary candidates consisted of three categories: "Class 'A': those willing to pay all their election expenses (£400–£1,200) and to subscribe £500–£1,000 a year to the local association; Class 'B': those willing to pay half their election expenses and to subscribe £250–400 per annum; Class 'C': those unable to pay any election expenses or to pay more than £100 per annum."[74] According to the memorandum, " 'A' Class have always an excellent chance of being adopted . . . 'C' Class hardly any at all."

Harvey acknowledged during subsequent correspondence in the press that the situation varied between constituencies and between different parts of the country. When a member of the Leeds (Yorkshire) Conservative Association asserted that Conservative candidates in Yorkshire were not obliged to make exorbitant contributions to their local parties, Harvey conceded that the evil was much worse in the Home Counties.[75]

The Harvey memorandum shows that the democratization of local party finance still had a considerable way to go at the outbreak of the Second World War.[76] It also indicates that important changes had taken place. Twenty years earlier, it had been a normal assumption that candidates should meet all or most of the costs of their campaigns. In 1939 it had become a matter of complaint.

[74] Ibid., p. 241.

[75] Ibid.

[76] The demands still made on some Conservative candidates in the 1930s are illustrated in Barbara Cartland's biography of *Ronald Cartland* (London: Hutchinson, n.d.). While candidate for the Birmingham constituency of King's Norton, Cartland had been required to give a contribution of £250 a year to the constituency association. He obtained this sum from "a friend who was interested in Ronald's future" and who "offered to give him an annual sum instead of contributing it to the party funds" (p. 79). A "staunch friend," Lord Carlow, also gave him, "his first Christmas at King's Norton, two tons of beef to distribute among the poorest families. He was to continue his gifts every year" (p. 86).

Cartland's methods of raising money for the constituency association also illustrate the survival of old methods: "Sir Herbert Austin [the motor manufacturer] gave a dinner for [Ronald Cartland]. . . . Twenty-four of the leading citizens of King's Norton were present. . . . Approximately £2,000 was subscribed that evening" (p. 60).

The Davidson Papers contain documents from an MP for a Norfolk constituency who set out his various expenditures, presumably to forward his claims for a political title. He estimated his running expenses as a candidate as £1,000 per annum and as an MP as £1,500 per annum. His election expenses averaged £1,100 for each campaign. In addition, he included over £14,000 spent on the *Norfolk Chronicle* as a political outlay. Other costs included the gift of four village halls, one Salvation Army hall, "dispatch of 6,000 Xmas cards, presents to every inmate of workhouses and 2 hospitals annually" and "entertaining in London to lunch at Lyons about 1,000 constituents (including special train) each summer."

Note: Lloyd George's Political Fund

The Political Fund was raised by Lloyd George's representatives (particularly his whips) during his premiership between 1916 and 1922. The money was ostensibly given to help Lloyd George to combat socialism. In reality, most of it seems to have been collected in return for honors[77]—a traffic that was conducted partly through go-betweens such as Henry Shaw and Maundy Gregory, who passed on the donations of the candidates for titles, keeping a commission for themselves.

Not all the money given by would-be recipients of titles went to Lloyd George. A portion also went to the Conservative partners in the 1916–1922 coalition. It is estimated by Sir Charles Mallet that the amount accumulated by Lloyd George by the time he fell from office in 1922 was nearly £1½ million.[78] This is a reasonable estimate. As mentioned in chapter 2, the Liberal chief whip between 1906 and 1908 saved about £½ million (apart from the routine costs of the central Liberal organization). Because of the inflation between 1906 and 1916, the 1906–1908 haul would have been worth over £1 million in post–First World War values. Thus, if Lloyd George made a profit from honors sales of £1½ million during his six years of office, this was not much more than the sum amassed by the official Liberals during two years under Campbell-Bannerman.

In the early days after Lloyd George's rise to the office of prime minister, the main item of spending from the Political Fund was the cost of running his personal political organization and the expense of an ex-servicemen's inquiry bureau. In addition, the bulk of the money was invested in 1918 in the *Daily Chronicle*. The expense of Lloyd George's personal machine is estimated by Owen as £20,000 a year.[79] According to Herbert Gladstone's memorandum about a conversation with Lloyd George in 1924, the cost of Lloyd George's organization in that year was £48,000.[80]

In each of the three general elections of 1922, 1923, and 1924, the Lloyd George Political Fund contributed to the election expenses

---

[77] It is clear from his papers that Lloyd George was well aware of the fact that many of those recommended by his whips for titles appeared on the list because of their payments to his Political Fund. See, for example, the letter from Guest, guiltily marked on the envelope "*Secret*, Only to Be Opened by the Prime Minister" (May 17, 1920, Lloyd George Papers, LG F/21/1/38).

[78] Mallet, *Mr. Lloyd George*, p. 254.

[79] Frank Owen, *Tempestuous Journey: Lloyd George, His Life and Times* (London: Hutchinson, 1954), pp. 687ff.

[80] Maclean Papers, 468, fo. 35.

116

of candidates. In 1922, before Liberal reunion, the help went to Lloyd George's National Liberal candidates alone. In 1923 and 1924, Lloyd George also gave money to the official Liberal headquarters. The amounts are in dispute. The Asquith Papers record donations of £90,000 in 1923 and £50,000 in 1924. Lloyd George later claimed that this understated his total contributions. He claimed that he had spent £155,000 on the 1923 campaign. (This larger sum may have included money given by the Political Fund in direct grants to candidates as well as the £90,000 channeled through the official Liberal organization.) One of Lloyd George's representatives claimed during the 1924 negotiations that he had altogether spent "not less than £650,000" from the fund during the previous two years.[81]

From the mid-1920s, the Political Fund spent heavily on the Land and Nation League, an organization that propagated Lloyd George's land policies. The sponsorship of economic inquiries into unemployment was another expense in the late 1920s. By 1927 the money from the fund was mostly gone, apart from the large investment in the *Daily Chronicle*. When Lloyd George decided to give heavy backing to the coming Liberal general election campaign (of 1929), he sold a large block of his newspaper shares at a handsome profit. According to Mallet, the Political Fund's holdings were sold for £2,888,000 in 1927. In exchange, £1,743,000 was received in cash and £1,145,000 in shares.[82] With this money, Lloyd George spent very heavily during 1927–1929.[83]

After 1929, however, the fund was hit by the depression, and the value of its investments fell so sharply that a purge of Lloyd George's

[81] Memorandum by Herbert Gladstone, Maclean Papers, 468, fo. 38. Sir J. T. Davies reportedly claimed on March 17, 1924, that "there was not more than £200,000 loose money now at the outside." This was exclusive of the money invested in the *Daily Chronicle* and presumably also excluded the interest from this investment, which Maclean gathered was running at £50,000 a year (Maclean Papers, 468, fo. 39).

[82] Mallet's figures are derived from *The Times* of July 21, 1927, and December 3, 1927. The advertisement of the sale of United Newspapers to the Daily Chronicle Investment Corporation revealed, according to Mallet "the fact that Mr. Lloyd George was the owner of at least 610,000 shares in United Newspapers Ltd., and that he had arranged to sell his holdings for £2,888,000 to the new company and to receive in exchange £1,743,000 in cash and £1,145,000 in fully paid ordinary shares of £1 each" (Mallet, *Mr. Lloyd George*, pp. 286-87).

[83] Besides the payments to the National Liberal Federation for routine and campaign costs, there were additional costs for his personal staff, and further sums must presumably be added for his activities in connection with the unemployment Yellow Books. According to a letter from Lord St. Davids (a trustee of the Lloyd George Fund) to Herbert Samuel shortly after the 1929 poll (July 7, 1929), the fund then stood at £765,000, and there were, in addition, 279,000 *Daily Chronicle* shares (Owen, *Tempestuous Journey*, p. 689).

personal staff was carried out at the beginning of 1931.[84] Lloyd George's alarm about the diminished size of his reserves was one reason—not the only reason—why he refused to give any support to Liberal candidates in the general election of 1931.

During the 1930s, the financial position of the fund seems to have improved, presumably as the value of investments recovered, even though Lloyd George was no longer interested solely in the Liberal party as a vehicle for his political interests. In the 1935 general election, he appears to have spent a staggering amount of money (estimated by Owen and Cross at £400,000) in organizing a "Council of Action." A network of regional councils was set up, and 362 candidates from all parties were "endorsed."[85]

The Political Fund was, according to Sylvester, still worth £¼ million by 1938 and over £75,000 in 1943.[86] In the later days, it was used to pay Lloyd George's political retainers and to meet the election expenses of Lloyd George and of members of his family.

The legal status of the fund was intentionally ambiguous. In order to avoid personal income taxes and death duties, it was a trust, although care was taken to ensure that the trustees were compliant.[87]

Table 27 gives estimates of known expenditure from the Lloyd George Political Fund. They do not include the routine costs of maintaining his personal staff or the costs of special projects such as the ex-servicemen's inquiry bureau.[88]

[84] See Colin Cross, ed., *Life with Lloyd George: The Dairy of A. J. Sylvester, 1931-45* (London: Macmillan, 1975), pp. 23-24.

[85] Ibid., pp. 123-24.

[86] Ibid., pp. 206, 314.

[87] For early discussions about the fund's legal status, see Guest to Lloyd George, November 26, 1921 (Lloyd George Papers, LG F/22/3/35). The fund's status remained ambiguous until the 1930s. In 1938 Lloyd George's advancing age and deteriorating health stimulated further legal inquiries. Sylvester, a Lloyd George intimate, wrote in his diary for July 8, 1938, "The documents have been looked up and there seems to be no document which gives precise information on the point of exact ownership. It is a question which in former days was always burked" (Cross, *Life with Lloyd George*, p. 213). On July 26, 1938, "L. G. received this morning a written decision from the Public Trustee saying that the Fund was his property" (p. 213). Sylvester described Lloyd George's dilemma about the legal standing of the fund as follows:

> He is confronted with two positions; (a) to have the Fund in his own name, or his nominees, arranged in such a way as he could do what he liked with it. In this case he would have to pay death duties. . . . (b) He could have a proper trust, but the difficulty would then be that he could not do as he liked with the money. L. G. wants to keep his cake and eat it (pp. 206-7).

[88] Table 27 also excludes the campaign expenses of Lloyd George's National Liberals in the elections of 1918 and 1922. If all these items are included, the total spent out of the fund between 1917 and the Second World War may have reached £2½-3 million.

TABLE 27

SOME ESTIMATED EXPENSES OF THE LLOYD GEORGE POLITICAL FUND
(in thousands of pounds)

	Amount	Purpose
	Payments for Liberal party purposes	
1923	100	For general election expenses (in a letter written to Reading in 1929, Lloyd George put the figure at £160,000)
1924	50	For general election expenses
1927	300	For forthcoming general election
1929	20	For extra election expenses
1927 1930	60	For Liberal headquarters expenses
Total	530	
	Additional disbursements recorded by Major Gwilym Lloyd George in a 1939 statement to the Liberal party	
	105	Toward the Liberal party Million Fund (receipt of this was disputed)
	240	Over several years for the Land and Nation League (1925–)
	400	For the Council of Action (Lloyd George's non-party campaign in the 1930s)
	100	For 1935 general election expenses
Total	845	

SOURCE: Owen, *Tempestuous Journey*, p. 692.

Note: The National Publicity Bureau (NPB)

As outlined in this chapter, most Conservative party publicity in the 1935 general election and before the election intended for 1939 (but not held because of the outbreak of war) was conducted by an organization called the National Publicity Bureau.[89] As mentioned in chapter 6, the NPB also arranged for Conservative publicity, though on a far smaller scale, in the election of 1945.

The pretext for setting up the NPB in 1934 was that the Conservatives were in coalition with Ramsay MacDonald's National

[89] Except where otherwise stated, the sources of information for this note are Ball's four memoranda listed in footnote 27.

Labour MPs and with Sir John Simon's National Liberals. The three parties forming the National government therefore needed a joint propaganda organization for the coming election. In fact, this was only one reason for setting up the NPB, and probably not the most important. It is significant that plans for such a front organization had already been made in the late 1920s, years before the formation of the National government, and that the NPB remained in existence well after the National government had disappeared.

The importance of the NPB in the eyes of Ball, the first director of the Conservative research department, is indicated in one of the last letters he wrote to Chamberlain in 1940. By that time, Chamberlain was the ex-premier and was in poor health, and Ball therefore took the opportunity to sum up his own achievements during the previous decade. He put "the establishment, the organization & direction of the National Publicity Bureau" on a par with the work of the Conservative research department.[90] In a later memorandum, apparently written in 1946 by Ball for Churchill (the current Conservative leader), Ball once again stressed the achievements of the NPB. It must therefore rate as an enterprise that deserves attention it has so far not received in studies of British interwar politics.

The NPB operated from 1934 to 1940 out of an office at 3, Central Chambers, a short walk from the Conservative research department's office in Old Queen Street, Westminster. It had a small permanent staff. When the NPB office was shut down after the outbreak of the war, the staff was retained on the payroll on the same basis as that of the Conservative research department. The arrangement was that employees should be released for war work and, if their salaries from the government fell below what they had been earning before the war, the shortfall would be met from the funds of the organization. This arrangement applied both to the NPB and to the Conservative research department and can be seen as evidence of the intention to reactivate the NPB after the war.

The full-time staff was directed by a committee. Sir Kingsley Wood, a leading Conservative politician, was chairman, and Ball acted as his deputy. Other members appear to have included Lord Luke and Sir Andrew Caird. The director of the NPB was Sir Patrick Gower. Since Gower was also director of publicity at the Conservative Central Office, he provided a working link between the NPB and Central Office's publicity department (though, as shown below, the intention was to keep political propaganda as far as possible out of

[90] Ball to Neville Chamberlain, 1940 (Neville Chamberlain Papers, NC/7/11/33/19).

the clutches of the Central Office). In order to establish the NPB's credentials as a nonparty body, Malcolm MacDonald (Ramsay MacDonald's son) acted as the National Labour representative, and Lord Hutchison represented the National Liberals. The body was, nevertheless, like the National government itself, to all intents and purposes Conservative. As Ramsay MacDonald had noted in his diary about earlier attempts at joint propaganda, "most of the joint propaganda & elections . . . have been pure Tory concerns."[91] This was hardly surprising in view of the fact that the National government consisted of 473 Conservative, 13 National Labour, and 35 National Liberal MPs.

Wood remained chairman of the NPB until his death in 1943, and Ball continued as his deputy. Wood was replaced as chairman by Geoffrey Lloyd (later Lord Geoffrey-Lloyd), a prominent Birmingham Conservative MP. The NPB remained in existence after the 1945 election but, during Lord Woolton's tenure as Conservative party chairman (from 1946), did not regain its former importance as the main body responsible for Conservative propaganda. The publicity campaign for the 1950 election was organized from the Central Office, and the NPB retained only marginal functions as an ancillary fund-raising organization, which supplied money mainly for the Conservative research department. By the postwar period, the NPB came to be known in Conservative fund-raising circles as the "Birmingham fund," because it was in that city that Lloyd, the chairman, had his closest connections.[92] In its heyday in the 1930s, it seems that the NPB raised most of its money in London, and it had a special City Committee for this purpose.

Why was Ball, who was the main inspiration of the NPB, so anxious to organize publicity through a body that was distinct from the Central Office? There are perhaps four main reasons. First, from the late 1920s onward, Davidson and Ball were convinced that Central Office, dominated as it was by men who had spent their careers as constituency party agents, did not grasp the importance of mass propaganda. This theme occurs again and again in the internal memoranda of the 1920s and 1930s. Davidson wrote of the "dead hand" of the party agents; Sir Leigh Maclachlan (who was the party's principal agent until he was dismissed by Davidson in 1928) was criticized because he was "ignorant of possibilities of new forms of propaganda."[93] Ball's memoranda of the 1930s are equally scathing.

[91] Marquand, *Ramsay MacDonald*, p. 746.
[92] This information was supplied by a former Conservative party treasurer.
[93] Unsigned memorandum in the Davidson Papers.

As he wrote to Chamberlain in 1938:

> It is, I think, clear that the Conservative Party organisation as a whole (and in this I include both our constituency organisations and the Central Office) has not realised the vital importance of propaganda under modern conditions. . . . At the Central Office . . . little money appears to be allocated for propaganda purposes . . . and . . . what money has been available has been spent mainly on organisation and on the political education of our own supporters.[94]

A way to guarantee the allocation of funds for mass propaganda was to collect a special fund earmarked for this purpose.

Second, the establishment of the NPB was part of a personal power struggle between Ball and the general director of the Central Office, Sir Robert Topping. Interviews with those who worked in the Conservative organization in the 1930s confirm that the two men were hardly on speaking terms, and this is the implication of the memoranda of the time. Topping was a career party agent who was appointed Central Office principal agent in 1928. In 1931 Topping's position was upgraded to that of general director of the Central Office. Since the newly formed Conservative research department was run independently of the Central Office (and, after the initial period, was separately financed), Ball did not work under Topping. Gower, the director of publicity, did. The formation of the NPB had the effect of removing the responsibility for most campaign publicity from Topping and putting it into Ball's hands. This may also have been congenial to Gower who, as a former senior civil servant, may have preferred working with Ball to working with Topping. These internal tensions are reflected in Ball's memorandum of 1938: "I am afraid that, with the exception of Gower, those in control of Central Office at the top are unnecessarily jealous and suspicious of the National Publicity Bureau."[95]

Third, Ball, an ex-officer of the Secret Service, was particularly security conscious and appears to have believed that publicity would be most effective if arranged in confidential surroundings. This could more easily be arranged at an inconspicuous office away from the main party headquarters.

Fourth, Ball argued that the formation of a nonparty organization would overcome the inhibitions of some corporations about subscribing directly to the funds of a political party: "The funds col-

[94] Memorandum no. 3.
[95] Ibid.

lected by the Bureau come to a very large extent from Joint Stock Companies, the executives of which regard themselves as precluded from subscribing to any *party* organisation." [96]

Notable features of the propaganda organized by the NPB in the 1930s were (1) the use of sustained publicity during a relatively long period before the announcement of the election date, (2) the heavy reliance upon professional advertising agencies, and (3) the sheer amount of the money reportedly raised and spent.

According to Ball, the methods of propaganda used in 1934–1935 were:

- posters
- broadsheets
- films (by outdoor and indoor projection)
- local press service (propaganda articles and news items)
- special pamphlets (written for and sent by direct mail to selected classes of the electorate)
- special paid canvassers in selected "key" constituencies [97]

Propaganda was concentrated in "330 key constituencies." It is not known which advertising agency was employed. The NPB may have continued to deal with S. H. Benson, the company used in 1929. Alternatively, it is possible that use was made of Charles Higham and Company, because Gower was later to become a director of this agency after leaving the Central Office.

Besides its activities in the 1935 campaign, the NPB contributed to Conservative publicity after the election. As Ball reported in 1938, the NPB "has borne the whole cost of every film campaign which has been undertaken since the last General Election; it has maintained its service of special articles for the local press; and it has, at lengthy intervals, publicised and distributed an issue of 3½ million copies of the National Broadsheet." [98]

Finally, some comments about the political context within which the NPB operated and its connection with the policy of appeasement of Adolf Hitler.

The very large expenditure on preelection publicity in 1935 has already been emphasized. It is surprising that Baldwin, who enjoyed such an overwhelming majority after the previous general election (1931), should have felt it necessary to sanction (and presumably to encourage) propaganda spending on such a scale. This heavy spending

[96] Ibid.
[97] Ibid.
[98] Ibid.

would seem to indicate the insecurity in Baldwin's mind about his prospects of reelection, and this may have influenced his program of rearmament, making him reluctant to sanction a rapid expansion of defense spending for fear of offending public opinion.

Lists of contributors to the NPB have not been located (and probably have not survived); so only speculative conclusions can be drawn about a link between NPB fund raising and appeasement. Such a connection does seem to have existed, however. Wood and Lloyd were both members of the Conservative party's proappeasement establishment. Ball himself strongly supported appeasement. After Chamberlain became prime minister in 1937, Ball sometimes carried out unofficial diplomatic missions on his behalf in furtherance of the appeasement policy. A much-reported incident was Ball's activity as intermediary between Chamberlain and the Italian ambassador in London, Count Grandi. In correspondence with Chamberlain, Ball later expressed himself "proud of having played a definite part of my own in helping you in your great search for peace." [99] Since Ball mentioned the NPB in the same sentence, it is reasonable to infer that its work was part of this "search for peace."

Ball's involvement with the appeasers is seen in his own business connections after his retirement from party service. Many of the most enthusiastic supporters of appeasement possessed business interests in the British Empire. They felt it was logical to reach an accommodation with Germany whereby Africa was recognized as a British sphere of influence while Germany was given a free hand in Eastern Europe. In this context, it is perhaps significant that from 1940 onward, Ball obtained directorships in several companies with interests in South and West Africa. [100]

The use of NPB funds to support appeasement is also implied in Ball's memorandum of 1938, in which he recommended that

> steps should be taken immediately to secure finance, possibly from National Publicity Bureau funds, for the formation of a national organisation, ostensibly non-political in character, with the avowed object of providing accurate and impartial information about foreign and international affairs, but with the secret objective of combating the dangerous propaganda of, and eventually smashing, the League of Nations Union and the pernicious Youth Organisation controlled by it.

[99] Ball to Neville Chamberlain (Neville Chamberlain Papers, NC/7/11/33/19).
[100] I am grateful to Lord Dacre for his views on this topic.

124

I should be prepared to submit a scheme for doing this ...
and I estimate that, while it might cost £15,000 annually
for a year or two, it could be made self-supporting in a year
or two.[101]

[101] Memorandum no. 3.

5

Conservative Party Finances
(1945-1979)

By the time British domestic politics was interrupted by the outbreak of the Second World War in 1939, the main patterns of modern British political finance were already emerging. Institutional sources of support had become (or were becoming) the mainstay of both major parties at the national level. Labour headquarters relied almost entirely on trade union political levies and, on the Conservative side, company donations to the Central Office were gradually replacing payments by individuals. Constituency finance in both the Labour and the Conservative parties was becoming more dependent on small-scale fund raising by ordinary party members. These important developments did not affect the Liberals. The Liberal party's failure to find new sources of money went hand in hand with its inability to establish a relevant role as the third party in a traditionally two-party system.

As far as expenditure by the parties was concerned, the main pre–Second World War trends had been (1) the increasing importance of national as compared with constituency spending and (2) the increasing proportion of total expenditure devoted to routine spending between elections. Despite the growing percentage of party money spent at the national level, however, constituency parties and their parliamentary candidates still accounted for the bulk of expenditure. A comparison of expenditure patterns in the aristocratic era and after the First World War shows that national-level spending in the Conservative party as a percentage of overall national and local spending grew from 2 percent in 1874–1880 to 26 percent in 1925–1929.[1] This meant that three-quarters of political money in 1925–1929 was spent at the constituency level. Local party needs were to remain vitally important after the Second World War. Consequently, the financial strength of the parties was to depend largely

[1] See table 73.

126

on their success in constituency fund raising. The story of British political finance since 1945 is mainly one of Conservative success and of Labour and Liberal failure in developing effective methods of collecting small political donations at the local level.

This chapter describes Conservative finances since the Second World War, and chapters 6 and 7 are devoted to the finances of the Labour and Liberal parties during the same period.

The Second World War and the difficult postwar years spurred the Conservative party to democratize its fund-raising methods. This process had begun before the war, but it was far from complete in 1939. During the six years of the war, normal politics came to an almost complete halt. There was an electoral truce between the main parties. The party headquarters continued to operate, but their functions were greatly reduced. At the constituency level, most party associations lost their full-time agents, who were required for war service. As victory against Germany approached, there was a partial resumption of political activity as the parties prepared for the general election, which had been postponed until the fighting ended. The Conservatives entered the 1945 campaign in a much more poorly organized state than usual. A private report presented after the 1945 general election by Ball pointed out that the party's central expenditure on election publicity (conducted by the National Publicity Bureau) was "some £20,000/£30,000 on posters and broadsheets."[2] This was a fraction of the £300,000 spent in 1935.

The Conservative party was faced in 1945 with the need to reestablish both its central and its local sources of money. The task was particularly important in view of the sweeping Labour victory in the election. There had been short-lived minority Labour governments before the war. In 1945 the Conservatives were opposed for the first time ever by a Labour government with a majority in the House of Commons and with the power to carry out the Labour party program.

The Second World War, unlike the first, produced no crop of new millionaires. Personal taxes were very high and profits strictly controlled. Thus, the potential for large individual donations to Conservative Central Office was reduced.[3] It was somewhat easier

[2] George Joseph Ball, "The Last General Election" (1946) (Woolton Papers, 21) (hereafter cited as Ball memorandum no. 4).

[3] The Central Office still benefited from large gifts from wealthy individuals. The Davidson Papers contain details of payments by one particular donor, an industrialist, who had earlier been knighted on party recommendation and whose untypical generosity appears to have been motivated by the desire for a peerage (which he was not awarded). Payments apparently included £100,000 in

to obtain donations from companies. In order to obtain sufficient funds to finance Central Office, it was considered necessary to collect medium-sized contributions from provincial businesses, as well as large sums of money from national corporations based in London and from the financial institutions in the City.

A treasurer's department within Central Office designed mainly to solicit provincial contributions had been set up shortly before the war. Its main function was "to deal with the collection of funds for Headquarters, and the giving of advice where requested to Area councils."[4] Previously, the raising of central funds had been an informal task entrusted to a handful of people: until 1911 to the chief whip in the House of Lords or the House of Commons and after 1911 to the party chairman and the party treasurer. This had been a workable arrangement as long as sufficient money could be raised from a small circle of donors. By the 1930s, it was becoming necessary to find a larger number of contributors, a job the party chairman and treasurers could not carry out without help.

In 1946 a central board of finance was established. It consisted of the party treasurers (normally backbench MPs or prominent figures able to solicit contributions at a national level), area treasurers (one from each area of Central Office's regional organization in England and Wales), and up to five co-opted members.[5] The dozen area treasurers were volunteer party workers with business contacts in the area of the country they represented. The central board of finance employed a paid representative in each area. These "collectors" were often retired military officers, and the intention was that they should

---

1944, £25,000 in 1946, £20,000 in 1951, and annual subscriptions of £1,000 to 1945 and thereafter of £2,000 a year. As the donor was chairman of a large manufacturing company, it is uncertain whether the payments came from him individually or were given in the company's name. The initiative for the contributions was clearly an individual one.

[4] John D. Hoffman, *The Conservative Party in Opposition, 1945-51* (London: MacGibbon and Kee, 1964), p. 55.

[5] This describes the CBF's composition by the 1950s. According to information kindly provided by George Carlyle, the original CBF was nominated *ad personam*. Neither the party treasurer nor area treasurers were members. Its chairman was Lord De L'isle, but he did not become a party treasurer until 1948. It should be noted that, like senior Central Office officers and officials, the party treasurers are appointees of the Conservative leader. Unlike his Labour and Liberal counterparts, the Conservative leader is subject to no formal restraints as far as decisions about party funds are concerned. In practice, the bureaucratic structure of the party organization restricts the leader's room for maneuver. The bulk of central party funds is devoted to the costs of the permanent headquarters and permanently employed staff. See Michael Pinto-Duschinsky, "Central Office and 'Power' in the Conservative Party," *Political Studies*, vol. 20 (1972), pp. 1ff.

systematically follow up the leads given by the area treasurers and by Central Office area agents.

A justification for the new system of provincial collections for Central Office was that businessmen would be willing to contribute considerably larger sums for the national organization than they would provide for a local party association. Therefore, it was argued, the central board of finance was not trespassing upon the traditional territory of the constituencies. The board's responsibility, in the words of an official Conservative publication, was to raise "for the Party money which would not normally be obtained by or go to the Constituencies." [6] Nevertheless, constituency organizations had good reason to feel that the Central Office was poaching some of their most generous supporters. The extended field of central fund raising imposed an extra burden on the local parties. Moreover, when the party chairman, Lord Woolton, made a special appeal in 1947 for £1 million, the proceeds were earmarked for the Central Office.

On top of their problems arising from the loss of many medium-sized business contributions to Central Office, constituency parties were asked to assume additional responsibilities. They were put under great pressure to forgo the payments that some of them still expected from their parliamentary candidates and MPs. The financial demands made by some constituency associations on their candidates limited their choice to wealthy men. This had been a source of complaint in the 1930s, as seen in Harvey's memorandum, which has already been quoted in chapter 4. There had been moves during the war to limit the payments that constituencies could ask of their candidates and MPs. After Labour's victory in the 1945 election, it seemed imperative to prove that the Conservatives were not a party of the rich by ending the sale of seats altogether. In June 1948, a Special Committee on Party Organisation was set up under the chairmanship of Sir David Maxwell-Fyfe (later Lord Kilmuir). Its interim and final reports were approved by the 1948 annual conference and by a special meeting of the party's central council in July 1949.

The main reform emerging from the Maxwell-Fyfe Committee was the ban on payments by parliamentary candidates to their local party associations. The new rules stipulated that:

> 1. The entire election expenses of Conservative candidates in every constituency shall be the responsibility of the constituency associations . . . and no subscription shall be

[6] Robert T. McKenzie, *British Political Parties: The Distribution of Power within the Conservative and Labour Parties* (London: Mercury Books, 1964), p. 215.

made directly or indirectly by the candidate to the fund for statutory election expenses. . . .

5. Candidates may, by arrangement with their constituency associations, make nominal subscriptions each year, but the subscriptions must in no case exceed £25; the annual subscriptions of Members of Parliament to their associations shall in no case exceed £50.

6. In no circumstances shall the question of an annual subscription be mentioned by any constituency selection committee to any candidate before he has been selected.

In his *Memoirs*, Lord Woolton explains the objective of the reform: "it was no use saying that the Conservative Party was not a 'class' party if a working-man Conservative could not afford to stand as a candidate." [7] In Lord Woolton's opinion, the ending of local subscriptions by candidates "was revolutionary and, in my view, did more than any single factor to save the Conservative Party." [8] Henceforth, the cost of constituency campaigns and of routine expenses between elections had to be found by the local parties.

This was not the end of the financial tasks that were heaped on the constituencies. Before the war, weak constituency associations had often been subsidized by Central Office. Now the flow was to be reversed. Local parties together were asked to pay £100,000 a year toward the upkeep of the party headquarters. This was to be collected by a system of quotas proposed by the Maxwell-Fife Com-

[7] Lord Woolton, *Memoirs* (London: Cassell, 1959), p. 345.

[8] Ibid., p. 346. The strict limits on financial contributions had some significant consequences. They had the effect of improving local Conservative organization. They probably increased the power of constituency associations over their MPs and candidates, a power generally used to enforce central party discipline. The new rules may have aided the selection of middle-class candidates without private means who, under the old system, might not have been able to afford the heavy costs of standing for Parliament. Nevertheless, the removal of financial barriers has not led to the selection of working-class Conservatives as parliamentary candidates. They have virtually never been accepted by the selection committees of constituency associations in winnable seats.

The failure of working-class Conservatives to win selection for the House of Commons after the Maxwell-Fyfe reforms illustrates the difficulty of assessing the effects of money in politics. Before the reforms were adopted, it was widely assumed that the most important barrier against the entry of working-class Conservatives into the House of Commons was financial. Experience since the 1950s indicates that social prejudice, not money, was the real barrier. The same possibly applies to the failure of Liberal constituency associations to select working-class candidates in the late nineteenth century and early twentieth century. See David E. Butler and Michael Pinto-Duschinsky, "The Conservative Elite, 1918-1978: Does Unrepresentativeness Matter?," in Zig Layton-Henry, ed., *Conservative Party Politics* (London: Macmillan, 1980).

mittee. Under the system eventually adopted, each constituency's voluntary quota was to be calculated according to a complicated formula based (1) on the size of the Conservative vote in the constituency and (2) on the ratio at the previous general election of Conservative votes to those cast for the most successful opposing candidate.[9] The heaviest burden was to fall on associations in the safely Conservative constituencies, which were likely to be most able to pay. An extra rule was that when an area collector of the central board of finance received a contribution, the first £10 (later the first £50 and, from 1977/1978, the first £100) was credited toward the quota of the constituency in which the contribution was made. The credit was intended to represent the maximum that the constituency treasurer would probably have received had he been soliciting the money for the local party.

A final burden placed on constituency associations in the postwar years was that of fighting local government elections. In many parts of the country, particularly the cities, these had been fought along party lines since the nineteenth century. Conservatives in suburban and rural areas resisted the idea of putting forward candidates for county and district councils. There was a widespread feeling in Conservative circles that local government issues should be separated from the national party struggle. Central Office made concerted efforts in the late 1940s to encourage Conservative constituency associations to participate in local government elections. This involved their raising money for the campaign expenses of the candidates.

The imposition of these varied fund-raising demands on local Conservative parties was a conscious policy, which had already been advocated by a Special Finance Committee set up in 1943. In his *Memoirs*, Lord Woolton (party chairman, 1946–1955) writes that he had "noticed that the organization of the party was weakest in those places where a wealthy candidate had made it unnecessary for the members to trouble to collect small subscriptions." [10] The re-

---

[9] According to a senior Central Office official, "the Maxwell-Fyfe Committee considered the reports of three earlier committees to see that their recommendations were compatible. In particular, the quota proposals were put forward by a committee whose chairman was Henry Brooke (now Lord Brooke of Cumnor). Its report recommended a quota target of £200,000, but Brooke took soundings of constituencies liable for the largest targets and concluded that it would be wise to halve the target to £100,000. Holland Martin [the party treasurer] and the general director agreed and he amended the recommendation before the Maxwell-Fyfe Committee met." The Maxwell-Fyfe Committee adopted the amended Brooke proposals.

[10] Woolton, *Memoirs*, p. 345.

moval of large contributions would oblige constituencies to recruit new members and to involve them in local party activity. The pressure on constituency associations to take part in local government campaigns had a similar objective: "I decided that from the point of view of party organization there was an overwhelming case for using the machinery of the party to support candidates for local elections—and to polish up the organization in the process."[11]

A national membership drive, Operation Knocker, was launched in 1946. About 300 constituency associations participated, and the party's total membership in England and Wales reportedly rose from under a million in 1946 to 1.2 million in 1947. In April 1948 a second campaign was launched to recruit a million extra members. By the end of June 1948, it was claimed that Conservative constituency membership in England and Wales stood at 2,249,031. Nineteen fifty-three produced an all-time high, 2,805,032 members in England and Wales. While these precise totals are open to serious question, there was undoubtedly a large increase in membership and in local Conservative activity in the late 1940s and early 1950s, and party membership was certainly burgeoning.[12]

The strategy of encouraging political participation by starving the local associations of easy money from candidates and from large contributors appears to have succeeded. In Lord Blake's judgment, "There can be no doubt that the need to collect a very large number of very small subscriptions, instead of relying on a very small number of very large subscriptions—perhaps only one—gave the

[11] Ibid., p. 341.

[12] There is a full discussion of Conservative party membership trends in the 1940s to the 1960s in Michael Pinto-Duschinsky, "The Role of Constituency Associations in the Conservative Party" (D.Phil. thesis, Oxford University, 1972), chap. 1. The statistics in this paragraph are taken from this source.

All Conservative party membership statistics must be treated with considerable reserve, because constituency associations are autonomous bodies and are not obliged to give information to Central Office. During a national recruitment campaign, constituency activists are likely to exaggerate their memberships. The difficulty of ensuring the accuracy of membership figures is increased by the fact that constituency-level officers and constituency agents themselves rely on totals submitted by committees in the ward branches. Usually ward branches do not insist on a minimum subscription and do not pass on to the constituency headquarters lists of the names and addresses of paid-up members. The objective of "membership" in the Conservative party is to involve as many people as possible and not to raise barriers to participation. Relatively little is raised from membership subscriptions, but members frequently take part in the small-scale social activities of ward and constituency associations, which, as argued later, have vital fund-raising functions.

132

constituency organisations a notable impetus towards the recruitment of members."[13]

It should be added that the political and social climate appears to have been ripe for mass participation in political parties. As described in chapter 6, Labour membership also reached its peak in the years after 1945. Other indicators of political activism (such as election turnout) reached high points.

There are two possible explanations of this high degree of political involvement after 1945. First, the result of the 1945 election produced an exceptionally clear confrontation between the two main parties. Labour's victory meant that for the first time it became—like the Conservatives—a party of government. Unlike previous decades, there was no third party (such as the Irish Nationalists in the late nineteenth century, Labour before the First World War, or the Liberals after 1922) to complicate the situation. The Liberals still existed but were politically weak. The election of the first majority Labour government appears to have stimulated both the enthusiasm of its supporters and the active opposition of ordinary Conservatives.

Social factors unconnected with politics also seem to have been important. During the years of postwar reconstruction, Britain was a drab place. Food rationing continued. Few forms of entertainment were available apart from the cinema. Participation in a local Conservative association was a welcome form of activity. The Young Conservatives became known as one of the best middle-class marriage markets. Competition from television and holidays abroad lay in the future.

Nevertheless, it would be a mistake to explain away the significance of the move toward small-scale constituency fund raising. The Conservative party managers, by denying the constituency organizations big donations, made them more democratic and more active. In all probability, this contributed to the improved Conservative performance in the 1950 election and the party's victories in the three general elections held between 1951 and 1959.

The importance of democratic fund raising for healthy party organization is illustrated by the fate of city Conservative associations, most of which resisted the financial reforms of the late 1940s and remained dependent on business money.[14] In major cities, such

[13] Robert Blake, *The Conservative Party from Peel to Churchill* (London: Fontana, 1972), p. 261.

[14] The finances of city associations in the 1950s and 1960s are described in Pinto-Duschinsky, "Role of Constituency Associations."

as Birmingham and Manchester, which each contained several parliamentary constituencies, the separate constituency associations had traditionally banded together to form city associations. Normally, a city association provided office accommodation for all the constituency organizations, and the constituency agents were subordinate to a chief city agent. City funds were generally raised from the contributions of local businessmen. The city associations strongly resisted attempts by Central Office to collect funds for national purposes within their bailiwicks. In the late 1940s business money permitted some of the city associations to employ large staffs and to accumulate hefty reserves.

The gigantic Conservative city organization in Birmingham at the time of the 1950 general election is detailed by Nicholas. Besides the chief agent and the administrative secretary, there were a women's organizer, a Young Conservative organizer, a publicity officer, a political education officer, and an organization officer. Each of the thirteen Birmingham constituency associations had a full-time agent with secretarial assistance. There were thirty-six ward organizers and thirty or more paid canvassers and subscription collectors.[15]

During the late 1950s and the 1960s, the financial position of the Birmingham city organization declined. Middle-class families gradually lost their involvement in city politics. Amalgamations and takeovers of family businesses by national corporations led to the loss of their financial support. For years the city association lived off its plentiful reserves. When these were depleted, the organization nearly collapsed.[16] In the words of a senior Central Office official in the West Midlands interviewed by the author in the 1960s, the Birmingham organization had in the postwar years "committed the worst sin of all":

> [it had] a staff of almost dropsical size. There were too many full-time people. There was just not enough work for the agents to do. There were thirty paid collectors who collected subscriptions. Birmingham tried to run a voluntary organization without giving the members any work to do. It absolutely sapped the moral fibre of the Association. Eventually the Birmingham people would not do anything at all.

[15] Herbert G. Nicholas, *The British General Election of 1950* (London: Macmillan, 1951), pp. 25-26.
[16] See David J. Wilson and Michael Pinto-Duschinsky, "Conservative Party City Machines: The End of an Era," *British Journal of Political Science*, vol. 6 (1976), p. 242.

The Birmingham pattern was repeated in other city associations, most of which eventually collapsed in the 1960s and early 1970s. The experience of these city organizations is direct evidence of the demoralizing effects of overfinancing. It shows how ordinary constituency associations outside cities might have decayed had they too been cushioned by business money (or by state aid) from the need to raise small-scale contributions from individual members.[17]

Amid the postwar spate of Conservative financial reforms, one traditional stance was maintained. The party treasurers refused in the late 1940s to publish the income and expenditure of the central Conservative organization. The publication of the accounts was advocated by the Maxwell-Fyfe Committee when it recommended the introduction of constituency quota payments to Central Office. In order to demonstrate to local activists that Central Office was short of money, the committee recommended that "the Treasurer of the Party should publish an annual financial statement. This is the only effective basis from which to explain to Conservative supporters the main facts about Party Finance. People will subscribe more generously when they can see how their contributions are spent."

The idea was rejected by the party managers. The objections must have been strong enough to convince Lord Woolton, who was not normally prone to unnecessary secrecy. There seem to have been two main objections to publishing the Central Office accounts. First, it was feared that publicity would inhibit some companies from contributing for fear of offending their workers. (The Ball memorandum quoted earlier [chapter 4, footnote 94] refers to the reluctance in the 1930s of some pro-Conservative organizations to subscribe directly to ordinary party funds—a reluctance that would be increased if donations were publicized.) Second, it was felt that the Labour party benefited from large "politically relevant" expenditures that did not show up in the Labour party's published accounts of its national-level expenditure. Thus, the parallel publication of Central Office accounts would give a misleading impression that the Conservatives were richer than Labour. This position was argued by the general director of Central Office, S. H. Pierssené, in a symposium on "Political Party Funds" published in the journal *Parliamentary Affairs* in 1948. Pierssené maintained that publication of the Conservative accounts would be "completely misleading":

[17] It would be a mistake, however, to ignore other factors that contributed to the decline of Conservative organization in some of the major cities, in particular the movement of the middle classes to the suburbs.

In a true comparison, it would be necessary to have regard to the activities and resources of such bodies as the Trade Unions, the Co-operative Societies, the Fabian Society . . . all of which take an active part in political work, in some cases spending large sums of money in promoting their interests.[18]

The existence of "these quasi-political bodies" increased "the difficulty of defining a political party." Without a satisfactory solution to this problem, it was impossible to define what constituted party finance and thus useless to introduce legislation to enforce publication of party accounts.

It was not until 1968 that Central Office accounts were published. The decision to end the tradition of secrecy followed the enactment by Harold Wilson's Labour government of the Companies Act, 1967. This obliged companies to declare all political donations in excess of £50 in their annual reports.[19] Since such contributions accounted for most of Central Office's income, there was little to gain by continued secrecy.

[18] S. H. Pierssené, "Political Party Funds. II—The Conservative View," *Parliamentary Affairs*, vol. 1 (1947-1948), p. 50.

On "politically relevant" expenditures, see chapter 8. Pierssené's argument was also made by the Conservative spokesman in the House of Commons debate on December 15, 1949, on the publication of political party funds. Quintin Hogg (Lord Hailsham) complained that the "Labour Party publishes accounts and they are cooked" (House of Commons Debates, 5th series, 470, col. 2994). The accounts were misleading, he argued, because they omitted the benefits received from the Labour movement. Hogg mentioned (1) payments from trade union political levy funds (the annual reports of these funds failed "to say where the money goes"), (2) services in kind given to the Labour party by "paid members of the trade union movement," (3) the educational expenditure of the Co-operative movement, which was "very largely directly political . . . yet no reference is contained in the [Co-operative party] accounts to this item," and (4) "What about the Left Book Club?" (cols. 2997-99).

In the same debate, Maxwell-Fyfe complained that trade unions could finance "pro-Socialist pamphlets" out of their general funds. Union journals, which were also "used as vehicles for Socialist propaganda," were also financed out of general union funds (cols. 3023-24). These arguments reflect the view put forward in the Ball memoranda, cited in chapter 4, that the published Labour party accounts showed only the tip of the iceberg of left-wing political finance.

The point has considerable justification. The compulsory publication of party accounts is bound to be misleading unless (1) there is a definition of what constitutes a political party that applies consistently to the opposing party organizations and (2) other organizations undertaking political action are also obliged to publish their accounts. Of course, it is not only the political left that has benefited from "politically relevant" spending. As mentioned in chapter 8, business organizations have also spent heavily on political advertising in favor of free enterprise.

[19] For a discussion of political payments by companies, see chapter 8.

Central Office has, for the purposes of this study, released previously unpublished party accounts for 1950–1964. Therefore, it is possible to give a reasonably comprehensive description of Conservative central finances during most of the postwar period. In addition, information about Conservative constituency finance has been obtained from two major studies: (1) a collection of over 400 constituency accounts for 1966/1967 collected by Central Office and analyzed by the author [20] and (2) a sample survey of 82 local accounts for 1973 and 1974 carried out for the Houghton Committee.

Central Party Finances, 1950–1979/1980

Official Central Office accounts since 1950 are given in table 28. The statistics of party income are presented in an unadjusted form. Accounts for years until 1976/1977 are for England and Wales. The figures from 1977/1978 include Scotland.[21] The statistics of constituency quota payments include quota credits (see table 28, note b) and thus slightly overstate the amounts actually donated by local parties.

Central Office Income. Most of the Central Office's income is under the broad heading of "donations" (84.3 percent between 1950 and 1964, and 74.7 percent between 1967/1968 and 1977/1978). According to the Central Office, individual contributions account for about 20 percent of donations, and the rest comes from companies and from other institutional sources, such as merchant banks and stockbroking partnerships. This suggests that about three-fifths of Central Office income since 1950 has come from business institutions.[22] This is shown in table 29.

Constituency quotas have been an item of growing importance for the central party organization. Between 1950 and 1964, they accounted for slightly over £1½ million (an average of £103,000 a year). Between 1967/1968 and 1974/1975, constituencies gave over £2.3 million to the Central Office (£289,000 a year). This increase owed much to constituency efforts during a special national financial appeal launched by Lord Carrington in 1967. In the four years between 1975/1976 and 1978/1979, quotas totaled about £2,215,000 (£554,000 a year).

20 Pinto-Duschinsky, "Role of Constituency Associations."

21 For a guide to the interpretation of published central party accounts, see appendix F.

22 It should be noted, however, that the Central Office accounts somewhat understate the amounts received in "donations," since the published figures are net of fund-raising costs.

TABLE 28

Conservative Central Income and Expenditure, 1950–1979/1980
(in thousands of pounds)

Year	Income				Expenditure		
	Dona-tions (net)[a]	Consti-tuency quotas[b]	Interest (net)	Total	Routine[c]	General election	Total
1950*	884	88	13	985	743	135	878
1951*	877	107	14	998	713	112	825
1952	397	93	24	513	601	—	601
1953	421	104	21	545	530	—	530
1954	458	125	17	600	538	—	538
1955*	1,064	133	39	1,236	594	142	736
1956	343	109	61	513	673	—	673
1957	485	111	36	633	597	88	685
1958	566	113	24	703	724	131	855
1959*	1,460	181	31	1,672	768	412	1,180
1960	282	130	60	472	695	—	695
1961	422	123	45	590	789	—	789
1962	423	113	41	576	863	—	863
1963	753	118	37	909	967	249	1,216
1964*	1,877	170	45	2,092	1,296	984	2,280
1967/68	545	278	20	845	1,071	—	1,071
1968/69	1,414	661	24	2,099	1,054	—	1,054
1969/70	670	286	46	1,001	(1,053)	(300)	1,353
1970/71*	1,507	298	55	1,860	(1,338)	(330)	1,668
1971/72	623	255	52	930	1,249	—	1,249
1972/73	893	267	39	1,199	(1,431)	(50)	1,481
1973/74*	2,379	377	63	2,819	(1,504)	(630)	2,134
1974/75*	1,213	299	74	1,624[d]	(1,955)	950	2,905
1975/76	1,137	574	28	1,889[d]	1,874	—	1,874
1976/77	1,306	587	50	2,094[d]	2,177	—	2,177
1977/78	1,944	663	33	2,794[d]	(2,754)	(—)	2,754
1978/79	2,420	782	35	3,402[d]	3,741	1,034	4,775
1979/80*	4,263	907	108	5,292[d]	4,586	1,299	5,885

NOTES: Asterisks denote general election years. Figures for 1977/1978 onward include Scotland; for other years, England and Wales only. The income and expenditure of the independently run Scottish Central Office amounted to about 6½ percent of that of the Central Office in London. The accounts include the income and expenditure of the Central Office's area offices, of the party leader's office, and, when the party is in opposition, of the whips' offices in Parliament. In 1966/1967 the accounting year was changed from January 1-December 31 to

April 1-March 31. For technical reasons, figures for 1965 and 1966 are unavailable.

a Statistics of donations exclude costs of fund raising.

b Constituency quotas include quota credits. According to the Central Office, these credits generally amount to 15 percent of quota payments.

c Total expenditure less general election expenditure.

d From 1974/1975, Central Office received annual state grants to cover the costs of the party as the official parliamentary opposition. These grants are included in total income. The party received £37,500 in 1974/1975, £150,000 a year for 1975/1976 and 1976/1977, £153,750 for 1977/1978, £165,000 for 1978/1979, and £14,335 for 1980.

SOURCES: 1950-1964—previously unpublished figures provided by the treasurer's department of Central Office. 1967/1968-1979/1980—columns 1-4 and 7 are published party accounts; column 6 is based on total spending for each general election provided by the treasurer's department. The allocation of election expenditure to particular years (for figures shown in parentheses) is based on assumptions made by the author.

Contributions from individuals, though much less important than before the war, seem to have a significant residual role. Little is known about the donors. Presumably the most generous are businessmen who do not wish their contributions to be declared in their company accounts and who are therefore willing to pay the

TABLE 29

ESTIMATED SOURCES OF CONSERVATIVE CENTRAL OFFICE INCOME,
1950–1977/1978
(percent)

Source	1950–64	1967/68–1973/74	1974/75–1977/78
Contributions by institutions (companies, banks, and partnerships)	67.4	62.5	56.3
Individual donations	16.9	15.6	14.1
Constituency quotas	11.9	19.2	21.5
Interest	3.9	2.8	2.2
State grant for parliamentary services inside the Palace of Westminster	—	—	5.8
Total	100.0	100.0	100.0

NOTES: 15 percent of constituency quotas has been added to "donations" to cover estimated quota credits. It is assumed that institutional contributions are 80 percent of "donations."

SOURCES: As for table 28.

heavy personal taxes involved in contributing on a private rather than on a company basis.[23] Individual donations were an estimated £300,000 a year between 1975/1976 and 1977/1978.

Between 1975 and 1979, the Conservatives received a state grant toward maintaining research and other expenses incurred by the party in its capacity as the official opposition in Parliament.[24] A total of £670,585 was received in the financial years 1974/1975 to 1979/1980.

Central Office Expenditure. The bulk of the party's central budget is committed to the *routine* expenditure involved in maintaining its permanent headquarters in London, the separately housed Conservative research department,[25] eleven area offices in England and Wales, and, recently, the Scottish Central Office in Edinburgh. The extra expenses of a general election campaign are only a fraction of the party's central expenditure over a complete parliamentary cycle. According to Central Office estimates of general election costs, national campaigns amounted to 17 percent of total central expenditure in the three parliamentary cycles between 1952 and 1964. In the eleven years 1967/1968–1977/1978, during which there were three general elections, campaign expenditure was 11.5 percent of total spending.

Besides the costs of the offices of the senior officers of the party and of the general administrative expenditure of the headquarters building, the main items of routine Central Office spending are (1) costs of promoting local party organization (maintaining an organization department at Central Office and eleven area offices and giving various kinds of direct assistance to constituencies), (2) routine publicity and press relations, and (3) research. The breakdown of routine expenditure during four recent nonelection years is given in table 30.

[23] (1) Generous reliefs from capital transfer tax (death duties) are available for bequests to political parties (see chap. 9, "Indirect Subsidies"). (2) In its internal accounts, Central Office apparently does not distinguish between company and individual contributions. Officials maintain that when a check is received from a businessman, it is often not possible to tell whether it has been given in a personal or a company capacity. Under the Companies Act, 1967, the obligation to declare a political donation is placed on the company concerned and not on the political party to which it is given.

[24] See chapter 9.

[25] It was decided after the 1979 general election to move the research department out of its premises at Old Queen Street, Westminster, and into the main headquarters building at 32, Smith Square, Westminster.

140

TABLE 30

TYPES OF ROUTINE EXPENDITURE BY THE CONSERVATIVE CENTRAL OFFICE, NONELECTION YEARS, 1967/1968–1975/1976

Average expenditure (£)	1,274,000
Type of expenditure (percent)	
Promoting constituency organization[a]	42.5
Research and policy formulation	15.8
Publicity and press relations	9.6
Senior headquarters staff	7.7
Other[b]	24.4
Total	100.0

NOTE: Figures for 1975/1976 are net of expenditure from the state grant of £150,000 for parliamentary services within the Palace of Westminster.

[a] The main cost of promoting constituency organization was the upkeep of the eleven area offices of the Central Office. About 6 percent of total expenditure was devoted to direct financial aid to constituency associations.

[b] The main item in this category is general administrative expenditure of the headquarters.

SOURCE: Percentages are based on published party accounts for 1967/1968, 1968/ 1969, 1971/1972, and 1975/1976.

Two points about the central party's routine expenditure should be noted:

1. Although Central Office's most costly function is the encouragement and promotion of local party activity, little money is given in direct financial aid to constituency associations. Central Office provides a variety of services: it maintains eleven area offices, recruits and trains constituency agents, provides literature and legal advice, and so on. But financial subsidies are limited. A study of the parliamentary cycle leading up to the general election of 1970 has suggested that financial grants to constituencies by Central Office between April 1966 and June 1970 totaled only about £200,000 [26]—that is, about 4 percent of Central Office expenditure (and 2 percent of total constituency income). During the 1970s, there has been some increase in Central Office financial aid to constituency organizations, though the percentage of total constituency income received in direct grants from the office is still small. According to statistics of constituency incomes drawn up by the Houghton Committee, Central Office grants average £151 per constituency (that is, under £100,000 in total) in the preelection year of 1973 and £255 per constituency (about £160,000) in 1974 (a year of two general

[26] Pinto-Duschinsky, "Role of Constituency Associations," p. 206.

elections).[27] Most Central Office aid is directed toward associations in Labour-held constituencies.[28]

2. The limited amounts spent on routine party publicity are largely accounted for by the fact that free television and radio time is generously provided to the main parties in electoral peacetime as well as during campaigns. One of the main functions of the party's publicity department is to prepare films and tapes for these free party political broadcasts.[29]

The Central Office's routine activities have given rise to little public comment, but its *campaign spending* has been hotly debated and criticized. In particular, Central Office advertising before some general elections has aroused the anger of the Labour party and of some academic observers.[30] During the long run-up periods to the polls of 1959 and 1964, Central Office employed professional public relations consultants to plan expensive publicity campaigns. It was widely argued that this type of spending gave an unfair electoral advantage to the Tories and made a mockery of the strict legal limitations on local campaign spending.

The official figures for spending in modern elections, including the controversial 1959 and 1964 elections, are given in table 31. The table includes estimates of the costs of other campaigns for which official figures are not available. Table 31 shows that central campaign expenditure varies greatly between one election and the next. Elections called at short notice are usually cheaper. During the postwar period, Central Office's campaign budgets have usually been low by pre-1939 standards. The most expensive general elections since 1945 have been those of 1959 and 1964.[31] Expenditure on preelection

27 Committee on Financial Aid to Political Parties, *Report*, Cmnd. 6601 (London: Her Majesty's Stationery Office, 1976), pp. 178-79 (Houghton Report).

28 An analysis of Central Office grants to constituency associations in the non-election year 1966/1967 shows that seventy-nine grants were given, averaging £472 each. Only ten went to associations in Conservative-held seats, and most (forty-seven of seventy-nine) went to associations in safe Labour constituencies. Of total grants of £37,366, £20,269 (54 percent) went to associations in safe Labour constituencies and £10,891 (29 percent) to associations in Labour-held marginal constituencies (Pinto-Duschinsky, "Role of Constituency Associations," p. 204).

29 The importance attached to these free party political broadcasts is indicated by Central Office's heavy investment in producing material for them. These production costs in the financial year 1978/1979 and in the 1979 general election campaign reached a total of £425,000 (see table 33).

30 See Introduction and chapter 10.

31 The campaign of 1950 may also have been relatively costly. Statistics of pre-campaign spending in 1949 are not yet available.

TABLE 31

CONSERVATIVE CENTRAL OFFICE EXPENDITURE IN SOME GENERAL
ELECTION CAMPAIGNS, 1910–1979

(in thousands of pounds)

General Election	Current Prices	1980 Prices
1910 (Dec.)	136[a]	3,477
1929	290[b]	4,339
1935	(about 450)[c]	(about 7,746)
1945	(50–100)[d]	(483–966)
1950	(at least 135)[e]	(at least 1,034)
1951	112	792
1955	142	887
1959	631	3,569
1964	1,233	6,102
1966	(350?)[f]	(1,583?)
1970	630	2,365
1974 (Feb.)	680	1,667
1974 (Oct.)	950	2,086
1979	2,333	2,710

NOTES: Figures are for Central Office spending and, except for 1979, exclude the independent spending of the Scottish Central Office. Figures in parentheses are estimates. All figures supplied by Central Office unless otherwise noted.
SOURCES: [a] Chapter 2, footnotes 36-37. [b] Robert Rhodes James, *Memoirs of a Conservative: J. C. C. Davidson's Memoirs and Papers, 1910-37* (London: Weidenfeld and Nicolson, 1969), p. 303. [c] According to the Ball memorandum, spending on propaganda amounted to £300,000. It is assumed that other central spending was at the same level as in 1929. [d] Only £20,000-30,000 was spent on propaganda (see chap. 5). It is assumed that other central spending was also modest. [e] This is the Central Office figure for election spending during the calendar year 1950. Figures for 1949 are not available, and the total given in the table thus excludes preelection spending before 1950. [f] Ramsden estimates that £300,000 was spent, apart from aid to constituencies. The total in the table includes estimated grants to constituencies (John A. Ramsden, "The Organisation of the Conservative and Unionist Party in Britain, 1910-1930" [D.Phil. thesis, Oxford University, 1974], p. 369).

publicity has been pruned since the costly campaign of 1964.[32]

Conservative Central Office (like Labour headquarters) does not publish an itemized breakdown of general election expenditure. An indication of the main costs of central Conservative campaigning in the general election of 1970 is given in table 32. The

[32] The figures in col. 6 of table 28 may underestimate campaign costs for some general elections, particularly 1964. This is suggested by the fact that "routine" expenditure in 1964 was, in real terms, considerably higher than that for

TABLE 32

Types of Campaign Expenditure by the Conservative Central Office in the General Election, 1970

	Percentage of Total Campaign Spending[a]
Publicity	68
Broadcasting costs[b]	14
Private opinion polls	5
Extra costs of party headquarters[c]	7
Party leader's election tour	1
Grants to constituencies	6

Notes: Apparent inconsistency in the total is due to rounding. Three-quarters of the spending on publicity was on newspaper advertisements; the rest went for posters, loss on election publications, and direct mail of literature to selected "opinion formers."

[a] Estimated.

[b] This large item was for monitoring broadcasts and for preparing material to enable the party to make good use of its allocation of free time on television and radio.

[c] The main item was the traditional campaign bonus paid to permanent Central Office staff.

Source: Interviews with party officers and officials.

percentages are based on interviews with senior Conservative officers and officials.

The most striking aspect of table 32 is the small percentage (6 percent) of the Central Office campaign budget devoted to grants for constituency election expenses. In the aristocratic and plutocratic eras, this was the main, and virtually the only, item of central campaign spending. The highest percentage was for central publicity, but the low level of the budget (relative to 1959 and 1964) means that the extent of political advertising was limited.

Detailed statistics of Conservative central precampaign and campaign spending for the general election of 1979 have been released by Central Office. The figures are shown in table 33.

1963. Some spending categorized as routine was probably stepped up for campaign purposes.

The distinction between routine and campaign spending is difficult to make. It is possible to make accurate costings of certain campaign activities (such as advertising). It is much harder to allocate other types of spending (such as staff costs, headquarters' overheads, and aid to constituencies) to routine and campaign categories, because the election period merely involves intensifying activities that are also carried out between elections (see Introduction).

TABLE 33

Conservative Party Central Precampaign and Campaign Expenditure, 1978–1979
(in thousands of pounds)

	Pre-campaign	Campaign	Total	Percentage of Total
Grants to constituencies	—	42	42	2
Advertising				
Posters	(380)	(211)	(591)	(25)
Press	(267)	(499)	(766)	(33)
Cinema	(111)	(33)	(144)	(6)
Total	758	743	1,501	64
Producing political broadcasts	276[a]	149	425	18
Opinion research[b]	—	70	70	3
Party publications (net of receipts)	—	113	113	5
Leaders' tours[c] and meetings	—	13	13	1
Staff[d] and administration costs	—	169	169	7
Total	1,034	1,299	2,333	100

Note: Parentheses indicate subtotals.

[a] Includes expenditure April 1978-March 1979.

[b] Opinion research in the precampaign period was classified by Central Office as a routine item.

[c] Thatcher's tour cost an estimated £10,000 net of receipts from journalists for seats on the campaign airplane.

[d] Cost of additional staff and overtime payments for routine staff.

Source: Director of finance and resources, Conservative Central Office.

As in the 1970 campaign, the main feature of the Central Office 1979 election budget were (1) the very low percentage devoted to grants to constituency campaigns (2 percent) and (2) the large proportion devoted to political advertising (64 percent).[33]

[33] For a detailed discussion of party finance in the 1979 election, see Michael Pinto-Duschinsky, "Financing the British General Election of 1979, " in Howard R. Penniman, ed., *Britain at the Polls, 1979: A Study of the General Election* (Washington, D.C.: American Enterprise Institute, 1981). Statistics on the 1979 campaign in this and in subsequent chapters are taken from this source. See also Michael Pinto-Duschinsky, "What Should Be the Cost of a Vote?," *The Times*, March 10, 1980.

Including the cost of producing political broadcasts and the costs of party publications, the total Central Office expenditure on political advertising for the 1979 general election amounted to £2,039,000. This was considerably less than the notional value of free broadcasting time received by both the Conservative and the Labour parties for the election. As suggested in chapter 9, this subsidy-in-kind was worth about £2.7 million for each party.

Conservative Constituency Finance

It is almost impossible to establish precisely how much the 623 Conservative and Labour constituency associations raise and spend each year. The assessment of long-term trends is even more problematic. First, the independence of local parties means that they normally do not submit copies of their accounts to the national headquarters except when occasionally bullied into doing so. Second, even if balance sheets are collected, it is difficult to analyze them because they are drawn up in many different ways. The fact that treasurers are voluntary party workers makes some local accounts unreliable. Third, constituency accounts do not give a picture of money raised and spent at the branch level. There has so far been no systematic study of the finances of ward branches in any party. Local government elections are frequently paid for by the branches; so it is also not possible, at present, to assess the costs of such elections. For these reasons, estimates of local-level finance need to be treated with reserve.

Constituency Income. During the postwar period, most of the money raised by Conservative associations has come from small-scale fund-raising events. Membership subscriptions have been of relatively minor importance.

Much modern Tory fund raising is carried out by branch committees in each ward.[34] Each branch committee is responsible for a small geographical area. Over three-quarters of the meetings run by the branches are social events.[35] Though not primarily political, they have the function of keeping together an organization of helpers in readiness for election campaigns. They also provide funds for maintaining a constituency office and paying for a full-time agent.

[34] The size of a ward varies. Conservative associations in large cities have an average of six ward branches. In rural constituencies the average is forty-eight (Pinto-Duschinsky, "Role of Constituency Associations," p. 39).
[35] Ibid., chap. 2.

TABLE 34

Sources of Conservative Constituency Income, 1973

Average total income (£)	4,713
Source (percent)	
Branch grants (raised mainly by social events)	32.8
Constituency level	
Social functions	18.4
Gambling schemes	8.5
Subscriptions and donations[a]	27.0
Grants from headquarters	3.3
Other	10.0
Total	100.0

[a] 6.2 percent of total income was from company donations.
Source: Houghton Report, p. 178.

Typically, the ward branches are allocated annual quotas that they are encouraged to raise for the constituency association. The branches run a whole range of coffee mornings, wine and quiche parties, jumble sales, bazaars, card meetings, dances, and outings. These efforts are topped up by occasional large-scale events organized at constituency level (a Christmas bazaar, a summer garden party, or a dinner). An analysis of over 400 constituency budgets for 1966/1967 indicates that branch quotas (mainly from small social events)[36] were the largest component of constituency income (44 percent of the total) and the next largest was the proceeds of constituency-level activities (24 percent). Subscriptions and donations produced only 20 percent of total income.

The same pattern emerges from the sample survey carried out for the Houghton Committee of constituency budgets for 1973. This is shown in table 34. Comparable figures for constituency Labour parties are given in table 43 and for Liberal constituency associations in table 54.

Constituency Expenditure. The further tightening in 1948 of limits on permitted campaign expenditure by parliamentary candidates and postwar inflation have meant that the historical trend toward lower

[36] Absence of comprehensive information about ward-level finance makes it impossible to determine the precise proportion of income derived from small-scale social events and the proportion from membership subscriptions.

TABLE 35
Types of Routine Expenditure by Conservative Constituency Associations, 1973

	Constituencies with Full-Time Paid Agents	All Constituencies
Average expenditure (£)	6,414	4,572
Type of expenditure (percent)		
Salaries	50.3	46.7
Office expenses	30.1	29.2
Local elections	6.8	8.4
Other	12.8	15.6
Total	100.0	100.0

Source: As for table 34.

election expenses has continued.[37] During a parliamentary cycle, the expenses of putting forward a candidate in the general election have become insignificant. For example, it is estimated that Conservative constituency associations spent a total of nearly £10 million during the parliamentary cycle 1966–1970.[38] The campaign expenses of Tory candidates in the general election of 1970 came to a mere 6 percent of this amount.[39]

For nearly half of constituency associations, as shown in table 35, the most important *routine* expenditures are those involved in the upkeep of a full-time agent and a constituency office.[40] Other associations share an agent or have no agent. Their budgets are much lower. The main components of local Conservative expenditure emerge from the Houghton Committee's survey.

The tight limit on *campaign* spending at the constituency level means that most of the permitted budget for election expenses is used for printing an election leaflet, which is normally sent to each elector and is delivered free by the Post Office, and for printing stickers and posters for display by party supporters. It is virtually impossible to pay for commercial advertising in local newspapers or on hoardings or to pay for campaign workers without exceeding the

[37] See appendix C.

[38] Pinto-Duschinsky, "Role of Constituency Associations," p. 206.

[39] See table 73.

[40] In May 1980 there were about 330 full-time Conservative constituency agents serving 412 constituencies. About 290 associations had a full-time agent of their own (47 percent of the total) (information provided by the Central Office).

148

permitted maximum. The legal restrictions make constituency campaigns almost completely dependent upon the unpaid efforts of voluntary party workers.

The Modern Pattern

The overall pattern of Conservative expenditure is shown in table 36. This is parallel to the similar tables in previous chapters for the aristocratic, plutocratic, and transitional periods.

The following long-term trends emerge from a comparison between the statistics for 1970 and the preceding four-year period and those for parliamentary cycles during previous eras: [41]

1. The rise in overall central and local expenditure between 1925–1929 and 1966–1970 was almost entirely a result of inflation. In real terms, overall expenditure rose by 8 percent. The rise in overall Conservative expenditure (in real terms) between 1876–1880 and 1966–1970 was about 31 percent.

2. Constituency campaign expenditure fell sharply from 14 percent of overall spending in 1925–1929 to 4 percent of total spending in 1966–1970. Between 1876–1880 and 1966–1970, this item declined from 77 percent to 4 percent of overall expenditure.

3. The trends toward routine spending and toward national-level spending continued (see also table 73).

4. Despite the move toward national-level spending, it still accounted for only 35 percent of overall spending in 1966–1970. In other words, about twice as much was spent locally as nationally (see also appendix D).[42]

5. The 8 percent growth in overall expenditure in real terms between 1925–1929 and 1966–1970 was accompanied by a further growth (albeit smaller than in previous eras) in the size of the electorate. This meant that the overall cost per vote at 1980 prices decreased from £6.4 to £4.5. The decrease between 1876–1880 and 1966–1970 was from £51.8 to £4.5.

[41] Estimates of routine central and constituency expenditures have been adjusted to represent spending over a standard four-year parliamentary cycle.

[42] The proportion of money spent locally is greater than indicated by the statistics, because "local" expenditure includes only constituency-level spending and excludes expenditure by ward committees. An important item of spending by many Conservative ward branches is on local government elections.

Since the ward network is more fully developed in the Conservative party than in the Labour and Liberal parties, the amount and proportion of unrecorded ward expenditure is probably greatest in the Conservative party. This means that the Tories' financial advantage at local level is probably even greater than shown in table 77.

TABLE 36

THE MODERN PATTERN: OVERALL CONSERVATIVE EXPENDITURE
(APPROXIMATE) DURING THE PARLIAMENTARY CYCLE 1966–1970
(in pounds)

	Routine Expenditure	Campaign Expenditure
Central	About 4,370,000	640,000
Local	Over 9 million	590,000

NOTES: This table is drawn up on the same basis as tables 4, 12, and 26; 6½ percent has been added to estimated Central Office expenditure for estimated expenditure of the Scottish Central Office. The totals of central spending are net of estimated grants to constituencies, and estimates of constituency spending are net of estimated constituency payments to Central Office. See tables 31 and 32.

SOURCES: Routine central expenditure is based on published party accounts for 1967/1968-1969/1970. Spending for 1966/1967 is estimated at £1,100,000. Routine spending April 1970-June 1970 is estimated at £265,000. For routine constituency spending, Pinto-Duschinsky, "Role of Constituency Associations," p. 206. This estimate is a revised version of that published in Pinto-Duschinsky, "Central Office and 'Power.'" For constituency campaign spending, David E. Butler and Anne Sloman, *British Political Facts, 1900-1979* (London: Macmillan, 1980), p. 229; for central campaign spending, interviews with party officers and officials.

Central Dependence upon Constituency Finance

The postwar period has seen an important development that table 36 does not show. The Central Office has become dependent to a considerable extent on locally raised funds. This is a reversal of the traditional relationship between the center and the periphery.[43]

During the aristocratic and plutocratic periods, parliamentary candidates became increasingly reliant on central money for their election expenses. Lowell, whose study of *The Government of England* was published in 1908, wrote that the Central Office war chest "holds many constituencies in a state of more or less dependence. . . . The power of Central Office is based to no small extent on its financial resources."[44]

Lowell undoubtedly exaggerated the extent of the Central Office's financial power. Nevertheless, central grants toward the election costs of Conservative candidates and toward the routine costs of constituency associations were considerable. They amounted to approximately £200,000 between 1906 and 1910—that is, over £5 million in 1980 values and 13 percent of total constituency income. During the 1925–1929 cycle, Central Office grants to candidates and local party organizations amounted to about £250,000 (including estimated grants by the Scottish Central Office). This amounted to over £3½ million in 1980 values and about 9 percent of total local income.

In the postwar years, the flow of money has reversed. As described above, Central Office financial grants to local associations have declined sharply (they seem to have amounted during the 1966–1970 cycle to less than £1 million in 1980 values). By the 1960s, Central Office subsidies to weak constituencies had been outstripped by the sums it was itself receiving from financially stronger local associations through the quota scheme. It received approximately £1¼ million from associations in England and Wales during 1966–1970 and paid out only about £200,000 in grants.[45] As shown in table 29, quota payments by constituencies have accounted for about a fifth of the party's central income over the past decade. There is no evidence that the constituencies have demanded (or obtained) any power over the central organization as a result of their fund-raising prowess. The financial independence of the local associations has nevertheless reinforced their independence of the center.

[43] The financial dependence of the Central Office on constituency associations is analyzed in Pinto-Duschinsky, "Central Office and 'Power.'" See also the note on Conservative finances in Michael Pinto-Duschinsky, "The Conservative Campaign: New Techniques versus Old," in Howard R. Penniman, ed., *Britain at the Polls: The Parliamentary Elections of 1974* (Washington, D.C.: American Enterprise Institute, 1975).

[44] A. Lawrence Lowell, *The Government of England* (New York: Macmillan, 1908), vol. 1, p. 568, and vol. 2, p. 4.

[45] Pinto-Duschinsky, "Role of Constituency Associations," p. 206.

Recent Developments

The main feature of Conservative finance since 1945 has been the party's relative success in harnessing the enthusiasm of local party members for fund-raising purposes. In recent decades, small-scale social events have yielded as much money for the Conservative party as company contributions. Conservative jumble-sale riches have been vital in three ways: they have enabled a high proportion of local Conservative associations to employ full-time agents; they have provided a useful source of central party income; and they have enabled company contributions to be directed very largely toward the national organization.

Despite this general success story, Conservative finances have come under strain since the 1960s. First, as shown in table 28, the party suffered considerable financial losses in the general elections of 1964, October 1974, and 1979. Normally the Central Office has relied on making sufficient profit on its election-year appeals to carry it through the years between elections. In 1964 exceptionally heavy campaign spending on preelection publicity meant that, despite a generous response to the election-year appeal, the Central Office suffered a loss of nearly £200,000. The deficit for the 1960–1964 cycle was over £1,200,000 (about £6 million at 1980 values).

The party's central reserve was sufficient to withstand this drain. Expenditure was sharply pruned for the 1966 election, and in 1967 a major national appeal was launched. The professional fund-raising consultants Hooker Craigmyle were called in. During 1968/1969, when the main appeal was in progress, £2,099,000 was raised. This was slightly over £1 million more than the Central Office's routine spending and helped to replenish the reserves.

In 1974 the reserves suffered a second blow, from which they have not recovered. In 1973 the party conducted its normal pre-election appeal, which enabled the Central Office to finance the February 1974 general election and to make an adequate profit, but no extra money seems to have been gathered for the second general election held in October 1974. Consequently, the Central Office ran a huge loss of nearly £1.3 million during the financial year 1974/1975, and the reserves had fallen by March 1975 to £649,000, which was equivalent to only four months' routine running costs of the central party organization.

After three years (1975/1976–1977/1978) during which income balanced expenditure, the Central Office has suffered further serious deficits in the past two years (1978/1979 and 1979/1980). During this time, spending exceeded income by £1,966,000. That a loss of this magnitude should have been incurred at the time of the 1979 general election—when a surplus could normally have been hoped for—indicates that the Conservative party treasurers will be hard pressed to raise funds for the routine expenses of the Central Office in the lean period that normally follows a campaign.

Unlike most previously published Central Office accounts, those for 1978/1979 and 1979/1980 do not include information on the state of the party's reserves. The magnitude of the deficits incurred between 1978 and 1980 and the low level of the reserves at the start of this period suggest that the central organization has exhausted its funds and that it has been obliged to seek bank loans to cover its day-to-day operations.

The fund-raising difficulties experienced by the Central Office during the 1970s led to a number of economy measures, such as the closure of Swinton Conservative College after the general elections of 1974. The search for savings also played a large part in the controversial decision after the 1979 election to move the research department from its separate buildings in Old Queen Street to the main headquarters at 32, Smith Square. The imminence of further cuts was announced in the party's annual report for 1979/1980.

The financial problems of the national organization seem to have resulted mainly from the decline of business contributions. During the most recent parliamentary cycle, 1975/1976–1979/1980, average annual company payments to Central Office were, in real terms, about 24 percent lower than in the 1951–1955 cycle, 29 percent lower than in 1960–1964 or in 1967/1968–1970/1971, and 17 percent lower than in 1971/1972–1974/1975.[46]

The inability of the Conservative party managers to rebuild the reserves during 1975 to 1979 (as they were able to do in 1968/1969) and the failure to collect a surplus in the election year 1979/1980 must be a cause for concern to them and raises the question whether past levels of donations are likely to be achieved in the future. Financial uncertainty on the Conservative side comes at a time when the trade unions have already committed themselves to substantial increases in their affiliations to the Labour party headquarters.

There have been problems in the constituencies. Although the level of local activity has remained high by pre–Second World War standards and by comparison with other political parties, there has been a substantial drop in membership since the mid-1950s. By 1974 total membership was about half that claimed at the all-time high

---

[46] Derived from column 1 of table 28. The fall in overall Central Office income has been smaller (see chapter 10, figure 4).

period of 1953. This seems to have affected local finances. In 1966/1967 it is estimated that the annual income of constituency associations averaged nearly £3,600 (£16,000 at 1980 values). In 1973 average income, according to the Houghton Committee's survey, was £4,700 (£13,700 in 1977 values). In 1977/1978, a more approximate estimate by the Central Office put average constituency income at over £8,000 (£10,500 at 1980 values). These figures need to be treated with caution in view of the problems involved in assessing local party income. If they are correct, however, they indicate a fall of about 50 percent in real terms in local party incomes since the 1960s.

One sign of strain within the local party organizations has been the fall in the number of full-time agents since the 1960s. In 1966 there were 421 full-time agents.[47] By May 1980 there were about 330. The loss of agents was concentrated in Conservative associations in Labour-held seats [48] and appears to have been accompanied by (and probably caused by) a fall in the size of party membership. By the early 1970s, the party had only about half as many members as at the time of the temporary peak reached in the early 1950s.

Concern about the departure of constituency agents from party service led in the early 1970s to a short-lived scheme for their central employment. It was hoped that agents would obtain greater financial security if they received their salaries from the Central Office and not from individual constituency associations. The central employment scheme had to be abandoned because constituencies proved unwilling to pass on to the Central Office the money they would otherwise have raised for agents' salaries and the Central Office could not find the extra funds needed for these salaries from other sources.

Between 1977 and 1980, the downward trend in the number of full-time agents was halted. Nevertheless, the party's agency service is still vulnerable and will be threatened by any further significant fall in party membership.

[47] David E. Butler and Michael Pinto-Duschinsky, *The British General Election of 1970* (London: Macmillan, 1971), p. 281.

[48] See Michael Pinto-Duschinsky, "The Limits of Professional Influence: A Study of Constituency Agents in the British Conservative Party," paper presented to the colloquium on party professionals (Paris: Association Française de Science Politique, 1977).

6
Labour Party Finances (1945-1979)

The main contrast between Labour and Conservative finances since the Second World War has been Labour's relative failure in raising small-scale funds at the constituency level. Constituency Labour parties have, like their Conservative counterparts, come to depend on the proceeds of local fund-raising efforts, and they often collect money from lotteries. Yet Labour has had far fewer individual members than the Tories. This has severely limited constituency Labour party budgets.

Labour's disadvantage at the local level has helped to disguise the party's increasingly favorable central finances. The income of Labour headquarters (Transport House)[1] has grown markedly since 1945. This has been the direct result of the expansion of the political levy funds of trade unions and of union willingness to hand over an increasing proportion of these funds to Transport House.[2] The combination of strong union funding and weak voluntary efforts has made it impossible for Labour to escape from its dependence upon the trade unions, which was already becoming burdensome in the 1930s.

Labour finances benefited from the political truce during the Second World War. Although normal party politics was suspended, the political levy continued to be collected by trade unions. This gave a welcome boost to their political levy fund reserves. Official statistics indicate that these reserves grew from £481,000 at the end of 1939 to £668,000 at the end of 1944. The actual increase was greater than appears. Much of the money registered as "expenditure" by unions merely represented transfers from their central political levy funds to local union branches, which kept the money received for

---

[1] The Labour party headquarters for many years occupied offices rented from the Transport and General Workers' Union at the union's headquarters, Transport House, situated at Smith Square, Westminster. Recently the Labour party has moved into a new headquarters building in South London.

[2] See chapter 8, especially tables 58 and 60.

use in the general election to be held after the war.[3] This meant that, from a financial point of view, the Labour party was well prepared for the general election of 1945. By contrast, Conservative campaign spending was far below the normal pre-1939 level. Consequently, the huge disparity between Labour and Conservative campaign spending in 1935 largely disappeared in 1945.[4]

Labour's clear victory in the 1945 election brought a further improvement in the party's financial position; the incoming Labour government soon passed an act of Parliament that reinstated "contracting out" of trade union levy funds, as had been the practice between 1913 and 1927. This led to a considerable jump in the proportion of union members paying the levy. In 1945, the last year of "contracting in," 48 percent contributed, compared with 76 percent in 1947, the first complete year in which the Trade Disputes and Trade Unions Act, 1946, was operating.[5] Political levy funds also benefited from the slightly increasing trade unon membership after the war. The overall result was a growth in the number paying the levy from 2.9 million in 1945 to 5.6 million in 1947 and a corresponding growth in the political levy fund income from £224,000 in 1945 to £401,000 in 1947. The amount paid in trade union affiliations to Labour headquarters increased from £51,000 in 1945 to £130,000 by 1948 and to over £200,000 in 1957.

Alongside this financial boost from the unions, Labour's local organization improved after the war as a result of unprecedented grass-roots enthusiasm. The individual membership of local Labour parties grew rapidly.[6] The number belonging to constituency Labour

[3] See Martin Harrison, *Trade Unions and the Labour Party since 1945* (London: Allen and Unwin, 1960), pp. 59-60.

[4] See table 75.

[5] See chapter 8.

[6] Labour party annual reports record the total number of party members under three categories: (1) trade union members, (2) individual members of constituency Labour parties, and (3) members of affiliated socialist societies (this last category is very small). The published totals are doubly misleading. First, as described in chapters 3, 8, and 10, the indirect members of the party, who are affiliated on the basis of their membership of a trade union, are not in any meaningful sense members at all. Second, the published membership totals of constituency Labour parties have often caused confusion. These totals record the number of votes that constituency parties are entitled to cast at the annual party conference and not their actual number of individual members.

According to a rule implemented in 1957, each constituency Labour party was affiliated to the national party on the basis of a minimum of 800 members (that is, each received a minimum of 800 votes at the annual conference) no matter how small its actual membership. The increase in total published constituency membership from 845,129 in 1956 to 912,987 in 1957 was a result of the new

parties increased from 266,000 in 1944 to a record 487,000 in 1945 and reached a peak of 1,015,000 in 1952. This surge of members was accompanied by a record growth in the number of full-time constituency agents. In 1951 there were 296. Possible reasons for the high level of political participation after the war have already been discussed. What needs to be stressed is, first, that even at its height Labour membership was well below that of the Conservatives and, second, that the number of members and full-time agents dropped quickly during the 1950s. There was a short respite in the early 1960s, but local organization declined much further during Harold Wilson's Labour governments of 1964–1970.[7] This is shown in figure 1.

The drop in local enthusiasm during the 1950s undoubtedly owed much to the disappointments of party supporters at Labour's loss of seats in the election of 1950, to its defeats in 1951, 1955, and 1959, to the doctrinal quarrels that plagued the party while it was in opposi-

---

rule. (According to the party's 1957 annual report, the actual increase in membership between 1956 and 1957 was only 15,000, which suggests a real total in 1957 of about 860,000.)

Between 1962 and 1963 the minimum constituency affiliation was raised from 800 to 1,000, which raised total recorded "membership" from 767,459 in 1962 to 830,346 in 1963. The published membership totals became progressively less accurate during the 1960s as ever more constituency Labour parties (CLPs) had real memberships below 1,000. By 1966, 394 CLPs had memberships of less than 1,000, although they continued to be credited with the notional minimum of 1,000. By 1976, 537 CLPs recorded the formal minimum of 1,000 members. Only the figures of 86 CLPs with over 1,000 members in that year could be regarded as even approximately accurate. The gross inaccuracy of the published membership totals is indicated by the figures for 1974. The Labour party's annual report recorded a total of 691,889, whereas the Houghton Committee's constituency survey produced an estimated total of 310,000. Recent changes in the rules relating to CLP affiliation fees to the national executive committee may make published membership totals somewhat less inaccurate in the future.

For the purposes of figure 1, the following assumptions have been made: (1) that the totals published in Labour party annual reports were accurate until 1956 (the recorded totals for these years were probably overestimates, but the exaggerations were relatively slight); (2) that membership in 1957 was 15,000 higher than in 1956 (as indicated by the 1957 annual report); (3) that membership in 1963 is assumed to have been the same as in 1962; (4) that membership in 1974 was 310,000 (as suggested by the Houghton Committee's constituency survey); (5) that, for years between 1957 and 1962, actual changes in membership were 1.5 times as great as recorded changes; and (6) that, since 1963, actual membership changes have been 2.4 times as great as recorded changes.

[7] A survey conducted for the 1970 Nuffield election study indicated that total individual Labour membership had fallen to a little over 300,000 by the late 1960s (David E. Butler and Michael Pinto-Duschinsky, *The British General Election of 1970* [London: Macmillan, 1971], p. 265). A broadly similar total is shown in figure 1.

FIGURE 1

NUMBER OF INDIVIDUAL MEMBERS OF THE LABOUR PARTY, 1928–1977,
AND NUMBER OF FULL-TIME CONSTITUENCY AGENTS, 1920–1978

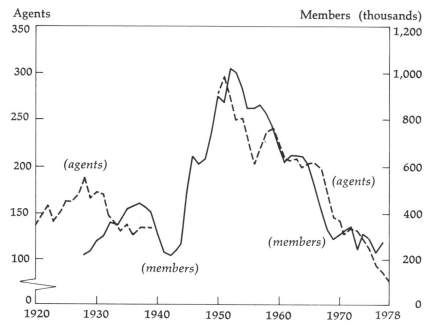

NOTE: The basis of calculation of constituency membership is described in footnote 6. Statistics about the number of constituency agents are not available in the Labour party annual reports for 1938 or 1940-1949. The number of agents in May 1970 is taken from the 1970 Nuffield election study.

SOURCES: Labour party annual reports, the Houghton Report, and Butler and Pinto-Duschinsky, *British General Election of 1970*, p. 269.

tion during the 1950s, and to the social developments mentioned in chapter 5.

Labour's inability or unwillingness to resist the loss of members also resulted from the fact that many constituency organizations had wasted the opportunities of the postwar years. They remained unnecessarily dependent upon trade union subsidies and were often inward-looking cliques. According to Harrison, routine union grants to local Labour parties amounted to about £145,000 a year in the late 1950s, that is, an average of about £250 per annum per constituency, or nearly a third of estimated constituency income. On top of these subsidies, constituencies received substantial annual sums (estimated at £30,000 in 1957) from cooperative societies.[8]

[8] Harrison, *Trade Unions and the Labour Party*, p. 99.

The effects of these payments were widely debated and disputed. They were criticized on several grounds. First, trade unions concentrated their money in safely Labour-held constituencies where it was needed least. The prime interest of unions in sponsoring parliamentary candidates was to place their representatives in the House of Commons. They usually considered it a waste to give grants for unwinnable or marginal seats. Second, there were complaints that the prospect of union money unduly influenced some constituency Labour parties when they selected parliamentary candidates. In effect, the unions "bought" the seats. Third, it was frequently claimed that union grants had enervating effects on local organizations.

Grants by unions and cooperative societies were not the only cause for concern. Until the 1950s, a number of Labour candidates also made substantial personal contributions to their constituency Labour parties (CLPs), a practice that had been firmly stamped upon in the Conservative party. According to a committee under Harold Wilson, which investigated the state of Labour organization after the 1955 election:

> We are disturbed at the number of candidates who, out of their own pockets, are required to make annual contributions toward Constituency Party finances. Quite apart from the undesirability of this practice on general grounds, the dependence of CLPs finances on such a source of income has a detrimental effect on organisation.[9]

In 1957 the national executive committee of the Labour party decided that finance must not be mentioned at selection conferences and forbade unsponsored candidates to give more than fifty pounds a year to constituency funds. However, this restriction did not apply to candidates sponsored by the trade unions. The choice of a union nominee as a parliamentary candidate remained an easy way for lazy CLPs to obtain money and to avoid the need to recruit individual subscribers.

The original rationale for trade union backing of particular parliamentary candidates had completely disappeared after the war. By 1955 the average election expenses of Labour candidates were about one-sixth (in real terms) of the expenses of the pioneers who contested seats in January 1910. Yet the habit of sponsorship survived (see table 37), although the payments made by unions were usually less, in real terms, than in the past.

[9] Quoted ibid., p. 277.

TABLE 37

Number of Labour Members of Parliament Sponsored by Trade Unions and Cooperative Societies, 1918–1979

General Election	Sponsored by Unions	Sponsored by Cooperative Societies	Total Sponsored MPs	Total Labour MPs
1918	49	1	50	57
1922	86	4	90	142
1923	102	6	108	191
1924	88	5	93	151
1929	114	9	123	287
1931	35	1	36	46
1935	78	9	87	154
1945	120	23	143	393
1950	111	18	129	315
1951	108	16	124	295
1955	95	18	113	277
1959	92	16	108	258
1964	120	20	140	317
1966	132	18	150	363
1970	112	17	129	288
1974 (February)	127	16	143	301
1974 (October)	126	16	142	319
1979	134	17	151	269

Source: David E. Butler and Anne Sloman, *British Political Facts, 1900-1979* (London: Macmillan, 1980), p. 146.

In the 1960s the decline in the membership of local Labour parties and the associated fall in the number of full-time Labour agents accelerated. By 1970 CLPs had barely 300,000 individual members, and there were only 141 constituency agents.[10] The causes of the sharp deterioration in Labour's local organization in the late 1960s are complex and uncertain. Disappointment among party activists at the performance of Harold Wilson's Labour government was undoubtedly a factor. It is unlikely, however, that this political dissatisfaction would have led to such a precipitous fall in membership and to the desertion of so many agents had the CLPs been in a healthier state to begin with.

Crumbling local organization posed considerable financial problems for many CLPs. The declining number of members restricted

[10] Butler and Pinto-Duschinsky, *British General Election of 1970*, p. 269.

160

income from subscriptions. Moreover, union grants to constituencies seem to have declined in real terms as political levy money was directed increasingly to the national party organization. By the late 1960s, gambling schemes were the major source of constituency income. The most popular were football totes. Other variations were horse-racing draws, Christmas raffles, and pontoon. These fund-raising methods were surprisingly successful and have prevented the financial collapse that might otherwise have been expected.

In order to bolster some of the deteriorating CLPs, especially those in marginal constituencies, Labour headquarters implemented a scheme in 1969 to provide salaries for full-time agents out of central funds. Forty appointments to the national agency service were made before the 1970 election.

During the 1970s, central employment gave a measure of security to some Labour agents, but it did not solve the problems facing the constituency organizations. Labour membership has not risen. There were probably about 250,000–300,000 members in 1979. The flight of agents has continued. The party's annual report of 1978 announced a record low of seventy-seven full-time constituency agents. As argued later, shortage of members, not lack of money, has been the root problem for CLPs.

By contrast with the local scene, the Labour headquarters has enjoyed a period of enviable strength. Central party income has grown considerably in real terms, although the relatively healthy financial state of Transport House has not alleviated the deep crisis in the constituency organizations.

This chapter analyzes Labour's central and local finances in the modern period in a manner similar to the analysis of Conservative finances in the previous chapter. This task presents several problems, despite the fact that Labour's central accounts, unlike those of the Conservatives, have always been published. First, the figures that appear in the annual reports of the Labour party include only the responsibilities of the national executive committee. Separate central funds received by the party leader, by the parliamentary party, and by regional organizations are not included. Second, the published accounts are complex and potentially misleading. The central finances are separated into a number of different accounts (in 1977 they were the general fund, development fund, general election fund, by-election fund, deposit insurance fund, and building fund). Details about the sources of income and categories of expenditure are given for the general fund, but similar information is not regularly available about other funds. This means that, although it is possible to tell how much trade unions and CLPs gave to the general fund, it is not possible to assess their total contributions to Transport House. Similarly, the published accounts have not regularly given breakdowns of expenditure from the special accounts, such as the general election fund.

Labour's central accounts present further difficulties: (1) There are periodical payments from one fund to another (for example, from the general election fund to the general fund). (2) Although special funds have particular objectives, they are not always used to carry them out. For instance, not all of the general election fund is used for campaign expenditure, while some money in the general fund is devoted to electioneering. (3) The breakdown of expenditure given for the general fund does not make it possible to assess the amounts allocated to different types of central spending (such as organization, research, and publicity).

The severe problems involved in compiling constituency incomes and expenditures are similar to those described in chapter 5 for the Conservative party.

Central Labour Party Finances, 1940–1979

Official Labour accounts since 1940 are summarized in table 38. The totals do not include the independent income of regional organizations. These amount to approximately 5 percent of Transport House income during a complete parliamentary cycle.[11] It should also be noted that the affiliation fees of trade unions are only one component of their contributions to the central Labour organization. Especially large extra payments are made by the union for general elections. It is for this reason that the percentage of total income coming from trade union affiliation fees is relatively low in election years.

Headquarters Income. As shown in table 39, most central party income is from affiliation fees paid by trade unions. These fees are supplemented by other union money. At least 90 percent of the party's general election funds normally come from special union grants. The estimated sources of Labour income during 1974–1977 are given in table 39. The percentages include estimated income of

---

[11] The independent income of regional councils is considerably higher in general election years than in nonelection years. As for the national headquarters, the main sources of regional funds are the unions.

TABLE 38

Labour Central Income and Expenditure, 1940–1979
(in thousands of pounds)

| | Income | | | Expenditure | |
	Total	Trade union affiliation fees	Affiliation fees as % of total[a]	Total	General election
1940	51	39	76	48	
1941	60	48	80	47	
1942	58	46	79	54	
1943	60	41	78	59	
1944	97	49	51	57	
1945*	166	51	31	100	51
1946	79	51	64	92	
1947	166	81	50	107	
1948	235	130	55	133	
1949	350	126	37	201	6
1950*	197	127	64	292	78
1951*	280	124	44	244	80
1952	172	126	73	202	
1953	172	126	73	173	
1954	179	139	77	183	
1955*	284	141	50	219	73
1956	186	141	76	183	
1957	258	209	81	275	
1958	378	210	55	329	37
1959*	498	213	43	485	202
1960	225	206	81	299	
1961	255	208	82	281	
1962	296	207	70	301	20
1963	344	276	80	516	213
1964*	573	276	48	583	305
1965	351	281	80	350	37
1966*	725	274	38	420	159
1967	352	277	79	384	
1968	342	270	79	408	26
1969	345	272	79	601	108
1970*	1,034	402	39	948	392
1971	585	423	72	702	
1972	692	551	80	787	9

(Table continues)

163

TABLE 38 (continued)

	Income			Expenditure	
	Total	Trade union affiliation fees	Affiliation fees as % of total[a]	Total	General election
1973	842	670	80	886	19
1974*	1,781	738	41	1,865	935
1975	1,371	1,118	82	1,226	
1976	1,527	1,221	80	1,315	
1977	1,536	1,268	83	1,530	
1978	2,124	1,501	71	2,174	204
1979	3,113	1,842	59	3,358	1,228

NOTE: Asterisks denote general election years.

[a] These percentages considerably underestimate total union contributions, especially in general election years, because they do not take account of union payments to special central Labour funds such as the general election fund. The figures are calculated on the same basis as those for table 16.

SOURCE: Labour party annual reports.

all Transport House funds (general fund, general election fund, and so on).[12]

[12] Businessmen have occasionally backed the Labour party, but their contributions have not normally been identified in the published party accounts because they have usually been earmarked for one of the special funds and not the general fund.

After Labour's defeat in the 1970 general election, Wilson supplemented the small allowance he received from Transport House for his political office as party leader by collecting funds of his own. The fact that the Labour leader felt obliged to raise independent money illustrates his lack of control over the allocation of funds by the party headquarters. The Labour party treasurer, unlike his Tory counterpart, is not an appointee of the leader but is responsible to a finance committee, which, in turn, is accountable to the national executive committee and the annual party conference.

The special funds raised on Wilson's behalf came mainly from businessmen (see chap. 8, footnote 43). According to Lord Wilfred Brown, the main trust was "low profile": "We did not want the Labour party to know about it because they would have wanted to get their fingers into it. It was for Harold Wilson as Opposition Leader. If it had gone through Transport House, we could not have been sure it would have got to him" (Andrew Roth, *Sir Harold Wilson: Yorkshire Walter Mitty* [London: Macdonald and Jane's, 1977], p. 35). A separate research fund was also set up to serve Wilson and other Labour front benchers. This, too, benefited from business donations.

TABLE 39

Estimated Sources of Transport House Income, 1974–1977

Average annual income (£)	1,554,000
Source (percent)	
Trade unions	90
Constituency Labour parties	8
Interest (net)	1
Other	2
Total	100

Note: Includes estimated contributions to special funds.

Sources: Derived from Labour party annual reports and information provided by the finance officer of the Labour party.

Headquarters Expenditure. Labour's central spending, like that of the Conservative Central Office, is devoted predominantly to routine, nonelection activities. During the parliamentary cycle 1970–1974, for example, 86 percent went for routine spending and 14 percent for the campaign of February 1974.

The types of routine expenditure by Transport House, estimated in table 40, are similar to those of the central Conservative organiza-

TABLE 40

Types of Routine Expenditure by Transport House, 1972

Total expenditure (£)	767,000
Type of expenditure (percent)	
Promoting constituency organization[a]	45.8
Research[b]	18.4
Publicity and press relations	7.0
Headquarters staff	7.3
Other[c]	21.5
Total	100.0

Note: It is assumed that the staff costs for each department were proportional to the numbers of administrative staff employed. For staff numbers at Transport House, see Rose, *The Problem of Party Government*, p. 169.

[a] The main cost was the maintenance of Labour's regional organization. The regional organizations themselves raised additional money, which is not included in these accounts. Grants to constituencies amounted to 9.4 percent of total expenditure.

[b] Includes work of the research and international departments.

[c] This item consists largely of "general administration expenses."

Sources: Richard Rose, *The Problem of Party Government* (New York: Free Press, 1975); and Labour party annual report.

tion. The figures are based on the assumption that staff costs for each function in the year covered by the table were proportional to the numbers employed in each department of Transport House.

A striking feature of Transport House's routine expenditure is that less than 10 percent is devoted to direct financial payments to constituencies.[13] This is higher than the equivalent percentage of Central Office expenditure, but in view of the parlous state of Labour's constituency organization and the relative wealth of Transport House, it is surprising that more money has not been channeled to the grass roots.

The postwar pattern of Labour's central spending on election campaigns is given in table 41.

The Labour headquarters, like the Conservative Central Office, has usually made a profit on general elections. Money from the special general election fund has frequently been used for the party's routine activities.[14]

The party has felt reluctantly obliged to compete with Conservative preelection advertising. This accounts for its relatively high campaign spending in 1958–1959, 1963–1964, and 1978–1979. Labour's political advertising has been on a considerably smaller scale than that of the Tories. For example, David Butler and Richard Rose estimate that in 1958–1959 Labour spent about £103,000 on campaign publicity and the Conservatives £468,000.[15] In 1978–1979, Labour's political advertising cost about £0.6 million and the Tories' £1.5 million.

These points about Labour's central campaign spending should be noted:

1. As shown in table 41, the party's election spending has grown in real terms since the postwar years.

2. The gap between the election budgets of the two main parties has been much smaller in recent campaigns than before the Second World War (table 75).

3. Labour's financial disadvantage could have been narrowed still further had trade unions relaxed their traditional caution about

[13] It is not possible to determine from the published accounts the precise amounts devoted by the headquarters to direct financial payments to local parties.

[14] For instance, interest from the general election fund reserves has since 1956 been automatically credited to the general fund. Uses of the general election fund for noncampaign purposes appear to include the transfer from the fund in 1962 of £34,183 for the marginal constituency aid scheme for 1960 and 1961 and, in 1968, the transfer of £150,000 to the national agency service reserve.

[15] David E. Butler and Richard Rose, *The British General Election of 1959* (London: Macmillan, 1960), p. 281.

TABLE 41

LABOUR CENTRAL SPENDING ON GENERAL ELECTIONS, 1900–1979

(in thousands of pounds)

General Election	Current Prices	1980 Prices
1900	a	
1906	2	55
1910 (January)	3.5 [b]	89
1910 (December)	3.5	89
1918	18	218
1922	7	98
1923	22	311
1924	32.5	456
1929	45	673
1931	31	518
1935	26	448
1945	51	493
1950	84	643
1951	80	566
1955	73	456
1959	239	1,352
1964	538	2,663
1966	196	887
1970	526	1,975
1974 (February)	440 [c]	1,078
1974 (October)	524	1,150
1979	1,566	1,819

NOTE: Totals exclude spending by regional councils except for 1979, for which an estimate of such spending has been included. See note to table 42.

[a] Negligible.

[b] It is assumed that central spending was the same in each of the general elections of 1910.

[c] Published party accounts do not separate the amounts spent on each of the 1974 elections. The totals in the table are based on information supplied by the finance officer of the Labour party.

SOURCES: Labour party annual reports and, for 1979, as for table 42.

handing over money to Transport House for campaign use from their political levy fund reserves. The "squirrel" instincts of the unions and of Transport House are emphasized by Harrison with reference to the 1955 and 1959 general elections.[16] In 1978–1979,

[16] Harrison, *Trade Unions and the Labour Party*, pp. 68-70.

too, union leaders showed reluctance to earmark money for the election campaign despite the fact that their political levy fund reserves were at record levels.[17]

4. Labour's capacity to devote money to political advertising has been limited by its need to spend heavily on direct financial aid to weak constituency organizations. Campaign grants to constituencies came to £139,000 in February 1974 and £158,000 in October 1974,[18] that is, about 31 percent of Labour's central campaign and precampaign spending (excluding regional councils) for the two 1974 elections. This compared with 6 percent of Conservative central spending that went to such subsidies during the 1970 campaign.[19]

In 1979 Transport House's grants for constituency election expenses amounted to £213,000 (16 percent of its election budget). If estimated spending by regional councils is added, constituency subsidies totaled about £363,000 (23 percent of the overall central election budget). By contrast, the Conservative Central Office spent only £42,000 in the same election on grants to local campaigns (2 percent of the total).[20]

5. The consequences of Labour's lower spending on campaign publicity are minimized by the fact that, like the Conservatives, it receives free time on radio and television for party political broadcasts. Including the notional value of these broadcasts, Labour's total spending on political advertising in the 1978–1979 campaign came to £3.3 million and that of the Conservatives to £4.2 million—that is, a Conservative advantage of only 27 percent.

Statistics of Labour's central spending for the 1979 general election are given in table 42.

Local Labour Finance

Constituency Income. According to Harrison's estimates, constituency Labour parties raised a total of about £450,000 in the nonelection year 1957. Of this total, about £145,000 came from trade unions, £30,000 from cooperative societies, and £275,000 was raised by the local organizations themselves. CLPs collected about £150,000 in

---

[17] Michael Pinto-Duschinsky, "Financing the British General Election of 1979," in Howard R. Penniman, ed., *Britain at the Polls, 1979: A Study of the General Election* (Washington, D.C.: American Enterprise Institute, 1981), pp. 217-18.

[18] Interview with the finance officer of the Labour party.

[19] See table 32.

[20] See table 33.

168

TABLE 42

LABOUR PARTY NATIONAL EXECUTIVE COMMITTEE PRECAMPAIGN AND CAMPAIGN EXPENDITURE, 1978–1979

(in thousands of pounds)

	Pre-campaign	Campaign	Total	% of Total
Grants to constituencies	—	213	213	16
Advertising				
Posters[a]	(224)	(130)	(354)	(26)
Press	(—)	(260)	(260)	(19)
Total	224	390	614	45
Producing political broadcasts	2[b]	71	72	5
Opinion research	48[b]	39	87	6
Party publications[a]	40	54	95	7
Leaders' tours and meetings	—	45	45	3
Staff and administrative costs	—	190	190	14
Miscellaneous	1	48	48	4
Total	315	1,050	1,366[c]	100

NOTES: Parentheses indicate subtotals. Figures exclude independent spending by regional councils; to make realistic comparisons with central Conservative campaign spending, it is necessary to add to the figures given in this table estimates of the additional amounts spent by the regional councils. Evidence from interviews indicated that this may have amounted to an additional £200,000, most of it devoted to grants by regional councils to constituency campaigns. Including regional councils, Labour's total election spending was an estimated £1,566,000. The estimated subtotals (in thousands of pounds) were as follows: grants to constituencies, 363; advertising, 619; producing political broadcasts, 72; opinion research, 87; party publications, 120; leaders' tours and meetings, 50; staff and administrative costs, 200; miscellaneous, 55. These are, however, crude estimates and subject to later revision (see Pinto-Duschinsky, "Financing the General Election of 1979," table 7.4).

The totals in this table and in table 33 of staff and administrative costs are somewhat arbitrary. Since the parties maintain permanent staffs and permanent headquarters, there is no objective way of demarcating routine and campaign costs for them. The higher figure for staff and administration for Labour than for the Conservatives may, therefore, indicate different accounting conventions and does not necessarily mean that Labour spent more heavily on these items.

[a] There may be marginal errors in assigning spending in these categories to the precampaign and campaign phases.

[b] These particular figures are not readily comparable with those for the Conservative party given in table 33 since the two parties used different definitions of precampaign expenditure for these categories. The Conservatives included all broadcasting production costs during the year before the election as precampaign while Labour did not; vice versa for opinion research.

[c] Apparent inconsistency in the total is due to rounding. This total is slightly lower than that given in table 38. This is because it is based on the unaudited accounts made available by the finance officer of the Labour party before the publication of the annual report for 1979. According to that report, NEC spending on the 1979 election totaled £1,432,000.

SOURCE: Finance officer of the Labour party.

TABLE 43

Sources of Labour Constituency Income, 1973

Average constituency income (£)	1,804
Source (percent)	
Branch payments	5.1
Constituency-level	
Social events	8.1
Gambling schemes	38.7
Subscriptions and donations	
Trade union and cooperative affiliations, grants, and donations	17.8
Individual subscriptions	12.1
Other	4.4
Grants from headquarters and regions	2.4
Other	11.4
Total	100.0

Source: Houghton Report, p. 178.

subscriptions and £125,000 from gifts, social events, and gambling.[21]

The Houghton Committee's constituency survey, based on a sample of seventy-five CLPs, gives the figures in table 43 for 1973 (also a nonelection year).

A comparison between these figures for 1973 and Harrison's estimates for 1957 suggests that trade union grants and individual subscriptions have become less important sources of local Labour income and that CLPs have become more dependent than before upon gambling schemes. These conclusions need to be treated with caution, as the estimates for 1957 and 1973 were derived differently and the Houghton Committee's survey may not have shown the full extent of contributions by trade unions to local Labour organizations.

Union money to constituencies, though probably less significant than before, nevertheless remains more considerable than indicated by table 43. First, trade union money is directed to specific constitu-

[21] Harrison, *Trade Unions and the Labour Party*, p. 99. This estimate differs from that of Dick (R. L.) Leonard, *Elections in Britain* (Princeton, N.J.: Van Nostrand, 1968). Based on about two dozen local balance sheets for 1962-1963, Leonard estimates the average annual income of CLPs at £2,000. According to Butler and Pinto-Duschinsky, average CLP income before the 1970 election was about £1,200 (*British General Election of 1970*, pp. 282-83). In the absence of systematic surveys of local Labour party finance in the 1940s and 1950s, it is difficult accurately to assess trends. For the purposes of this chapter, calculations of trends have been based on Harrison's estimates for 1957.

encies, many of them safe Labour seats. In these particular CLPs, union funding is often crucial. According to the Houghton Committee's constituency survey, 27 percent of CLPs were in receipt of special trade union or Co-operative party grants in 1973 and 1974. In these seats, trade union (or Co-operative) backing accounted for a third of total income in the nonelection year of 1973. Second, constituency accounts exclude union money, particularly for local government elections, which are paid directly to ward committees. Third, the importance of trade unions and cooperatives increases at general elections. In the general election year of 1974, union and cooperative donations, grants, and affiliations amounted to 22 percent of total constituency income and, in constituencies receiving grants, to 39 percent of income. Fourth, some constituency income is categorized as "miscellaneous" in the Houghton Report, and this probably includes some further union money.

Considering their low membership, the financial performance of CLPs has not been discreditable. Largely thanks to gambling profits, their income per member is about twice as high as that of Conservative constituency associations.[22] Moreover, their budgets seem to have kept pace with inflation since the late 1950s,[23] a notable achievement in view of the great fall in membership they have suffered. Nevertheless, too much has depended on the efforts of small groups of activists. The number of local participants has become too small to provide sufficient money or security to constituency agents who, in an age of increasing prosperity, have expected salaries that CLPs have usually been unable (or unprepared) to pay.

The problem of local Labour organization was summed up well in the annual report of one CLP in 1970:

> The trend has been for the not so active Parties to become inactive, and the active Parties to become not so active. Most Parties have suffered a drop in membership. . . . [The reason] is just that the majority of members of this Party are not membership minded, and therefore they have not bothered to try to recruit new members, and in some cases they have not even bothered to collect subscriptions from existing members.[24]

[22] See table 34.

[23] This is based on a comparison between Harrison's estimate quoted above for 1957 and the Houghton Committee's estimate for 1973. See also Samuel E. Finer, *The Changing British Party System, 1945-1979* (Washington, D.C.: American Enterprise Institute, 1980), p. 108.

[24] Annual report of the Yeovil Labour party.

It is no coincidence that the deficiency of CLPs as compared with Conservative constituency associations is most apparent in categories of income dependent upon large membership. The Houghton Committee indicates that in 1973 CLPs obtained more from trade unions than Conservative associations received from companies. However, CLP income from individual membership subscriptions, branch payments, and constituency-level social activities amounted to only £457 per constituency. The average income of Conservative associations from these items was £3,167. This means that across the nation the 623 CLPs raised less than £300,000 from those activities dependent on the size of their memberships, compared with nearly £2 million raised by Conservative constituency associations (that is, a deficiency of £5 million at 1980 values).

Constituency Expenditure. Local Labour parties have, like their Conservative counterparts, been helped by the tight limits on permitted spending on election campaigns. This has meant that money that, in the prewar period, would have been earmarked for electioneering has been used for routine purposes. In the parliamentary cycle 1970–February 1974, CLPs probably spent a total of about £4¼ million,[25] of which £702,000 (16.5 percent of the total) was used for constituency campaigning in the general election of February 1974.

The most important items of routine spending, as for the Conservatives, are the upkeep of constituency offices and of full-time agents. CLPs devote a higher proportion of their constituency budgets than Conservative constituency associations to local government elections.

The average expenditures of all CLPs and of the minority with full-time agents are given in table 44.

The Pattern of Labour Finance

The estimated pattern of Labour spending in the parliamentary cycle 1970–February 1974, is given in table 45.

This has been drawn up on the same basis as table 36, which shows Conservative spending in the parliamentary cycle 1966–1970.

The Labour pattern is broadly similar to that of the Tories insofar as routine costs account in both parties for the lion's share of spending during a parliamentary cycle (86 percent for Labour in the 1970–1974 cycle, compared with the Conservative 91.5 percent in

[25] This figure has been adjusted to represent spending over a standard four-year parliamentary cycle.

TABLE 44

Types of Routine Expenditure by Constituency Labour Parties, 1973

	Constituencies with Full-Time Paid Agents	All Constituencies
Average expenditure (£)	4,585	1,761
Type of expenditure (percent)		
Salaries	43.2	29.6
Office expenses	32.5	35.2
Local elections	15.0	18.8
Other	9.3	16.5
Total	100.0	100.0

Source: as for table 43.

1966–1970).[26] There are some significant differences, however, which reflect the relative weakness of constituency Labour parties. Whereas Conservative local associations account for nearly two-thirds of overall Conservative spending (64.7 percent), CLPs account for little over half of total Labour spending (56.5 percent in 1970–1974). Second, campaign costs are somewhat more important for CLPs than for Conservative associations. In the parliamentary cycles under review, general election campaigns consumed 16.5 percent of CLP budgets and 6.2 percent of Conservative local spending.

The weakness of CLPs affects the financial relationship between center and periphery. As shown in chapter 5, Conservative Central Office receives far more in quotas from strong local associations than it gives in financial grants to weak ones. In the Labour party, the center does not benefit in this way. In the parliamentary cycle 1970–1974, the outflow of grants from the center was about the same as the amount received from constituencies (mainly in affiliation fees).

Recent Trends

If the orchestrated cries of alarm are to be believed, the Labour party is in a state of grave financial crisis. In the words of one article, published shortly after the 1979 general election, Labour was "bank-

[26] For the purposes of this paragraph, totals of routine spending have been adjusted to represent spending over a standard four-year parliamentary cycle.

TABLE 45

The Modern Pattern: Overall Labour Party Expenditure (approximate) during the Parliamentary Cycle 1970–1974
(in pounds)

	Routine Expenditure	Campaign Expenditure
Central	2.7 million	315,000
Local	3¼ million	700,000

NOTES: This table has been drawn up on the same basis as table 36. Routine central expenditure includes estimated routine regional expenditure and expenditure of leader's office. The totals are net of estimated grants to constituencies. The totals of routine spending cover the period July 1970-February 1974.

SOURCES: Labour party annual reports; Houghton Report; and Butler and Sloman, *British Political Facts, 1900-1979*, p. 229.

rupt and bruised." [27] The party treasurer warned the 1979 annual conference that, without strong remedial action, the organization's deficit would "threaten the party's existence." [28] The 1980 annual

[27] Patrick Wintour, "Bankrupt and Bruised," *New Statesman*, September 28, 1979.

[28] *Daily Telegraph*, October 4, 1979. The threatened deficit resulted not from a contraction of Transport House income, but from the rapid growth of spending. After the 1979 general election, Transport House staff claimed hefty salary increases and benefits. According to one report, these included a salary increase of 41 percent, £5,000 a year extra for heads of department, and £150,000 for new cars (Wintour, "Bankrupt and Bruised"). By threatening to go into deficit

conference heard a statement by David Basnett, union leader and co-chairman of the Labour Party Commission of Enquiry, referring to "the party's desperate financial difficulties." It was important, he said, that "the conference should recognize their enormity." [29]

Such rhetoric contrasts starkly with the buoyant state of affairs emerging from the published accounts of the national executive committee (NEC). As shown in table 38, Labour's central income has increased greatly since the Second World War and particularly during the 1970s. The growth has easily outstripped inflation. Between 1946 and 1978 (both nonelection years), NEC income jumped from £79,000 to £2,124,000—a twenty-seven-fold increase. In real terms, this meant that NEC income in 1978 was nearly four times as large as in 1946. The growth has continued during the recent decade of inflation. Between 1969 and 1978 there was a sixfold increase in NEC income, from £345,000 to £2,124,000. When account is taken of inflation, this represents a real growth of 96 percent.

Transport House's income has grown as the direct result of successive increases in the affiliation fees and grants paid by the trade unions. The affiliation fee was one penny per member (0.417p) in 1912, two pennies in 1918, three in 1920, four in 1932, 4½ in 1937, and five (one shilling) in 1941. Affiliation rates since the Second World War and agreed increases to 1981 are given in table 46. The affiliation rate in 1981 (40p) is eight times as much as that of 1969 (5p).

The unions' ability to increase their contributions to the party centrally resulted partly from the growth of their political levy in comes (this is discussed in chapter 8) and partly from the fact that they have directed a higher proportion of their political money to the center rather than to the constituencies as in the past. Labour's national executive committee has for many years tried to persuade unions to hand over money to them rather than to fritter it away on various local Labour causes. The argument has been that the national party is in a better position to use the money where it is needed most; for example, in marginal seats rather than the Labour strongholds that traditionally had been the recipients of union sponsorship. The attempt to persuade unions to direct their money to the center led in 1933 to the Hastings Agreement, which restricted

to meet these extra expenses, Transport House was putting pressure on the trade unions to hand over money lying idle in their political levy fund reserves. Transport House evidently expected that higher spending would induce the unions to increase their affiliation fees still further.

[29] *The Times*, October 1, 1980.

TABLE 46
Affiliation Rates to the Labour Party (Transport House), 1945–1981

	Rate per Member (pence)
1945	5d (2.08)
1948	6d (2.5)
1955	9d (3.75)
1961	12d (5)
1970	7½
1972	10
1973	12½
1974	15
1975	17
1976	21
1978	24
1979	28
1980	32
1981	40

Note: New pence (p) are given in parentheses until 1970. "d" denotes an old penny. There were 240 old pence to the pound sterling. There are 100 new pennies to the pound sterling.
Source: Labour party annual reports.

the amounts a union was permitted to spend on sponsored constituencies (see chapter 3). These limits have gradually had the desired effect. In 1933 trade union affiliations to Transport House were under 20 percent of total political levy income; by 1976 this had risen to 41 percent. Trade union affiliation fees to Transport House rose from £51,000 in 1946 to £272,000 in 1969. By 1979 they had jumped to £1,842,000. On the basis of the further increases in affiliation rates that have already been agreed, the fees are likely to rise to about £2.4 million for 1981. Between 1946 and 1979, trade union fees to Transport House increased thirty-six-fold (a fourfold growth in real terms). To these fees must be added other hefty, but usually undisclosed, contributions to Transport House's special funds, such as the £1 million contributed by unions to Transport House and to the regional organizations for the 1974 election funds. The growth in Labour's central income between 1968 and 1979 is shown in figure 2.

Shortage of information makes it hard to draw reliable conclusions about the party's finances at the constituency level. Consider-

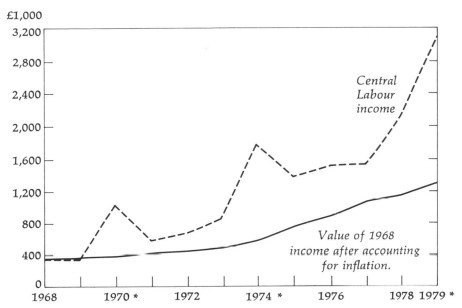

FIGURE 2
TRANSPORT HOUSE'S GROWING INCOME, 1968–1979

£1,000

*Central
Labour
income*

*Value of 1968
income after accounting
for inflation.*

| 1968 | 1970 * | 1972 | 1974 * | 1976 | 1978 1979 * |

NOTE: Asterisk denotes general election year.
SOURCE: Labour party annual reports.

ing the steep fall in party membership, local Labour finances seem
to have held up surprisingly well. Comparisons between the 1950s
and the 1970s suggest that CLP budgets may have kept pace with
the cost of living. This means that income per member has risen
sharply in real terms. Nevertheless, CLPs have remained financially
weak in comparison with their Conservative counterparts, and few
of them have been able to provide sufficient financial security to
retain the services of a full-time agent. As shown in figure 1, there
has been a steep decline in the number of Labour agents since the
general election of 1959. This cannot be attributed to the severe
inflation of the 1970s, since the downward trend was well established
by the 1960s.

The enlarged sums that have come into the central coffers of the
Labour party have been used to only a very limited extent for pump
priming at the constituency level. Although there has been a great
deal of public concern about the desertion of constituency agents
and the need to give them better pay and more security, Transport
House funds have been used sparingly for this purpose. Statistics of
administrative staff employed by Transport House indicate that be-

177

tween 1963 and 1974 the payroll of the national organization grew, while the number of full-time agents working in constituencies nearly halved. This has led to a top-heavy organization. In 1963 there were over 200 full-time agents and seventy-eight administrative officers at national and regional levels. By 1974 there were only 120 agents in the field but eighty-eight administrators in the national and regional bureaucracy. Since then, the headquarters/constituency ratio has deteriorated still further.[30]

The expansionist, bureaucratic tendencies of the party's central organization have become apparent in other ways. For instance, the project of collecting money for a new, purpose-made headquarters building took priority in the 1970s over local Labour enhancement. Shortly after the 1979 general election, the central organization moved from Transport House to elegant offices in Southwark. In order to relieve the party of the burden of this major project, financial responsibility was undertaken by a consortium of trade unions, which provided the money for the newly renovated building in addition to their usual affiliation fees and grants to the NEC. (The capital expenditure on the new head office incurred by the trade union consortium was reportedly taken from general union funds rather than from their political levy fund reserves, on the grounds that the project was a normal commercial venture and that the party's national executive committee would pay a fair rent for the building. It is fair to speculate that the motives of the unions involved in supporting the building project were not exclusively commercial.)[31]

The prospect of further increases in union affiliation fees and the healthy reserves of the trade union political levy funds (shown in table 58) allow Labour's central organization to look forward with some confidence to the future. While its income remains smaller than that of Conservative Central Office, the gap has narrowed greatly and, on present trends, is likely to narrow further in the 1980s.

[30] Finer, *Changing British Party System*, p. 102.
[31] Wintour, "Bankrupt and Bruised."

7
Liberal Party Finances (1945-1979)

Since before the Second World War, Liberals have complained about the poverty-stricken state of their party. Lack of money has consistently been cited as a "main obstacle to the rapid surge forward of the Liberal Party."[1] The Conservatives are nurtured by big business and Labour by the trade unions; the Liberals, it is argued, have no institutional support.[2] In matters of finance, as in so many other respects, the political system is loaded against them, and they are obliged to rely on small donations from rank-and-file supporters.[3] Finally, Liberals have often emphasized that, because there has been nothing to hide, their funds have been open—in contrast to the traditional secrecy of the Tories.

An examination of these claims reveals that they are only partly justified. The Liberals have, in matters of party finance, been neither as poor nor as pure as they have suggested. The party's income has in many years probably been double the amount shown in its published accounts. Publicly declared money has been supplemented by a confusion of unpublished or secret funds. The party has benefited from donations by wealthy individuals and from company

---

[1] Quoted in the Liberal party's memorandum to the Houghton Committee (1975) from a Liberal Party Organisation pamphlet of 1960, "This Is Your Party." Similar views are put forward in Jorgen Rasmussen, *Retrenchment and Revival: A Study of the Contemporary Liberal Party* (Tucson: University of Arizona Press, 1964), p. 29: "The one major obstacle preventing the more rapid surge forward of the Liberal Party is money." See also William Wallace, "The Liberal Revival: The Liberal Party in Britain, 1955-1966" (Ph.D. dissertation, Cornell University, 1968), p. 182. Wallace viewed lack of money as the Liberals' "first and largest organizational handicap."

[2] Philip Fothergill, "Political Party Funds. III—The Liberal View," *Parliamentary Affairs*, vol. 1 (1947-1948), pp. 51-52: "The Liberal Party is poor, only because it has no wealthy pressure group to finance it." Fothergill gives a typical Liberal attack on political financing by institutions: "The modern political machine backed by pressure finance is a thoroughly cynical political instrument. . . . It is important for the health of democracy that this problem should be tackled."

[3] Ibid.

179

contributions to a greater extent that its leaders have cared to reveal.[4] Nevertheless it would be wrong to understate the financial difficulties with which the Liberals have been confronted. These stem from a combination of three disadvantages: inability to attract a solid, active following of members in the constituencies, lack of reliable (as opposed to intermittent) support from institutional sources, and— probably most important—the Liberals' failure to make any lasting electoral impact. Liberal difficulties in raising money seem, in general, to have been the consequence and not the cause of political failure.

The mood of political enthusiasm that followed the Second World War enabled the Liberals to make considerable, if temporary, strides toward a popular pattern of fund raising. An appeals committee was set up and a major financial campaign, the Foundation Fund, was launched in 1946. It was to be the largest appeal since the Million Fund of 1925.[5] A particularly encouraging aspect of fund-raising efforts between 1945 and 1950 was that, in William Wallace's words, they succeeded "in widening radically the party's pool of subscribers."[6] Largely because of the Foundation Fund, 475 Liberal candidates were put forward in the general election of 1950.

The result of the 1950 campaign was a Liberal disaster. No fewer than 319 Liberal candidates obtained less than 12.5 percent of the votes cast in their constituencies and suffered the humiliation of losing their £150 deposits.[7] The advent of a majority Labour ministry in 1945 had focused politics on the two-party battle between Labour and Conservative. The Liberals, even more than before, were seen as irrelevant.

The 1950 result demoralized the party.[8] In the elections of 1951 and 1955, barely a hundred constituencies put forward a Liberal

---

[4] As Wallace comments, "ideological commitment to widespread individual participation led the Party Treasurers on occasions to underplay the importance of the large subscribers" ("Liberal Revival," p. 195).

[5] Liberal News, March 18, 1949, quoted in Rasmussen, Retrenchment and Revival, p. 15.

[6] Wallace, "Liberal Revival," p. 185.

[7] The Liberals had fortunately paid £5,000 to Lloyds' for an insurance policy against the loss of deposits. Lloyds' undertook to pay for all lost deposits over those incurred in 50 constituencies and up to 250 (Rasmussen, Retrenchment and Revival, p. 16).

[8] "The collapse of party morale and organization which followed the 1950 election brought down with it much of the fund-raising structure which [the appeals committee responsible for the Foundation Fund] had erected" (Wallace, "Liberal Revival," p. 185).

candidate. Local membership dropped by 1953 to an all-time low.[9] The Liberal disintegration ruined all hopes of raising money from small subscriptions. Wallace reports that "the party was most heavily dependent in the early fifties upon the continued support of relatively small groups of large subscribers."[10]

In 1960–1966, the Liberals enjoyed a spectacular but short-lived political revival. It was caused mainly by public discontent against the Conservatives, who had been in office for a decade. As the popularity of the Tories declined, Liberal performance in local government and by-elections improved. In March 1962 the Liberal candidate won a sensational victory in the by-election at Orpington, a suburban Tory stronghold. This success had an electric effect on Liberal organization and finance. While there seemed to be a prospect of a major Liberal breakthrough, subscriptions and donations—often unsolicited—flooded into the local Liberal associations and the central party.[11] After the disappointing Liberal performance in the 1966 general election, the enthusiasm flagged, and the payments stopped growing. By 1969 the central organization, which had been extravagantly expanded, faced a major financial crisis and was bailed out by five "exceptionally large" gifts.[12]

There was a similar financial pattern during the second Liberal upsurge, which occurred between 1972 and 1975 and was even more meteoric. As before, the Liberal breakthrough was the reaction to an unpopular Conservative government. Once again political success led to financial success and, as in the 1960s, political decline produced a corresponding financial decline. By the late 1970s, the Liberals had still made only limited progress toward the goal put forward in the 1920s of raising a sufficient amount in small subscriptions to provide a steady source of income and to remove the party's dependence on a circle of wealthy benefactors.

This chapter analyzes the main patterns of Liberal expenditure and sources of income. It begins with a description of the party's accounting procedures. This is necessary to show why the published accounts are incomplete and potentially misleading.

[9] Ibid., p. 268.

[10] Ibid., p. 185.

[11] "Orpington brought in a flood which doubled the party's subscription rate for a period . . . every turn of the party's fortunes affected its subscription rate" (ibid., p. 194).

[12] Sir Frank Medlicott, "Finance Report: The Challenges Ahead," *Liberal News*, July 9, 1970.

Why the Published Liberal Party Accounts Are
Potentially Misleading

It has been a longstanding Liberal claim that the party's accounts have been available for public inspection. The decision to open the books was reportedly taken in the 1920s by the official (that is, anti–Lloyd George) Liberals as a reaction against the scandals surrounding the Lloyd George Fund. Ramsay Muir (a prominent political scientist and a leading Liberal official) wrote in a textbook published in 1930 that the headquarters organization of the Liberals "since 1924 has been democratically controlled, and is required to give periodical accounts of the way in which money is spent. It is a curious fact that the Liberal party, in these years, has been the only political party which has ever made its finances openly and publicly known." [13]

A similar statement was forcefully made after the Second World War by the chairman of the executive of the Liberal Party Organisation (LPO). The Liberals, he wrote, had "nothing to lose by publicity." He called for "the compulsory publication in detail of political accounts. Publicity is an antiseptic. Only by means of publicity can the grosser forms of patronage and endowment be stamped out." [14] In December 1949, when the House of Commons debated a motion calling for the publication of central party funds, the Liberal spokesman, Frank Byers (later Lord Byers), asserted:

> The fact that we in the Liberal Party have published our accounts for a considerable number of years—over 25— makes us a good deal holier than the Conservative Party. . . . The electorate has the right to know which vested interests are behind a political party.[15]

Byers said that the Liberals had given both a list of donors and a statement of accounts, "with this exception . . . that where a man or woman has come to us and said 'Will you please keep my gift anonymous,' we have definitely respected that anonymity." Byers added, however, that if a gift was a very large one, the party would "hesitate to keep it anonymous." [16] He concluded:

[13] Ramsay Muir, *How Britain Is Governed* (London: Constable, 1930), p. 136. Muir's statement is, of course, incorrect: the Labour party accounts had been published since 1900.

[14] Fothergill, "Political Party Funds," p. 52.

[15] House of Commons Debates, 5th series, 470, col. 3004ff., December 15, 1949.

[16] It is current LPO policy to keep the identity of all donors confidential (interview with secretary general, LPO).

The Liberal Party publish annually, as part of the report to the assembly meeting every year, their statement of receipts and payments and details of all expenditures by their organisation on publications, publicity, committees, appeals and so on . . . and those accounts are audited by Deloitte, Griffiths and Co., chartered accountants. Why cannot the Conservative Party do that? Why not? Are they suggesting that those accounts are not accurate, because if they do, it is a direct slur on the auditors.

Despite such statements, the annually published Liberal accounts do not give a complete picture and give the impression that the party is considerably poorer and more dependent on small subscriptions and donations than is actually the case.

Since the reorganization of 1936, the published accounts have been those of the Liberal Party Organisation (LPO). The LPO replaced the old National Liberal Federation. Commentators have all too often been misled by the title Liberal Party Organisation into supposing that the body bearing that name constitutes the entire central organization of the party. In fact, it is only one part of the national Liberal machine among several others. Moreover, the activities of the LPO itself have not been fully included in the published balance sheets. The difficulty in interpreting the accounts is compounded by frequent changes in accounting conventions. These mean that certain activities (such as those of the regional federations) are included for some years and largely omitted for others.

The basic difficulty arises because the Liberal party has a far more fragmented central structure than the two main parties, and it is incorrect to cite the accounts of the unit termed the LPO as a direct indication of the party's total central resources. Yet it is only the routine finances of this one section of the Liberal party that have been readily made available to the public in the published annual reports.

The major categories of income and expenditure that have usually been left out of the LPO accounts are listed below:

1. LPO spending at national and regional levels on general election campaigns has usually been excluded. The published statistics are of the income and expenditure account, which includes only routine spending. Election accounts for the campaigns of 1974 have been issued, but there do not appear to have been any published LPO election accounts for 1950, 1951, 1955, 1959, 1964, 1966, or 1970.

2. The LPO is responsible for England alone. There are sep-

arate organizations for Scotland and Wales. Perhaps 95 percent of the LPO's services do not cover Scotland, and perhaps 80 percent do not cover Wales.[17] These omissions are significant, as these have traditionally been areas of Liberal strength.

3. The accounts have usually included little of the income or expenditure of the party's regional federations. (The independence of the regional federations is itself an expression of the Liberal belief in governmental decentralization.)

4. Several "recognized units" of the national extraparliamentary organization are independently financed, for instance, the Women's Liberal Federation, the Association of Liberal Trade Unionists, and the Young Liberals. Grants to these bodies out of LPO funds are, however, included in the LPO accounts.[18]

5. The accounts of some departments of the LPO headquarters have at some periods been excluded from the LPO accounts. According to Michael Steed, the LPO accounts in the 1950s and 1960s excluded the costs of the departments of the party headquarters dealing with candidates and research. (These were a responsibility of the Liberal Central Association, which is described below.)[19] More recently, the LPO accounts have excluded the Liberal publication

---

[17] Michael Steed, "Report on the Liberal Party of the United Kingdom of Great Britain and Northern Ireland," paper presented to the colloquium on party professionals (Paris: Association Française de Science Politique, 1977), p. 2.

[18] Some of the exclusions from LPO accounts are noted in the LPO annual report of 1980:

Scope of the Accounts
These accounts deal solely with those activities of the Finance and Administration Board of the Liberal Party as relate to the running of the Liberal Party Organisation Headquarters and therefore do not include the assets, liabilities, expenditure and revenue of:—
  a) the following Constitutional Organs of the Liberal Party and other activities of the Finance and Administration Board:
  Constituency Associations
  Regional Parties
  The Centenary Fund
  Liberal Central Association
  The Liberal Publication Department
  The Liberal News
  The By-Election Guarantee Fund
  The Pooled Fares Scheme
  b) various other bodies recognised by the Constitution as revised in 1978 (Section A paragraph 3) and 1978.

A similar note attached to the LPO annual report of 1975 includes among the funds excluded in the financial year 1974 "The Direct Aid Fund (now named the Marginal Seats Fund)."

[19] Steed, "Report on the Liberal Party," p. 2.

184

department (LPD). Another independent unit of the national organization is the Association of Liberal Councillors.

6. The published accounts omit a number of special funds. In 1976, these included the centenary fund, the by-election guarantee fund, and the pooled fares scheme.

7. The Liberal Central Association (LCA) has continued to operate independently of the LPO, and its finances were until 1979 a strict secret. Its origins are mentioned in chapters 1 and 2. During the modern era, it was especially important in the Second World War. According to R. M. Sommer, "since the L.P.O. was almost inert during these years, there was in effect, an aggrandisement of the Liberal Central Association, which was the only portion of the Party organization in full operation." [20] By the 1950s, the LCA had, according to Steed, "come to be a fund controlled by the Chief Whip, through which limited servicing of the Liberal MPs was performed, but it also had financial and organisational responsibilities for two departments in the party headquarters—candidates and research." [21] By the early 1970s, the importance of the LCA had apparently declined. It increased again after 1975, when it obtained responsibility for administering the Liberal share of the newly introduced state grant to opposition parties in the House of Commons.

8. The party leader and the Liberal parliamentary party (that is, the Liberal MPs) have sometimes collected funds of their own. These have been used to support the leader's office in the House of Commons and to enable him to make grants for extraparliamentary purposes free from LPO control or knowledge. The right of the leader and of the Liberal MPs to raise independent funds was specifically stated when the LPO was set up in 1936. In the words of the *Liberal Magazine* of May 1936:

> The Reorganization Committee [which recommended the setting up of the LPO] have quite rightly made hardly any reference to the Parliamentary Party. Indeed it does not come within their subject . . . the Leader of the Party must have his own office and organization.[22]

Recent examples of important contributions given directly to the party leader and the parliamentary party were the £55,000 allocated in April 1977 and a further £45,000 allocated between September

[20] R. M. Sommer, "The Organization of the Liberal Party, 1936-1960," (Ph.D. thesis, London School of Economics, 1962), pp. 67-68.
[21] Steed, "Report on the Liberal Party," p. 2.
[22] *Liberal Magazine*, May 1936, p. 131.

1978 and May 1979 by the Joseph Rowntree Social Service Trust Ltd. The expenditures made out of these grants were not included in the LPO accounts, and it appears that senior LPO officials were not informed about the existence of the grants.

9. For many years during the postwar period, leading Liberals have collected funds, usually secret, earmarked for particular purposes. The accounts of some of these funds have been concealed even from the LPO treasurer. According to Wallace, tied contributions in the late 1950s and early 1960s "included the financing of a research project by Harry Ferguson, the inventor and tractor manufacturer, in 1958; in 1963 Rudolph Detsinyi, the Treasurer of the Liberal International, paid for an advertising campaign in certain newspapers." [23]

The most important "tied fund" in recent years appears to have been the "special fund for winnable seats" (sometimes called the Direct Aid Committee or marginal seats fund). According to an official statement by the Liberal party president in 1979, "The Direct Aid Committee operated successfully for many years. . . . Its accounts were not published." [24] The main object of the Direct Aid Committee was to raise money in secret to be given to constituencies already held by Liberal MPs or those considered most promising. A further aim was to raise funds for national election publicity. One of the most active fund raisers was Jeremy Thorpe, who was involved from the early 1960s, that is, before he became party treasurer (1966–1967) and party leader (1967–1976).

It should be noted that, among these types of income and expenditure that are not included in the LPO accounts, some are published elsewhere (for example the accounts of some "recognized units"), though the collection of the statistics presents insuperable practical problems. Other accounts (such as those of the LCA and the Direct Aid Committee) have deliberately been kept secret.

Most of the expenditures omitted from the LPO accounts are included in the central accounts of the Conservative and Labour parties given in chapters 5 and 6. An uncritical comparison between the published accounts of the three parties gives the impression that the Liberal disadvantage is considerably greater than is actually the case. Since the Liberals have projected an image of David facing the twin Goliaths of Conservative and Labour, it has been convenient

[23] Wallace, "Liberal Revival," p. 189.

[24] Statement by Michael Steed, chairman of Liberal Party's Committee of Enquiry—June 26, 1979 (LPO press release).

for them to understate their resources by omitting to publicize the money that has been separated from the LPO accounts. The Liberal case for state subsidies presented to the Houghton Committee in 1975 must have been helped by the artificially low figures of Liberal central income and spending that were presented to the committee.

There has, however, been a more important internal reason for the collection of special, secret funds. They have been important weapons in the personal power struggles and factional fights that have typified Liberal politics. The control of funds has been a convenient way for particular MPs and their backers to bypass the democratic structure of the LPO. For instance, the fact that a fund was raised over a long period to aid a small number of winnable seats ensured that the money could be directed specifically to the constituencies chosen by those in charge of the fund. Had the same money been channeled through the ordinary LPO funds, they would (in the judgment of those collecting the special fund) have been squandered on the routine expenses of the headquarters or on subsidizing candidates in unwinnable constituencies.

Another instance of a contribution that was intentionally steered away from the LPO for internal party purposes was the substantial donation given by the Rowntree Trust in 1977. The trust's chief executive, Lord Chitnis, was a former senior official of LPO who had resigned in 1969 in protest against the extravagance of the headquarters bureaucracy. It is therefore not surprising that the trust's money was intentionally made available not to the LPO but to the party leader and the Liberal parliamentary party. The contribution, coinciding as it did with the controversial Lib-Lab pact, must have strengthened the hand of the party leader, David Steel, with his fellow Liberal MPs and helped him to explain his strategy to the party outside the House of Commons.

The existence of secret funds has repeatedly led to bitterness, controversy, and rumors of corruption. The existence of such funds was an important factor in Sir Frank Medlicott's resignation as LPO treasurer in 1972. Medlicott's private papers, which were made available for this study, show the extreme acrimony which came to characterize his dealings with Thorpe and Byers. In one report, Medlicott referred to his "constant tug of war" [25] with Thorpe over the allocation of funds. He felt that Thorpe placed as much money as possible in secret accounts so that it would be out of the control of the LPO's democratically chosen finance and administration board (FAB). In

[25] *Strictly Confidential* to the Members of the FAB [finance and administration board] only—subject: *Financial Control*," memorandum, September 8, 1970.

particular, the finances of the Direct Aid Committee were concealed from the LPO treasurer and from the FAB. Another source of complaint was "the unwillingness of the parliamentary party to accept any kind of financial supervision from L.P.O."[26]

The alleged abuse of funds donated secretly to Thorpe during 1974 received extended publicity before Thorpe's trial in 1979 for conspiracy to murder. It was suggested that Thorpe had used two donations of £10,000 each to pay the hit man allegedly hired to kill the male model, Norman Scott. Thorpe was acquitted.[27] This was probably the first time it had been suggested that a large contribution for Liberal party purposes had been used to finance a murder plot. The Liberal controversies of the 1970s about the use of personally controlled political funds are in many ways reminiscent of, and in every way as acrimonious as, the quarrels over the Lloyd George Fund before the Second World War.

Besides leading to friction, the division of fund-raising responsibilities between so many separate, competing bodies has arguably meant the inefficient use of party resources. In Medlicott's words, written in 1970, "The present division of financial responsibility between the Party Organisation, the Parliamentary Party and the Liberal Central Association is a source of weakness and confusion, and should be ended."[28] There have been a number of attempts to unify the party's structure of financial control. They have not wholly succeeded. In 1974, after "considerable private pressure within the Party," Thorpe agreed to the LPO treasurer's becoming one of the signatories to the "direct aid" account (though its income and expenditure were still not made public). However, these changes "were not applied to a second Direct Aid Committee [sic] at Lloyd's Bank, Finsbury Circus, of whose operation Mr. Thorpe was in exclusive charge."[29] The existence of this additional account, which contained donations of £49,000 from Jack Haywood and other smaller sums, only came to light amid the investigations preceding Thorpe's trial. After David Steel's election as party leader in 1976, further reforms were introduced to ensure that no special funds remained concealed

---

[26] Ibid.

[27] For accounts of the Norman Scott affair and attendant speculations about Liberal party finances, see Barrie Penrose and Roger Courtiour, *The Pencourt File* (London: Secker and Warburg, 1978); Peter Chippindale and David Leigh, *The Thorpe Committal: The Full Story of the Minehead Proceedings* (London: Arrow Books, 1979); and Lewis Chester, Magnus Linklater, and David May, *Jeremy Thorpe: A Secret Life* (London: Fontana, 1979).

[28] Medlicott, "Finance Report."

[29] Statement by Michael Steed—June 26, 1979 (LPO press release).

from the LPO treasurer. It is unclear whether these have been followed, because sizable funds (such as the Rowntree grants mentioned above) remain out of the control of the LPO treasurer and have not been included in the annual LPO accounts.[30]

There has been a strong tendency within Liberal circles to blame Thorpe for the internal conflicts over party funds. In my opinion, this criticism is somewhat unfair. While Thorpe was certainly unwilling to hand over the money he collected for use at the discretion of the party organization, he is by no means the only party leader to have adopted this attitude. The tug of war between the LPO (representing the headquarters staff and the constituency parties) on the one hand and the leader and his parliamentary colleagues on the other hand has been a constant feature of Liberal politics for half a century.[31] The party leader has typically protected his freedom to use the money collected by him or on his behalf by concealing its existence from the constituency parties and from the LPO.

Central Liberal Finances, 1949–1979

Since no comprehensive central Liberal accounts exist, it is necessary to deal separately with those parts of the central organization for which there is information.

The income and expenditure account of the LPO. This account is summarized in table 47. The statistics exclude general election costs. The figures are not strictly comparable from year to year because of alterations in accounting procedures. The salary costs of the parliamentary party office and of the regional federations appear to be included during the 1960s and generally excluded for other years.[32]

[30] The existence of such a profusion of accounts has sometimes led to great internal confusion. In 1970, the £206,500 received from seven major donors went in and out of at least ten central and regional accounts. A special account, called the general fund, was established to hold some of the money received from these donations pending its allocation to other funds. It then went to the LPO's ordinary income and expenditure account, the LPO's general election fund, the special seats fund, the direct aid account, the party leader's fund, and so on (Medlicott Papers).

[31] The Committee on Party Reconstruction, which reported in 1946, stated that "uncertainty of control has been aggravated by the divided responsibility between the Whips' Office (Liberal Central Association) and the Liberal Party Organisation, for the selection and placing of candidates, the financing of their campaigns, and the supply of speakers" (*Coats Off for the Future* [London: Liberal Publication Department, 1946], p. 7, quoted in Rasmussen, *Retrenchment and Revival*, p. 55).

[32] LPO income 1936-1948 was as follows: 1936, £14,652; 1937, £12,546; 1938,

189

TABLE 47
Liberal Party Organisation Routine Income and Expenditure, 1949–1979
(in pounds)

	Income	Expenditure		Income	Expenditure
1949[a]	28,422	34,581	1965	66,137	92,161
1950[a]	15,566	17,219	1966	113,547	115,582
1951[a]	10,931	13,889	1967	90,611	130,311
1952	16,624	17,630	1968	95,752	118,165
1953	17,517	18,267	1969	114,130	102,383
1954	18,943	17,370	1970	213,630	96,699
1955	19,431	17,826	1971	75,059	82,691
1956	16,933	20,920	1972	72,050	86,371
1957	24,173	21,431	1973	125,190	97,126
1958	21,774	23,933	1974	87,074	119,241
1959	28,275	27,057	1975	100,698	106,176
1960	48,892	39,894	1976	81,322	111,296
1961	52,373	50,341	1977	129,670	105,002
1962	73,693	87,713	1978	169,271[b]	156,771[c]
1963	82,672	87,270	1979	299,101[b]	252,089[c]
1964	82,965	82,784			

Note: Income and expenditure for 1959-1969 include constituency affiliation fees and quotas, of which half was transferred to regional federations. For total LPO income net of these transfers, see table 50.

[a] Investment income excluded.

[b] Includes funds received from the European Liberal and Democratic Group.

[c] Includes the disbursement of a proportion of those funds (about £25,000 in 1978) to the regional, Scottish, Welsh, and Ulster Liberal parties.

Sources: LPO annual reports; statistics for 1949-1965 are derived from Wallace, "Liberal Revival," p. 190, and those for 1966-1976 have been prepared by John Curtice.

LPO general election funds. These funds, which are excluded from the routine accounts in table 47, have normally been unpublished. The LPO treasurer kindly authorized the release of accounts for elections before 1974 for the purposes of this study. As no records survived in the LPO's files or in those of the party's auditors, this authorization produced no new information.

£11,217; 1939, £10,560; 1940, £8,046; 1941, £7,328; 1942, £8,862; 1943, £9,719; 1944, £18,295; 1945, £12,453; 1946, £26,172; 1947, £23,442; 1948, £37,349 (derived from LPO annual reports by Sommer, "Organization of the Liberal Party").

LPO accounts for four recent campaigns are available—those for 1970 are in the Medlicott Papers, for February and October 1974 in the LPO's annual report for that year, and unaudited estimates for 1979 have kindly been provided by the LPO. In 1970 the LPO's general election spending was £34,234. This included £6,100 for Lord Beaumont's "Special Help Constituencies" scheme. LPO expenditure in February 1974 totaled £73,893 and, in October 1974, £127,817. For the 1979 campaign, LPO spending amounted to about £137,000.

These sums do not represent the party's overall central campaign spending. In 1970 and 1974, substantial amounts were spent in addition to the LPO general election fund from the direct aid account. The Medlicott Papers show that items totaling £90,500 were paid into this account in 1970 and that this was only part of its income.[33] It is uncertain how much was spent on "direct aid" to Liberal constituency campaigns in the 1970 election. If estimated direct aid expenditure and spending by regional federations are added to that of LPO, the central Liberal campaign probably cost a total of £70,000–100,000.

The Direct Aid Committee appears to have spent about £60,000 in the two elections of 1974. At least £49,000 was spent from a second direct aid account maintained by the party leader.[34] In total, central Liberal spending for the two 1974 campaigns was about £300,000.[35]

In the election of 1979, central spending consisted of LPO, £137,000; campaign expenditure out of the Rowntree grants to the party leader, about £50,000; and spending by regional federations,

[33] It is uncertain whether some of the amounts shown by Medlicott as having been paid into the direct aid account were subsequently transferred to other accounts. Medlicott, though LPO treasurer, did not have access to the direct aid accounts.

[34] No clear picture of flows of money in and out of the direct aid accounts has yet emerged. The figures in this paragraph are based on interviews with senior Liberals. The second direct aid account at Finsbury Circus probably contained about £20,000 in addition to Hayward's contributions totaling £49,000.

[35] This sum is mentioned in a letter from Thorpe to Hayward written on November 28, 1974. The letter was subsequently made public during the committal proceedings in 1978 at Minehead magistrates' court before Thorpe's trial. See Chippindale and Leigh, *Thorpe Committal*, p. 72.

Some information about central Liberal campaign funds in the 1960s is given in Wallace, "Liberal Revival," p. 189. The special fund for winnable seats (that is, the direct aid account) "is said to have raised about £40,000 between 1962 and 1966, mainly from large contributors." In addition, the party's general election appeals in 1964 and 1966 "reached about £25,000 each, mostly raised from rallies" (p. 201).

TABLE 48
LIBERAL CENTRAL ASSOCIATION ACCOUNTS, 1972–1978
(in pounds)

| | Income | | Expenditure | |
	Total	Received from public funds[a]	Total	Spent on staff salaries and fees to research staff
1972	7,133	—	6,975	5,567
1973	8,840	—	12,927	11,103
1974	7,718	—	9,234	7,664
1975	35,493	33,234	39,517	33,206
1976	34,877	33,234	33,234	29,588
1977	34,197	33,234	33,536	25,961
1978	38,107	36,558	36,501	29,812

[a] State grant to opposition parties in the House of Commons for services within the Palace of Westminster.
SOURCE: Finance officer of the LPO.

recognized units, and Scottish and Welsh Liberals, approximately £15,000–25,000. This makes a total of slightly over £200,000.[36]

Liberal Central Association. This account has traditionally been kept strictly secret. It has usually been under the control of the party's chief whip in the House of Commons and has provided money for the parliamentary party and for candidates for the House of Commons. Authorization was kindly given for me to receive past LCA accounts for publication in this study. Like the LPO's general election fund accounts, LCA balance sheets could not be located, except for years since 1972. These figures are given in table 48. The totals do not tally with information given by the Rowntree Trust (table 51). It

[36] According to the secretary general of the LPO, expenditure was lower than the £213,000 shown in table 53. In his estimate, spending by regional federations and by the Scottish and Welsh organizations totaled an estimated £12,300, not £25,000 as estimated for the purposes of table 53. He suggests that campaign (as distinct from routine) spending out of the Rowntree grants amounted to only £18,000, not £50,000 as estimated for table 53. This large discrepancy stems from different definitions of what constituted "precampaign" expenditures. See Michael Pinto-Duschinsky, "Financing the British General Election of 1979," in Howard R. Penniman, ed., *Britain at the Polls, 1979: A Study of the General Election* (Washington, D.C.: American Enterprise Institute, 1981), p. 224. The total of £137,000 spent by the LPO is an unaudited estimate and differs slightly from the total in the subsequently published LPO annual report.

would appear that certain grants allocated by the trust to the LCA have not been included in the LCA accounts.

The party leader and the parliamentary party. Since the introduction in 1975 of the scheme of state aid to opposition parties in the House of Commons, the leader and the Liberal MPs have relied largely on this money, administered by the LCA, to finance their secretarial and research staff. In the early 1970s, the Rowntree Trust provided grants for "political fellowships" to enable opposition parties and shadow ministers to employ larger staffs. The Labour and Liberal parties were the main beneficiaries of this scheme, which was intended to encourage the introduction of state finance for party organizations in Parliament.

Liberal MPs and, in particular, the party leader have supplemented this money by raising further special funds. These have generally been used for their office and research expenses, for special projects (such as the campaign in the 1970s for the introduction of proportional representation), for subsidies to their constituency organizations, and for aid to Liberal parliamentary candidates. In the 1960s and early 1970s, the direct aid fund met some of these needs. In the late 1970s, the Rowntree Trust provided substantial sums for Steel and the Liberal parliamentary party. As mentioned, these grants totaled £100,000 between 1977 and the general election of May 1979.

Regional federations, Scottish and Welsh organizations, and recognized units. In order to assess total central Liberal resources, it is necessary to estimate the funds of these bodies, as the accounts of the equivalent Conservative and Labour organizations are largely or wholly included in their central accounts. The task of collecting these additional Liberal accounts presents formidable practical problems, because the LPO headquarters does not collect them and it is, in any case, uncertain whether they are public or private.

The LPO's routine and general election accounts include the sums spent by the headquarters on supporting regional federations and "recognized units." It is unclear how large a proportion of the income of these units comes from the LPO, though it is evident that this varies largely from year to year.

In the 1970s the party's organization at the regional level was patchy. Several regional federations had no paid staff, and this greatly reduced their running costs. Nevertheless, the ratio of staff employed at headquarters to staff employed at the regional level seems to have been only slightly smaller in the Liberal party than in the Conservative and Labour organizations.

TABLE 49
LIBERAL PARTY CENTRAL STAFF, JULY 1979

On LPO payroll	17
LPO staff independently financed	3
Employed by Liberal leader and MPs	8 (including 2 part-time)
Employed by Scottish and Welsh parties and by regional federations	18 (including 8 part-time)
Total	46 (including 10 part-time)

SOURCES: Secretary general of the LPO and chief whip's secretary.

The number of staff on the LPO payroll compared with the numbers employed by the Liberal parliamentary party and by the regional federations in July 1979 is shown in table 49. This table is included because, in the absence of accounts for the party's regional organizations and recognized units, it gives an impression of the proportion of the party's central staff whose salaries and costs are not included in the published LPO accounts.

Table 49 indicates that the LPO payroll in 1979 included only seventeen of the estimated total of forty-six employees of the central party. This somewhat underestimates the LPO's role because (1) limited grants were given by the LPO to the regional federations, and (2) some of the employees of the parliamentary party and of the regional federations were part-timers. As a broad approximation, it would seem that the LPO accounts included about half of the party's routine central expenditure.

In calculating Liberal central funds in the 1970s, it is reasonable as a rule of thumb to say that they have been double the sums shown in the LPO income and expenditure account in nonelection years and about treble in general election years.

The following comparisons between central Liberal finances and those of the two main parties emerge. (1) As far as routine finances are concerned, the Liberals in the 1970s raised and spent approximately one-tenth to one-eighth as much as the Conservatives and about one-fifth as much as Labour. (2) In recent elections, the ratio of Liberal:Labour:Conservative central spending seems to have been 1:6:8 in 1970, 1:3:5 in the elections of 1974, and 1:7:12 in 1979.

Sources of Central Income. A major feature of Liberal fund raising is that contributions by a "few very wealthy individuals"[37] have

[37] Liberal party memorandum to the Houghton Committee.

194

continued to be considerably more important than in the two main parties. Some of these rich backers have themselves been Liberal politicians or former politicians. In other cases, appeals on sentimental grounds have been made to descendants of leading Liberal figures. Occasionally it has been rumored that the prospect of a peerage has encouraged a generous donation.

According to Sommer, the Liberal party in the late 1930s was still dependent on its rich subscribers. Liberal MPs such as Harcourt Johnstone "for many years contributed a great percentage of the money which kept the organization alive."[38] Wallace stresses the important role of large contributions during the period 1955–1966. Among the postwar benefactors whom he mentions are Lord Sherwood, Graham White, Lawrence Cadbury, and James de Rothschild.[39]

The vital role of a few large contributors emerges in an article by Medlicott in *Liberal News* shortly after the 1970 election in which he describes the emergency fund-raising exercise carried out between autumn 1969 and summer 1970.[40] The large amounts raised were sufficient to wipe out a deficit of £93,000 accumulated by the LPO in the 1960s, to fight the 1970 election, to finance the routine activities of the LPO, and to leave a reserve of "at least £50,000." Some of the money had been collected by various appeals for small and medium-sized donations: a £25-a-head fund-raising effort by the party leader; an Operation Overdraft appeal and a £1-a-head appeal by the LPO executive; and a special approach by the party's appeals organizer and his team to "those people who might be prepared to donate smaller sums." In addition, there had been three schemes to raise larger sums: (1) "A number of distinguished Liberals responded generously to a private appeal." (2) Some Liberals who had previously lent sums to the party converted their loans into gifts. "Lord Beaumont was prominent in this group, with a gift of £10,000." (3) A group of senior party figures approached "people and companies who might be prepared to contribute large sums to Party funds."

> Mr. Jeremy Thorpe [party leader], Lord Beaumont [former treasurer, chairman, and head of the LPO], Lord Byers [Liberal leader in the House of Lords], and Mr Peter Bessell

[38] Sommer, "Organization of the Liberal Party," pp. 94-95. The Committee on Party Reconstruction reported in 1946 that Liberal funds had for the previous fifteen years been collected mainly by the whips' office from "a comparatively limited circle of generous subscribers" (*Coats Off for the Future*, p. 38, quoted in Rasmussen, *Retrenchment and Revival*, p. 14).

[39] Wallace, "Liberal Revival," p. 186.

[40] Medlicott, "Finance Report."

[a Liberal MP] initiated discussions which resulted in five donations of exceptional size being received shortly before the election.[41]

The most important of these gifts was £150,000 given by Hayward. This was about three times as much as the amount raised by all the appeals for small and medium-sized contributions. The other major donors were Simon Mackay (£25,000), Geoffrey Edwards (£15,000), and, as mentioned, Beaumont (£10,000).[42] (As detailed later, large sums were also given to the Liberal party in 1970 as in other years by the Joseph Rowntree Social Service Trust Ltd.) Medlicott viewed the party's reliance on its wealthy supporters with misgiving, pointing out that "85% OF ALL MONEY THAT HAS BEEN SUBSCRIBED DURING THE LAST EIGHT MONTHS HAS BEEN GIVEN BY LESS THAN 25 PEOPLE."[43] The LPO's finance and administration board, in its report and accounts for 1971, reiterated this worry:

> It would . . . be a profound error to think that the figures for 1970 give any cause for complacency. They do, in fact, constitute both a warning and a challenge: a warning that unless the Party can maintain an adequate level of income from the grass roots it may in future years face yet another financial crisis.

In 1975 the Liberal party, in its memorandum to the Houghton Committee, claimed that such a crisis had again arisen and gave as a major cause the fact that some of its wealthy contributors had "been impoverished by the collapse of share values and are inhibited by changes in taxation from being as generous as usual."

There have been constant efforts since the war to encourage the flow of small subscriptions to the various organs of the central party. Besides the rallies and fetes arranged by regional federations and by "recognized units" of the party such as the Women's Liberal Federation, the LPO has collected money from ordinary Liberal supporters in two ways: by direct appeals to individual Liberal activists and through affiliation fees and quotas from constituency associations. Known Liberals have been regularly solicited for annual subscriptions to the LPO and, before elections, for contributions to the general election appeal. The financial appeal during the LPO's annual assembly is also an important event in the fund-raising calendar. Rose

[41] Ibid.

[42] Medlicott Papers. Other contributors in 1970 included Mrs. James de Rothschild, £3,000; Eric Lippman, £2,500; and Percy Bibby, £1,000.

[43] Medlicott, "Finance Report."

196

estimated in the 1960s that about half the totals raised in subscriptions and by assembly appeals came from small sums and the other half from "a hundred or so wealthy Liberal sympathizers."[44]

Since the late 1950s, these direct contributions by individual Liberals have been supplemented (and to some extent replaced) by payments to the center from constituency associations. It must be assumed that much of this constituency money is raised from small subscriptions and local fund-raising events. Until 1958 the affiliation fees paid by local associations were small—about £2,000 a year to the LPO and the regional federations. In 1958 a scheme of constituency quotas and assessments was introduced, similar to that of the Conservatives. The view was taken that "the bulk of party funds must ultimately come from the constituencies."[45] The quota scheme was a moderate success. According to Wallace, by 1966 the scheme "had not fulfilled the hopes of its promotors nor had it yet proved capable of providing the bulk of the party's central funds; but the total raised was nevertheless substantial by Liberal standards." Under the rules of the scheme, the LPO passed on half the amounts received from the constituencies to the regional federations. In 1969 the quota scheme was abandoned, and in its place a new system was introduced. Constituencies were to pay affiliation fees to the LPO, which would retain all the money; they were also to contribute separately to regional federations. The annual sums raised by the LPO are given in table 50. A feature of the 1970s has been the steady growth of constituency payments to the LPO headquarters.

Company contributions have been another significant source of central Liberal income. They have benefited the party to a greater extent than has been acknowledged. The party's main corporate contributor has been the Rowntree Social Service Trust Ltd. This was originally established before the First World War out of the profits of the Rowntree family's chocolate factories in York. Unlike several charitable trusts set up by the Rowntrees, the Social Service Trust was formed as a limited company. This meant sacrificing the tax reliefs of a charity but permitted political contributions. The trust has given donations to politicians of all the main parties and to a number of fringe parties and pressure groups as well. The lion's share has gone to Liberal causes. The trust has maintained a special subcommittee to allocate its contributions to various Liberal party organizations. In the 1970s the subcommittee pursued definite policies,

[44] Richard Rose, *Influencing Voters: A Study of Campaign Rationality* (London: Faber, 1967), p. 269.
[45] *Liberal News*, November 6, 1958, quoted in Wallace, "Liberal Revival," p. 198.

197

TABLE 50

QUOTAS AND AFFILIATION FEES PAID BY CONSTITUENCY ASSOCIATIONS TO THE LIBERAL PARTY ORGANISATION, 1959–1979
(in pounds)

	Constituency Quotas and Affiliation Fees	Constituency Payments Retained by LPO[a]	Total LPO Income[b]	Col. 2 as % of Col. 3
	(LPO and regions)			
1959	9,404	4,702	23,573	20
1960	11,000	5,500	43,392	13
1961	10,998	5,499	47,874	11
1962	16,713	8,357	65,336	13
1963	18,139	9,070	73,602	12
1964	15,153	7,577	75,388	10
1965	22,469	11,235	54,902	20
1966	25,214	12,607	100,940	12
1967	24,442	12,221	78,390	16
1968	22,059	11,030	84,722	13
1969	16,665	8,333	105,797	8
	(LPO only)			
1970	7,367	7,367	213,630	3
1971	7,957	7,957	75,059	11
1972	7,441	7,441	72,050	10
1973	9,222	9,222	125,190	7
1974	13,896	13,896	87,074	16
1975	19,662	19,662	100,698	20
1976	29,984	29,984	81,322	37
1977	28,001	28,001	129,670	22
1978	39,759	39,759	169,271	23
1979	39,120	39,120	299,101	13

[a] Half of col. 1.

[b] Net of income received through constituency quotas and affiliations and transferred to regional federations.

SOURCE: Liberal Party Organisation annual reports.

and in some respects it acted, in effect, as an alternative party headquarters. The trust generally criticized the role of the LPO headquarters and, as mentioned later, directed its gifts away from it. At the same time, the trust gave help to the Liberal publication depart-

TABLE 51

GRANTS TO THE LIBERAL PARTY BY THE JOSEPH ROWNTREE SOCIAL SERVICE
TRUST LTD., BY RECEIVING BODY, 1969–1978

(in pounds)

	Liberal Party Organisation			Liberal Central Associa- tion[b]	Grants Distributed by the Trust		Total
	General purposes	Election	Other[a]		General grants[c]	Election grants	
1969	17,163				2,347		19,510
1970	27,750	6,000[d]			3,592	1,500	38,842
1971	9,250		125	1,829	4,059		15,263
1972	20,000		4,250	5,854	12,747		42,851
1973	25,000		4,250	11,531	17,022		57,803
1974	7,500	34,650	125	18,488	21,897	9,250[e]	91,910
1975	2,500		10,945	6,550	18,133		38,128
1976	1,000		4,250	3,500	19,089		27,839
1977				415	52,676		53,091
1978					39,716	6,495	46,211
Total, 1969– 1978	110,163	40,650	23,945	48,167	191,278	17,245	431,448

[a] Routine grants to LPO for specific purposes.

[b] Most of the grants to the LCA were for the trust's political fellowship scheme.

[c] Includes grants to the party leader and parliamentary party, to regional federations, and to city and constituency parties. Some were devoted to campaign purposes, although they were not specifically earmarked for campaign use.

[d] The Medlicott Papers show that only £3,000 went to the LPO's general election fund and the remaining £3,000 to the direct aid account.

[e] Paid to the direct aid account.

SOURCE: The Joseph Rowntree Social Service Trust Ltd.

ment (LPD) and the Association of Liberal Councillors. Influential trustees appear to have favored the establishment of a "center party," and it was probably for this reason that the trust gave financial backing to the Lib-Lab pact of 1977. Table 51 lists the trust's contributions to the Liberal party between 1969 and 1978 and the organizations to which they have been given. These payments to the Liberals appear to have been at least as great as those of any single company to the Tories.

Besides the Rowntree Trust, the Liberals have sometimes tapped other business funds. Party leaders made an exceptionally concentrated and successful effort to raise contributions from companies after the encouraging Liberal performance in the general election of February 1974. Among large firms that gave donations were General Electric, Bowater, Cadbury Schweppes, Marks and Spencer, and Inchcape. According to press reports, Liberals have also attempted to obtain contributions from small companies, but with relatively little success.

Finally, as mentioned, a useful source of income since 1975 has been the state grant to opposition parties in the House of Commons. This grant, which amounted in 1975–1977 to £33,234 and in 1978 to £36,558, went to the Liberal Central Association and was not, therefore, included in the LPO accounts.

An impressionistic assessment suggests that, apart from the state grant, central Liberal income between the late 1960s and the late 1970s was obtained as follows: about 35 percent in constituency quotas and other sums collected in small amounts from rank-and-file supporters; about 35 percent in medium and large donations from individuals; and about 30 percent from companies. These percentages include all central and regional organs of the party.

Central Expenditure. It is not possible to be as precise about the main types of central Liberal spending as about those of the two main parties (tables 30 and 40). It appears that the Liberal pattern of *routine expenditure* is broadly similar to those of the Conservative and Labour parties. The main costs are maintaining the services of the party headquarters, which is situated within the National Liberal Club at Whitehall Place, and the regional federations and Scottish and Welsh party organizations. The percentage of total central funds spent on maintaining these regional offices seems to be comparable to that in the two major parties, though the extent of regional Liberal organization has fluctuated in recent years.

A special feature of Liberal central spending is the relatively high proportion devoted to the parliamentary staff. The functions of research and publicity, which are entrusted by the Conservative and Labour parties to departments of their central organizations, are largely carried out within the Liberal party by staff employed directly by the party leader and the chief whip. The duplication of functions by the LPO headquarters and by parliamentary staffs has given rise to the tensions described earlier in the chapter.

Central expenditure on general election campaigns. The main characteristics of Liberal central campaigns are the relatively large

TABLE 52

ESTIMATED CENTRAL LIBERAL SPENDING IN THE GENERAL ELECTION OF OCTOBER 1974
(in pounds)

Grants to constituencies	49,000
General administration	28,000
Leader's press conferences	19,000
Advertising	17,000

NOTE: There are several conflicting estimates of total central Liberal campaign spending. The Liberal party's evidence to the Houghton Committee gave the total as £106,000, the LPO's annual report as £127,817, and the Nuffield election study as £115,000. All these are undoubtedly too low since they exclude spending from secret accounts that was revealed later. The breakdown given in the table does, however, given an impression of the main categories of spending.

SOURCE: David E. Butler and Dennis Kavanagh, *The British General Election of October 1974* (London: Macmillan, 1975), p. 242.

proportions devoted to (1) grants to local campaigns and (2) headquarters administration and the low percentage devoted to advertising.

A breakdown of estimated Liberal central spending in the campaign of October 1974 is shown in table 52. The figures are based on those given in the Nuffield election study and are derived from information given by a senior party official.

Estimated central Liberal spending for the 1979 election is shown in table 53. The totals include LPO spending (£137,000), campaign expenditure out of the Rowntree grants to the party leader, and spending by regional organs of the party. The figures are only approximate because precise information has not been collected about the spending of the regional organizations and recognized units.

The large portion of the campaign budget devoted to constituency grants has two explanations. Since the party possesses no safe seats, it is obliged to give financial aid to bolster its organization in those few constituencies it holds and in those considered most winnable. At the same time, party leaders have during the 1970s felt it vital that there should be a Liberal candidate for virtually every constituency. The object has been to maximize the total Liberal vote throughout the country and thereby to strengthen the case for electoral reform. In numbers of hopeless seats, it has been necessary to guarantee the candidate against the loss of the £150 deposit in order to induce him to stand. The low advertising budget is made possible by the fact that the Liberals benefit largely from the system of free party political broadcasts, which is described in chapter 9.

TABLE 53

Liberal Party Central Precampaign and Campaign Expenditure, 1978–1979

(in thousands of pounds)

	Precampaign	Campaign	Total
Grants and guarantees to constituencies	30	54	84
Advertising (press and posters)	9	26	35
Producing political broadcasts	—	1.5	1.5
Literature (including manifesto)[a]	8.5	7	15.5
Tours and travel	1.5	16.5	18
Central operating expenses[b]	9	44	53
Miscellaneous	1	5	6
Total	59	154	213

NOTES: Includes spending by the LPO, leader's office, regional federations, and other central organizations. See footnote 36.

[a] Consists mainly of free copies of the manifesto and leaflets.

[b] Includes the cost of hiring accommodation for press conferences, because the Liberals did not have sufficient room on their own premises. Other significant items included in this category are postage, telephone, printing and stationery, security and hire of equipment, and the operating expenses of regional organizations.

SOURCES: LPO; Scottish Liberal party; and the Joseph Rowntree Social Service Trust Ltd.

Liberal Constituency Finance

For the Liberals, whose national impact has been so weak, the establishment of a strong political and financial base in the constituencies has been vital. The party's general inability to build up a solid local organization is a key to many of its problems. In parts of the country there has been no organization at all over long periods of time. In many constituencies, Liberal associations have not existed or have remained "little more than a self-appointed committee."[46]

A particular problem has been the unreliability of the local associations during times of political misfortune. For example, the relative enthusiasm of the late 1940s evaporated after the poor Liberal performances in the 1950 and 1951 elections, which "left most local associations in complete disorder."[47] The party's failure to consolidate its position after the Orpington by-election was in

[46] Wallace, "Liberal Revival," p. 248.
[47] Ibid., p. 253.

large measure due to flagging constituency activity when it became apparent that a sudden political breakthrough was not in the offing. In Wallace's words, local Liberal organizations by 1966 "remained throughout most of the country at the periphery of the political fabric maintaining a shadowy existence."[48]

The generally low level of Liberal activity in the constituencies is indicated in several ways. Many local parties do not even affiliate to the LPO. This is usually a sign that they are very weak or non-existent. At the height of Liberal postwar enthusiasm in 1949, only 400 of 542 constituencies in England and Wales affiliated.[49] This total declined to 341 in 1955 and to 330 in 1959. After rising again in the early 1960s, the number dropped to 375 in 1966. In 1974 the LPO's annual report noted affiliations by 320 of 516 constituencies in England. The Liberal memorandum in 1975 to the Houghton Committee stated that "it is doubtful whether there are 300 constituency Liberal Associations who have maintained a continuous existence over the last ten years."

According to Jorgen Rasmussen, "a more accurate index of the number of active local associations is the total bothering to appoint delegates to the party's annual assembly."[50] In the mid-1950s this varied between 175 and 181. The fluctuations in the number of constituencies putting forward parliamentary candidates are seen in table 56. During the postwar nadir in the 1950s, less than sixty constituencies in the United Kingdom (under one in ten) had a Liberal candidate in both 1951 and 1955.

Very few Liberal constituency associations have employed a paid full-time or part-time agent on a permanent basis. Information gathered from various sources yields the following pattern (it should be noted that several of the figures represent temporary election peaks): October 1949, 140 agents, about half of whom had their agents' certificates; 1951, 44; 1955, 27; 1959, 32; 1964, 70; 1966, 60; 1966 (postelection), 20; 1969, 17; 1970, 24; February 1974, 31; October 1974, about 20; 1975, under 30 full-time and part-time; 1979 (postelection), 23.[51]

According to a subsequent LPO estimate, party membership (England and Wales) was only 76,000 in 1953.[52] By 1959, it was

---

48 Ibid., p. 266.

49 Ibid., p. 274.

50 Rasmussen, *Retrenchment and Revival*, p. 20.

51 Derived from Nuffield election studies; Rose, *Influencing Voters*, p. 269; Wallace, "Liberal Revival," pp. 268, 273, 276; unpublished work by Curtice; and interviews with party officials.

52 Wallace, "Liberal Revival," pp. 268, 273, 278.

about 150,000. It reached a peak in the post-Orpington phase,[53] though there are conflicting estimates. According to the LPO's annual report for 1964 and 1965, membership was "the highest ever at 351,280." Retrospectively, the Liberal memorandum to the Houghton Committee gave an estimate for 1964–1965 of "about 250,000." Membership then declined until 1972. The constituency survey by the Houghton Committee gave a Liberal membership of approximately 300 per constituency in 1974; that is, about 165,000 for England and Wales and nearly 190,000 for Great Britain.

These various indicators all show the erratic nature and low level of local Liberalism in most of the country. There have been some notable exceptions to this pattern. A handful of the best Liberal constituency organizations have been on a par with some of the top Conservative associations, for example, the Liberal associations in North Cornwall and North Devon. Most of the centers of Liberal activism have been in rural or suburban areas. In city-center districts, Liberals have occasionally built up highly successful organizations by concentrating on pressing local government issues. In the past decade, bridgeheads were created by this means in Birmingham and Liverpool. These exceptional local examples do little more than highlight the barren picture elsewhere.

Small membership and sporadic activity have obviously limited local Liberal finance. Many constituencies have relied on a handful of patrons. Wallace records that in the late 1950s, "many constituencies were heavily dependent on the generosity of one or two large contributors for the provision of the bulk of their funds. Where no such wealthy supporters existed, the employment of professional staff was generally out of the question."[54]

Routine Finance. Poor Liberal organization has gone hand in hand with rudimentary record keeping. A survey of local finances carried out in 1966 by the Oxford University Liberal Club showed that, even among the active associations, many "still did not have detailed accounts, or any budgetary planning of income and expenditure." A consequence is that a relatively small proportion of associations—presumably the better organized—have responded to questionnaires and surveys. This has tended to produce exaggerated estimates of local Liberal finance. This applies to the Oxford University Liberal Club survey (which found that Liberal constituency income averaged £576 in 1966) and also to the Houghton Committee's constituency

[53] Ibid., p. 269.
[54] Ibid.

TABLE 54

SOURCES OF LIBERAL CONSTITUENCY INCOME, 1973 AND 1974

	1973	1974
Average total income (£)	964	2,189
Source (percent)		
Subscriptions	7.7	3.0
Individual donations	14.1	24.9
Grants from headquarters and from regional federations	11.0	7.0
Ward/branch grants, social functions, and lotteries	61.2	40.7
Other	6.0	24.3
Total	100.0	100.0

SOURCE: Houghton Report, p. 178.

survey. Out of questionnaires issued to ninety-nine Liberal constituency associations, the Houghton Committee received sufficient information to analyze only thirty-seven. The findings need therefore to be treated with caution as they probably overestimate local Liberal resources both absolutely and in relation to the main parties.

According to the Houghton Committee's survey, the annual income of local Liberal parties in 1973 averaged £964 (compared with £1,804 for Labour and £4,713 for the Conservatives). The main categories of Liberal income in the nonelection year 1973 and in 1974, when there were two general elections, are given in table 54.

The pattern of local Liberal income is similar to that in the two main parties insofar as membership subscriptions are unimportant and social functions, lotteries, and branch fund-raising efforts are the most significant sources. Statistics on Liberal constituency expenditure are given in table 55.

The main characteristics of routine spending by local Liberal parties are, first, the small amounts devoted to salaries and, second, the relative importance of local government elections. The low salary costs reflect the fact that so few Liberal associations employ paid agents or secretaries.

Campaign Spending. A comparison of the three parties' local spending shows that the Liberal disadvantage is smaller in parliamentary campaigns than in routine spending. In the 1979 general election,

TABLE 55

TYPES OF EXPENDITURE BY LIBERAL CONSTITUENCY ASSOCIATIONS, 1973 AND 1974

	1973	1974
Average total expenditure (£)	872	2,603
Type of expenditure (percent)		
Salaries	22.1	13.2
Office administration	39.2	20.9
Local government elections	22.9	3.5
General elections		56.3
Other	15.7	6.2
Total	100.0	100.0

SOURCE: Houghton Report, p. 181.

Liberal candidates spent on average about half as much as candidates of the two major parties. In the most marginal constituencies, where money was potentially of greatest importance, Liberal candidates spent as much as their opponents.[55]

Liberal associations have frequently been unprepared to foot the bill of a parliamentary campaign without assistance from central party funds or from the candidates themselves. Where money has been unavailable from these sources, many Liberal associations have simply declined to put forward a candidate. The variable number of Liberal candidates in general elections between 1945 and 1979 is shown in table 56.

The pressures on Liberal candidates to underwrite their own campaigns are described by Rasmussen on the basis of interviews carried out after the 1959 general election. He writes that "in a good number of cases being a Liberal parliamentary candidate clearly involved considerably greater personal expense than being a candidate for either of the major parties. . . . [S]pecifically mentioned sums ranged from £50 to £500. In other cases respondents characterized their contributions as 'sizeable' or 'substantial.' "[56]

[55] According to *The British General Election of 1979*, Liberals spent 91 percent of the maximum permitted sum in their thirty best constituencies. In the sixty-two most marginal Conservative/Labour contests, Conservatives spent 91 percent of the maximum and Labour candidates 87 percent (David E. Butler and Dennis Kavanagh, *The British General Election of 1979* [London: Macmillan, 1980], p. 316).

[56] Rasmussen, *Retrenchment and Revival*, p. 210.

TABLE 56

Number of Liberal Candidates and Their Election Expenses in General Elections, 1945–1979

General Election	Number of Candidates	Average Expenditure per Candidate (pounds)	Number of Forfeited Deposits
1945	306	532	76
1950	475	459	319
1951	109	488	66
1955	110	423	60
1959	216	532	55
1964	365	579	52
1966	311	501	104
1970	332	828	184
1974 (February)	517	745	23
1974 (October)	619	725	125
1979	576	1,013	304

NOTE: Average expenditure per candidate generally excludes the cost of forfeited deposits. The cost of each forfeited deposit was £150.
SOURCE: Derived from David E. Butler and Anne Sloman, *British Political Facts, 1900-1979* (London: Macmillan, 1980), p. 229.

There is no reason to suppose that candidates have been relieved of this burden in more recent elections, but the real cost of contesting parliamentary elections has fallen. The legal ceiling on election expenses has risen more slowly than inflation. The deposit has remained set at £150—far less in real terms in the 1970s than immediately after the Second World War. These factors have combined to reduce the financial burden of fighting Liberal parliamentary campaigns, and this partly accounts for the growing number of Liberal candidatures in recent elections.

The Pattern of Liberal Finance

The approximate pattern of Liberal spending in the parliamentary cycle 1970–February 1974 is given in table 57. It has been drawn up on the same basis as tables 36 and 45 for the Conservative and Labour parties.

A noteworthy aspect of modern Liberal finance as shown in table 57 is its decentralization. Central spending (including the LPO

TABLE 57

The Modern Pattern: Overall Liberal Party Expenditure (approximate) during the Parliamentary Cycle 1970–1974
(in pounds)

	Routine Expenditure	Campaign Expenditure
Central	550,000	75,000
Local	1½ million	385,000

Notes: Includes LPO spending and estimated spending by other units of central party organization. Routine central and constituency spending covers the period July 1970-February 1974. The totals have been calculated on the same basis as those for table 36.
Sources: As for tables 47, 48, 49, 52, 55, and 56.

and other national and regional party organs) accounted for only 25 percent of estimated total Liberal spending and local-level expenditure for 75 percent (compared with 57 percent for Labour and 65 percent for the Conservatives).[57] The weakness of central Liberal spending is seen by a comparison with the Labour party. During 1970–1974, Labour spent roughly twice as much as the Liberals at the local level but five times as much centrally.

Another point about Liberal spending is that, like that of the major parties, it is devoted mainly to routine activities (83 percent

[57] In calculating the percentages in this paragraph, the routine totals in table 57 have been adjusted to cover a standard four-year parliamentary cycle.

of the total). However, campaign expenditure is relatively more important in the Liberal party. At the constituency level, campaign spending in February 1974 accounted for 19 percent of local Liberal spending over the parliamentary cycle (compared with 16.5 percent of constituency Labour budgets and 6 percent of Conservative local spending).

Recent Trends

The central Liberal party has not been bereft of support from some companies and from individual subscribers. However, these sources have been erratic. The Labour party receives regular payments from trade unions, which are institutionalized by the regulations concerning the political levy. Company payments to the Conservative party are more volatile than union funds to the Labour party; but the Tories can nevertheless depend on business contributions to provide for most day-to-day expenses of the Central Office. The Liberals suffer from the fact that they have no similar source of regular central income. The party has benefited from bursts of generosity by individuals and companies—such as the large gifts received in 1970—but it has not been able to make long-term financial commitments in anticipation of obtaining such donations.

The absence of reliable sources of support has made the various organs of central Liberal organization especially vunerable to short-term problems. A crop of difficulties arose shortly after the general elections of 1974. Filled as it was with political enthusiasm for the Liberals, 1974 was a vintage year for fund raising. (This is not apparent from the LPO's routine accounts, because the bulk of the party's central income went into the LPO's general election funds and into the special funds.) The first blow was provided by the party's failure in the election of October 1974 to maintain the momentum established in the campaign of February 1974. The Liberals received fewer votes in October than in February. They failed to gain the block of new seats in the House of Commons for which they had been aiming.

This political setback damaged the party's chances of obtaining a considerable number of donations from large companies. This had been a realistic prospect over the summer of 1974, when an anti-socialist coalition of Conservatives and Liberals appeared to be a possibility.

To make matters worse, the October 1974 result led to a rapid collapse of Liberal morale. There was serious bickering about the desirable role of the LPO and controversy about the competence of senior personnel. A committee of influential Liberals debated whether the LPO headquarters should be abolished altogether. According to one view, it was a waste of money to maintain the expensive apparatus of an extraparliamentary headquarters and far better to decentralize the party's organization and expenditure.

This recommendation was narrowly defeated. It was decided to retain the LPO's headquarters organization, albeit with a different chief executive and new premises. The anti-LPO faction appears to have included members of the Rowntree Trust's Liberal subcommittee, which decided the trust's donations to various Liberal party causes. Consequently, the trust adopted an important change of policy. It would no longer support the routine upkeep of the LPO but would channel its donations to other Liberal causes. This decision eliminated the LPO's most important source of institutional funds.

The central party's financial position was helped by the introduction in 1975 of the "Short money," that is, the system of state aid to opposition parties in the House of Commons. The Liberal share of this money in 1975 was £33,234, a sum equivalent to one-third of the LPO's total income for that year. However, this significant new source benefited the parliamentary party and not the LPO.

Amid the controversy over the role of the LPO came the first rumblings of what was to grow into the "Thorpe affair." The speculations and revelations concerning Thorpe's private life and his replacement in 1976 as Liberal leader were politically harmful to the party and created an atmosphere that was hardly conducive to fund raising. Second, as mentioned earlier, the investigations into the supposed murder plot specifically involved allegations about the use of Liberal party funds. One of those accused alongside Thorpe had formerly been assistant LPO treasurer.

As if the Thorpe affair were insufficient, the Liberals were implicated in a second financial and sexual scandal involving the National Liberal Club, where the LPO's offices were moved after the 1974 campaigns. Although the club was not formally connected with the LPO, the existence of shared premises, similar title, and some overlap of officers could not have been helpful to the LPO's search for funds. It should be emphasized that the police investigations into the affairs of the National Liberal Club resulted in no prosecutions.

At first sight, it would seem that the party's central funds were severely affected by these problems. A casual examination of LPO income (table 47) suggests that it failed to grow significantly between 1966 and 1978, during which time there was a fourfold increase in the cost of living. However, the trend of overall central Liberal spending was probably considerably less adverse, taking into account items of central Liberal spending not included in the LPO accounts. As full information about the "secret funds" is not available, an accurate assessment is not possible.[58]

Nevertheless, the central Liberal finances do not appear by the 1970s to have fully kept pace with increases in the cost of living since the 1960s. The party's disadvantage in comparison with the central funds of the Labour party had grown considerably. The disadvantage compared with Conservative Central Office had probably increased moderately.

At the local level, the post-Orpington Liberal upsurge of the mid-1960s produced a temporary peak of party membership, organization, and finance. This grass-roots enthusiasm was never recaptured in the 1970s, despite the party's improved performance in general elections. Votes received by the party in the 1970s came largely from electors who were dissatisfied with the Conservatives and with Labour but had little positive attachment to the Liberal cause. Had there been a larger pool of active Liberal supporters, the party's finances would have been considerably stronger.

[58] It would appear that the LPO accounts were more inclusive in the late 1960s than in the late 1970s. It is not possible to be certain about this, however, without fuller information about the "secret funds" in the 1960s than is so far available.

8

Trade Union versus Company Donations

Following the description of the finances of the three main parties in the postwar years, the next two chapters focus on special features of political funding in Britain. This chapter analyzes political payments by trade unions and by companies. Chapter 9 deals with the system of regulating political finance and, in particular, the existing subsidies-in-kind to political parties.

The reliance of Conservative and Labour on institutional backers has attracted much criticism.[1] A common picture has been of one party in the clutches of big business, the other under the sway of union bosses. How accurate is this view? How do the political donations of unions compare with those of businesses?

Trade Union Political Levy Funds

As shown in chapter 3, money from the unions has been the basis of Labour party funds ever since the party's formation in 1900. Political payments by unions are regulated by the Trade Union Act, 1913, and by subsequent amendments (see chapter 3). A union is permitted to make political contributions only under set conditions. It must first establish a "political fund," and this must be kept separate from general union funds. A political fund may be established only after a successful ballot of the union's members. Any members not wishing to subscribe to the political funds must be permitted to "contract out" of doing so. Finally, the political fund accounts must be declared each year to the governmental body responsible for auditing the accounts of trade unions, building societies, and other similar institutions.[2]

[1] In discussing "institutional" support for the Conservative and Labour parties, it should be remembered that the institutions concerned are individual unions and individual companies. The organizations that represent the collective voices of the unions (the Trade Union Congress) and business (the Confederation of British Industry) do not act as channels for donations to political parties.

[2] See chapters 3, 9.

As already mentioned, there have been modifications in the laws governing political payments. In 1927 a system of contracting in was introduced,[3] but this was replaced in 1946 by the original system of contracting out. The name of the governmental institution responsible for overseeing trade union accounts has also altered. Until 1970 and for 1974, the overall income and expenditure of union political funds were listed in the reports of the chief registrar of friendly societies. These were normally issued annually. For 1971–1973, information was included in the annual report of the chief registrar of trade unions and employers' associations. No figures were collected for 1973 because of conflicts (not directly connected with the political funds) following the passage by the Heath government of the Industrial Relations Act, 1971. Information about trade union political funds is currently collected by the certification officer for trade unions and employers' associations. The certification officer's first annual report was issued in 1977.

The official reports of the bodies listed above are the most convenient source of information about trade union political levies. They give annual totals of the amounts raised and spent and the total reserves of the funds at the end of the year. The reports do not give breakdowns of political levy expenditure, nor are they wholly reliable, and frequent changes in their format make it difficult to compare statistics for different years. An alternative source of information is the annual reports of the individual unions with political levy funds. Apart from the severe practical problems involved in obtaining nearly a hundred separate reports, variations in the way unions draw up their published accounts make it difficult to calculate overall totals of income and expenditure and even harder to give accurate breakdowns of categories of spending. The statistics, in table 58, are therefore drawn mainly from the official reports.[4]

As shown in table 58, the overall income from trade union levies has grown steadily since the Second World War. The total for 1977 (£3.4 million) was nearly fifteen times as large as that for 1943 (£0.2 million). If inflation is taken into account, it is apparent that there have been two significant increases in the real value of the levies: the first came in the late 1940s, when the Labour government introduced legislation to restore the system of contracting out. This led to a sharp rise in the number and percentage of trade unionists

[3] See chapter 3.

[4] The problems involved in interpreting official reports of political levy income and expenditure are admirably described in Martin Harrison, *Trade Unions and the Labour Party since 1945* (London: Allen and Unwin, 1960), pp. 59-60. See also the note to table 20.

TABLE 58
TRADE UNION POLITICAL LEVY FUNDS, 1943–1978

	Total Trade Union Member-ship (thousands)	Total Member-ship of Trade Unions with Political Funds (thousands)	Total Contrib-uting to Political Funds (thousands)	Political Funds Total (£1,000)		
				Income[a]	Expendi-ture	Reserves at end of year
1943[b]	7,867	5,706	2,901	204[c]	163	664
1944	8,174	5,620	2,950	207[c]	206	668
1945*	8,087	6,034	2,903	230	353	460
1946	7,875	6,904	n.a.	254	207	506
1947	8,803	7,413	5,613	409	325	590
1948	9,145	7,529	5,773	466	390	666
1949	9,319	7,477	5,821	496	534	626
1950*	9,274	7,433	5,833	492	472	647
1951*	9,289	7,688	5,936	490	583	554
1952	9,535	7,712	5,962	507	374	689
1953	9,383	7,678	5,924	546	405	834
1954	9,523	7,707	5,949	547	410	981
1955*	9,556	7,854	6,173	561	638	906
1956	9,726	7,859	6,245	588	416	1,078
1957	9,829	7,923	6,329	753	535	1,298
1958	9,639	7,735	6,280	773	707	1,366
1959*	9,623	7,688	6,305[d]	763	891	1,234
1960	9,835	7,843	6,373[d]	767	543	1,451
1961	9,916	7,851	6,473[d]	771	628	1,596
1962	10,014	7,835	6,410	803	625	1,764
1963	10,067	7,928	6,439	870	1,110	1,525
1964*	10,218	8,013	6,457	925	1,003	1,444
1965	10,325	8,112	6,615	950	685	1,707
1966*	10,261	7,997	6,423	982	1,192	1,494
1967	10,190	7,802	6,194	970	725	1,758
1968	10,193	7,741	6,160	955	733	1,979
1969	10,472	7,940	6,332	984	738	2,227
1970*	11,179	8,446	6,738	1,105	1,616	1,703
1971	11,128	n.a.	n.a.	1,260	1,027	1,891

TABLE 58 (continued)

	Total Trade Union Membership (thousands)	Total Membership of Trade Unions with Political Funds (thousands)	Total Contributing to Political Funds (thousands)	Political Funds Total (£1,000)		
				Income[a]	Expenditure	Reserves at end of year
1972	11,353	n.a.	n.a.	1,492	1,183	2,171
1973	11,449	n.a.	n.a.	n.a.	n.a.	n.a.
1974*	11,756	8,715	7,120	1,964	3,026	1,499
1975	11,950	n.a.	n.a.	2,335	1,893	2,000[e]
1976	12,133	n.a.	n.a.	2,942	2,278	3,176[f]
1977	12,719	9,715	7,915	3,392	2,460	4,108
1978	13,054	9,888	8,082	4,045	3,417	4,530

NOTES: Asterisks denote general election years. n.a. = not available.

[a] Except for 1943 and 1944, "income" includes contributions and gross investment income. Taxes paid on investment income are included under expenditure. It is not possible to give investment income net of tax. Were this done, the totals of annual income and expenditure would be reduced by about 1 percent.

[b] No statistics were issued for 1940-1942.

[c] Income from contributions only.

[d] The total contributing to political funds is 465,000 less than that given by the chief registrar. This is based on the chief registrar's estimate that, apart from union members not exempted from paying the political levy, another 465,000 (including honorary members, retired members, free-card members, and members in the armed forces) did not contribute. See *Report of the Chief Registrar of Friendly Societies for the Year 1969* (London: Her Majesty's Stationery Office, 1971), pt. 4, p. 17.

[e] Estimated.

[f] The large increase in reserves reported for this year is partly a result of a change in accounting procedures by some major unions that had previously overestimated their expenditure and had thereby underestimated their reserves.

SOURCES: Except where otherwise stated, statistics are derived from the reports of the chief registrar of friendly societies, the chief registrar of trade unions and employers' associations, and the certification officer for trade unions and employers' associations. Other sources: col. 1: 1945-1960, David E. Butler and Jennie Freeman, *British Political Facts, 1900-1968* (London: Macmillan, 1969), p. 220; 1961-1975, Central Statistical Office, *Annual Abstract of Statistics* (London: Her Majesty's Stationery Office); col. 3: 1945-1958, Harrison, *Trade Unions and the Labour Party*, p. 62.

paying the levy and to a considerable increase in the amount collected. The second sharp rise was in 1957. Since then the increases in the total income of political levy funds have broadly kept pace with inflation.

Political fund revenue in the 1970s was, in real terms, twice as great as revenue until 1945. Revenue per member has not kept pace with the cost of living, and the increase in the total collected has resulted from the large rise in the total numbers paying the levy. Between 1945 and 1977, the number of members contributing to political levy funds increased by 173 percent, from 2.9 million to 7.9 million. This growth was the result of three factors: (1) the growth in the number of trade unionists from 8.1 million in 1945 to 12.7 million in 1977 (an increase of 57 percent), (2) a corresponding growth in the number of members belonging to unions with political funds, from 6 million in 1945 to 9.7 million in 1977 (an increase of 61 percent), and (3) the introduction of contracting out and the consequent increase in the percentage of members paying the political levy from 48 percent in 1945 to 76 percent in 1947. Since 1947 this percentage has remained almost constant. In 1977, 81 percent of members of unions with political funds paid the levy. This is broadly in line with the percentages contributing during the period of contracting out between 1914 and 1927.[5] The large growth in the numbers paying the levy has compensated for the fact that the average amount paid per member has fallen in real terms from 75 pence per member in 1945 (in 1980 values) to 59 pence per member in 1977.

Unions have tended to hoard their political levy income. Between 1945 and 1978, over 10 percent of total income was devoted to building up reserves. The high reserves at the end of 1978 were partly a reflection of the fact that the reserves are normally built up during a parliamentary cycle and depleted during the year of a general election. The total political levy reserves probably touched £5 million before the general election of 1979 and had probably been reduced to £3–4 million by the end of 1979. The hoarding instinct of the trade unions has been a subject of discussion and complaint. There have been variations over time. In the postwar years, union levy reserves grew steadily until the early 1960s; expenditure balanced income between 1964 and 1974 (both general election years); in the middle and late 1970s the reserves again grew rapidly.

In addition to the overall picture, it is useful to look at the contributions of separate trade unions. The political funds of the main unions in 1977 are shown in table 59. Several major points

[5] See table 22.

216

TABLE 59
Political Levy Funds of the Twenty Largest Trade Unions, 1977

Union	Members (thousands)	Contributing to Political Fund No. (thousands)	Per-cent	Income[a] (£1,000)	Income per Member[a] (pence)	Expenditure (£1,000)	Reserves at End of Year (£1,000)
TGWU	2,023	1,963	97	572	29	356	876
AEUW[b]	1,449	1,028	71	449	44	320	398
GMWU	945	926	98	327	35	255	315
NALGO[c]	709						
NUPE	693	682	98	476	70	378[d]	315
USDAW	442	402	91	147	37	115	172
ASTMS	441	147	33	60	41	45	57
EETPU	433	365	84	80	22	74	14
NUM[e]	411	268	65	355	132	211	1,021
UCATT	306	200	65	64	32	56	29
NUT[c]	296						
CPSA[c]	226						
COHSE	212	194	91	39	20	37	12
SOGAT	198	49	25	27	55	17	71
UPOW	197	187	95	84	45	67	18
NUR	172	164	95	109	66	93	194
APEX	146	109	74	68	62	48	124
Boilermakers	130	82	63	66	80	24	93
NAS/UWT[c]	127						
POEU	123	89	72	78	88	71	52
All unions with political levy funds	9,715	7,915	81	3,392	43	2,460	4,108

Note: Individual unions are as follows: TGWU, transport and general workers; AEUW, engineering workers; GMWU, general and municipal workers; NALGO, local government officers; NUPE, public service employees; USDAW, shop workers; ASTMS, clerical and technical workers; EETPU, electricians; NUM, miners; UCATT, construction workers; NUT, teachers; CPSA, lower-grade civil servants; COHSE, health service employees; SOGAT, printers; UPOW, Post Office workers; NUR, railwaymen; APEX, clerical and executive workers; NAS/UWT, teachers; POEU, Post Office engineers.

[a] Includes gross investment income.
[b] Includes the separate accounts of the four sections of the union.
[c] No political fund.
[d] The union devotes an unusually high percentage of its political levy fund expenditure to "administration."
[e] Includes the separate accounts of the National Union of Mineworkers (Durham Area).

Source: Certification officer's annual report.

about the pattern of union political funds emerge from this table.

1. Almost all the large unions have political funds. The only unions in the top twenty that do not are four white-collar unions (local government officers, civil and public servants, and two teachers' unions).

2. Among unions with political funds, there are large variations in the percentages of members contributing and the amounts contributed. In some unions virtually all the members pay the political levy. For example, in 1977 all but 169 of the 61,416 members of the National Union of Dyers, Bleachers and Textile Workers were reported as having paid the political levy—nearly 100 percent. In other unions, the proportion contributing is much lower; for example, no more than 25 percent of the members of the printing union, SOGAT. These differences are only partially explained by variations in percentages of members formally contracting out of paying the levy. Some unions include several categories of member who are not expected to pay contributions but who are nevertheless included in the total belonging to the union—retired, unemployed, and apprenticed members. Their inclusion lowers the percentage of total membership contributing to the levy fund. The percentages given in column 3 of table 59 do not therefore give a good indication of political feelings in the different unions listed. Unfortunately, statistics of numbers contracting out of the levy in each union are not collected by the certification officer.[6]

3. There are large variations in the average amounts contributed by members of different unions. In 1977 this ranged between a low of 20 pence and a maximum of 132 pence per member of the mineworkers' union. The large amount contributed by the National Union of Mineworkers is perhaps explained by the fact that in the early years of the twentieth century, the union was the largest and most powerful in the country. In a time of decreasing membership, the union has shown increasing militancy and appears to have been determined to retain some of its old influence within the Labour movement.

4. Another important aspect of the political levy is the high proportion of the total that comes from a handful of the largest unions. In 1977 the top five contributing unions accounted for 61 percent of members contributing to political funds, 64 percent of total income, 62 percent of expenditure, and 71 percent of total reserves. This concentration is largely a consequence of the fact that 57 percent of all members of unions with political levy funds belong to these five unions.

[6] For statistics of contracting out in 1924, see table 18.

The task of assessing how trade unions spend the money in their political funds is complicated by the fact that the accounts submitted by unions to the certification officer and the accounts published by unions in their annual reports vary greatly in their format and detail. A particular difficulty is that unions frequently hand over money out of their political funds to be spent by their regional, district, and branch organizations. In these cases, the annual reports of the union do not normally show how the money has been spent.

Broadly speaking, union levies are spent in three ways: (1) on administrative and allied costs, (2) for political purposes not connected with the Labour party, and (3) for Labour party purposes. The lion's share is devoted to helping the Labour party in a number of ways and at every level of the Labour party organization.

Administrative costs. Although unions are not legally bound to make a return of their administrative costs against the political fund, approximately 10 percent of their expenditure is classed as "administration."[7] An exceptional union such as NUPE, the public employees' union, usually allocates about half of its political fund expenditure to the administrative costs of collecting subscriptions and running its political fund. Other unions make no administrative charge at all. Harrison estimated that, in the late 1950s, it was probable that the reported administrative costs of unions represented only about half of their true overheads in organizing their political funds and that "the unions' political efforts were to that extent underestimated."[8]

To the cost of administration must be added the tax paid by unions on the investment income from their political funds reserves. As mentioned above, this amounts to about 1 percent of total expenditure, though it is not possible on the basis of currently available information to be more precise.[9]

Expenditure for political purposes not connected with the Labour party. Unions regularly give contributions to a variety of political causes apart from the Labour party—gifts to memorial appeals and affiliations to bodies like the Fabian Society. The total of these "other" contributions is small—under 5 percent of total expenditure. It is virtually unknown for a union, at national or district level, to give any money out of its political fund to the Conservative or Liberal parties.

[7] Harrison, *Trade Unions and the Labour Party*, p. 94.
[8] Ibid.
[9] See table 58, note *a*.

Trade union payments for Labour party purposes. Most expenditure from the unions' political funds—probably over 85 percent of the total—is devoted to Labour party purposes. Money is pumped into the party at all levels of its organization and for many separate purposes. This adds to the difficulty of assessing precisely how much trade unions give to the Labour party. However, the variety of union giving has the practical political effect of making every level of the Labour party organization heavily dependent on the unions.

Unions make payments to the Labour party's national executive committee, to regional councils, to constituency Labour parties, and to individually sponsored members of Parliament. Money is given for routine affiliation fees, for election campaigns (parliamentary and municipal), and for special purposes. In addition to these different forms of direct payment, unions spend money on sending delegations to the annual Labour party conference and on paying for union members to attend Labour party summer schools and other party-sponsored educational activities.

1. Unions pay regular affiliation fees to the Labour party's national executive committee. The affiliation rate per member is approved by the annual Labour party conference. The rates are shown in table 46. A union need not affiliate on the basis of all of its members who pay the political levy. For example, in the 1970s nearly 2 million members of the Transport and General Workers' Union contributed to the union's political fund. However, the union affiliated to the national Labour organization on the basis of only 1 million members.[10] This meant that the union had a block of just over 1 million votes at the party conference—considerably less than the total it would otherwise have received. At the same time, the union, by reducing the amount it paid in affiliation fees to the national Labour organization, left more in reserve to spend for general election purposes and at other levels of the party.

In 1977, trade unions paid affiliation fees to Transport House for a total of 5,913,000 members. Although this amounted to only three-quarters of the 7,915,000 contributing to political levy funds, it

[10] This illustrates that the concept of membership does not meaningfully apply to trade union affiliations to the Labour party. The fact that a particular union affiliates on the basis of a particular number of "members" means nothing more than that it is willing to pay a certain total amount of money to the party. The Transport and General Workers' Union (TGWU) has recently increased its affiliation to the party from 1 million to 1¼ million. This sudden jump did not mean that a ¼ million extra Labour party members had been recruited but that the union had agreed to step up its routine payments to Transport House: it had, as it were, increased its total number of "shares" in the Labour party (see chapter 10, "The Real Abuses").

TABLE 60

TABLE 60

TRADE UNION AFFILIATION FEES TO THE NATIONAL EXECUTIVE
COMMITTEE OF THE LABOUR PARTY, 1945–1977

	Total Union Members Contributing to Political Levy Funds (thousands)	Total Union Members Affiliated to Labour Party NEC (thousands)	Col. 2 as % of Col. 1	Affiliation Fees Paid by Unions to Transport House[a]		Votes at Labour Party Conference Controlled by Unions (%)
				Amount (£1,000)	Percentage of political levy income	
1945	2,903	2,510	86	51	22	83
1949	5,821	4,946	85	126	25	87
1952	5,962	5,072	85	126	25	83
1955	6,173	5,606	91	141	25	86
1958	6,280	5,628	90	210	27	86
1961	6,473	5,550	86	208	27	88
1964	6,457	5,502	85	276	30	87
1967	6,194	5,340	86	277	29	88
1970	6,738	5,518	82	402	36	89
1974	7,120	5,787	81	738	38	89
1977	7,915	5,913	75	1,268	37	89

[a] That is, the national executive committee of the Labour party.

SOURCES: Labour party annual report, 1979, pp. 97–98; and tables 38 and 58.

still gave trade unions 89 percent of the votes at the annual party conference. Had the unions affiliated on the basis of all the members contributing to the political levy, they would have controlled 92 percent of the votes at the party conference. Table 60 shows the postwar trends of union affiliations to the national executive committee (NEC) of the Labour party. The number of trade union members affiliated has remained roughly constant since the mid-1950s. Because of sharply rising affiliation rates (as shown in table 46), the total contributed by unions to the NEC has grown fast, and the percentage of political levy income devoted to affiliations to the NEC has increased markedly, from about a quarter in the late 1940s to almost 40 percent in the 1970s. The table shows that the control of the unions over votes at the party conference has tightened still further since the 1950s. This is because the number of union votes (deter-

221

TABLE 61

ESTIMATED MAJOR CONTRIBUTIONS TO THE GENERAL ELECTION FUND OF THE
LABOUR PARTY NATIONAL EXECUTIVE COMMITTEE, 1978–1979
(in thousands of pounds)

	Donation	Percentage of Total
Trade unions[a]		
Transport workers (TGWU)	150	(12)
Municipal workers (GMWU)	150	(12)
Engineering workers (AEUW)	102	(8)
Miners (NUM)	100	(8)
Technicians (ASTMS)	50	(4)
Public employees (NUPE)	50	(4)
Other union donations	496	(41)
Total union donations	1,098	91
League against Cruel Sports	80	7
Other nonunion donations	25	2
Total	1,203	100

NOTE: Parentheses indicate subtotals.

[a] These figures possibly underestimate the totals given by some of the major unions listed to the NEC general election fund. Although individual unions eventually publish their political fund accounts and although the Labour party is, in theory, in favor of the publication of individual donations to its funds, there was on this occasion reluctance both by some individual unions and by the Labour party to reveal the totals donated by the major unions. The figures in the table are therefore based on estimates in Butler and Kavanagh, *The British General Election of 1979.*

SOURCES: Finance officer of the Labour party; and David E. Butler and Dennis Kavanagh, *The British General Election of 1979* (London: Macmillan, 1980), p. 57.

mined by numbers affiliated) has remained constant at a time when individual membership has dropped.

Besides their regular affiliation fees to Transport House, the union donations are virtually the only source of money for the party's special general election fund. This is illustrated in table 61, which shows union contributions to the NEC's general election fund for the 1979 election.

From time to time, Transport House makes special financial appeals—for example, the general secretary's appeal after the general elections of 1974 and, more recently, the building fund. Almost invariably it is the unions that subscribe most of the money out of their political fund reserves.

2. At the regional level, unions pay affiliation fees on the national

TABLE 62

LABOUR MEMBERS OF PARLIAMENT SPONSORED BY MAJOR TRADE UNIONS AND BY THE CO-OPERATIVE PARTY, 1979

	Number of MPs
Transport workers (TGWU)	22
Engineering workers (AEUW)	21
Miners (NUM)	16
Municipal workers (GMWU)	14
Railwaymen (NUR)	12
Other unions	49
Co-operative party	17
Total sponsored MPs	151
Total Labour MPs	269

SOURCE: David E. Butler and Anne Sloman, *British Political Facts, 1900-1979* (London: Macmillan, 1980), p. 146.

model and contribute extra sums during general elections. The routine affiliation fees are small, and it is at elections that union donations at the regional level are significant.

3. At the constituency level, unions pay routine affiliation fees. This entitles them to representaion on constituency Labour party general management committees and thus to a say in the selection of parliamentary and local government candidates. Unions contribute heavily to parliamentary and local government campaigns.

4. A special form of financial payment, which has no counterpart in the Conservative and Liberal parties, is the system of union sponsorship of candidates. This is especially important at the parliamentary level but exists at the municipal level as well. When a union sponsors a particular candidate, it can make a variety of payments on his behalf: payments toward election expenses, routine donations between elections to the candidate's constituency Labour party, and payments directly to the candidate after his election to Parliament. These direct payments frequently take the form of a retainer or of a grant toward secretarial or other expenses. After the general election of 1979, 151 Labour MPs (out of 269) were sponsored by a union or by the Co-operative party.[11] The main blocks of sponsored MPs are listed in table 62.

[11] Why do trade unions continue to sponsor MPs? Do they exert undesirable pressures on them? These questions are considered in detail in Harrison, *Trade Unions and the Labour Party,* and in William D. Muller, *The Kept Men? The First Century of Trade Union Representation in the British House of Commons*

5. Unions devote considerable sums from their political levy funds to sending delegates to party meetings, particularly the annual Labour party conference. Smaller sums are spent on sponsoring union members and activists wishing to attend summer schools and other educational activities organized by the Labour party. The money in this last category is not paid directly to Labour party funds but is used to support Labour party purposes.

According to detailed calculations made by Harrison for 1955–1958 (a four-year period including one general election), the breakdown of total trade union political fund expenditure was as shown in table 63. These figures suggest that nearly 90 percent of political levy expenditure was devoted to Labour party purposes. If payments to sponsored candidates and for "other Labour party purposes" are excluded, nearly 80 percent of total spending from the political levy funds went into direct payments to the national, regional, and constituency organizations of the Labour party.[12] Since the late 1950s, there appears to

(Atlantic Highlands, N.J.: Humanities Press, 1977).

These authors seek to allay some popular fears about sponsorship. Demands on sponsored MPs have apparently lessened over time; the funding given to sponsored MPs is relatively modest; unions have increasingly sponsored political stars and not merely time-serving union officials; unions enjoy ready access to the government and do not need sponsored MPs to gain this objective; and in any case a union is not permitted to threaten an MP with the denial of future sponsorship if he refuses to vote or act as directed by the union.

In my view, there are nevertheless some undesirable features about sponsorship: (1) Although sponsored MPs are not given direct orders about their behavior in Parliament, there is obviously an underlying expectation that they will act on their sponsor's behalf—by speaking in the House of Commons on union matters, by interesting themselves in the work of committees considering legislation affecting the union, by addressing meetings of union members, by writing for union journals, and so on. Some unions have assigned officials to liaison with their contingents of sponsored MPs, presumably to help them to work for the unions' interests. (2) Although the secretarial and other allowances received by sponsored MPs from their unions are usually modest and although union contributions toward their campaign expenses are relatively unimportant at a period when such expenses have fallen drastically in real terms, a sponsoring union nevertheless has great potential power over its MPs. A union that sponsors an MP is normally well represented on the general management committee of his constituency Labour party. This representation is itself the result of the union's financial payments to the CLP. The general management committee selects the MP and may refuse to renominate him. A sponsored MP who falls out with his union therefore faces the threat that he will not be renominated—a mighty threat. Companies that make payments to MPs do not have similar leverage.

12 Rose estimates the allocation of trade union political levy funds between 1960 and 1964 as follows: to Transport House (apart from general election grants) 31 percent, to regional councils 2 percent, to constituency Labour parties 23 percent, to the general election 14 percent, to administration and other activities 25 percent, and to reserves 5 percent (Richard Rose, *Influencing Voters: A Study of Campaign Rationality* [London: Faber, 1967], p. 276).

TABLE 63

(percent)

Payments for Labour party purposes	
To national organization	(44)
To regional councils	(3)
To constituency Labour parties (including payments on behalf of sponsored candidates)	(32)
To sponsored candidates and MPs	(2)
For other Labour party purposes (conference delegates' expenses and political education)	(8)
Total payments for Labour party purposes	88
Expenditure for political purposes not connected with the Labour party	3
Administration and tax	9

NOTE: Parentheses indicate subtotals.
SOURCE: Derived from Harrison, *Trade Unions and the Labour Party*.

have been a shift of union political fund spending toward the national level of the party organization. This has been accompanied by a reduction in the percentage of total spending at the constituency level, but the percentage of total spending devoted to Labour party purposes appears to have remained about the same.

It is not possible to gauge precisely the extent to which the Labor party relies on trade union money. Trade union payments to the Labour party at all levels can only be estimated. There is, equally, uncertainty about the overall income of the Labour party, since there is no firm information about the totals spent annually by constituency Labour parties. According to Harrison's estimates for 1957, union contributions accounted for between 40 percent and 55 percent of the Labour party's total central, regional, and constituency income.[13]

Estimates by Rose suggest that unions provided 50 percent of Labour's overall income between 1967 and 1970 and 53 percent in 1972.[14] A calculation by the present author for the parliamentary cycle July 1970–February 1974 suggests that trade union payments accounted for 56 percent of Labour's total central, regional, and local income during this period. These estimates need to be treated with

[13] Harrison, *Trade Unions and the Labour Party*, p. 99.
[14] Richard Rose, *The Problem of Party Government* (New York: Free Press, 1975), p. 236.

caution. A broad picture does emerge: in the postwar period, the unions appear to have been the source of slightly over half of the Labour party's overall income. As shown in chapter 6, the central organization has remained dependent on the unions for about 90 percent of its income, while constituency parties have on average obtained less than half of their income from this source.

By directing their donations to the center and to safely held Labour constituencies, the unions have ensured very good value for money in terms of their power within the party. Harrison remarked in the late 1950s that "due to the unusual system of affiliation the unions can control eight out of ten votes at the Party Conference although they contribute only about half the Party's income."[15] This imbalance has increased during the 1960s and 1970s. At present the unions appear to contribute about 55 percent of overall Labour party income, but they control nine votes out of ten at the annual Labour conference. In the House of Commons, over half the party's MPs are sponsored by unions, despite the fact that union money provides considerably less than half of the party's income at constituency level. The unions evidently invest their money where the political return is greatest.

A constitutional change voted in January 1981 will mean that in future the unions will have an important additional power. They will have 40 percent of the votes in the newly devised electoral college that will select the party leader. This selection was in the past the prerogative of Labour MPs alone. The extension of trade union power was itself the decision of a special party conference dominated by the block votes of the big unions.

Apart from the fact that unions have such extensive control of the Labour party's constitutional machinery, it is questionable whether their financial contributions should entitle them to any voting privileges at all. This is discussed more fully in "The Real Abuses," in chapter 10.

Before analyzing company donations to the Tories, two additional, separate points about Labour party reliance on its institutional backers ought to be briefly mentioned. First, the scope of the Trade Union Act, 1913, is narrow. It merely stipulates that union expenditure on a number of specifically defined "political objects" must be channeled

---

[15] Harrison, *Trade Unions and the Labour Party*, p. 107. Individual members may not directly join the national party. They must subscribe to a constituency Labour party, which in turn pays a part of the membership subscription to the national party. Trade unions are permitted, by contrast, to affiliate directly to the party at the national level. It is thus cheaper for the unions than for individual party supporters to obtain votes at the annual party conference.

through a special "political fund." There are important political activities not regulated by the act, which unions are permitted to finance through their ordinary general funds. Most trade unions, for example, produce newspapers that openly urge members to vote Labour. These are financed out of unions' general funds.[16] Similarly, the Labour-oriented educational facilities provided by many unions need not be financed out of the political levy funds.

The overall effect of the law is that union contributions to the Labour party and to parliamentary and local government candidates must come out of the political fund, whereas general political education and propaganda—even if it openly urges members to vote Labour—may come out of ordinary union funds. The financial contributions of unions to the Labour cause are therefore greater than the amounts that have been estimated in this chapter. In practice, it is difficult to define, yet alone to measure, the extent of these extra, "politically relevant" activities. It is for this reason that they have not been considered in this study. Similarly, the section of this chapter on company donations restricts itself to payments for party political purposes and excludes spending on politically relevant advertising, such as the campaigns opposing nationalization financed by some threatened industries during the 1950s and 1960s.[17]

16 See chapter 9.

17 Each party characteristically points out the "politically relevant" spending of the other side. Labour spokesmen and sympathetic commentators have concentrated on political advertising sponsored by some business interests. Elections of the 1950s and 1960s saw heavy spending on antinationalization publicity, such as that commissioned by steel companies before the general election of 1964. (These campaigns are described in detail in Rose, *Influencing Voters*.)

The right of companies to spend money on antinationalization advertising during general election campaigns was challenged in the courts in the 1950s. It was decided that such spending was allowable and did not contravene the spending limits for parliamentary candidates because the advertisements did not directly support particular parliamentary candidates or parties. (See Alfred P. Brainard, "The Law of Elections and Business Interest Groups in Britain," *Western Political Quarterly*, vol. 13 (1960); chap. 9, footnotes 10 and 12; and chap. 10, footnote 4.)

By contrast, Conservatives have repeatedly stressed that the financial support given by the Labour movement to the Labour party far exceeds the amounts shown in the Labour party accounts or trade union political levy accounts. As described in chapters 4 and 5, Conservatives have repeatedly cited left-wing educational activities and union expenditure out of their general funds on pro-Labour journals as examples of such additional expenditures. (See the quotation in chap. 4 from Ball's memorandum on "The Present Situation" and chap. 5, footnote 18.)

A left-wing reply is that the political impact of trade union journals is dwarfed by that of Tory-owned national newspapers, the costs of which are, like those of union journals, not included in party budgets despite their political

A second point about the Labour party's institutional backers is that money from trade unions is supplemented by funds from the cooperative societies. These are supermarkets and retail stores that devote a portion of their trading profits to Labour party activities. The cooperative societies have a complex internal organization consisting of local societies, regional organizations, the Co-operative Union, and the Co-operative party, which is the political branch of the movement. It is not possible to give an accurate assessment of the movement's financial contribution to the Labour party because most donations are given at the constituency level by regional Co-operative parties, which do not publish their accounts. According to Rose, the Co-operative movement had political funds with an average overall annual income of £180,000 a year in 1967–1970. It gave an estimated £46,000 a year to the Labour party, including £45,000 a year to constituency Labour parties.[18] This amounted to about 3 percent of overall Labour party income.

By agreement with the Labour party, the Co-operative party sponsors up to thirty Labour candidates at general elections, financing them on the same basis as trade unions sponsoring candidates. The Co-operative party also sponsors a large number of local government candidates. If contributions from the Co-operative movement are added to those of the unions, Labour would appear to obtain nearly 60 percent of its funds from these two institutional sources.

Company Donations to the Conservative Party

During the period between the two World Wars, donations from companies gradually replaced payments by rich individuals as the main source of Conservative central income. Political payments by companies—unlike those of trade unions—remained strictly confidential and, until the passage of the Companies Act, 1967, were subject to no special governmental regulation.

There appear to have been several reasons for the traditional secrecy surrounding political payments by companies. Some company

---

relevance.

It will be evident that there is a whole spectrum of expenditures that are more or less "politically relevant." There is no easy dividing line between items that should be included in an examination of political finance and those that should not. The problem of defining what is politically relevant has been avoided in this study, since only party funds have been dealt with. Whatever definition of politically relevant spending is used, it should be applied equally to all parties. This appears obvious enough but has been widely ignored in writings on political finance in Britain.

[18] Rose, *Problem of Party Government*, pp. 233, 236.

directors were uncertain whether their company regulations and objectives permitted donations to political parties. There were fears about unfavorable reactions from workers if a company's financial support for the Conservative party became known. Firms hoping to obtain local government contracts felt that they risked discrimination from Labour-controlled local councils if their political donations became known. Possibly most important, secrecy was a habit.

A desire to avoid publicity has remained. Many companies continue to channel their donations to the Conservative party through intermediary organizations. The most important is called British United Industrialists, a body whose main purpose is to collect money that is then passed directly to the Conservative party.[19] A company giving a donation to British United Industrialists can truthfully—though misleadingly—claim that it is not paying money to a political party. In the provinces, a number of "industrialists' councils" collect money from local businesses for transmission to the Conservative Central Office.

Apart from British United Industrialists and the industrialists' councils, Conservative Central Office maintains a fund-raising organization of its own. There are about a dozen paid collectors, one for each area of the country, whose responsibility is to solicit contributions, mainly from the industrial community.

In 1967 the Labour government introduced legislation that compelled companies to declare all political donations exceeding £50 in their annual reports. An important side effect was that Conservative Central Office decided to publish its accounts, though it did so in a form that gave no information about specific company donations or even about the total of such payments.

Since the Companies Act, 1967, much information about political payments by companies has become available for the first time, though two barriers still make it impossible to assess precisely how much business spends each year for political purposes. First, private companies and partnerships are not covered by the provisions of the Companies Act, 1967. This means that stockbrokers' partnerships, for example, need not declare political contributions. Second, there are so many companies that it is not practical to scrutinize the annual

[19] "This organization, formed by a merger of two fund-raising groups founded in 1948, solicits contributions from large companies, in order to promote free enterprise. As the organization has no programme of activities, and its only official is Col. Juan Hobbs, the secretary, it is reasonable to assume that funds collected are transferred, with Central Office receiving most" (Rose, *Influencing Voters*, p. 264). According to the Central Office, about 80 percent of the funds collected by British United Industrialists are probably transferred to the Conservative party.

reports of all of them. The Labour party's research department and an independent organization, the Labour Research Department, both regularly survey the annual reports of about 1,000 of the largest companies, but even these painstaking efforts fail to unearth many important political donations by smaller enterprises. The reports published annually by these two bodies do not, therefore, establish the total of political donations by companies, although they provide useful information about payments by particular firms.[20]

The estimates of total company donations that are used in this chapter have been derived from the published accounts of Conservative Central Office for the period since 1967/1968, from previously unpublished accounts for 1950–1964 provided for this study, and from information given in interviews. The technicalities of the calculation are set out in a footnote.[21] It has been assumed that 80 percent of the total listed in the central party accounts as "donations" comes from companies. In addition, it is assumed (on the

[20] A further problem is that the accounting years of companies vary and do not necessarily correspond with that of Conservative Central Office. It is therefore not always possible to tell from the annual report of a company during which Central Office accounting year a contribution has been received.

[21] The annual accounts of Conservative Central Office give the total of "donations" received. This category includes bequests and donations by individuals as well as by companies. The published total of donations has underestimated the amounts actually received because (1) donations are listed net of the costs of fund raising, (2) some payments by companies to the central party organization are partly credited toward constituency quotas and are therefore listed as payments by constituency associations, and (3) until 1977/1978, Central Office accounts excluded the separate Scottish Central Office. The following amendments and additions have therefore been made to the total of donations given in the annual central party accounts:

1. Fifteen percent of the amounts listed as payments by constituencies has been added to the published total of donations to take account of quota credits.
2. It is assumed that 80 percent of donations are from companies.
3. It is assumed that, between 1950 and 1964, companies annually contributed £150,000 to city and constituency associations in election years and £110,000 in nonelection years.
4. It is assumed, on the basis of the Houghton Committee's constituency survey, that companies have provided 6 percent of estimated local party income since 1967/1968 (see the Houghton Report, pp. 178-79).
5. It is assumed that total local party routine income grew from £1.8 million in 1967/1968 to £7 million in 1979/1980 and that local parties raised additional sums in election years to cover the declared expenses of Conservative parliamentary candidates, as listed in the Nuffield election study for the relevant election.
6. It is assumed that fund-raising costs attributable to business donations rose from £25,000 in 1950 to £230,000 in 1979/1980 (this is slightly lower than Rose's estimate that collection costs have averaged 15 percent of total contributions [see Rose, *Problem of Party Government*, p. 217]).
7. For years until 1976/1977, 6½ percent has been added to account for company donations in Scotland.

TABLE 64

ESTIMATED TOTAL COMPANY DONATIONS TO THE CONSERVATIVE PARTY,
1950–1979/1980
(in thousands of pounds)

	Amount	At 1980 Values		Amount	At 1980 Values
1950*	951	7,285	1964*	1,834	9,078
1951*	947	6,696	1967/68	668	3,000
1952	494	3,260	1968/69[a]	1,543	6,299
1953	516	3,405	1969/70	812	3,126
1954	550	3,564	1970/71*	1,566	5,702
1955*	1,115	6,964	1971/72	773	2,540
1956	455	2,681	1972/73	1,023	3,132
1957	582	3,361	1973/74*	2,374	6,527
1958	615	3,479	1974/75*	1,393	2,979
1959*	1,469	8,309	1975/76	1,377	2,440
1960	417	2,310	1976/77	1,603	2,426
1961	535	2,897	1977/78	2,105	2,779
1962	539	2,794	1978/79	2,590	3,243
1963	827	4,191	1979/80*	4,251	4,569

NOTE: Asterisks denote general election years. For the basis of calculation, see footnote 21.
[a] A special national financial appeal was made during this year.
SOURCE: As for table 28.

basis of the Houghton Committee's constituency survey) that companies provide 6 percent of the income of Conservative constituency associations. This calculation possibly slightly overestimates the extent of company payments to the Conservative Central Office, as the proportion of donations that comes from companies may be somewhat lower than 80 percent.[22] Estimated total company payments to the Conservative party since 1950 are given in table 64. The figures include payments to all levels of the party organization.

Table 64 shows that company contributions reach a peak in general election years. This normally enables the Conservative party to build up a reserve to cover the routine expenses of the Central Office between elections. This pattern contrasts with that of the

22 As mentioned in chapter 5, the party treasurers cannot always tell whether a contribution comes from a company or from a businessman in his personal capacity. This makes it impossible to specify the precise proportion of donations that comes from companies.

unions, whose political fund income does not vary between election and nonelection years.

Over the last thirty years, company contributions have not fully kept up with increases in the cost of living. During the eight-year period 1952–1959, which included two general elections, company donations amounted to about £35 million at 1980 values. During the eight-year period 1971/1972–1978/1979, which includes two general elections, companies contributed about £26 million at 1980 values. A decline, in real terms, in the level of payments has been particularly marked since the Conservative defeat in the election of February 1974.[23]

During peak years company donations to the Conservatives have considerably exceeded union political levies. Yet companies have been less regular and less dependable as political backers. This is apparent not only from the statistics of overall contributions, given in table 64, but also from an analysis of payments by individual companies. In 1976 sixteen of the twenty largest unions had political funds. During the same financial year, only three of the top twenty industrial companies gave any political donations to the Conservative party, British United Industrialists, or regional industrialists' councils. Of the largest 100 industrial companies in the United Kingdom, 29 made political donations, and of the top 800, 148 (less than 19 percent) made donations. The pattern is given in table 65.

Surveys for the years 1973–1978 indicate that the majority of large enterprises did not make any contributions, direct or indirect, to the Conservative party. A particular feature is the absence of political payments by the British branches of multinational corporations. Among major industrial companies that appear to have made no political payments between 1973 and 1978[24] are (by rank order): British Petroleum, Shell, British-American Tobacco, Imperial Chemical Industries, Unilever, Imperial Group, British Leyland, Esso, Rio Tinto-Zinc, Cavenham (Associated British Foods),[25] Ford, Courtaulds, Grand Metropolitan, George Weston, Dunlop Holdings, Rothmans, C. Czarnikow, Gallaher, Reed International, Amalgamated Metal, Lonrho, Texaco, Hawker Siddeley, Thorn Electrical Industries, Great Universal Stores, Bass Charrington, Sears, S. and W. Berisford,

[23] This trend is reflected in the decline in company and individual donations to Conservative Central Office. See chapter 5, "Recent Developments."

[24] The absence of a recorded donation does not, of course, preclude the possibility that individual directors or shareholders contributed in their individual capacities.

[25] A contribution is recorded to the Conservative-oriented Centre for Policy Studies.

TABLE 65
Number of Top Industrial, Commercial, and Financial Institutions Donating to the Conservative Party and to Conservative Fund-raising Organizations, 1976/1977

	Number Donating to:			Total Making Political Donations
	Conserv-ative party	British United Industrialists	Industrialists' councils	

800 largest industrial companies (by rank order)				
1–100	21	14	2	29
(1–20)	(3)	(3)	—	(3)
(21–40)	(6)	(3)	—	(7)
(41–60)	(3)	(3)	—	(5)
(61–100)	(9)	(5)	(2)	(14)
101–200	18	10	4	30
201–300	16	4	4	22
301–400	13	4	1	17
401–500	9	—	5	12
501–600	10	—	1	11
601–700	11	—	3	14
701–800	12	—	2	13
Total	110	32	22	148

153 largest financial and commercial institutions				
25 insurance companies	3	6	—	9
50 investment trusts	14	1	—	15
7 clearing banks	—	—	—	—
11 discount houses	4	—	1	5
16 accepting houses	7	—	—	7
24 finance houses	1	—	—	1
20 property companies	3	—	—	3
Total	32	7	1	40

Notes: The table does not include donations to right-wing bodies largely or wholly independent of the Conservative party, such as Aims for Freedom and Enterprise, Economic League, and so on. The table includes all donations from January 1976 listed in company annual reports published by September 1977. Some companies donated both to the Conservative party and to an industrialists' council or to British United Industrialists. Parentheses indicate subtotals.

Sources: Derived from *The Times, 1,000 Largest United Kingdom Industrial Companies, 1976/1977;* and Labour Party Research Department, *Company Donations to the Tory Party and Their Allies,* Information Paper no. 8 (London: Labour Party, September 1977).

233

Unigate, Rank Xerox, Boots, Tube Investments, Metal Box, Distillers, EMI, F. W. Woolworth, J. Sainsbury, and Dalgety.[26]

Among the minority of large companies that contributed to the Conservative party in 1973–1978, the average sums involved were small when compared with political levies collected by the big unions. The 188 companies and enterprises listed in table 65 gave a total of £988,113 in 1976/1977—an average of £5,256 for each company. Of the 29 companies in the top 100 that contributed, payments averaged £13,809. The largest contributions for 1977 and 1978 are listed in table 66. The list is taken from the Labour party research department's survey of the top 800 companies and of the major financial and commercial institutions. It may therefore omit some large contributions given by smaller enterprises not covered by the survey.

Besides collecting money from large firms, the Conservative party's central board of finance actively solicits funds from small and medium-sized businesses. Most of the total raised from the business community, however, comes from the more substantial enterprises. The thousand top British companies surveyed by the Labour party's research department in 1976/1977, 1977/1978, and 1978/1979 contributed about 60 percent of total company donations.[27]

Over the twelve years from 1967/1968 to 1978/1979, company donations to the Conservative party totaled nearly £18 million. An estimated £15½ million went to the party at the center (86 percent of company donations) and approximately £2½ million to local Conservative organizations. During this period, company money accounted for about 30 percent of the overall central and local income of the Conservative party.

Donations to the Conservative party represent the vast bulk of political payments by companies. As noted in chapter 7, however, a sprinkling of money has gone to the Liberals. In some years Liberals have received up to 5 percent of total company donations to political parties. The odd company payment has found its way into Labour coffers.

[26] Several of these corporations did, however, contribute to Britain in Europe, the pro-Common Market organization in the 1975 referendum. Among companies contributing at least £10,000 were Imperial Chemical Industries, Shell, Ford, Reed International, Cavenham, Unilever, Bass Charrington, and Metal Box (David E. Butler and Uwe Kitzinger, *The 1975 Referendum* [London: Macmillan, 1976], p. 85).

[27] This percentage was fairly constant in each of the three years. The percentage was derived from (1) the estimated annual total of company donations, given in table 64, and (2) the annual surveys of donations by top companies issued by the Labour party research department.

TABLE 66
LARGEST CONTRIBUTIONS BY TOP COMPANIES TO THE CONSERVATIVE PARTY, 1977 AND 1978
(in pounds)

1977		1978[a]	
Taylor Woodrow	30,000	Taylor Woodrow	64,050
Newarthill	27,380	Rank Hovis MacDougall	30,000
Allied Breweries	26,500	Rank Organisation	30,000
Guardian Royal Exchange	25,756	Inchcape	28,600
Glaxo	25,000	Newarthill	26,000
GKN	25,000	Guardian Royal Exchange	25,750
Trust Houses Forte	25,000	Charter Consolidated	25,400
British and Commonwealth		Glaxo	25,000
Shipping	23,545	GKN	25,000
Consolidated Goldfields	22,000	Norwest Holst	25,000
Inchcape	20,328	Royal Insurance	25,000
Beechams	20,000	George Wimpey	25,000
Marks and Spencer	20,000	British and Commonwealth	
Rank Hovis MacDougall	20,000	Shipping	23,605
Rank Organisation	20,000	United Biscuits	21,500
Reckitt and Colman	20,000	Consolidated Goldfields	21,000
Royal Insurance	20,000	Beechams	20,000
Trafalgar House	20,000	Commercial Union	20,000
United Biscuits	20,000	General Accident	20,000
		Marks and Spencer	20,000
		Marley	20,000
		Reckitt and Colman	20,000
		Sun Alliance	20,000
		Thorn Electrical	20,000
		Trafalgar House	20,000

NOTES: Includes the 800 largest companies and the financial and commercial institutions listed in table 65. Includes donations to the Conservative party, British United Industrialists, and industrialists' councils.

[a] Excludes Allied Breweries. This company continued to contribute but did not issue an annual report for 1978.

SOURCES: Labour Research Department, *Labour Research* (London, September 1978); Labour Party Research Department, *Company Donations to the Tory Party and Other Political Organisations*, Information Paper no. 4a (London: Labour Party, November 1978); and Information Paper no. 17, September 1979.

Union versus Company Donations

The data that have been presented reveal important differences between union and company donations. The link between the unions and the Labour party is far closer than that between companies and the Conservative party.

1. It is usually assumed that political donations by companies are far larger than those of trade unions. This has not been the case since the Second World War. During the 1950s and 1960s, company donations only slightly outpaced those of the unions. Since the 1970s the position has been reversed, and union political levies have overtaken company payments.

A precise comparison depends on two technical factors concerning the treatment of union political funds. These are discussed in a footnote.[28] It will be assumed that 87 percent of the annual income of political levy funds is raised for Labour party purposes. This excludes the estimated costs of administration, tax on investment income, and donations to other causes. During the eight years 1952–1959, company payments to the Conservatives (net of fund-raising costs) were 27 percent greater than union money raised for the Labour party and, in 1960–1970, 23 percent. However, during the seven years 1971–1978, the amount received by the Conservative party from companies was 27 percent less than that raised by the unions for Labour. The recent trend of union and company donations is shown in figure 3.[29]

2. Company donations provide approximately 30 percent of overall Conservative income, but unions give well over 50 percent of

[28] (1) Besides making direct payments to the Labour party at national, regional, and local levels, union political levy funds are devoted, as described earlier in the chapter, to a variety of other Labour party purposes for which there is no parallel on the Conservative side. These include union payments to sponsored Labour MPs, expenses of delegates to Labour party conferences, and grants to those attending Labour party education courses. If all these payments are included, an estimated 87 percent of the political levy is devoted to the Labour party. Alternatively, if these expenditures are excluded and account is taken only of direct union payments to organs of the party, the proportion of the political levy devoted to the Labour party falls to an estimated 78 percent. These figures assume that the proportion of the levy devoted to Labour party purposes is marginally lower than Harrison's statistics for 1955-1958 given in table 63. (2) Political levy fund reserves have increased; however, it is natural to assume that almost all these reserves will eventually be used for Labour party purposes, as has happened in the past. Therefore the percentages of the political levy devoted to Labour party purposes calculated for the purposes of figure 3 are the percentages of political levy *income* for the year concerned.

[29] If union money for sponsored MPs, delegates' expenses, and so on is excluded and account is taken only of money raised for direct financial donations to units of the Labour party organization, the comparisons are as follows: 1952-1958, company donations 42 percent greater than union funds for the Labour party; 1959-1964, 21 percent greater; 1967-1970, 37 percent greater; and 1971-1978, company donations 18 percent smaller than union funds for the Labour party.

FIGURE 3
COMPANY PAYMENTS TO THE CONSERVATIVE PARTY COMPARED WITH UNION MONEY FOR LABOUR PARTY PURPOSES, 1967–1978

£ million

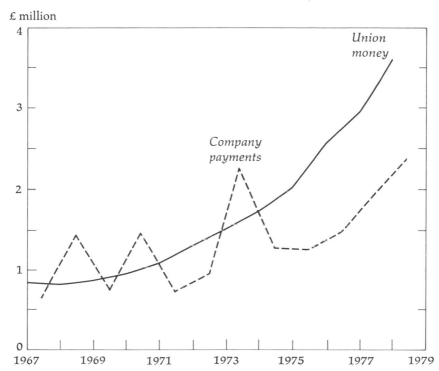

NOTE: Totals are net of estimated administrative and fund-raising costs. Payments by companies have been calculated on the same basis as for table 64 except that estimated fund-raising costs have been subtracted. Trade union money for Labour party purposes consists of 87 percent of total political levy fund income for the year concerned.

SOURCES: As for tables 58 and 64.

total Labour party income. If local parties are excluded, companies provide about 60 percent of central Conservative income and unions about 90 percent of Labour's central income.

3. Individual company donations are smaller than those of the big unions. This is partly a reflection of the differing structure of unions and of companies. The largest unions have more members than the top companies have employees. The consequence is that the leaders of the main unions have a financial power over the Labour party organization that has no counterpart on the Conservative side. In the late 1970s, the three top unions raised more money for

237

Labour than the top 800 companies combined for the Conservatives. As shown in table 59, five unions provided 64 percent of total political levy income in 1977 and 62 percent of political levy expenditure. These five unions donated approximately one-third of the Labour party's overall national, regional, and local income. In the Conservative party, the top five company donations provided a little over 1 percent of overall party income.

4. The most fundamental distinction is that the Labour party constitution gives powers to its institutional benefactors for which there is no parallel in the Conservative party. Their affiliation fees to the national Labour organization entitle unions to nearly 90 percent of the votes at the annual party conference. (The Transport and General Workers' Union has a block vote of almost twice as many as the votes of all the constituency Labour parties put together.) Payments to constituency Labour parties enable unions to sponsor over half of the party's MPs and to control a majority of seats on the party's national executive committee and, as mentioned, give them 40 percent of the votes in the new electoral college to select the party leader.

In combination, these differences make it unrealistic to treat institutional financing of British parties as if it were a single phenomenon. Although companies play a vital role in financing the central organization of the Conservative party, the connection between trade unions and the Labour party is far more intimate and significant. For those with worries about the undesirable consequences of political payments by institutions, union money provides a more realistic basis for concern.

The existing system of Labour party funding, which permits trade unions literally to buy power over the party, is, in my view, indefensible and constitutes the most important single abuse relating to British political finance. The problem is considered further in chapter 10.

Personal Payments to Members of Parliament

Apart from trade union political funds, the most serious problems connected with money in politics within the British system do not involve campaign finance or payments for the routine upkeep of the party organizations. They concern the personal finances of politicians.

Under modern conditions, companies, unions, and pressure groups wishing to purchase political influence frequently make payments—direct or indirect—to individual legislators who have already been elected to the House of Commons. Such payments can provide more leverage than contributions to a parliamentary campaign or to a party headquarters.[30]

Most MPs supplement their official salaries and allowances by accepting outside employment or sponsorship. Labour MPs are typically sponsored by trade unions, while Conservative MPs frequently accept company directorships. In addition, members sometimes act as public relations consultants or as spokesmen for pressure groups and foreign organizations.

MPs are not only permitted to have outside employers, they may also forward their interests in the House of Commons. They act as contact men or read speeches in Parliament, sometimes drafted for them by a group or trade union from which they receive fees or contributions.

Although they lack executive power, MPs possess influence and access that seem to have become increasingly valuable to outside bodies. The widening scope of government and the complex discretionary powers of the bureaucracy have increased the value of MPs as brokers. As Francis Noel-Baker put it:

> Speaking in debate is only one of many ways in which a Member may promote an interest. A note on House of Commons writing paper, a word in a Minister's ear, a party in one of the House's private dining rooms, and invitations to foreign hospitality and free travel . . . these are often far more effective weapons.[31]

Worries have frequently been expressed in general terms about the potential conflicts between the duties of MPs to their constituents and their obligations to outside paymasters, but there is no code of conduct for MPs. "Members have little formal guidance on the rules and customs of Parliament that govern their activities as Members in relation to influence and interests."[32] Nor is there

[30] This section deals with potential conflicts of interests involving MPs. There are similar problems, which are not dealt with in this study, relating to civil servants. The promise of a postretirement job or consultancy to a well-placed civil servant or local government official can prove an excellent investment for a company or foreign government.

[31] Francis Noel-Baker, " 'The Grey Zone': The Problems of Business Affiliations of Members of Parliament," *Parliamentary Affairs*, vol. 15 (1961-1962), p. 93. For an earlier discussion of problems about MPs' interests, see Frank C. Newman, "Reflections on Money and Politics in Britain," *Parliamentary Affairs*, vol. 10 (1956-1957).

[32] Alan Doig, "Self-Discipline in the House of Commons: The Poulson Affair in a Parliamentary Perspective," *Parliamentary Affairs*, vol. 32 (1979), p. 255.

any clear set of rules or procedures to cover allegations of misconduct or conflict of interest. MPs are not subject to the relatively tight codes of conduct for ministers, civil servants, local government councilors, and local government officers. According to a common interpretation, they are also exempt from the laws relating to bribery.[33] Their freedom contrasts with the strict limitations on the outside interests and earnings of congressmen and senators in the United States.

Broadly speaking, there are only two limitations on a British MP. First, an MP may not receive a direct instruction from a financial sponsor to vote or act in a particular way, nor may a sponsor give such an order. (In other words, there must be no explicit quid pro quo though, in practice, an implicit one is all right.) Second, when speaking in the House of Commons on a matter in which he has a pecuniary interest, a member must declare it. As mentioned later, MPs have since 1975 also been required to register certain categories of interests and benefits.

Discussion about alleged conflicts of interest is greatly hindered by the stringent British libel laws and by the regulations relating to parliamentary privilege. As a result, debate has centered on a few examples of alleged misconduct, which have somehow emerged into the public domain, even though the MPs concerned have often done little that has been out of the ordinary.

The wide-reaching nature of "parliamentary privilege" is illustrated by the fact that, in 1965, the Select Committee of Privileges even discussed a complaint by an MP against James Callaghan, who was chancellor of the exchequer at the time, on the grounds that he had referred in a speech (in very general terms) to the fact that some MPs were influenced by their business interests. Callaghan was exonerated.[34] In 1974 another MP was not so lucky. Joe Ashton, MP for Bassetlaw, was hauled before the Committee of Privileges for writing in the magazine *Labour Weekly* to the effect that he knew the names of six Labour MPs whose services in the House of Commons were for hire by outside organizations. The committee reported that Ashton had committed a "serious contempt" against the privileges of the House, and he was compelled to give an apology, though, in the words of *The Times*, it was "by no means unqualified."[35]

[33] See Geoffrey Marshall, "The House of Commons and Its Privileges," in S. A. Walkland, ed., *The House of Commons in the Twentieth Century: Essays by Members of the Study of Parliament Group* (Oxford: Oxford University Press, 1979), p. 222.

[34] *The Times*, July 6, 1965.

[35] *The Times*, April 29, 1974. See also Edward J. Milne, *No Shining Armour:*

In this sensitive environment, it is hardly surprising that discussions about financial problems relating to members have generally taken place behind closed doors and private concerns have usually not been aired openly. One MP wrote in the early 1960s in the academic journal *Parliamentary Affairs* of the cases "which members discuss in private" and added: "Because of the risks involved it is difficult to discuss specific cases publicly, but I should be glad to supply more detailed evidence in confidence."[36]

During recent years, several examples of allegedly undesirable (or potentially undesirable) payments to MPs have been publicized, despite the inhibitions against reporting. Some of these are mentioned below. The examples are of three types: (1) allegations that MPs have carried out specific actions connected with their parliamentary duties in return for payment, (2) unacknowledged interests, and (3) allegedly "inappropriate" interests. It should be stressed that the examples in categories (2) and (3) have, with the exception of the Stonehouse case, involved no allegations of breaches of existing law or of parliamentary privilege.

MPs for hire? The most serious charges have involved suggestions that certain MPs have used their parliamentary positions for direct financial gain. In July 1977, a Conservative MP, John Cordle, resigned from the House of Commons after a report of an all-party Select Committee on Conduct of Members. This committee had investigated the conduct of several MPs employed by an architect, John Poulson, who had been imprisoned for corruption. A letter had been found in Poulson's files in which Cordle asked for payment from the architect partly on the ground that he had given a speech in Parliament forwarding Poulson's interests. In the speech, Cordle had pressed for building contracts in West Africa financed by British aid to be allocated to British contractors—a policy that would benefit Poulson. In the words of the select committee: "What your Committee find objectionable about Mr Cordle's conduct is that his motive in pressing the interests of the Gambia in the House was to further his own unavowed commercial interests, that is to say, that he was raising a matter in Parliament for reward."[37]

An earlier case involved a Labour MP, Will Owen, who was tried in 1970 at the Old Bailey for allegedly selling secret information to the Czech embassy. Owen testified that he had never passed

The Story of One Man's Fight against Corruption in Public Life (London: John Calder, 1976), p. 177.

36 Noel-Baker, "Grey Zone," pp. 91-92.

37 *The Times*, July 15, 1977, and July 23, 1977.

classified information to two Czech intelligence officers working in London. At the same time, he acknowledged that during a period of up to nine years he had been paid about £2,300 but claimed that often he would invent information when they pumped him during lunchtime appointments. He was found not guilty on all counts but did not resume his political career.[38]

Unacknowledged interests. In 1968 the *Sunday Times* obtained a copy of a report by a London public relations firm working on behalf of the colonels' regime in Greece. In this report the company claimed that it had secured the services of a British MP who was working behind the scenes to influence other MPs on behalf of the Greek regime. It was revealed shortly afterward that the member in question was a Labour MP, Gordon Bagier. Bagier then acknowledged that he had been employed by the public relations firm. He disclaimed ever having exercised any influence on its behalf, and this was accepted. There was a considerable volume of press and television comment about the affair. In particular, concern was expressed that the rules governing the behavior of MPs, as they stood at the time, did not oblige a member to declare his financial interests except when making a speech in the House of Commons. In May 1969 a Select Committee on Members' Interests (Declaration) was set up to consider remedies.[39]

In 1977 the select committee investigating the conduct of MPs employed by the imprisoned architect Poulson issued a report criticizing Albert Roberts, a Labour MP, and Reginald Maudling, formerly the deputy Conservative party leader, for their lack of frankness in acknowledging their business connections with the architect while carrying out their official duties. (Both members strongly rejected the committee's criticisms.)[40]

Allegedly inappropriate interests. Several forms of financial interest have given rise to concern, even though they have not been kept private. First, payments to MPs to act as public relations consultants to outside political organizations and foreign governments.

[38] Milne, *No Shining Armour*, p. 77; and *The Times*, April 21 and 23, 1970, and May 7, 1970.

[39] *The Times*, October 4, 1968; Ivan Yates, "Public Men, Private Interests," *Observer*, July 9, 1972; Royal Commission on Standards of Conduct in Public Life, *Report*, Cmnd. 6524 (London: Her Majesty's Stationery Office, 1976), p. 97 and appendix 14 (the Salmon Report); and K. I. Vijay, "The Declaration of Interests by MPs: An Analysis of the Current Campaign for Reform," *Political Quarterly*, vol. 14 (1973).

[40] *The Times*, July 15, 1977.

Second, the employment of MPs to gain trade contracts in Soviet countries or right-wing dictatorships. These dealings indirectly give the members concerned a financial stake in these regimes. Third, there has been criticism of some members' associations with fringe banking or property speculation. It has sometimes been felt that MPs have, without due care and for financial gain, lent their names to provide respectability (or contacts) for unworthy enterprises. Fourth, the personal finances of some ex-ministers have sometimes been the object of comment.

In 1976 a former Labour minister, John Stonehouse, whose ambitious business enterprises had collapsed, was imprisoned for seven years for theft and deception. While his offenses had not been directly related to his membership in the House of Commons, his financial dealings had been based to a large extent on his public contacts and on his reputation as an MP and former government minister. Inspectors of the Department of Trade and Industry, who later reported on the "offences, irregularities and improprieties" of Stonehouse's London Capital Group, emphasized that he had used his political position for personal advantage: "Most held Mr Stonehouse in awe and great respect. He treated them well, took them for walks along the corridors of power and enabled them to rub shoulders with men of considerable eminence."[41]

Thorpe's connection with the fringe bank London and County Securities almost certainly harmed his political standing after the bank collapsed in 1973. This was a factor in his fall as Liberal leader.

In 1977 there was widespread press concern and some comment at the annual Labour party conference about the financial connections between several MPs and Sir Eric Miller, whose apparent suicide had coincided with police investigations into his activities while head of the Peachey property empire. Miller had come to an arrangement with Maudling whereby the Conservative politician had sold his house to the property developer, who had then rented it back to him at a token rent. This was the third time that Maudling's personal dealings had become an object of criticism. He had, as mentioned, been employed by the imprisoned architect Poulson, and he had also acted briefly (during 1969) as a director of a company that managed an offshore fund, the Real Estate Fund of America (REFA). In 1970, over a year after his resignation from the management company, REFA collapsed, and Maudling was later named in a suit brought in

41 *The Times*, December 14, 1977. For reports on Stonehouse's business interests, see the *Sunday Times*, December 22, 1974, and *The Times*, February 21, 1975.

New York on behalf of the stockholders. Maudling's unhappy business connections damaged his political career. After he left the cabinet in 1972, he never returned to real prominence.[42]

The instances that have been cited are not a complete catalog, nor is it intended to imply that the MPs mentioned were at fault.[43] It is clear, however, that MPs have considerable financial difficulties, which sometimes lead them into speculative or undesirable enterprises, and there are grounds for suspecting that members have sometimes been paid to use their political influence. In Noel-Baker's words, membership in the House of Commons "has often led to profitable financial spoils. One can point to a good many contemporary examples as evidence that it sometimes still does."[44]

There has been a gradual awakening to the problem, and one step has been taken toward tackling it. Following the recommendations of the Select Committee on Members' Interests (Declaration), endorsed by the House on June 12, 1975, a member is required to register nine specific classes of pecuniary and other benefit. These are listed in chapter 9. Although the register is a distinct advance, there are still loopholes, and there remains a resistance to requiring MPs to make public details of their personal finances or those of their families.

[42] The *Economist*, October 1, 1977; *The Times*, October 3, 1977; and the *Sunday Times*, October 2, 1977. See also *The Times*, May 26, 1978. For Maudling's connection with REFA, see *The Times*, July 22, 1972, and May 7, 1974; and M. Gillard and Paul Foot, *A Little Pot of Gold: The Story of Reginald Maudling and the Real Estate Fund of America* (London: Private Eye and André Deutsch, 1974).

[43] Shortly after Wilson's resignation as prime minister in 1976, there was considerable comment about a fund raised after the general election of 1970 to finance his political office as leader of the opposition. It was revealed that separate funds had also been raised to provide research support for some Labour shadow ministers. At the time the Wilson fund was set up, he had been at odds with the party headquarters, which had not been prepared to allocate sufficient money for his personal political staff. A group of business supporters supplied the necessary finance. The arrangement was later criticized on several grounds: (1) it was considered inappropriate by many in the party that the Labour leader should have sought financial help from capitalist sources; (2) the accounts of the fund had not been publicly known (in the words of one of the fund's officer's, "it was not kept secret, but we kept a low profile"); (3) some of the contributors were to be involved in financial scandals or legal proceedings about their business affairs; and (4) several received knighthoods or peerages during Wilson's tenure as premier (1964-1970 and 1974-1976). See *The Times*, May 29, 1976, February 18 and 19, 1977, and May 27, 1977. The fund and the controversy about Wilson's award of honors are discussed in Andrew Roth, *Sir Harold Wilson: Yorkshire Walter Mitty* (London: Macdonald and Jane's, 1977), and Joe Haines, *The Politics of Power* (London: Hodder and Stoughton, 1977). (See chap. 6, footnote 12.)

[44] Noel-Baker, "Grey Zone," p. 88.

TABLE 67

How Members of Parliament Supplement Their Official Salaries
(percent)

	Conservative	Labour	Liberal	Total[a]
Directorships of companies	54	9	46	29
Paid employment	33	11	23	21
Paid trades or professions	56	32	54	43
Professional client related to membership of the Commons	6	2	—	4
Financial sponsorships by:				
Trade unions	1	45	—	22
Co-operative party	—	5	—	2
Overseas visits not paid for by the MP or public funds	29	22	15	24
Payments or material benefits from abroad	5	3	—	4
Land and property of "substantial" value	23	4	31	13
Declarable shareholdings (i.e., more than 1% of the nominal share capital of any company)	30	6	23	17
Nil interests declared	3	19	15	12
Total number of MPs	278	316	13	634

[a] Includes minor parties.

Source: Compiled from the *Register of Members' Interests as on 26 May 1976* (London: Her Majesty's Stationery Office, 1976). See the *Economist*, July 23, 1977.

A list of declared interests has been compiled by the *Economist* and is reproduced as table 67.

The register of interests is a useful device (even though it is not sufficiently stringent). Even so, it does not, in my opinion, deal with the basic fault in the existing system. Problems will inevitably arise as long as MPs are permitted to act and vote on behalf of outside sponsors and employers, no matter how open they are about their associations.

It is a long-established tradition that MPs pursue careers outside Parliament and that they need not be full-time professional politicians. There are advantages to such a practice, and it is not necessary to limit or to ban outside occupations. What is objectionable is that an

MP should use his elective office for the benefit of an employer or sponsor.

A solution to the problem is to apply to MPs codes similar to those for local government councilors. An MP not only should be required to declare his outside interests but should not be allowed to speak, vote, or in any other way use his elective office to promote the cause of a sponsor. For instance, MPs employed as public relations consultants should never use House of Commons notepaper or the official dining rooms on their sponsors' behalf. They should make no approaches to ministers, civil servants, or fellow MPs. These new rules would still permit trade unions to sponsor MPs, as at present. But an MP sponsored by a particular union would not be allowed to lobby, speak, or vote on any matter pertaining to its affairs or interests. Likewise, members would still be permitted to receive benefits from corporations, but only on similar conditions. Such restrictions would not inhibit backers with altruistic motives or employers from using MPs for reasons unconnected with their elective positions. They would deter those expecting a political return for their money. This proposal is considered further in chapter 10.

9
Regulating Political Finance: British Style

Political finance can be regulated or reformed in many different ways. A survey of legislation in different countries reveals these categories:

1. limits on permitted expenditure by candidates or parties (spending ceilings)
2. restrictions on stated types of expenditure, even if they are within permitted spending limits
3. disclosure requirements
4. regulations or prohibitions against political payments from certain sources (such as corporations, unions, government employees)
5. cash subsidies to candidates and/or parties
6. indirect subsidies (typically, tax relief for political donors)
7. subsidies-in-kind (for example, free mail, free publicity, free broadcasting time)
8. limits on individual or group donations to candidates or parties (contribution limits)[1]

Regulations exist in Britain of the first seven types listed above. The main feature of the British system, however, is its combination of strict spending limits strictly applied (category 1) and subsidies-in-kind (category 7). This chapter describes and assesses the existing laws and practices concerning political finance. The object is to set

[1] See Herbert E. Alexander, "Political Finance Regulation in International Perspective," and Khayyam Z. Paltiel, "Public Financing Abroad: Contrasts and Effects," in Michael J. Malbin, ed., *Parties, Interest Groups, and Campaign Finance Laws* (Washington, D.C.: American Enterprise Institute, 1980). See also United States Library of Congress Law Library, *Government Financing of National Elections, Political Parties, and Campaign Spending in Various Foreign Countries* (Washington, D.C., 1979); and Khayyam Z. Paltiel, "Campaign Finance: Contrasting Practices and Reforms," in David E. Butler, Howard R. Penniman, and Austin Ranney, eds., *Democracy at the Polls: A Comparative Study of Competitive National Elections* (Washington, D.C.: American Enterprise Institute, 1981).

the scene for the discussion about proposals for reform in the next chapter.

Expense Limits for Parliamentary Elections

Since 1883 successive acts of Parliament have imposed limits on permitted election expenditure by candidates for the House of Commons.[2] These limits have varied according to the number of electors in a constituency. Higher expenditure has been permitted in rural (county) than in urban (borough) constituencies.

Under the relevant acts, the restrictions apply not only to campaign spending but also to expenditure incurred in promoting a candidate's election at any time before the poll.[3] In practice, it is easy for a candidate to avoid incurring election expenses, as defined by the law, during the precampaign period. Expenditures before the election date is announced[4] are permitted if they are designed to promote the fortunes of the local party association rather than the candidate personally.[5]

Besides setting strict expenditure limits, the acts have backed them up by strong regulations to ensure that they are enforced. In particular, no expense may, with a view to promoting or procuring the election of a candidate at an election, be incurred by any person other than the candidate, his election agent, or a person authorized in writing by the election agent.[6] This stipulation prevents the establishment, on the American model, of separate committees with sepa-

[2] For an account of the Corrupt and Illegal Practices Prevention Act, 1883, see Cornelius O'Leary, *The Elimination of Corrupt Practices in British Elections, 1868-1911* (Oxford: Oxford University Press, 1962), chap. 6. Modern election law is fully described in H. W. Wollaston, ed., *Parker's Conduct of Parliamentary Elections* (London: Charles Knight, 1970), and Lord Hailsham, ed., *Halsbury's Laws of England*, 4th ed. (London: Butterworth's, 1977), vol. 15, section on "Elections." The major political parties also produce useful guides to the law for the use of candidates and local party workers. See, for example, Donald Storer, *Conduct of Parliamentary Elections*, 8th ed. (London: Labour Party, 1977).

[3] Representation of the People Act, 1949, s. 103. See also Hailsham, *Halsbury's Laws of England*, vol. 15, para. 710.

[4] In practice, the announcement by the prime minister of the date of the poll is usually regarded as marking the start of the general election period. Technically, this announcement has no legal significance as far as candidates' permitted election expenses are concerned. See Hailsham, *Halsbury's Laws of England*, vol. 15, para. 712. See also Conservative and Unionist Central Office, *Parliamentary Election Manual*, 11th ed. (London, 1963), pp. 47ff.

[5] Hailsham, *Halsbury's Laws of England*, vol. 15, para. 713.

[6] Representation of the People Act, 1949, s. 64. The strict laws about agency are set out in Wollaston, *Parker's Conduct of Elections*, chap. 1, and Hailsham, *Halsbury's Laws of England*, vol. 15, paras. 691-704 and para. 721, notes 4-9.

rate accounts on behalf of a candidate. The law also restricts the provision of gifts in kind; for example, the notional cost of using election day committee rooms must be included in the expense limit, even though such rooms are usually in the private homes of volunteers and are free of charge.[7]

The law is not watertight. An experienced election agent can normally find ways of stretching permitted expenditures. Printers are persuaded to give low quotations for election literature with the promise of further business after the campaign. Paper is purchased before the start of the campaign on behalf of the local party association and then sold to the candidate as secondhand stock. Election agents' fees are frequently artificially low. These devices can, where required, provide an extra 20 percent of expenditure. It is not possible, however, to abuse the limits on a large scale without risking the draconian penalty of having his election declared void.[8]

The limits shown in table 68 have involved a reduction in real terms in the limits when consideration is taken of inflation and of the increasing number of votes in an average constituency. The remarkable fall in the cost of candidates' election expenses following the 1883 act was shown in tables 5 and 7.[9]

The only expenditures restricted by the 1883 act and its successors are those of the candidate. Neither local nor national party organizations are directly subject to the legal limits.[10] However, the rule forbidding expenditure not authorized by the candidate or his agent makes it difficult in practice for a local party association to operate during an election campaign without risking contravening the law. It is normal for local party associations to dissolve themselves completely for the duration of the campaign so as to avoid the possibility that some of their routine, noncampaign activities might be construed as promoting the candidate's election and thus be subject to the legal restrictions.[11]

---

[7] Hailsham, *Halsbury's Laws of England*, vol. 15, para. 719, notes 2, 3.

[8] Representation of the People Act, 1949, s. 139(1). See also Hailsham, *Halsbury's Laws of England*, vol. 15, paras, 808-10.

[9] See also appendix C.

[10] R v. Tronoh Mines Ltd [1952], 1 All England Law Reports, p. 697. However, see also Director of Public Prosecutions v. Luft [1976], All England Law Reports, p. 569.

[11] "It is a prudent step for a political association to suspend its activities as soon as an election commences" (Hailsham, *Halsbury's Laws of England*, vol. 15, para. 715). According to the Conservative and Unionist Central Office, *Parliamentary Election Manual:*

In most cases where the rules of the association do not automatically suspend the operations of the association and its branches when the

TABLE 68
Maximum Permitted Expenditure for Each Parliamentary Candidate, 1883–1978

Date Enacted	Type of Constituency	Expense Limit[a]
1883[b]	Boroughs	Less than 200 electors—£350 More than 200 electors—£380, plus £30 for every additional 1,000 electors
	Counties	Less than 2,000 electors—£650 More than 2,000 electors—£710, plus £60 for every additional 1,000 electors
1918[c]	Boroughs	5d per elector
	Counties	7d per elector
1928[c]	Boroughs	5d per elector
	Counties	6d per elector
1949	Boroughs	£450 plus 1½d per elector
	Counties	£450 plus 2d per elector
1969	Boroughs	£750 plus 1½d per elector
	Counties	£750 plus 2d per elector
1974	Boroughs	£1,075 plus 6p for every 8 electors
	Counties	£1,075 plus 6p for every 6 electors
1978	Boroughs	£1,750 plus 1½p per elector
	Counties	£1,750 plus 2p per elector

Note: "d" denotes an old penny and "p" a new penny. There were 240 old pence to the pound sterling. There are 100 new pennies to the pound sterling.

[a] Permitted expense limits exclude candidates' personal expenses, which may be incurred in addition.

[b] Slightly different limits have applied to Ireland (until 1918), to Ulster (from 1922), and to multimember constituencies (until 1945).

[c] An additional election agent's fee of up to £50 in boroughs and £75 in counties was allowed until the general election of 1945. Under the Representation of the People Act, 1949, sch. 5., the election agent's fee had to be included in the legal maximum.

Sources: Corrupt and Illegal Practices Prevention Act, 1883, sch. 1, pt. 4 and pt. 5, para. 3; Representation of the People Act, 1918, sch. 4; Representation of the People (Equal Franchise) Act, 1928, s. 5; Representation of the People Act, 1949, s. 64(2)(a); Representation of the People Act, 1969, s. 24(1) and sch. 2, para. 16; Representation of the People Act, 1974, s. 1; Representation of the People Act, 1978, s. 1.

The limits on parliamentary candidates also limit certain activities of the national party organizations[12] in the period between the announcement of the general election date and the poll; for example, election grants by the central parties to candidates and centrally financed advertisements promoting specific candidates must be included in the permitted expenditure of the candidates concerned.

For many years the central party organizations refrained from all forms of press and poster advertising during an election campaign for fear that it might be construed as promoting the election of the party's candidates and thus be subject to the legal spending limits. Since 1974 the three main parties have taken a more daring view of the law.[13] In the 1979 election, the Conservative and Labour parties both advertised extensively during the campaign period. According to the legal advice given to Conservative Central Office, press and

---

candidate is adopted, a special resolution should be passed. The effect of this is to make it clear to all sections of the Party that all operations except those connected with the election campaign must cease until polling day (p. 41).

All association and branch activities must cease absolutely as soon as the campaign commences (p. 46).

[12] Existing election law has been criticized on the ground that it leaves national-level campaign spending unaffected and uncontrolled. The point was forcefully made in David E. Butler and Richard Rose, *The British General Election of 1959* (London: Macmillan, 1960), appendix 5, "The Condition of Election Law." In practice, there are some major legal limitations—as shown in this chapter—on campaign expenditures by the central party organizations.

The concern of Butler, Rose, and other commentators of the early 1960s about unregulated national-level spending by parties and pressure groups stemmed largely from the assumption that it allowed an imbalance between the two main parties. The Tronoh case of 1952 was seen as opening the way to unlimited advertising by business groups that effectively supported the Conservative cause—advertising that, it was felt, Labour could not hope to match (see Alfred P. Brainard, "The Law of Elections and Business Interest Groups in Britain," *Western Political Quarterly*, vol. 13 [1960]). Probusiness advertising was largely balanced by the propaganda of union newspapers, however, which supported the Labour party case in general and even recommended particular union-sponsored parliamentary candidates. Not only was this expenditure exempt from the limitations on spending by parliamentary candidates, but it also came from general union funds rather than from their political levy funds. The ability of unions to use their general funds for partisan political purposes was confirmed by an earlier case, Forster v. National Amalgamated Union of Shop Assistants, Warehousemen and Clerks. (See [1927], 1 All England Law Reports, p. 618). (See also footnote 31.)

[13] During the general election of February 1974, the Liberal party launched a £25,000 advertising campaign in the *Daily Express* and was not taken to court for violating the spending limits for candidates set out in the Representation of the People Act, 1974, s. 1. See David E. Butler and Dennis Kavanagh, *The British General Election of February 1974* (London: Macmillan, 1974), pp. 240-42. See also Wollaston, *Parker's Conduct of Elections*, pp. 78-79, and Hailsham, *Halsbury's Laws of England*, vol. 15, para. 721.

poster advertisements would not be subject to the spending restrictions on candidates provided that they publicized the party as a whole and did not mention the name of particular candidates and provided that any poster advertisements were distributed equally around the country and not concentrated in certain types of constituency (such as marginal constituencies).[14] The Labour party was bolder and placed advertisements in regional newspapers including target marginal seats in their areas of circulation.

Restrictions on Types of Political Expenditure

There are restrictions on certain types of political spending even if they are within the permitted spending limits.

Constituency Election Campaigns. Candidates and their election agents are not permitted to make or authorize payments of several kinds. These include (1) payments for the conveyance of voters to or from the poll,[15] (2) payments for the exhibition of posters,[16] (3) the use of a wireless station abroad,[17] (4) bribery,[18] and (5) "treating" (that is, the offer of inducements of meat, drink, or entertainment).[19] Most of these restrictions were introduced by the Corrupt Practices Act, 1883.

Radio and Television Advertising. Radio and television in Britain are controlled by the British Broadcasting Corporation (BBC) and by the Independent Broadcasting Authority (IBA). Neither permits political advertising.

The BBC came into operation at the beginning of 1927 under royal charter. It was to be a public service body "acting in the national interest" and financed by license fees paid by all owners of radio receivers. The first director general, Sir J. (later Lord) Reith, considered that this charter prevented the BBC from accepting pay-

---

[14] Interview with Central Office official.

[15] Representation of the People Act, 1949, ss. 89 and 90. See also Hailsham, *Halsbury's Laws of England*, vol. 15, paras. 765-66.

[16] Representation of the People Act, 1949, s. 94(1). See also Hailsham, *Halsbury's Laws of England*, vol. 15, para. 756. Commercial poster sites are exempt from the ban.

[17] Representation of the People Act, 1949, s. 80.

[18] Ibid., s. 99. See also Hailsham, *Halsbury's Laws of England*, vol. 15, paras. 767-80.

[19] Representation of the People Act, 1949, s. 100. See also Hailsham, *Halsbury's Laws of England*, vol. 15, paras. 781-83.

252

ments for advertising. Accordingly, when Winston Churchill wrote to Reith in 1929 offering to pay £100 to be able to broadcast a ten-minute appeal on India, Reith refused, explaining that he was unwilling to introduce "American" methods into British broadcasting.[20] The Television Act, 1954, set up the Independent Television Authority (later called the Independent Broadcasting Authority) to license program contracting companies that would depend on advertising revenue. The same restrictions on the political content of political broadcasts were applied under the act as for the BBC.[21] Accordingly, political advertising is not accepted.[22] This is an extremely important restriction on the national party organizations. It means that the most powerful advertising medium is not available for purchase, no matter how much money a party is prepared to pay.

Payments to Secure Titles and Peerages. The Honours (Prevention of Abuses) Act, 1925, provides for the "punishment of abuses in connection with the grant of honours." The scandals that led to its enactment are outlined in chapter 4. The act lays down a penalty of up to two years' imprisonment for any person found guilty of trading in honors. The act makes it illegal to accept "any gift, money or valuable consideration as an inducement or reward for procuring or assisting ... to procure the grant of a dignity or title of honour."[23] The act also makes it an offense to give or offer such an inducement.[24]

Disclosure Requirements

Parliamentary Candidates. Parliamentary (and local government) candidates are required by law to make detailed returns of their election expenses. Failure to submit a comprehensive return of expenses is an illegal practice, and if a successful candidate fails to transmit the declaration of expenses to the returning officer within thirty-five days after the declaration of the election result, he cannot sit or vote in the House of Commons.[25] The returning officer is directed by law

[20] See Martin Gilbert, *Winston S. Churchill*, vol. 5, *1922-1939* (London: Heinemann, 1976), pp. 358-59; and Asa Briggs, *The History of Broadcasting in the United Kingdom*, vol. 2, *The Golden Age of Wireless* (Oxford: Oxford University Press, 1965), pp. 131-41.

[21] Television Act, 1954, s. 3(1).

[22] See Colin Seymour-Ure, *The Political Impact of Mass Media* (London: Constable, 1974), pp. 209ff.

[23] Honours (Prevention of Abuses) Act, 1925, s. 1(1).

[24] Ibid., s. 1(2).

[25] Representation of the People Act, 1949, ss. 69, 73.

to publish the accounts and make them available for inspection for two years.[26]

Trade Unions. Unions are bound by statute to make an annual financial statement, including an account of the political fund, to the certification officer.[27] Unions are not obliged to detail their expenditure on political objects and, Harrison points out, "a few unions are still so afraid of giving anything away to 'the other side' that they withhold the most elementary facts from their own members."[28] "Political objects," the income and expenditure for which must be included in the separate political fund account, are defined as follows:

- paying expenses incurred directly or indirectly by a candidate or prospective candidate for any public office
- holding meetings or distributing literature or documents in support of a candidate
- maintaining any member of Parliament or other holder of public office
- selection of a candidate for Parliament or any public office
- "the holding of public meetings of any kind, or the distribution of political literature or political documents of any kind, unless the main purpose of the meetings or of the literature or documents is the furtherance of statutory objects within the meanings of this Act"[29]

Although contributions to political parties are not mentioned in this definition, they are interpreted as political purposes under the terms of the act. As mentioned in chapter 8, however, the exclusion from the political levy fund regulations of expenditure by unions in the furtherance of their "statutory objects" is a major loophole. These statutory objects are loosely defined and include, for instance, "the regulation of the relations between workmen and masters" and "the provision of benefits to members."[30] According to a subsequent interpretation:

[26] Representation of the People Act, 1969, s. 8.
[27] Trade Union and Labour Relations Act, 1974, s. 11 and sch. 2; Employment Protection Act, 1975, s. 125.
[28] Martin Harrison, *Trade Unions and the Labour Party since 1945* (London: Allen and Unwin, 1960), p. 59. Harrison comments that "statute binds them [unions] to make an annual financial statement to their members—but nothing binds them to make it either comprehensive or comprehensible" (p. 59).
[29] Trade Union Act, 1913, s. 3(3).
[30] Ibid., s. 1(2).

If a matter lies within the statutory objects of a trade union it is not "political" although it may be part of the programme of a political party. The "political" objects, therefore, which are contrasted by the proviso with statutory objects must be those party political objects which are not also statutory objects.[31]

This gives unions considerable scope to exclude expenditures from their political funds on the grounds that, though political, they also have the objective of furthering an industrial policy. Under this ruling, unions were, for instance, permitted to subsidize the Labour party newspaper, the *Daily Herald*, out of their general funds. Union newspapers and publications are considered industrial and not political, even if they openly exhort members to vote for the Labour party or for specific trade-union-sponsored candidates.

Companies. The Companies Act, 1967, as amended, obliges companies to record political contributions of more than £200 in their annual reports of the directors.[32] The definition of "political purposes" is as follows:

a company shall be treated as giving money for political purposes if, directly or indirectly,—
(a) it gives a donation or subscription to a political party of the United Kingdom or any part thereof; or
(b) it gives a donation or subscription to a person who, to its knowledge, is carrying on, or proposing to carry on, any activities which can, at the time at which the donation or subscription was given, reasonably be regarded as likely to affect support for such a political party as aforesaid.[33]

Under subsection (a), companies are required to declare payments to front organizations, such as British United Industrialists. Such organizations, however, if they do not themselves have the legal status of a company, are not obliged to declare the purposes to which they devote the political payments they receive.

Because of the wide definition of "political purposes" under subsection (b), companies must report donations not only to political

[31] Report of the chief registrar of friendly societies, 1925, p. 3. Quoted in Harrison, *Trade Unions and the Labour Party*, p. 57. This liberal interpretation accorded with the judgment in the Forster case (see footnote 12). Harrison rightly comments that "this ruling offers an engaging number of loopholes" and permits the use of general union funds for "essentially political campaigns" (p. 57).
[32] Companies Act, 1967, s. 19.
[33] Ibid., s. 19(3).

parties and their front organizations but also to a number of right-wing pressure groups. In this respect, the law regulating disclosures of donations by companies is more stringent than that for trade unions.

Members of Parliament. The recently introduced rules are set out in the following extract from Erskine May.

> *Classes of interest to be registered.* Following the recommendations of the Select Committee on Members' Interests (Declaration), endorsed by the House on 12 June 1975, a Member is required to register nine specific classes of pecuniary interest or other benefit. They are:—
>
> (1) remunerated directorships of companies, public or private;
> (2) remunerated employments or offices;
> (3) remunerated trades, professions or vocations;
> (4) the names of clients when the interests referred to above include personal services by the Member which arise out of or are related in any manner to his membership of the House;
> (5) financial sponsorships, (a) as a Parliamentary candidate where to the knowledge of the Member the sponsorship in any case exceeds 25 per cent of the candidate's election expenses, or (b) as a Member of Parliament, by any person or organization, stating whether any such sponsorship includes any payment to the Member or any material benefit or advantage direct or indirect;
> (6) overseas visits relating to or arising out of membership of the House where the cost of any such visit has not been wholly borne by the Member or by public funds;
> (7) any payments or any material benefits or advantages received from or on behalf of foreign Governments, organizations or persons;
> (8) land and property of substantial value or from which a substantial income is derived;
> (9) the names of companies, or other bodies in which the Member has, to his knowledge, either himself or with or on behalf of his spouse or infant children, a beneficial interest in shareholdings of a nominal value greater than one-hundredth of the issued share capital.

A Member is only required to enter the source of the re-muneration or benefit and not the amount received.[34]

These disclosure requirements have a number of limitations:

1. Parliamentary candidates are not required to state their sources of income.

2. It is not possible to determine accurately, on the basis of the disclosure requirements, the totals given by unions and companies to specific political parties. This is because the reporting onus is on individual unions and companies and not on the political parties re-ceiving the payments. Neither unions nor companies are obliged to give the final destination of their declared political expenditures.

There are severe practical problems in collecting union and com-pany accounts, as described in chapter 8. On the union side, the total income, expenditure, and reserves of political levy funds are given in the annual reports of the certification officer. These do not give the purposes for which money was spent. This information has to be gleaned from the accounts of individual unions. As far as companies are concerned, there is no official compilation of political payments.[35]

---

[34] Sir David Lidderdale, ed., *Erskine May's Treatise on the Law, Privileges, Pro-ceedings, and Usage of Parliament*, 19th ed. (London: Butterworth's 1976), pp. 1087-88.

[35] Individual union accounts (published in their annual reports) and political levy fund returns to the certification officer vary in their detail and their presen-tation. They do not permit any precise conclusions about total union payments to the Labour party or to political pressure groups. There is a strong case for requiring unions to give fuller and prompter information about their political levy funds to the certification officer.

Several improvements in the reporting of political payments by unions and by companies are needed: (1) It is reasonable to require unions and companies to reveal the ultimate recipients of their political payments. If a union or com-pany makes a payment to an intermediary body, that body should be required in turn to declare the political use to which the payment is put. (2) Procedures for collecting and publishing information about trade union political levy funds should be improved: (a) The annual reports of the certification officer should give the numbers in each union "contracting out" of paying the levy. (b) Income from members' contributions should be shown separately from investment in-come. (c) For each union, the contribution rate per member should be given. (d) Investment income should be recorded net of tax. (e) Totals of reserves should include funds held at all levels of the relevant unions—that is, by regional and branch units of the union organizations as well as by headquarters. (f) Transfers from a union nationally to regional or branch organizations of the union should not be recorded as "expenditures." (g) The certification officer's reports ought to show the overall amount of political levy fund expenditure on the Labour party at various levels of its organization and also the sums given to other bodies. (h) The amounts entered as spending on administration ought to reflect the sums actually spent for this purpose. (i) Changes in accounting procedures between one annual report and the next ought to be noted and

3. The existing legislation does not require disclosure of payments to British parties by foreign unions, companies, or individuals.

4. The new register of MPs' interests leaves a number of loopholes, and there remains resistance to requiring MPs to make public details of their personal finances or those of their families.[36]

Regulations or Prohibitions against Political Payments from Certain Sources

Unlike the United States, Britain does not prohibit political donations by companies, unions, or banks. However, the conditions under which unions are permitted to make payments for political objects are regulated by the Trade Unions Act, 1913, as described in chapter 3 and chapter 8.[37]

Cash Subsidies to Candidates and/or Parties

There has been a traditional reluctance in Britain to give direct cash grants out of public funds for political purposes. Where such payments have been made, they have normally been to enable MPs and ministers to carry out their public duties once elected to the House of Commons, but they have not been given to finance campaigns or

---

sufficient information given to permit standard comparisons over time. (j) All unions (including those without political levy funds) should be required to declare and specify expenditures out of their general funds devoted to "political purposes" as defined in the Companies Act, 1967, s. 19(3). (3) The registrar of companies should enter political payments declared in company annual reports in a special register of such payments. The task of collecting the information should not be the responsibility of independent researchers.

[36] (1) There is no effective sanction against noncompliance by MPs (see Lidderdale, *Erskine May's Treatise*, pp. 1088-89). (2) Members may decide for themselves whether particular pecuniary interests are "relevant" and need therefore to be registered. (3) As mentioned, MPs are not required to state the source of their remuneration or benefit or the amount received. (4) The interests of MPs' wives and children are excluded (except for shareholdings). The shortcomings of the existing arrangements have attracted understandable criticism. According to one MP, "some of the information given in the present register was ludicrous" (*Daily Telegraph*, July 27, 1979).

[37] For regulations about the establishment and operation of trade union political levy funds, see the Trade Union Act, 1913, ss. 3-5. In 1927 the provision about contracting out was replaced by "contracting in" (Trade Disputes and Trade Unions Act, 1927, s. 4.) Contracting out was again restored by the Trade Disputes and Trade Unions Act, 1946, sch. 1, para. 2. In the 1950 general election, the Conservatives pledged that they would reverse the law yet again if they were elected to office. They narrowly lost the election, and the pledge was not repeated in the 1951 general election campaign. Contracting out was left untouched by Conservative governments from 1951 onward (see Harrison, *Trade Unions and the Labour Party*, pp. 29-31).

extraparliamentary party organizations. Payments have been introduced for these uses:

Salaries for Government Ministers. These have been given throughout the period covered by this book. The Ministers of the Crown Act, 1937, provided a salary for the leader of the opposition.[38] The Ministerial Salaries Consolidation Act, 1965, provided a salary for the leader of the opposition in the House of Lords and the opposition chief whips in each house. The Ministerial and Other Salaries Act, 1972, introduced salaries for two opposition assistant whips in the House of Commons.[39]

Payments to the Government Chief Whip. Under legislation enacted in 1782 and 1837, the government chief whip received an annual sum of £10,000 for "Secret Service," of which he was not obliged to give any account. The grants were intended to help the chief whip carry out his official duties of providing for the business of the House of Commons. Only part of the £10,000 was needed for this purpose, however, and the rest was used to finance other party activities. As described in chapter 1, the use of the Secret Service money for party purposes was seen as an abuse in the 1880s. The grant was discontinued in 1886. From this time, the government has paid directly for the expenses of the government chief whip's office. The £10,000 per annum grant until 1886 was the closest approach to a direct government subsidy for extraparliamentary party uses that has existed until the present time.[40]

MPs' Salaries. Payment for MPs was first introduced in 1911, when the rate was set at £400 per annum.[41] Salaries have risen periodically

---

[38] Ministers of the Crown Act, 1937, s. 5.

[39] See Lidderdale, *Erskine May's Treatise*, p. 14; and R. Malcolm Punnett, *Front-Bench Opposition: The Role of the Leader of the Opposition, the Shadow Cabinet, and Shadow Government in British Politics* (London: Heinemann, 1973), pp. 77-78. See also Ministerial Salaries Consolidation Act, 1965, s. 1, and Ministerial and Other Salaries Act, 1972. The current provisions are contained in the Ministerial and Other Salaries Act, 1975.

[40] See Lord Chilston, "Aretas Akers-Douglas: 1st Viscount Chilston (1851-1926): A Great Whip," *Parliamentary Affairs*, vol. 15 (1961-1962), pp. 55-57. The acts providing for the Secret Service grants were 22 Geo. 3, ch. 82, 1782, and An Act for the Support of Her Majesty's Household, and of the Honour and the Dignity of the Crown of Great Britain and Ireland, 1837. The grants were abolished by the Secret Service Money (Repeal) Act, 1886.

[41] A provision for MPs' salaries was first made in the Appropriation Act, 1911, sch. B, pt. 7. For a useful historical account, see William B. Gwyn, *Democracy and the Cost of Politics in Britain, 1832-1959* (London: Athlone Press, 1962), chap. 8, "Payment of Members."

but have always been relatively modest.[42] Other financial benefits and allowances have also been introduced. They include free travel for MPs between London and their constituencies (introduced in 1924), pension provisions (1965), a secretarial allowance and free telephone calls within the United Kingdom (1969), terminal grants to MPs losing their seats in a general election (1972), and housing allowances (1972).

Financial Aid to Opposition Parties in the House of Commons. In 1975 the House of Commons approved a scheme to give financial aid to opposition parties in Parliament. The scheme enabled opposition parties to claim financial assistance in respect of expenses incurred in carrying out their parliamentary business. The amount of aid was based on a formula taking account of the number of votes gained by each party at the previous general election and the number of seats won. In order to qualify for assistance, a party had to have at least two MPs elected at the previous general election or one MP and a minimum of 150,000 votes. When the scheme was introduced, the grant consisted of £500 per annum per seat won and £1 for every 200 votes cast for the party's candidates at the preceding general election, subject to a maximum of £150,000. This meant that the Conservatives received £150,000 and the other opposition parties a total of £53,570 per annum. Since the introduction of the scheme, the grants have been regularly raised.[43]

[42] The growth of MPs' salaries and allowances is detailed in David E. Butler and Anne Sloman, *British Political Facts, 1900-1979* (London: Macmillan, 1980), p. 194. Though still ungenerous by international standards, MPs' pay has recently increased rapidly. In July 1980 MPs voted themselves an annual salary of £11,750, with a further raise to £13,150 to take effect in June 1981 (*The Times*, July 22, 1980). As late as June 1979, the salary had been only £6,879. In addition, there has been a significant growth of fringe benefits (see David Wood, "MPs' Pay and Growth of Expenses," *The Times*, July 31, 1978).

In July 1980 the allowance available to each MP for secretarial and research assistance was set at £7,859. This was to rise to £8,000 in 1981. An additional 10 percent was made available for employees' pension contributions. Other allowances include a maximum of £3,046 for MPs' overnight stays away from their main residences and a supplement of £424 for MPs representing constituencies in London.

[43] Committee on Financial Aid to Political Parties, *Report*, Cmnd. 6601 (London: Her Majesty's Stationery Office, 1976), p. 1 (Houghton Report). For the resolution of the House of Commons to introduce the grants, see House of Commons Debates, 5th series, 888, cols. 1933-34, March 20, 1975. In 1978 the maximum grant payable was raised to £165,000. See House of Commons Debates, 5th series, 944, col. 203, February 13, 1978. In reply to a parliamentary question, it was stated in 1979 that a total of £813,660 had been paid to opposition parties in Parliament. It had been distributed as follows: Conservatives, £615,000; Liberals, £136,259; Scottish National party, £39,762; Plaid Cymru, £9,557; United Ulster Unionist party, £7,875; Social Democratic and Labour party, £5,207. See

State Aid during the Common Market Referendum, 1975. Under the Referendum Act, 1975, grants of £125,000 each were authorized to the two main opposing campaign organizations, Britain in Europe and the National Referendum Campaign.[44] Each organization was permitted to supplement the amount received from the government with donations from individuals and institutions, but they were obliged as a condition of receiving the grant to publish their accounts. State aid was not provided for the 1979 referendums in Scotland and Wales on proposals for devolution or for the 1979 elections for the European Parliament. In the European elections, however, parties received aid from Common Market sources.

Indirect Subsidies

No provisions have been introduced in Britain to stimulate contributions to political parties by income tax relief or tax credits to the donors. The law relating to capital transfer tax (that is, gifts tax and inheritance tax), however, encourages payments to parties. This law could be considered a form of indirect political subsidy.

The Finance Act, 1975, provides exemptions from capital transfer tax for gifts to political parties. It lays down that

> transfers of value are exempt to the extent that the values transferred . . .
> (a) are attributable to property which becomes the property of a political party qualifying for exemption under this paragraph; and
> (b) so far as made on or within one year of the death of the transferor, do not exceed £100,000.[45]

In order to qualify for this benefit, a party must have the same minimum level of electoral support as needed to qualify for a grant under the scheme, described above, to aid opposition parties in the House of Commons;[46] that is, it must have won at least two seats at the

---

House of Commons Debates, 5th series, 962, col. 237 (Written Answers), February 8, 1979. In 1979 the amount per vote payable was raised by a further 75 percent and the maximum grant payable by 75¾ percent (that is, to £290,000). See House of Commons Debates, 5th series, 999, col. 155 (Written Answers), November 11, 1979.

[44] Referendum Act, 1975, s. 3. See also Privy Council Office, *Referendum on United Kingdom Membership of the European Community: Accounts of Campaigning Organisations*, Cmnd. 6251 (London: Her Majesty's Stationery Office, 1975).

[45] Finance Act, 1975, sch. 6, pt. 1 (11)(1).

[46] Ibid., pt. 1 (11)(2).

preceding general election or, alternatively, it must have won one seat and an aggregate of not less than 150,000 votes.[47]

Subsidies-in-Kind

Although candidates and parties do not receive direct financial aid from the government, they are entitled to a number of benefits that greatly reduce their financial burdens. Until 1918 the parliamentary candidates in each constituency were obliged to share among them the costs incurred by the returning officer in conducting the poll. In addition, the regulations concerning voter registration were so complex that prospective candidates or their local party associations had much to gain by helping potentially sympathetic electors to register and by raising objections to the registration of apparently hostile electors. The considerable costs of voter registration and payments to the returning officer during the aristocratic era are shown in table 1. Candidates and their local supporters were required under the pre-1918 system to bear the costs of running the formal machinery of an election, which could reasonably be regarded as a responsibility of the state. Under the Representation of the People Act, 1918, the government accepted financial responsibility for the conduct of the poll.[48] Candidates were no longer required to contribute toward the costs of the returning officer in conducting the ballot. The franchise was extended and simplified. This reduced the complexity of voter registration. Local government authorities became responsible for all aspects of registration, which almost entirely removed the burden from candidates and local party organizations.[49]

[47] The tax status of political parties was the subject of a recent case, in which Conservative Central Office won a decision on appeal against the inspector of taxes. The judgment permitted the Central Office to continue to pay income tax rather than corporation tax on its investment income. The case possibly had wider constitutional implications insofar as it raised the question of the legal definition of a "political party" (see Conservative and Unionist Central Office v. Burrell [Inspector of Taxes], *The Times*, April 3, 1980).

[48] For a discussion of the Representation of the People Act, 1918, see David E. Butler, *The Electoral System in Britain since 1918*, 2d ed. (Oxford: Oxford University Press, 1963), chaps. 1, 2.

[49] The costs of voter registration to the Treasury and the local authorities rose from £1,020,000 in 1922-1923 to £2,360,000 in 1961-1962 (ibid., p. 169). According to the Houghton Report, local authorities (excluding Northern Ireland) spent a total of £6,025,000 on all aspects of voter registration in 1973-1974 (p. 2). According to Home Office sources, this cost had trebled by the late 1970s.

Public expenditure on voter registration could be considered a form of subsidy-in-kind to parliamentary and local government candidates. It saves expenses regularly incurred before 1918. In countries such as the United States, parties

This 1918 act introduced two forms of aid for parliamentary candidates: free postal deliveries and free use of school halls and other public rooms for political meetings.[50]

Free Postage. A parliamentary candidate is entitled to send free of any postal charge to each elector one postal communication weighing not more than two ounces and containing matter related to the election.[51] The Houghton Committee recorded that in the general election of October 1974, the Post Office received £2.1 million from the Treasury to cover the cost of delivering 75 million communications.[52] By 1979 this sum probably rose to about £5 million, that is, some £2,000 for each candidate. This grossly overstates the commercial cost of a door-to-door delivery and the usefulness of this facility to candidates. Information from a commercial firm indicates that the charge for door-to-door delivery throughout an urban constituency was about £400 in 1979. The rural areas costs were higher. A national average of £500 per constituency is, therefore, a reasonable basis for calculation. This means that the value of the free postal delivery in the general election of 1979 was £311,000 for the Conservative and Labour parties and £288,000 for the Liberals.

Free Hire of Halls. During a parliamentary or local election campaign, a candidate is entitled to hold meetings in schools situated in his or an adjoining constituency. For parliamentary elections, this entitlement extends to any rooms available for public meetings that are maintained wholly or mainly out of public funds. The candidate is

---

still spend heavily on publicity drives on television and in the press to encourage voters to register. Nevertheless, I have not listed state spending on voter registration or on other aspects of electoral administration as subsidies-in-kind. There is a clear distinction between the costs of establishing the legal and administrative framework for elections and the costs of campaigning.

[50] The Representation of the People Act, 1918, not only released candidates from the responsibility of paying for the administration of the poll but also gave subsidies-in-kind of considerable value. In order to deter frivolous candidatures, the act therefore required from each candidate a deposit of £150, which was forfeited if he or she obtained less than 12.5 percent of the votes cast. Since 1918 the deposit has remained at its original level. Because of inflation, it has been reduced in real terms to under a tenth of its level in 1918. It no longer serves as a deterrent to the frivolous. There is a good case for raising the deposit substantially, possibly to £1,000, or to a quarter of the maximum permitted election expenses in the constituency concerned. (For the current legislation, see Representation of the People Act, 1949, sch. 2, Parliamentary Election Rules, r.10(1).)

[51] Representation of the People Act, 1949, s. 79.

[52] Houghton Report, p. 3.

not required to pay for the hire of the room, but he has to pay for any heating, lighting, and cleaning costs.[53]

Public meetings have gradually declined in importance, and election agents now attach more importance to canvassing and to informal "walkabouts" in marketplaces, shopping precincts, and other places where crowds gather. Formal meetings continue to play a part in constituency election campaigns, however, especially in rural areas. In the general election of February 1974, Conservative and Labour candidates held an average of eight meetings each and Liberal candidates six meetings each.[54] The value of the free hire of public halls was possibly about £100 per candidate in the election of 1979, that is, a total of £62,000 for the Conservative and Labour parties and £58,000 for the Liberals.

Party Political Broadcasts. Since before the Second World War, the BBC (and later the IBA) have made available free broadcasting time to the major political parties.

The broadcasting authorities have no specific statutory commitment to allocate air time to political parties, and they are not reimbursed by the Treasury for doing so. The provision of party political broadcasts has been viewed as a public service under the charter of the BBC and under the general terms of the Television Act, 1954 (which established commercial television).[55] To all intents and purposes, the free broadcasts are a subsidy-in-kind to the main parties.

The time allotted to each party is decided by informal but tough bargaining in a committee including representatives of the broadcasting authorities and the main political parties. The committee on political broadcasting includes Conservative, Labour, and Liberal representatives and, since the general election of February 1974, the Scottish Nationalist Party. The exact allocations to each party have varied over time. The pattern of the past two decades has been consistent: the Conservative and Labour parties have received equal time, and the Liberal party has been given less time than the two major parties but more than that to which it would be entitled on the basis of its electoral support. Since 1959 the Liberal party has received about twice the television time to which it would be entitled if allocations had been based on the number of votes received in general elections.

[53] Representation of the People Act, 1949, s. 82. See also Houghton Report, p. 3.

[54] Butler and Kavanagh, *British General Election of February 1974*, p. 224.

[55] There is a useful discussion about the status of party political broadcasts in Lord Hailsham, ed., *Halsbury's Laws of England*, 4th ed. (London: Butterworth's, 1974), vol. 8, para. 1135.

Party political broadcasts take place both during general election campaigns and in electoral peacetime. There are both radio and television broadcasts. The main election broadcasts are a series of ten-minute programs screened nationwide on all three television channels. Since 1964 the Conservative and Labour parties have received five broadcasts, and the Liberals have had three broadcasts. In the election of October 1974, the ratio was 5:5:4. More limited time has been given to the Scottish and Welsh Nationalists and to the National Front. The simultaneous screening of party political broadcasts during election campaigns (and of many such broadcasts between elections) is a device to deny politically apathetic viewers the option of avoiding the parties' messages by switching to another channel.

The number of minutes of television time allotted to the Conservative, Labour, and Liberal parties since the general election of 1959 is shown in table 69. Over time the length of party political broadcasts has been reduced. In the 1959 general election the Conservative and Labour parties each had five broadcasts, four lasting twenty minutes and one of fifteen minutes. In 1961–1962, the two main parties had four routine broadcasts each, two twenty-minute broadcasts and two of fifteen minutes. Since 1970 general election broadcasts by the Conservative, Labour, and Liberal parties have lasted ten minutes each, and ten minutes has become the usual length of broadcasts between elections.

It is hard to overstate the importance of party political broadcasts. They provide the main parties with their only opportunity for television advertising. Since the 1950s television has replaced radio and newspapers as the main medium of mass communication in Britain. A definitive estimate of the value of party political broadcasts cannot be given, as they have no commercial counterpart. An impression of the large sums involved is suggested by the following statistics for party political broadcasts in 1979:

1. In 1979 advertising time on the Independent Television network cost about £40,000 a minute.

2. Since the two BBC channels have the same total audience as the ITV, the cost of a minute's advertising on all three channels was a notional £80,000. The notional cost of ten minutes—the length of a party political broadcast—was £800,000.

3. The commercial cost of eleven broadcasts each (for Conservative and Labour) was about £8.8 million. This included six routine broadcasts and five general election broadcasts. The cost of the six Liberal

TABLE 69

Minutes of Free Television Time Allotted to the Conservative,
Labour, and Liberal Parties for Political Broadcasts, 1959–1979

	Routine			General Election		
	Conserv-ative	Labour	Liberal	Conserv-ative	Labour	Liberal
1959	n.a.	n.a.	n.a.	95	95	25
July 1960–June 1961	80	80	15			
July 1961–June 1962	80	80	15			
July 1962–June 1963	75	75	25			
July 1963–June 1964	75	75	25			
July 1964–Dec. 1964	40	40	15	75	75	45
1965	60	60	20			
1966	60	60	20	75	75	45
1967	60	60	20			
1968	60	60	20			
1969	60	60	20			
1970	60	60	20	50	50	30
1971	60	60	20			
1972	60	60	20			
1973	60	60	20			
1974	60	60	30	50[a]	50[a]	30[a]
				50[b]	50[b]	40[b]
1975	60	60	30			
1976	60	60	30			
1977	60	60	30			
1978	60	60	30			
1979	60	60	30	50	50	30

Notes: Party political broadcasts are shown on all national television channels, and the parties are also allocated time on radio.

n.a. = not ascertained.

[a] February 1974.

[b] October 1974.

Sources: Annual editions of British Broadcasting Corporation *Handbook;* and Nuffield election studies.

television broadcasts (three routine and three general election) was about £4.8 million.

4. So far, the notional commercial cost of television time has been calculated. The *value* to the parties of the time available was undoubtedly reduced, however, by the fact that they were obliged to

TABLE 70

Estimated Value of Subsidies-in-Kind in the General Election of 1979

(in thousands of pounds)

	Conservative	Labour	Liberal
Free postage	311	311	288
Free hire of halls	62	62	58
Party political broadcasts[a]	2,700	2,700	1,500
Total	3,073	3,073	1,846

[a] Includes general election broadcasts and precampaign broadcasts. Precampaign broadcasts are defined as the allocation of routine broadcasting time for eight months before the poll.
Source: The basis of the calculations for this table is given in the text.

take it in clumsy ten-minute slices. The value in terms of effectiveness of ten minutes together is less than that of ten separate minutes. Research in Europe apparently has calculated that the most effective length for a political broadcast is four minutes. It is therefore reasonable to calculate that the value of each party political broadcast was one-third to one-half of the number of minutes allotted. With this in mind, each ten-minute party political broadcast will be valued at £300,000.

5. In view of the crude nature of these estimates, no separate estimate is being made for radio time.

The calculated value of free broadcasts in the calendar year 1979 is as follows: for the Conservative and Labour parties, £3.3 million each (£1.5 million for campaign broadcasts and £1.8 million for routine broadcasts), and for the Liberal party £1.8 million (£0.9 million for campaign and £0.9 million for routine broadcasts).[56]

The estimated total value of subsidies-in-kind in the general election of 1979 is shown in table 70.

---

[56] What was the value of party political broadcasts in the general election of 1979? It is reasonable to regard the normal party political broadcasts in the eight months before the 1979 poll as "precampaign" broadcasts. On this basis, the Conservative and Labour parties each had nine party political broadcasts (campaign and precampaign), and the Liberals had five. Conservative and Labour party political broadcasts were, by this calculation, each worth £2.7 million and Liberal broadcasts £1.5 million.

Assessment

The best-known feature of British law relating to political finance is its imposition of a strict ceiling on the level of permitted spending by parliamentary candidates. As Heidenheimer points out in his introduction to *Comparative Political Finance*, Britain is the only country that has effectively controlled these election costs.[57] Other countries, such as Canada, Australia, Japan, and the Philippines, have regulations that limit campaign spending by candidates for political office. He suggests that the law in these countries can be short-circuited. Canadian and Australian practices leave the door open to a variety of nonregulated expenditures on the candidates' behalf. These loopholes hardly exist in Britain because legislation makes it illegal for anyone to spend on a candidate's behalf unless specifically authorized by the candidate or his election agent. One effect of the British legislation is to prevent ordinary electors from campaigning independently for or against parliamentary candidates. This could be considered an infringement of their right to free speech and their right to participate in the parliamentary campaign process.

The impact of spending ceilings is lessened by the fact that they apply directly only to constituency-level spending during campaigns. There is no similar limit on constituency spending between elections or on expenditure by national party organizations. These gaps have become more serious over time. When the spending limits were first introduced in 1883, expenditure by parliamentary candidates—which was subject to legal regulation—constituted about three-quarters of overall central and local, routine and campaign spending during a four-year parliamentary cycle. Campaign spending by candidates for the House of Commons had fallen to a third of overall expenditure by 1906–1910, to under 15 percent in 1925–1929, and to a mere 4 percent of total Conservative spending in 1966–1970. In other words, only one twenty-fifth of Conservative spending was covered by the law by the post–World War II period. In the parliamentary cycle 1970–1974, only 9 percent of overall Labour spending was devoted to constituency campaigning.

These statistics would appear to support the case of those who maintain that the legal ceilings on spending by parliamentary candidates do little under modern conditions to control political expenditure as a whole. Consequently, there have been demands over a

[57] Arnold J. Heidenheimer, "Major Modes of Raising, Spending, and Controlling Political Funds during and between Election Campaigns," in Arnold J. Heidenheimer, ed., *Comparative Political Finance: The Financing of Party Organizations and Election Campaigns* (Lexington, Mass.: D.C. Heath, 1970), p. 14.

TABLE 71

The Lack of Growth of Central Party Spendng on General Election Campaigns, 1910–1979

(in millions of pounds)

General Election	Combined Central Expenditure of Conservative, Labour, and Liberal Parties at Constant 1980 Prices[a]
1910 (December)	8.9
1929	11.4
1935	8.5
1959	5.2
1964	9.9
1970	5.1
1979	4.8

Note: To produce comparability, a number of additions have been made to the statistics of central party campaign spending given in chapters 2, 5, and 6. Adjustments have been made to account for estimated Liberal Unionist spending in 1910, Liberal party spending in 1935, 1959, and 1964, and spending by the Scottish Central Office and by Labour regional councils in 1959, 1964, and 1970. These additional estimates are rough and based on little firm evidence. However, the tentative nature of these adjustments does not significantly affect the pattern that emerges in this table.

[a] Approximate.

Sources: As for tables 9, 31, and 41.

considerable period of time that additional limits should be imposed on central party spending.[58]

This argument assumes that central party budgets have escalated because of the absence of legal controls. This is a misinterpretation. An examination of trends since the early twentieth century shows that (1) there has been a long-term decline in central Liberal finances (this is attributable to the party's political decline); (2) central Labour spending has gradually increased in real terms, allowing the party nearly to catch up with the Conservatives; and (3) Conservative central funds have remained roughly constant in real terms since before the First World War.

Table 71 shows the approximate combined total spent by the central organizations of the three main parties in some general elec-

[58] See footnote 12 and chap. 10, footnotes 1, 5, and 6. An article that expresses strong criticism of the loopholes in the existing election law is Frank C. Newman, "Money and Elections Law in Britain—Guide for America?" *Western Political Quarterly*, vol. 10 (1957).

TABLE 72

ROUTINE EXPENDITURE BY THE CONSERVATIVE CENTRAL OFFICE,
1909/1910–1976/1977
(in thousands of pounds)

	Expenditure	Expenditure at 1980 Prices
Prewar period		
1909/10	73	1,878
1910/11	96	2,446
1911/12	133	3,257
1912/13	126	3,080
1913/14	151	3,713
Interwar period		
1925	187	2,619
1926	180	2,567
1927	217	3,191
1928	248	3,685
1929	235	3,514
Postwar period		
1972/73	1,431	4,381
1973/74	1,504	4,135
1974/75	1,955	4,180
1975/76	1,874	3,321
1976/77	2,177	3,296

SOURCES: As for tables 11, 25, and 28.

tion campaigns between 1910 and 1979. The elections chosen include three of the costliest pre–Second World War contests, and the four postwar elections are likewise among the most expensive in this period. The figures clearly refute the common assumption that campaign spending by the central party machines has grown rapidly. A lack of significant growth is also seen by comparing the routine expenditure of the Conservative Central Office in the 1970s with the interwar years and with the period before the First World War. These statistics are given in table 72.

The absence of any explosion in political spending can be shown in a third way. Table 73 gives overall Conservative spending (central and local, routine and campaign) during the parliamentary cycles 1874–1880, 1906–1910, 1925–1929, and 1966–1970. The figures indicate that, although there has been a long-term move away from local

TABLE 73

The Falling Cost of Politics:
Overall Conservative Expenditure in the Aristocratic,
Plutocratic, Transitional, and Modern Eras,
1874/1880–1966/1970

	Aristocratic Era	Plutocratic Era	Transitional Era	Modern Era
Parliamentary cycle	1874–80	1906–10	1925–29	1966–70
Overall expenditure (thousands of pounds)	1,940	1,885	3,727	14,231
Overall expenditure at 1980 values (millions of pounds)	45.7	48.6	55.1	59.7
Total Conservative vote at subsequent general election (millions)	0.9	3.1	8.7	13.1
Overall cost per vote at 1980 values (pounds)	51.84	15.55	6.36	4.54
Percentage of overall expenditure devoted to				
Central				
Routine	2.1	16.4	20.7	30.8
Campaign	—	1.3	5.4	4.5
Constituency				
Routine	20.6	47.7	59.6	60.6
Campaign	77.3	34.5	14.4	4.1
Total	100.0	100.0	100.0	100.0
Percentage central	2.1	17.7	26.1	35.3
Percentage routine	22.7	64.1	80.3	91.4

Note: Estimates of routine central and constituency expenditures have been adjusted to represent spending over a four-year period.
Sources: As for tables 4, 12, 26, and 36.

campaign spending toward national-level spending, (1) the overall cost of politics in real terms has not significantly increased (this includes the categories of spending not directly affected by the limitations on expenditure by parliamentary candidates); and (2) expressed in terms of costs per vote, the overall level of political spending has continued to fall, even when central party outlays and routine constituency expenditures are taken into account.

Why has there been no escalation of political spending in Britain despite the major gaps in electoral law? There are several explanations. First, the spectacular reductions in the costs of constituency electioneering, which have resulted from the legally imposed ceilings, have made it possible for parties to devote money to other uses without raising the overall cost of politics. National party organizations have been able to find money to pay for national-level advertising because they have been largely relieved of the need to subsidize constituency campaigns. Second, subsidies-in-kind and the regulations about political broadcasting are of prime importance. On the one hand, British parties are banned from spending money on radio or television advertising. This is a severe restriction. On the other hand, the provision of free time for party political broadcasts is a very valuable subsidy-in-kind, especially in general election campaigns. Third, the incentives for large contributions and high spending are lacking in the British political system. Since British voters are influenced largely by national party loyalties, a constituency campaign is likely to have little impact on the result. At the national level, the fact that decisions about particular government contracts and regulations are usually taken by civil servants rather than by the political parties lessens the incentive for big political gifts. The success of British regulations about political money has stemmed not only from skillful drafting of legislation (although this has been an important factor) but also from the favorable political and economic context in which the law has operated.[59] Had similar laws been enacted in some other countries, the loopholes would undoubtedly have been exploited with greater vigor.

[59] See chapter 1, footnote 12.

10
Reforms

It will have become evident from the description of British political finance given in previous chapters that the case for introducing a new system of public subsidies is unjustified. It is based on a tangle of misconceptions and on false assumptions about the resources of the main parties.

The current obsession with the issue of state aid is doubly unfortunate. It ignores the notable success of the existing mechanism of controls and subsidies-in-kind. At the same time, it deflects attention from the two most important abuses relating to political money in Britain. These are, in my view, the financial control exercised by trade unions over the Labour party and the financial interests of MPs.

This chapter assesses the case for state aid to political parties and then discusses these two other areas in which the real abuses are to be found.

Should Political Parties Receive Cash Subventions from the Public Treasury?

The arguments about state aid will be considered under five headings:

- Is the existing system fair?
- Would public subsidies make British parties more effective?
- Would state aid lessen the undesirable influence of pressure groups?
- Do subsidy systems in other countries provide a good precedent for Britain?
- Is there a danger of legal gerrymandering?

(The first four of these items are the same as in the introduction.)

Is the Existing System Fair? In the 1960s the case for public subsidies was usually based on the argument that the existing controls on spending by parliamentary candidates did not regulate national-level political advertising This important loophole permitted marked inequality between the political parties.[1] Only the Conservatives, it was maintained, could afford to raise money for costly poster and press publicity or for an efficient party headquarters. This gave them an unfair advantage over their opponents.

Alarm was heightened by the assumption that political advertising was a new departure and that it was likely to revolutionize political campaigning. According to a standard textbook on British electioneering, the Conservatives resorted "for the first time to the professional public relations" in 1957–1959. The party's newspaper and advertising campaign before the 1959 election was held to be "unprecedented in both intensity and skill."[2] In a book on political advertising, published in 1967, Rose characterized it as a post–Second World War phenomenon.[3] Commentators were intrigued by the fact that the Conservative Central Office employed a professional advertising agency—Colman, Prentice and Varley—to conduct its 1959 campaign. This, too, was seen as an innovation.

The development of modern advertising techniques was held responsible for the disparity between the campaign spending of the rival party headquarters. For example, Rose suggested that the Conservatives and their business allies outspent Labour on advertising by a ratio of 9:1 before the 1964 election and "showed no apparent difficulty in finding hundreds of thousands of pounds extra as the pre-election campaign increased in length and intensity."[4] A leading

[1] Richard Rose, "Money and Election Law," *Political Studies*, vol. 9 (1961), p. 13.

[2] Peter G. J. Pulzer, *Political Representation and Elections in Britain* (London: Allen and Unwin, 1967), p. 83.

[3] "In the past fifteen years, a major change has occurred in the conduct of election campaigns. In efforts to influence voters, candidates and parties have increasingly relied upon the mass media and experts in modern media techniques. This development, occurring soon after totalitarian countries had demonstrated how the media could serve anti-democratic ends, has been a source of anxiety. . . . The change in campaign techniques first became prominent in America during the successful presidential campaign of Dwight D. Eisenhower in 1952" (Richard Rose, *Influencing Voters: A Study of Campaign Rationality* [London: Faber, 1967], pp. 13-14).

[4] This widely quoted 9:1 ratio is misleading. "Politically relevant" propaganda is included in the Conservative total but not in Labour's. Rose counts advertisements by the steel industry opposing nationalization as a Conservative party expense for the purposes of the comparison. But union spending on their newspapers, which openly advocated Labour victory, is not counted as a Labour expense. If politically relevant spending is excluded on both sides, the Conservative advertising advantage in 1963-1964 was just over 3:1. Including all campaign expenditures by party headquarters, Conservatives outspent Labour by somewhat over 2:1. (See Richard Rose, "Pre-Election Public Relations and Advertising," in David E. Butler and Anthony King, *The British General Election of 1964* [London: Macmillan, 1965]).

article in *The Times* referred to the supposedly new development of political public relations as "an embryonic abuse" that might grow into a "notorious scandal" unless the law regulating permitted election expenses was widened.[5] In similar vein, Robert McKenzie called for a reexamination of election law "perhaps by a Royal Commission" to consider the implications of uncontrolled Conservative spending on national-level propaganda.[6]

The actual trend of party expenditure has been very different from that depicted by commentators in the 1960s. The use of newspapers and poster sites for professional political advertising does not date from the general election of 1959. As described in chapter 4, it was highly developed in Britain before the Second World War. Professional advertising agents had been regularly employed at least since the 1920s. Spending on national party publicity probably reached an all-time peak (in real terms) in the general election of 1935.

The high spending (by postwar standards) on advertising before the general elections of 1959 and 1964 did not prove to be the start of a new trend. In the five general elections between 1966 and 1979, expenditure by the two main parties has not approached the level of the 1964 campaign. One reason for this decline, contrary to Rose's interpretation, is that the Conservatives found considerable difficulty in raising funds for their political advertisements in 1963–1964. The previously unpublished Conservative accounts for 1963 and 1964, which have been made available for this book, show that Central Office was obliged to use money normally reserved for its routine activities to pay for its publicity campaign.[7] Conservative reserves were so seriously depleted after the 1964 election that Central Office felt obliged to conduct an emergency fund-raising campaign in 1968–1969 to place its finances back on a firm footing. The experience of 1963–1964 was a warning to the Conservative party managers that publicity on a similar scale could not become a normal feature of the party's national election campaigns.

Another probable reason for the decline in expenditure on publicity since the election of 1964 is the growth of television. In some other countries, such as the United States, television advertising has become the most costly spending category. As Alexander has written of campaign expenditure in the United States during the

[5] *The Times*, June 9, 1960. Quoted in Rose, "Money and Election Law," p. 15.

[6] Robert T. McKenzie, *British Political Parties: The Distribution of Power within the Conservative and Labour Parties* (London: Mercury Books, 1964), p. 658. See also chap. 9, footnote 12.

[7] See chapter 5, "Central Party Finances, 1950-1978/1979."

1950s and 1960s, "the single item most responsible for the increase in campaign expenditure is the growing costs of, and increasing reliance placed upon, broadcasting." [8] In Britain, as in America, television has played an ever-widening role in national campaigns. The financial consequence in Britain appears to have been the opposite, however. Television has lessened the pressure for other forms of exposure (such as newspaper advertisements or nationwide poster campaigns). As broadcasting time is given free to the parties and as they are not permitted to advertise on television or radio, the cost of election publicity has been kept in check.

A comparison of Conservative and Labour finances since the 1950s shows (1) that there has been no explosion of spending in the areas not covered by election law (that is, routine and campaign expenditure by national party organizations and routine constituency expenditure); (2) that the Conservative advantage over Labour has been declining; (3) that the remaining gap between the two parties is reduced if account is taken of the notional value of subsidies-in-kind; and (4) that the Conservative advantage, such as it is, derives entirely from the fact that the party has many more members than the Labour party.

Conservative and Labour finances will be compared under three headings: constituency campaign finances; central party finances (routine and campaign); and routine constituency finances.

Constituency campaign finances. The strict legal control over constituency campaign spending has had two direct effects during recent decades. It has led to a further fall in the real cost of parliamentary campaigns, and it has ensured that spending by candidates of the two parties has been approximately equal (see table 74). In real terms, average spending by all candidates in the general election of 1979 fell to about a quarter of average spending in the constituency campaigns of 1945. The gap between expenditure by Conservative and Labour candidates, which was small even in 1945, narrowed still further. Moreover, the distance between the parties has normally been particularly small in the marginal constituencies.[9]

[8] Herbert E. Alexander, "Links and Contrasts among American Parties and Party Subsystems," in Arnold J. Heidenheimer, ed., *Comparative Political Finance: The Financing of Party Organizations and Election Campaigns* (Lexington, Mass.: D.C. Heath, 1970), p. 91.

[9] In 1966 "in close contests almost everyone returned expenses to within £50 of the legal maximum" (David E. Butler and Anthony King, *The British General Election of 1966* [London: Macmillan, 1966], pp. 202-3). In 1970 Labour candidates spent 86 percent of the permitted maximum in the fifty most marginal seats (David E. Butler and Michael Pinto-Duschinsky, *The British General Election of 1970* [London: Macmillan, 1971], p. 334). There was a similar pattern in 1979 (see chap. 7, footnote 55).

TABLE 74

Spending on Constituency Campaigns by Conservative and Labour Parliamentary Candidates, 1945–1979

General Election	Conservative Average Spending (pounds)	Labour Average Spending (pounds)	Conservative Expenditure as % of Labour Spending
1945	780	595	131
1950	777	694	112
1951	773	653	118
1955	692	611	113
1959	761	705	108
1964	790	751	105
1966	766	726	106
1970	949	828	115
1974 (February)	1,275	1,163	110
1974 (October)	1,197	1,127	106
1979	2,190	1,897	115

Source: David E. Butler and Anne Sloman, *British Political Facts, 1900-1979* (London: Macmillan, 1980), p. 229.

The continued fall in the cost of constituency electioneering has had an important indirect effect. It has allowed money previously devoted to parliamentary campaigns in the constituencies to be redirected to the central party organizations. Conservative constituency associations have been able to increase their donations to Central Office, and trade unions have devoted a greater proportion of their political levy expenditure to the national Labour party organization (as shown in table 60).

Central party routine and campaign finances since the 1950s. The main trends have been as follows: (1) central Conservative income has fallen slightly in real terms; (2) central Labour income has doubled in real terms; and (3) the gap between the finances of the two national party organizations has narrowed significantly. In the parliamentary cycle 1952–1955, the Conservatives raised three and a half times as much centrally as Labour. By 1975–1979 the Conservatives raised one and a half times as much. The trend of central income is shown in figure 4.

Central expenditure on *general election campaigns* has been volatile. The cost of particular elections has been affected by the length of the

FIGURE 4
Average Annual Central Conservative and Labour Income during Parliamentary Cycles, 1952–1979

£ million

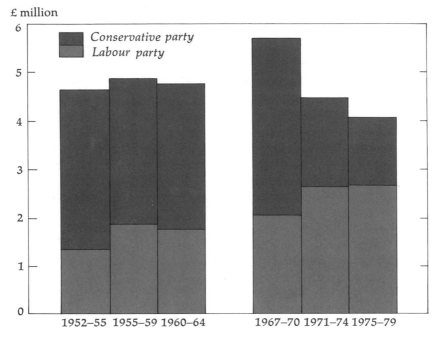

NOTE: At constant 1980 prices. Includes routine and campaign income.
SOURCES: As for tables 28 and 30.

preelection period. The cheaper postwar elections have been those called suddenly or after a short Parliament. The campaigns of 1951, 1955, 1966, February 1974, and October 1974 all fall into this category. Four general election campaigns have been held after a full-length Parliament: 1950, 1959, 1964, and 1979. Complete information is not available regarding Conservative spending before the 1950 election. The campaigns of 1959, 1964, and 1979 were among the most costly of the postwar period, especially the campaign of 1964.

Although it is not possible to be definite about trends of central campaign spending, the statistics suggest (1) that there has been a fall (in real terms) in the level of spending since the temporary peak of 1964, and (2) that the Conservatives have normally spent about 1½ to 2 times as much as Labour (see table 75). Extending the comparison to elections before the Second World War, it is evident

TABLE 75

CONSERVATIVE AND LABOUR CENTRAL SPENDING ON GENERAL ELECTION
CAMPAIGNS, 1929–1979
(in thousands of pounds)

General Election	Conservative Expenditure	Labour Expenditure	Conservative Expenditure as % of Labour Expenditure
Prewar period			
1929	290	45	644
1935	450 [a]	26	1,731
Postwar period			
1945	50–100 ?	51	?
1950	135 [b]	84	?
1951	112	80	140
1955	142	73	195
1959	631	239	264
1964	1,233	538	229
1966	350 ?	196	178 ?
1970	630	526	120
1974 (February)	680	440	155
1974 (October)	950	524	181
1979	2,333	1,566	149

NOTE: For elections up to 1974, Conservative totals exclude Scotland, and Labour totals exclude independent expenditures by regional councils.

[a] Approximate.

[b] At least.

SOURCES: As for table 31 and 41.

(1) that Labour party central campaign spending has grown in real terms since the 1920s and 1930s, (2) that Conservative central spending has not risen since before the First World War, and (3) that the Conservative advantage over Labour has lessened from about 6:1 in 1929, and 15:1 in 1935 to less than 2:1 in most campaigns since 1951.

Table 31 indicated that in only one of the nine elections between 1951 and 1979 did spending by Conservative Central Office exceed (in real terms) the level reached in the election of December 1910. In no postwar election has central Conservative spending equaled that of 1935.

TABLE 76

THE CONSERVATIVE ADVANTAGE DECLINES:
ROUTINE CENTRAL EXPENDITURE BY THE CONSERVATIVE AND LABOUR
PARTIES, 1952–1978

	Conservative Expenditure as % of Labour Expenditure
1952–54	299
1956–58	266
1960–63	285
1971–73	178
1975–78	175

SOURCES: Tables 28 and 38.

As far as *routine central spending* is concerned, the Conservative lead over Labour has been largely eroded since the 1950s. This is shown in table 76. (As shown in table 77, the Tory advantage in terms of *routine central income* has narrowed even more.)

Routine constituency finances. The Conservative advantage is most marked at this level. As constituency party accounts are not normally collected and as there is no common method of presentation, it is very difficult to give comprehensive and reliable statistics. There is a particular shortage of information on the finances of constituency Labour parties. The broad trends emerge clearly from several independent studies carried out in the 1960s and 1970s. According to a survey conducted for the Nuffield study of the 1970 general election, the budget of an average constituency Labour party in 1969 was about £1,200, compared with an average of over £4,000 for Conservative constituency associations. These estimates suggest that Conservative local associations raised and spent over three times as much as constituency Labour parties.[10] The Houghton Committee's constituency survey indicated that the expendiure of Conservative constituency associations averaged £4,572 in the nonelection year 1973, compared with a Labour average of £1,761—that is, Conservative constituency spending was over 2½ times as great as Labour's.

To sum up: this examination of central and local finances shows that the Conservatives have a financial advantage over Labour in

[10] Butler and Pinto-Duschinsky, *British General Election of 1970*, pp. 271, 282–83.

280

TABLE 77

COMPARISON BETWEEN CONSERVATIVE AND LABOUR FINANCES, 1975–1979

	Conservative Income as % of Labour Income[a]	
Level and Type of Income	Excluding notional value of subsidies-in-kind	Including notional value of subsidies-in-kind[b]
Constituency campaign[c]	115	112
Central campaign[c]	149	118
Central routine[d]	144	125
Constituency routine[e]	261	261

NOTES: Calculations are based on estimated routine Labour income 1975-1978 and Conservative income 1975/1976-1978/1979 plus campaign income for the 1979 general election. It is assumed that constituency income remained in real terms at the level reported for 1973 by the Houghton Committee.

[a] Estimated.

[b] For basis of calculation, see footnote 11.

[c] Campaign income is defined in this table as equal to campaign expenditure.

[d] Includes constituency payments to central parties.

[e] Includes estimated central payments to constituency parties.

SOURCES: Constituency campaign, table 74; central campaign, table 75; central routine, tables 28 and 38; constituency routine, tables 34 and 43; subsidies-in-kind, table 70 and chap. 10, footnote 11.

all aspects of party activity. The Conservative lead is smallest in constituency-level election campaigns. It is greatest at the level of routine constituency finance.

The value of subsidies-in-kind. The Conservative and Labour parties benefit equally from subsidies-in-kind. In the four years 1975–1978 and in the 1979 general election, each party received subsidies-in-kind of a notional value of £7¾ million.[11] The Conservative financial advantage over Labour is reduced if the value of these subsidies-in-kind is taken into account. Table 77 compares the incomes of the two major parties excluding and including subidies-in-kind. Table 77 indicates that, when account is taken of subsidies-in-kind, the Con-

[11] This includes the subsidies-in-kind for the 1979 general election shown in table 70 and the notional costs of routine party political broadcasts, 1975-1978. Overall Conservative income (central and local, routine and campaign) in the period 1975-1979 was about 1.9 times as large as Labour's. If the value of subsidies-in-kind is taken into account, Conservative income was 1.6 times that of Labour.

TABLE 78

The Financial Advantage of Mass Membership:
The Conservative Constituency Advantage, 1973

	Conservative	Labour
Total membership	1,495,000	312,000
Estimated income per member (pounds)	1.93	3.61
Total income of local party organizations (millions of pounds)	2.9	1.1

Source: Derived from the Houghton Report, pp. 31, 178.

servative advantage over Labour had by the late 1970s become small except at the level of routine constituency finance. As far as constituency campaigns were concerned and as far as the central incomes of the two parties were concerned (both routine and campaign), the Conservative party received only up to 1¼ times as much as Labour. Even if subsidies-in-kind are excluded from the reckoning, Conservative income was no more than 1½ times that of Labour at these levels of organization.

The only real area of Conservative advantage by 1975–1979 was at the level of routine constituency activity. Most constituency income in both parties comes from small-scale social activities and lotteries. The superior Conservative effectiveness in this enterprise results from the fact that the party has a far larger individual membership than Labour. According to the Houghton Committee's constituency survey, the average Conservative constituency association had 2,400 members in 1974, compared with a Labour average of only 500.

The financial advantages of a large membership are illustrated by table 78. This shows that the Conservatives raise less money per member but that the weight of numbers has ensured their financial superiority.

The contributions raised by those endless coffee mornings, jumble sales, and supper dances organized by Conservative branch committees strengthen not only constituency finances but Conservative central funds as well. The relative financial potency of the party's constituency organizations has two direct consequences: (1) it permits constituency associations to make substantial direct payments to Conservative Central Office, and (2) it permits over 80 percent of company contributions to be directed toward the

TABLE 79

The Effect of Labour's Weakness at the Constituency Level on Central Party Funds, 1971–1978
(in pounds)

	Affiliation Fees Paid by Constituency Labour Parties to Transport House	Quota Payments by Conservative Constituency Associations to Central Office
1971	59,000	217,000
1972	58,000	227,000
1973	77,000	320,000
1974	82,000	254,000
1975	119,000	488,000
1976	130,000	499,000
1977	136,000	564,000
1978	143,000	665,000
Total 1971–78	806,000	3,234,000

NOTES: Conservative payments are given net of estimated quota credits. It is assumed that quota credits constituted 15 percent of constituency quota payments as published in the annual accounts of Central Office. For years until 1977, Conservative payments exclude Scotland.

SOURCES: As for tables 28 and 38.

center. In the Labour party, constituency organizations contribute far less to the center; moreover, they soak up about a quarter of total political payments by trade unions. These two factors largely account for the financial superiority of Conservative Central Office over Transport House. Table 79 compares constituency payments to the center in the two main parties.

Table 79 slightly underestimates payments to the center by constituency Labour parties because it does not include contributions to special appeals and special funds. Assuming that they amounted to 10 percent of affiliation fees, this makes a total of £0.9 million contributed to the central organization by Labour's constituency parties, campared with £3.2 million contributed to the center by Conservative constituency associations.

It seems reasonable to conclude that, by comparison with Conservative Central Office, Labour's headquarters lost a sum in the region of £4 million during 1971–1978 from the weakness of its local organizations. It lost some £1.6 million through union payments to constituencies that would otherwise have found their way into the central coffers had the unions directed the same percentage of their contributions to the national party as company payments to Conservative Central Office. It lost a further £2.3 million representing the difference between payments by local Conservative and Labour organizations to party headquarters. Had the Labour party benefited from this extra £4 million, its central income would have approached that of Conservative Central Office.

Conservative popular strength at the grass roots not only accounts for the superior routine finances of the party's local associations but also explains the Conservative advantage at the central level.[12]

Liberal party finances. So far comparisons have been limited to the two main parties. Estimates of Liberal party finances during 1975–1979 indicate the following: (1) In the parliamentary cycle preceding the general election of 1979, overall Liberal income (central and local, routine and campaign) was one-sixth of Conservative income and one-third of Labour income. (2) If the notional value of subsidies-in-kind is taken into account, Liberal income was a quarter of Conservative income and two-fifths of Labour income. (3) If subsidies-in-kind are excluded, the Liberal disadvantage was particularly marked at the central level. The Conservative/Labour/Liberal ratio of central campaign income was 12:7:1, and the ratio of central routine income was similar. Liberal central finances [13] suffered from lack of institutional backing (the mainstay of the central income of the two main parties) and also from the relatively small financial support received from Liberal constituency associations.[14]

[12] The same point emerges from another analysis. In the four years 1975-1978, the Conservatives raised (centrally and locally) very little more than Labour in large contributions from individuals and from companies and unions but three times as much in small contributions. It is asssumed that donations to central party organizations are large while those to local parties (apart from those of companies and trade unions) are small. All figures are approximate:

	Conservative	Labour
	(millions of pounds)	
Small contributions	17.9	6.0
Large contributions	8.3	7.5
Interest and state grants	0.8	0.1
	27.0	13.6

[13] "Central" income includes regional federations, the Liberal Central Association, the leader's office, and so on.

[14] In 1975-1978 Liberal constituency contributions to headquarters totaled £117,000, and the equivalent Conservative and Labour totals were £2,216,000 and £581,000; that is, a Conservative/Labour/Liberal ratio of 19:5:1.

284

(4) According to the Houghton Committee's constituency survey, Liberal party membership in 1974 was 300 per constituency—that is, three-fifths of Labour membership and one-eighth of Conservative membership. In the 1979 general election, the Liberal vote was under two-fifths of the Labour vote and under one-third of the Conservative vote.

If it is assumed that levels of party membership remained constant between 1973 and 1979, it follows that overall Liberal expenditure *per member* was higher than Conservative expenditure *per member*. (This includes central and local, routine and campaign.) Liberal expenditure *per voter* was lower than in the Conservative party. The Liberals spent less than Labour *per member* but spent about the same as Labour *per voter*. These comparisons all exclude the notional values of subsidies-in-kind.

Summary. The comparisons of Conservative and Labour party funds given above show that attacks on the present system have normally been based on an exaggerated notion of the Conservative party's financial edge and on the false assumption that its lead derives from the backing of big business or from large donations from wealthy individuals.[15] In fact, the Conservative financial advantage over Labour derives almost entirely from fund raising in the constituencies, and this in turn results from the fact that local Conservative associations have several times more members than their Labour counterparts. Weight of numbers is essential, because local social activities have modest financial returns and therefore many events have to be organized if the total revenue is to be adequate. The revenue per member received by the Conservatives is small—less than Labour's. It is the relatively wide extent of the party's grass-roots support that ensured its financial superiority in the 1960s and 1970s. As far as the balance between Conservative and Labour is concerned, the existing system is not unfair.

[15] There is an obvious distinction between "equality" on the one hand and "fairness" or "justice" on the other hand. It is reasonable to expect political parties that enjoy greater popular support to have healthier finances than those that have less support. One measure of a party's appeal is the number of votes obtained, but popular participation takes other forms as well, for example, party membership and local party activity. A party that attracts a large number of individual members or activists can be expected to raise and spend more money than a party that does not.

If this is accepted, it follows that it is just and fair for a party to outspend its rivals, provided that its financial advantage derives from a large number of small donations and not from a small number of large ones. In order to establish that a system of financing political parties is unfair, it is necessary to show not only that a party has more money than its opponents but also that its superiority reflects the wealth and not the number or the enthusiasm of its followers.

The Liberals have more ground for complaint. Their central organization is handicapped by lack of the support from companies and unions enjoyed by the two main parties. The Liberals do, however, derive particular benefit from subsidies-in-kind, and this partly compensates for the absence of steady institutional finance. In general election campaigns, the free exposure received by the party on television makes up for the Liberals' inability to pay for large-scale press and poster advertising (the main element in the election budgets of the Conservative and Labour parties). Expressed in terms of costs per vote and including the estimated value of subsidies-in-kind, the Liberals spent more in the 1979 general election than the two main parties. The Liberals spent sixty-one pence per vote, the Conservatives forty-nine pence, and Labour forty-seven pence. This unexpected result is produced because the Liberals enjoyed a disproportionately generous allocation of free television time.[16]

These statistics demonstrate that the introduction of state payments to parties cannot be justified on the grounds that they would help to redress existing unfairness in the finances of the parties. Indeed, it could be argued that state aid would in itself be unfair if it denied the party with the largest membership the fruits of its strength at the grass roots.

Would Public Subsidies Make British Parties More Effective? In the 1970s the focus of debate about public subsidies changed. Proponents of reform placed greater emphasis on the need for state aid as a means to make political parties more "efficient" and "effective." This shift was typified by the work of Rose. In a major book published in 1974, he argued that many of Britain's difficulties resulted from weak political parties—hence the title *The Problem of Party Government*. In order to act effectively, parties needed to formulate policies more thoroughly, they required larger parliamentary secretariats to enable MPs to balance the growing power of civil servants, and they required more thorough constituency organizations in order to encourage popular participation in political life.

Rose proposed that, since parties had shown themselves incapable of finding the necessary money and since they had been badly hit by inflation, they should be substantially relieved of the burden of fund raising. Instead, "the cost of conducting party politics ought to be borne by the Treasury."[17] Public funds would help to meet

[16] Michael Pinto-Duschinsky, "Financing the British General Election of 1979," in Howard R. Penniman, ed., *Britain at the Polls, 1979: A Study of the General Election* (Washington, D.C.: American Enterprise Institute, 1981), p. 234.
[17] Richard Rose, *The Problem of Party Government* (New York: Free Press, 1975), p. 278.

the basic requirements of party organization, which were defined as (1) extra money for policy research, (2) enlarged party headquarters, and (3) a permanent, full-time Conservative and Labour agent in each constituency.

Rose's position was closely mirrored in the report of the Houghton Committee. The report emphasized that "(e)ffective political parties are the crux of democratic government. . . . The parties in opposition have the responsibility of scrutinising and checking all the actions of the Executive. . . . At election times, it is they who run the campaigns. . . . At all times they are the vital link between the government and the governed." The report argued that democracy itself would fail if parties lacked the resources to perform their functions of "research, policy formulation, publicity and communication."[18] To be effective, parties needed to "greatly expand their efforts and resources." Inflation and rising costs meant that state grants were "the only way of supporting the minimum standards of political activity and efficiency required to maintain the vitality of our system of representative government."[19]

This analysis is open to criticism on several grounds. It is based on an unduly bleak view of he parties' recent financial position; insofar as they have fund-raising difficulties, inflation has been a relatively minor cause; there is little evidence that the maintenance of larger party staffs out of state funds would give rise to better policy proposals at the center or to greater participation in the affairs of constituency organizations. Above all, the view that state aid can strengthen the parties shows a fundamental misunderstanding of the reasons for their decline over recent decades. It has not resulted from shortage of funds. The drop in membership and in the number of full-time constituency agents experienced by all parties—especially the Labour party—seems to have been a response to lackluster leadership and to the poor performance of government in the 1960s and 1970s. The disenchantment that manifested itself in these ways was essentially a political phenomenon. Reforms that ignore the essence of the problem and deal only with its institutional manifestations will not provide a solution. To increase the number of constituency agents by subsidizing them from the public purse is not likely, in itself, to increase popular participation in local party organizations. This injection of help would be like a drug that deals temporarily with the symptoms but leaves the disease itself uncured.

---

[18] Committee on Financial Aid to Political Parties, *Report*, Cmnd. 6601 (London: Her Majesty's Stationery Office, 1976), pp. 53-54 (Houghton Report).
[19] Ibid., p. xii.

Are the parties in a state of financial crisis? The thesis "that British political parties are today in a state of financial crisis" has been repeated so often that it has been accepted uncritically and has simply been assumed to be the case.[20] Yet the analysis of Conservative, Labour, and Liberal accounts presented in chapters 5 to 7 shows that the talk of a crisis has been considerably exaggerated.

The postwar trends of central Conservative and Labour income are shown in figure 4. Even if account is taken of rises in the cost of living, Labour's central income, far from declining, roughly doubled between the early 1950s and the 1970s.[21] During the 1970s—the decade of inflation—Labour's central income in real terms remained well ahead of its level in the 1960s (see figure 2).

Conservative central income is much less regular than that of Labour, and it is therefore harder to determine long-term trends. According to figure 4, average annual income in the parliamentary cycle 1975–1979 was, in real terms, 14 percent lower than in 1960–1964 and 12 percent lower than in 1952–1955.[22]

It is too soon to determine whether this drop in the 1970s was part of a long-term trend. The experience of these years must give concern to Conservative party managers, especially about the flagging support from the business community. Central Office will need to

[20] Dick (R.L.) Leonard, *Paying for Party Politics: The Case for Public Subsidies*, Broadsheet no. 555, vol. 41 (London: Political and Economic Planning, 1975), p. vii. Leonard suggests that the "real value of the incomes enjoyed by the political parties has probably . . . declined since the 1950s . . . probably because their incomes from other sources [than from members] have not kept pace with the level of inflation" (Leonard, "Contrasts in Selected Western Democracies: Germany, Sweden, Britain," in Herbert E. Alexander, ed., *Political Finance* [Beverly Hills, Calif.: Sage Publications, 1979], p. 66). As shown in this study, this assessment certainly does not apply to the Labour party and probably not to the Liberals either (see footnote 24). Leonard's statement that "the two largest political parties have become increasingly dependent on interest groups for their financial backing—particularly at the national level" (p. 66) is also not borne out by the facts (see table 29 for the Conservative party). As far as the Labour party is concerned, its heavy reliance on union money dates back to its foundation.

[21] It is sometimes suggested that the retail price index (RPI) is an unsatisfactory yardstick. Salaries, which are a major component of party expenditure, have risen faster than the RPI throughout much of the economy. Thus party incomes would have had to rise faster than the RPI to provide salary increases for party employees similar to those granted in many other sectors of the economy. On the other hand, other components of party spending (parliamentary elections, for instance) have not kept pace with the RPI. On balance, the RPI is the simplest and probably the best single measure of inflation as it has affected the party organizations.

[22] The decline between 1967-1970 and 1975-1979 was considerably larger; Conservative income in 1967-1970 was unusually high because of the major financial appeal of 1968/1969.

renew its appeal to these business donors or to find new sources of income or, if this proves impossible, to trim the scale of its operations. Even if it is forced into this last course of action, it probably will remain larger than Labour's national organization in the immediate future, though its former superiority will have been lost.

The absence of comprehensive accounts makes it impossible to give any precise assessment of postwar trends of central Liberal income. The party's resources at the center declined (in real terms) in the 1970s from the temporary peak of the 1960s, but the position was probably better than in the 1950s. As shown in chapter 7, the published Liberal Party Organisation accounts do not include a number of significant sources of central income. The party's position is somewhat better when account is taken of these extra funds, such as those at the disposal of the Liberal leader.

What are the trends of local party finance? As far as the Conservatives and Labour are concerned, their local associations appear to have fared worse than their central organizations. The income of Conservative constituency associations seems to have declined seriously. The statistics given in chapter 5 indicate that, by the late 1970s, their real income may have fallen to half that of the mid-1960s.[23] The funds of constituency Labour parties, though far behind those of the Conservatives, appear to have kept pace since the 1950s with the cost of living.[24] Liberal constituency associations (like the party centrally) are probably weaker financially than in the 1960s but stronger than in the 1950s. These estimates about constituency funds all need to be treated with caution because of the lack of firm data.

If the central incomes (in real terms) of the three main parties are added together, a surprising conclusion emerges. Between the parliamentary cycles of 1952–1955 and 1975–1979, they *rose* slightly.[25] During the same period, there was a considerable fall

[23] See chapter 5, "Recent Developments."

[24] See chapter 6, "Local Labour Finance."

[25] In 1952-1955 combined three-party central income (at 1980 values) averaged £6.2 million per annum (Conservative, £4,647,000; Labour, £1,301,000; and Liberal, £235,000). This includes routine and campaign income. In 1975-1979, the equivalent figure was £7.2 million (Conservative, £4,078,000; Labour, £2,679,000; and Liberal, £421,000). The figures are approximate as (1) they do not include the income of the Scottish Central Office until 1977/1978, (2) independent income of Labour regional councils is excluded, and (3) it is assumed that total Liberal central income was twice that shown in the LPO's routine income accounts. The trend shown in the figures above is nevertheless clear: (1) although there was no escalation of central party income in this period, it rose by about 16 percent in real terms; and (2) this overall increase

in their combined constituency incomes.[26] Although this is not an altogether happy state of affairs, it does not correspond to the picture of woe that has featured so prominently in much party rhetoric and political commentary.

The Conservative, Labour, and Liberal parties have all experienced a fall in party membership since the 1960s. This has been particularly severe in the Labour party. There is no evidence that lack of money has been responsible for this downward trend. Indeed, party funds have remained remarkably resilient in view of the narrowing popular base from which they have had to be raised. In particular, Labour headquarters has been shielded by rising trade union levies from the consequences of collapsing membership in the constituencies. The central Labour machine actually grew at a time when party membership fell to a third of its level in the 1950s.

Is the rampant inflation of the 1970s to blame for the parties' financial problems? The 1970s saw a fourfold rise in the cost of living. This inflation is often held responsible for the parties' "financial plight" and for the wastage of members. The implication is that inflation (a phenomenon for which the political machines cannot be blamed) has led to their money problems and that these have, in turn, led to falling memberships and to deteriorating organizations.

In fact, party membership and the number of full-time constituency agents contracted more sharply in the 1960s (that is, before inflation became severe) than in the 1970s. The 1960s saw growing disenchantment with the nation's political leaders and with the established parties. The size of party membership provides a good measure of this evaporating support. It is no accident that Conservative constituency organization appears to have suffered worst during the early 1960s (because of dissatisfaction with the governments of Macmillan and Home), while Labour experienced the most precipitous collapse of its membership during Wilson's premiership of 1964–1970 (see figure 1). Liberal membership also reflected the party's political fortunes, rising briefly during the early 1960s and then falling sharply in the late 1960s.

These trends suggest that falling membership has been a consequence not of financial stringency but of political unpopularity. The

---

resulted from the fact that the growth of Labour and Liberal central income more than offset the fall in Conservative income (see tables 28, 38, and 47 for the sources on which this footnote is based).

[26] While there has been a drop in overall constituency party income, income per member has probably risen in real terms.

parties' financial difficulties (which are in any case less severe than normally supposed) are the result, not the cause, of contracting popular support.

Have poor policies resulted from inadequately staffed research departments at the party headquarters? The research departments of the Conservative and Labour parties sometimes play a key role in the formulation of policy, particularly when a party is in opposition. However, there is no ready correlation between the size of research department staff and the quality of advice given. Indeed, a compact research unit is likely to be more effective than a very large one. The importance of the advice given by a research department depends on whether it has the confidence of the party leaders. A research department that grows too large and develops institutional loyalties of its own is likely to be regarded with mistrust by the party leader, and its influence will diminish. This situation has occurred for brief periods in recent years in both the main parties, and at these times party leaders have looked elsewhere for advice on new policies.[27]

Moreover, it is wrong to think of the research department of a political party as a rival civil service. Its function is not to work out the details of a proposal but to suggest general lines of approach.[28] It is not accidental that in the Conservative party two of the more significant and successful policy shifts engineered in cooperation with the Conservative research department involved very small staffs (the protective tariff of 1932 and the "New Conservatism" of 1946–1947), whereas one of the least successful exercises in policy making was the most detailed. This occurred when the Conservatives were in opposition between 1964 and 1970. The most painstaking care was devoted to the preparation of the party's proposals for the reform of industrial relations. These led to the act of 1971, by general agreement a failure.[29]

[27] Before the 1979 general election, the research department of the Labour party reportedly commissioned "2,000 research papers, 70 major statements and a 60,000 word policy declaration" (*Sunday Times*, December 30, 1979). They were "largely ignored by James Callaghan when the time came."

[28] The motive for detailed policy preparation has sometimes been to anticipate and confound objections from permanent civil servants; however, if party leaders need this prop when they enter government, they are in any case unlikely to be able to impose their will.

[29] Lloyd George's costly efforts before the 1929 election to work out striking and novel policies are a good illustration of the irrelevance of spending on research by a party that lacks public backing. Lloyd George used considerable sums from his Political Fund to gather together some of the finest brains in the country to formulate a program to combat inflation. Many historians consider that the resulting proposals were brilliant, but they were no substitute for the popular base of support that the Liberals had lost by the late 1920s.

The supporters of state aid assume that, as political parties play a vital role in a democracy, their organizations ought to be large and ought to be kept artifically in operation even if they lack popular backing. The effectiveness of a party cannot be separated, however, from its ability to command a popular base. No matter how thoroughly a party's research department may prepare policies, the exercise will be useless unless the party is able to attract a following in the electorate.

The danger of public funding is that it makes popular backing unnecessary and creates a gulf between the professional staff and the ordinary members.[30] Declining enthusiasm in the constituencies and falling contributions from members are salutary danger signals to party leaders. It is undesirable that the party managers at the center should have no financial stake in the constituency organizations, either because of large central contributions or because of state finance.

Robert Michel's classic analysis of political parties warned of the oligarchical and bureaucratic tendencies of party organizations. He gave a particular warning about the effects of placing control over finances in the hands of party leaders or senior party officials.[31] Once party professionals are released from the need to raise money from the ordinary members, a major incentive for recruitment is lost. The historical chapters of this study are filled with examples of the damaging effects of an excess of money on political activity and, conversely, of the salutory discipline of financial restrictions.

1. The limitation of constituency campaign costs by the Corrupt Practices Act, 1883, led to the formation of local party organizations. It became necessary to recruit members to carry out on a voluntary basis the tasks that had previously been allocated to paid agents and canvassers. The cut in permitted spending led directly to the growth of political participation. In McKenzie's words, the 1883 act "provided a very important stimulant to the development of the mass party in this country."[32]

2. As outlined in chapter 5, the extension of Conservative party activity at the constituency level after 1945 owed much to the ban on large contributions by parliamentary candidates and to the demand

[30] "There is nothing like the guarantee of public money—or even the sniff of it— for encouraging political apparatchiks and party bureaucrats to behave arrogantly" (Anthony Howard, "Political Parties and Public Funds," *New Statesman*, September 3, 1976).
[31] Robert Michels, *Political Parties: A Sociological Study of the Oligarchical Tendencies of Modern Democracy* (New York: Dover, 1959). esp. pt. 2, chap. 2.
[32] McKenzie, *British Political Parties*, p. 164. See also chapter 2, footnote 55.

placed on the local organizations to make quota payments to Conservative Central Office. The imposition of fund-raising demands on the local parties was a conscious strategy, since the party chairman, Lord Woolton, had "noticed that the organization of the party was weakest in those places where a wealthy candidate had made it unnecessary for the members to trouble to collect small subscriptions."[33]

3. In contrast to the relatively healthy state of local activity during the post–1945 period in a majority of Conservative constituency parties, Conservative associations in a number of cities have atrophied. It was these city associations that continued to rely on quite large business contributions. Their decline is direct evidence of the demoralizing effects of overfinancing.[34]

4. The rich haul received by the central Liberal organization between the 1890s and 1920s from the sale of titles damaged the party's local organizations. It was by general agreement a major cause of the political demoralization of the Liberal party. In the initial stages, the large payments to the national Liberal machine from plutocrats hoping for political honors probably dampened the enthusiasm of the local Liberal caucuses (though other important difficulties also faced local Liberalism after the split of 1886). After the Liberal victory in the election campaign of 1906, the bounty from the trade in titles led to a rapid expansion in the central and regional bureaucracy of the party, a development that does not, however, appear to have stimulated party organization at constituency level. Herbert Gladstone was later to attribute the decline of local Liberal organization before and during the First World War to "the multiplication of federations and officials" produced by the glut of money.[35] As quoted in chapter 4, Gladstone felt that "extravagance at H.Q. from 1910 to 1918 had discouraged local expenditure and contributions."[36]

The corrupting effects of extensive central reserves were most evident after the First World War when the Liberal organization remained supine for several years and when Gladstone could write, in 1924, to the party leader that "we have had no contributions from any quarter since 1916 and have been living on capital."[37] Not only did the easy money from seekers of honors act as a disincentive to other potential contributors, but the existence of huge central re-

[33] Lord Woolton, *Memoirs* (London: Cassell, 1959), p. 345.

[34] See chapter 5, footnotes 14-16.

[35] Sir Charles Mallet, *Herbert Gladstone: A Memoir* (London: Hutchinson, 1932), pp. 143-44.

[36] Maclean Papers, 468, fo. 28.

[37] Asquith Papers, 34, fo. 133.

serves led to intense quarrels about their control. Easy money from the state would probably have similar, damaging effects.

5. In the years before the Second World War, sizable payments to Labour candidates and constituency organizations by trade unions discouraged local initiative and, in the words of the party's national executive committee, frequently led "to dependence and in some cases to actual slackness" in constituency Labour parties.[38]

In many countries, socialist parties have provided the models of efficient mass organization financed by the subscriptions of large numbers of individual members. The Labour party in Britain has not conformed to this pattern and has had far fewer individual members than the British Conservative party. This Labour failure to secure a significant following of activists is hardly surprising in view of the ease with which money has regularly been obtained from trade unions.

6. In the 1960s and 1970s, there was a serious drop in Labour party membership. Thanks to trade union money, however, the income of the party's central organization remained unaffected by this weakness at constituency level. Had the finance of Labour's Transport House been damaged by declining constituency activity, it is probable that central party officials would have done far more to stimulate the local organizations, if only for their own financial self-interest.

An important effect of declining local Labour membership appears to have been that moderates have departed and extremists have remained. The fall in membership therefore has tended to be accompanied by an increase in political militancy within constituency Labour parties. Had Transport House been given a greater financial incentive to recruit more local members, it is reasonable to suppose that the political complexion of constituency Labour organizations would have been more moderate than it has been.[39]

[38] Chapter 3, footnote 32.

[39] Some of the most politically extreme local Labour parties in the 1970s were those with very small memberships, such as the Newham North East CLP, which dismissed its moderate MP, Reginald Prentice. In my opinion, the introduction of state subsidies would permit small, unrepresentative cliques to dominate constituency organizations and, if Rose's subsidy proposals were implemented, would allow them to pay for a full-time agent without any need to recruit new members. If constituency agents were paid out of public funds, a far-left agent in a safe Labour seat or a far-right agent in a safe Tory seat would have a great temptation to restrict party membership as much as possible. This would be a sinister development for Labour and Conservative moderates. For a summary of literature about conflicts within constituency Labour parties in the 1970s, see Anthony King, "Politics, Economics, and the Trade Unions, 1974-1979," in Penniman, *Britain at the Polls, 1979*, p. 89.

The lack of attention paid by the party headquarters to the task of maintaining

These historical precedents indicate that an injection of state aid would be likely to diminish fund-raising activities by party organizations and to foster undesirable reliance on the public purse. The Houghton Committee was aware of this objection but argued (1) that the proposed state funding would be too small to discourage additional fund raising by the parties and (2) that state aid would have a "pump-priming" effect on parties. It would give them a solid base on which to build their further activities.

Both these rationalizations need to be treated with suspicion and disbelief. Some advocates of state aid frankly admit what others prefer to conceal—that an initial small dose of public finance would establish a new system that would be extended later on. Once limited public payments to parties were introduced, it would be hard to resist arguments for their extension. The dissenting minority of the Houghton Committee correctly warned against this prospect: "the experience of European countries confirms that state aid, once started, never diminishes, and almost always increases. As one distinguished Swedish politician told us, in what was intended to be a piece of helpful advice: 'Start small—you can always increase it later.' " [40]

The argument that the pump-priming effect of state aid may actually increase the capacity of the parties to raise their own finances is also implausible. Pump priming implies a once-and-for-all payment to set an ailing organization on its feet. On this limited basis a grant can sometimes have the desired effect. The proposed state cash would not be short term, however, but would be given permanently.

The assumptions on which the Houghton Committee based its recommendation for state aid were that British parties by the mid-1970s were facing a permanent financial shortage and that this was not the fault of the parties themselves but had extraneous causes, particularly inflation. It has been shown that shouts of crisis have been exaggerated. Electioneering costs have declined, at the con-

membership and organization in the constituencies is commented upon in the recent Nuffield election study: "Many people inside and outside politics have a misleading picture of Transport House as an electoral force. In recent years headquarters had become entangled with matters of policy and the manifesto; the organisation and the party's popular base had been somewhat neglected. . . . In 1979, . . . ministers and advisers were openly despairing and even contemptuous of Transport House as a vote-winning organisation" (David E. Butler and Dennis Kavanagh, *The British General Election of 1979* [London: Macmillan, 1980], p. 133).

[40] Houghton Report, p. 81. The escalation of demands for public money has already begun: the Labour Party Commission of Enquiry has rejected the Houghton Committee's scheme as too "modest" and has called for higher levels of subsidy. See Introduction, footnote 8.

stituency level because of the strict legal limits and centrally because of the growing importance of free television and radio facilities. As far as routine income is concerned, the central income of the Labour party (and possibly the Liberal party) has grown, in real terms, during the postwar period. The only party whose central income has slightly declined—the Conservative party—opposes state aid. Moreover, insofar as the parties have experienced financial pressures, these have resulted not directly from inflation but from a decline in local support.

The real problem of party government in Britain in recent years is that the two main parties have performed poorly when in office and the Liberals have shown few signs that they would have done better. In particular, the failure of successive party leaders to cope effectively with the nation's economic problems has naturally led to disappointment and disillusionment. A way in which party followers can best voice their concern is by withdrawing their membership subscriptions and by refraining from local party activity. It would be greatly against the interests of democratic government if financial aid from public funds enabled party machines to dispense with the services of ordinary party members.

Would State Aid Lessen the Undesirable Influence of Pressure Groups?
A common argument for state subsidies is that they would reduce the parties' dependence on funding by powerful sectional interests. Even if it is accepted that organized groups ought not to play a dominant role in the funding of parties, this is not a decisive argument for state subsidies. Reliance on companies and unions might be preferable to dependence on the state.

Public funding would almost certainly increase the bureaucratic tendencies of party organizations. There would be pressure to gain for party officials the various advantages enjoyed by civil servants—security of tenure, inflation-proofed pension rights, and so on. It is, of course, wholly understandable that the permanent employees of party organizations should seek these benefits. But, if granted, they would insulate the party machines from ordinary party members and would, to all intents and purposes, make the party headquarters like government departments. As suggested in the next section, this already seems to have happened in some countries where public subsidies have been introduced. Once absorbed into the cosy atmosphere of Whitehall, the party machines would not be able to fulfill their democratic functions. Nor would the fact that there are rival party organizations be of much help. The opposing party headquarters would probably become like separate ministries—vying with each other, but within an enclosed civil service world of shared values, common career interests, and unified salary structures.

If a major motive of reform is to curb the undesirable influence of organized pressure groups, the measure proposed by the Houghton Committee and by Rose and Leonard would not achieve it. The scheme would produce the worst of both worlds. It would introduce state aid, with the damaging side effects that have been mentioned; at the same time, it would do little to reduce the parties' reliance on institutional backers. As pointed out in the introduction to this book, the Houghton Committee's proposals would still leave the Labour party's headquarters dependent on trade unions for two-thirds of its income.

A case could be made for linking a system of public subsidies with a ban on institutional donations to political parties. Though this would, in my opinion, be a retrograde step, it would possibly be an improvement on the Houghton Committee's projected scheme. (The question is considered further in the final section of this chapter.)

Do Subsidies in Other Countries Provide a Good Precedent for Britain? The main British proponents of state aid to political parties have referred enthusiastically to the schemes that have already been introduced in a number of countries. The majority report of the Houghton Committee was "impressed" by the experience of subsidies in several European countries, especially West Germany and Sweden. The introduction of state aid in these countries "had produced few adverse side-effects" and, in the four countries visited by the committee, "the public generally seemed to have accepted that some form of financial assistance was inevitable. . . . They saw the state subsidy as a more attractive alternative than the parties' dependence on business interests." The committee reported that the principle of state aid had been accepted "by virtually all the political parties, despite initial hesitation by some" and that subsidies "do not appear to have had any adverse effect on party membership or voluntary activity" in Sweden and West Germany.[41]

41 Houghton Report, pp. 47, 49, 51. It is perhaps not unrealistic to comment that some members of the Houghton Committee, already committed to the idea of subsidies, found the evidence for which they were seeking. Not all officials of parties and of party foundations in West Europe share the conclusion reported by the Houghton Committee. According to a recent statement by a West German official, "the German political parties, for all practical purposes, are bankrupt today, precisely because, for various reasons, individual and organizational contributions have dwindled; every party is deep in the red. . . . Perhaps in an indirect way what has happened in West Germany is that parties have relied too much on public funding and have overspent their resources. . . . People just

The Houghton Report and Leonard's survey both argued that foreign experience provided a favorable precedent for the introduction of state aid to parties in Britain. This view can be challenged on two grounds: first, foreign examples are not directly relevant to the situation in Britain and, second, the reforms introduced in several countries have had some damaging consequences. Public subsidies for political parties were introduced in several countries to solve problems that do not seriously exist in Britain. In Italy, for instance, an important objective was to control electoral corruption. Elsewhere a major objective was to enable parties to meet the rising costs of electioneering and, in particular, the growing expense of television advertising. As acknowledged by the Houghton Committee, "rising costs in the communications field . . . were common to most countries"[42] and were a major factor in the decision to introduce some form of public subsidy. Similarly, Paltiel cites "the reduction or restraining of rising costs" and "the assurance of probity" as two of the main motives usually advanced in favor of the regulation of campaign finances and public subsidies.[43]

As mentioned in chapter 1, the problem of corruption in the financing of parties and campaigns has largely been eliminated in Britain. As far as rising campaign costs are concerned, these have been effectively controlled by the combination of strict limits on campaign expenditure by parliamentary candidates and free television and radio time for the national party organizations. Moreover, recent studies, particularly by Paltiel, have given a far less rosy picture of public subsidies than that of Leonard and of the Houghton Committee. Paltiel's detailed examination of the experience of eleven countries in the late 1970s led to some disturbing conclusions:

> Subsidy systems and their accompanying regulations have made it difficult for new groups and individuals to enter the competitive electoral struggle and may be promoting the ossification of the party systems in certain states. To the extent that these schemes limit entry of new competitors

did not give as much money any more. Their disenchantment with the political process and the party system was reflected in dwindling contributions" (Manfred von Nordheim, director of the Washington office of the Konrad Adenauer Stiftung, verbatim report of a discussion on "Campaign Finance Regulation in International Perspective," in Michael J. Malbin, ed., *Parties, Interest Groups, and Campaign Finance Laws* [Washington, D.C.: American Enterprise Institute, 1980], p. 383).

[42] Houghton Report, p. 48.

[43] Khayyam Z. Paltiel, "Public Financing Abroad: Contrasts and Effects," in Malbin, *Parties, Interest Groups*, p. 354.

and new parties, they may well promote alienation from democratic methods of change and may stimulate recourse to extra-parliamentary opposition tactics of violent confrontation.[44]

These fears may be unduly alarmist, but they serve a useful function in highlighting some of the dangers of recent experiments. It is useful to survey Paltiel's findings about Europe and America, because they accord with some of the conclusions about Britain set out in the preceding chapters. According to Paltiel, "the biggest immediate beneficiaries of direct cash subsidies tend to be the central party organizations and the party staff professionals:"[45]

> Public subventions in Austria, Canada, Finland, Italy, Sweden and West Germany have been accompanied by a vast expansion in the apparatuses of the party organizations. No one who has visited Sweden or West Germany can fail to be impressed by the lavish quarters, numbers and quality of the personnel employed by the parties. . . . Increased dependence on professional expertise has led to the relative decline of middle-level party leaders and the restriction of party militants to routine tasks.[46]

[44] Ibid., p. 370. As outlined later in this section, one system that gives cause for long-term anxiety is that of West Germany. Its regulations about political finance have been formulated largely to prevent a repetition of the pattern that, it is considered, permitted the rise of Hitler. The Nazis obtained large funds from big business; therefore the new system of state funding is intended to diminish the role of corporate contributors. Weimar Germany was weakened by a multiplication of small fringe parties; therefore the new system prevents such parties from receiving the full benefits of public subventions.

So far, these political arrangements have had the desired effect. West Germany has remained stable. Political extremism has been held in check. This success can be attributed to the buoyant German economy, however, rather than to its political constitution. There remain worries, alluded to by Paltiel, about whether the existing political structures would be able to withstand major strains. Under current rules, the main parties—SPD, CDU/CSU, and FPD—form what is in effect a political cartel. They jointly benefit from very large payments from public funds, and they maintain extensive bureaucracies that, as mentioned in the text of this section, have many of the characteristics of government departments. The system has two potential dangers: (1) because the established party machines rely so heavily on state money and because their educational activities are generally sponsored from above, it is uncertain whether the three main parties have developed organic support that would survive if the financial props of state aid were ever to be removed; and (2) a gulf appears to have been created between the established parties and other forms of political expression; the fact that the main parties enjoy a monopoly of public financial support makes it more difficult for fringe organizations to mount an electoral challenge and encourages them to concentrate on unconstitutional action instead.

[45] Ibid., p. 367.

[46] Ibid.

In Italy, "public finance has not led to more openness but rather to greater bureaucratization of Italian parties."[47] Canadian observers "have noted a similar experience regarding the expansion of the role of paid party staffs following on the introduction of subsidies."

The situation in West Germany is especially remarkable. Not only do the main party organizations receive large public subventions, but extra funds are given to party research foundations. The foundations receive huge grants from several government ministries—the Federal Center for Political Education, the Ministry for Inner German Affairs, the Foreign Ministry, and the Ministry for Economic Cooperation.[48] Other public funds are granted by some of the *Länder* and communes. Besides carrying out research in West Germany, the foundations maintain offices in foreign countries and give support to political parties in some of these countries. They also hand out major grants for economic development. The finance for these activities is provided almost entirely by government ministries, and the party foundations are, therefore, to all intents and purposes, branches of the West German civil service. As Paltiel rightly comments:

> serious questions arise, first, as to the propriety of these international activities and, second, with regard to the identification of party and state as the foundations carry out projects using resources subject directly and indirectly to government control.[49]

Is There a Danger of Legal Gerrymandering? The committee established under Lord Houghton's chairmanship to consider the possibility of financial aid to political parties was advertised by the Labour government, which set it up in 1974, as an independent, nonparty body. It included members of the Conservative, Labour, Liberal, and Scottish Nationalist parties as well as others not publicly associated with any party. It emerges from subsequent research that considerable care was taken to ensure that a majority of those asked to serve on the committee had Labour party sympathies and, in particular, that they favored the idea of state subsidies.[50] There is evidence that some members were canvassed about their views on the subsidy question before being appointed to serve on the committee. In these circumstances, it is hardly surprising that a majority of the Houghton Committee found in favor of state aid.

[47] Ibid., p. 368.
[48] Ibid., p. 362.
[49] Ibid., p. 363.
[50] See F. Leslie D. Seidle, "State Aid for Political Parties," *Parliamentarian*, vol. 61 (1980), p. 86.

These remarks are in no way intended as criticisms of the members or staff of the Houghton Committee. Nor are Labour governments alone in attempting to ensure that "independent" committees are filled with partisans. The political bias of the Houghton Committee is typical of bias that is likely to affect all such bodies. Paltiel has argued that legislators (and their advisers) characteristically seek to "entrench their electoral positions" by introducing subsidies that will serve their own interests. Once the idea of public payments to parties is legitimized, there is a real danger that the governing party of the day—whichever it is—or the governing coalition of parties will manipulate the regulations for their own ends. In Paltiel's words:

> in every known instance public subventions have been introduced by the parties in office; given the nature of parliamentary regimes, this is inevitable, as only those parties commanding a majority in the legislature can assure the passage of the necessary legislation. It is scarcely to be expected, therefore, that incumbents will adopt measures to their own detriment.[51]

Acceptance of state payments to political parties and candidates is therefore likely to lead to the management of the rules of the political system—a potentially pernicious form of legal gerrymandering. This danger is one of the most important objections to state aid for parties, for it is a fallacy to regard money provided for political purposes by the state as "neutral" or pure.[52]

[51] Paltiel, "Public Financing Abroad," p. 366. See also Gary C. Jacobson, "Practical Consequences of Campaign Finance Reform: An Incumbent Protection Act?," *Public Policy*, vol. 24 (1976).

[52] An additional argument for a new system of public subsidies is that they are required to enable the parties to cope with the demands made by the new forms of campaigning introduced in the 1970s, in particular referenda (such as the 1973 Ulster referendum, the 1975 referendum on British membership in the European Community, and the 1979 referenda in Scotland and Wales on the government's proposals for devolution) and the direct elections for the European Parliament (first held in 1979). The argument is weak:

1. The new forms of campaigning are irregular and impose relatively little extra burden on the party organizations. They are a marginal development and should not be used as a pretext for introducing subsidies for traditional forms of campaigning.

2. Referenda cut across party lines and are not contested exclusively on a party political basis. For the 1975 referendum, (a) special state grants were allocated to the main (nonparty) campaign organizations, and (b) one of these organizations successfully tapped extra sources of funds in addition to those normally given to the parties.

3. The European elections were largely financed by grants provided by the European Community and, like the 1975 referendum, appear to have attracted

Summary. The main arguments for introducing state subventions for British parties are unfounded. The existing system of funding party politics is fair. The Conservatives are somewhat richer than their opponents. This advantage derives from the small contributions of Conservative members in the constituencies and not from big business. British parties, unlike many of their foreign counterparts, have not been faced by mounting campaign costs because the main expense of modern electioneering—television advertising—is provided free of charge. British central party organizations have not suffered severely from inflation. The supposed defects that subsidies would be intended to remedy therefore do not exist. Moreover, state cash for parties would be harmful. It would enable the parties to ignore the signs of discontent and inactivity at the grass roots. Judging by foreign experience, it would increase the power of central party bureaucrats and would diminish participation.

It is paradoxical that British commentators should be looking to foreign subsidy systems in view of the general success of the existing British regulations concerning political finance. The British combination of spending limits and subsidies-in-kind promotes equality of campaign spending, allows all the main parties to project their messages to the electorate, but, at the same time, avoids the bureaucratic dangers inherent in direct cash subventions.

The Real Abuses

The two areas in which there is a pressing need for reform concern, as outlined in chapter 8, the financial interests of members of Parliament and political payments by trade unions for Labour party purposes.

The Financial Interests of Members of Parliament. The strict limitations on campaign spending by parliamentary candidates, introduced in 1883, were designed largely to limit the scope for electoral corruption. In the modern period, the main opportunities for conflicts of

---

some additional funds of their own.

4. The total number of political campaigns did not increase in the 1970s. The introduction of referenda and the European election were balanced by the streamlining of the system of local government elections.

5. It is in any case a fallacy to assume that the introduction of new forms of political campaigning must necessarily impose new burdens on party organizations. They may have the effect of stimulating new sources of support. As mentioned in chapter 5, the practice of contesting local government elections adopted by many Conservative constituency associations in the postwar years seems to have improved their organization and finances.

interest (corruption is possibly too strong a term) appear to have moved from the hustings to the House of Commons itself.

While there is no objection to MPs' supplementing their public salaries, it is objectionable that their outside earnings should be linked or interlaced in any way with their official duties or privileges.

Three sets of reforms are needed. First, existing regulations about the registration and declaration of financial interests should be extended and tightened.[53] Second, as argued in chapter 8, MPs ought to be banned from advocating or advancing the interests of any person or body from which they draw money or other material benefits. This ban should apply to voting, speaking in the House of Commons, and using informal contacts for the benefit of an outside backer. Third, the draconian British law of libel and the conventions of parliamentary privilege need to be liberalized.

At present the investigative activities of the media in Britain are unduly hampered. There is an obvious need to protect politicians and their families from irresponsible personal attacks. Nevertheless, the best safeguard against skillful or unscrupulous evasion of codes of behavior by public figures is the threat of adverse publicity. Lord Shawcross has suggested a change in the law to protect journalists who, in the course of a publication about a matter of public interest, unwittingly commit a libel. This proposal has the support of Justice, the International Commission of Jurists. It provides for "a statutory defence of qualified privilege to be available in respect of matters which, if true, it would have been in the public interest to publicise" and "which were in fact published with an honest belief in their truths, based upon reasonable grounds and without malice."[54] Such a reform not only would guard against undesirable influence exerted upon MPs but would also protect against financial abuses in other parts of the political system.

Trade Unions and the Labour Party. The intimate financial and institutional bond between the trade unions and the Labour party has no British counterpart and can have few parallels in other democratic countries.

The system of political payments gives a handful of the largest unions a stranglehold on the Labour party. This arrangement has stunted the development of representative and active Labour organizations in the constituencies.

---

[53] See chapter 9, footnote 36.
[54] Lord Shawcross, letter to *The Times*, May 2, 1974.

The problem results not only from the high proportion of total Labour party funds (over 50 percent) that comes from the unions. Under the party constitution, financial payments entitle trade union leaders to almost all of the votes at the party conference, to a majority of seats on the party's national executive committee, and to a large say in the selection (and readoption) of the party leader and of Labour MPs. As related in chapter 8, the rules give the biggest union a block of votes at the party conference twice as large as the number at the disposal of all the constituency Labour parties together. Half a dozen unions possess between them well over half of the total conference votes.[55]

Commentators have sometimes justified the rules that permit this state of affairs on the ground that union votes are generally cast in favor of moderate policy planks at the annual party conference and on the national executive committee,[56] thereby preventing a takeover by extremists representing the constituency parties. It is open to doubt whether this interpretation is still correct, though it generally held good until the 1960s. In the long run, the domination of the party by the unions is probably one of the main reasons why individual membership is so pitifully small and why the local organizations are vulnerable to capture by small, unrepresentative groups of militants. Trade union power within the Labour party limits the role of the individual members and must act as a deterrent to constituency party activity.

The rationale for giving almost 90 percent of the votes at the party conference to trade union delegates is that they represent blocks of party members distinguished from the individual members only by the fact that their subscriptions are paid through a trade union political levy fund and not directly to a constituency Labour party (CLP).

This is a legal fiction. Trade union "membership" of the party does not exist in any meaningful sense. Its only function is to justify giving power to union leaders according to the size of their payments. The artificial nature of trade union "membership" of the party is seen in several ways:

---

[55] See Lewis Minkin, *The Labour Party Conference: A Study of Intra-Party Democracy* (London: Allen Lane, 1978), appendix 12. Minkin reports that the six largest unions possessed 3,647,000 votes of the total of 6,392,000 at the annual party conference of 1976. The fifty-four unions represented at the conference had 5,669,000 votes, constituency Labour parties 673,000, and nine socialist, cooperative, and professional organizations 50,000.

[56] This is a major theme of McKenzie, *British Political Parties*.

1. Each union might be expected to affiliate to the Labour party the full number of members who subscribe to the union's political levy fund. In practice there is no direct connection between the total affiliation fee paid by a union and the size of its political levy–paying membership. In 1978, 2,012,543 members of the Transport and General Workers' Union contributed to its political levy fund. Union leaders paid an affiliation fee to the Labour party in 1979 sufficient to represent only 1¼ million of them. Theoretically, 1¼ million TGWU members thus became members of the Labour party, while the other 762,543 did not. Lists were never drawn up by the union showing the names of the 1¼ million on whose behalf votes were cast at the 1978 party conference or of the other 762,543 for whom no affiliation fee was paid and no votes were cast.[57] The party rule, which gives unions voting power on the basis of their payments and not on the basis of their membership, has rightly been criticized by a union leader as "simply buying votes and buying influence."[58]

2. Unions affiliate not only to the Labour party nationally but also to regional and constituency Labour parties. These extra affiliations give them votes at these lower levels of the organization as well. The size of their votes depends on their subscriptions to the relevant regional and constituency parties. A result is that unions frequently affiliate to the national party a different number of members than to the regional parties. Applied to the individual union member, this means that some are theoretically affiliated to the national but not to the regional party organization (or vice versa).

3. Trade union members who subscribe to a political levy fund are also permitted to pay an individual subscription directly to their constituency organization. Technically, they are party members twice over, and two votes are cast on their behalf at the Labour conference. Once again, if the democratic implications of union membership were

---

[57] As mentioned in chapter 3, one peculiar feature of the system is that some unions affiliate to the Labour party on the basis of a larger number than the total of their members paying the political levy. The National Union of Railwaymen, for instance, paid an affiliation fee sufficient to obtain 180,000 votes at the 1979 party conference, despite the fact that only 164,406 of its members had paid the levy and that its total membership (including those not paying the levy) was 171,411. At the other end of the scale, some unions paid an affiliation fee that entitled them to a total vote representing only a fraction of their levy-paying membership (for example, the National Graphical Association affiliated on the basis of 22,000 members, even though 64,805 had paid the political levy). These figures are derived from the certification officer's report for 1979 and Labour party information department, news release no. AC3/79.

[58] Tom Jackson, general secretary of the Union of Communication Workers, quoted in *The Times*, February 2, 1981.

taken seriously, steps would be taken to ensure that members of CLPs were not counted in the union column as well.

4. As related in chapter 8, members of unions with political levy funds automatically subscribe unless they contract out. Administrative inconvenience and the moral pressures of the workplace mean that probably no more than 2 percent of union members contract out, despite the fact that nearly half of them do not vote Labour at general elections. This means that about 40 percent of the money raised by unions for Labour party purposes comes from members who oppose it.

These Conservatives, Liberals, Scottish and Welsh Nationalists, Communists, and National Front supporters who through inaction subscribe to political levy funds (and thus to Labour party funds) thereby become members of the Labour party. Votes are cast at party conferences—supposedly on their behalf—by trade union delegates.

Under the terms of the Labour party constitution, individual subscribers to constituency Labour parties must "accept and conform to the Constitution, Programme, Principles and Policy of the Party." Similar regulations do not apply to trade union members of the party. Were they applied, about 40 percent of trade union members would become ineligible to join.[59]

5. The connection between most individual trade unionists and the Labour party is so tenuous that few realize that they are, technically speaking, members of the party. This fact emerges from opinion surveys that show that the number regarding themselves as Labour members is a small fraction of the number on whose behalf votes are cast at the party conference.[60]

6. According to established practice, each union casts a block vote at Labour conferences. This system, described by Aneurin Bevan as a "travesty of the democratic vote,"[61] puts power in the

[59] Company contributions to the Conservative party are open to the same criticism. Individual shareholders have no real choice about whether their money is used to support the Conservative party. The essential difference is that political contributions do not entitle the companies involved to votes at the Conservative party conference or on constituency party committees.

[60] Special tabulation by the author of survey data for David E. Butler and Donald Stokes, *Political Change in Britain: Forces Shaping Electoral Choice* (London: Macmillan, 1969). See especially p. 488, question 44. Surveys carried out for this study in 1963 and 1964 also indicated that only a small minority of union members believed that trade unions should have close ties to the Labour party. The proportion of union members favoring such ties was 25 percent in 1963 and 31 percent in 1964 (ibid., p. 169).

[61] Speech delivered on September 29, 1954, quoted in Martin Harrison, *Trade Unions and the Labour Party since 1945* (London: Allen and Unwin, 1960), p. 56.

hands of small numbers of union leaders. Frequently, they refuse even to inform their members how the union's block vote has been cast.[62] The block vote—like the unit rule at former presidential nominating conventions in the United States—greatly increases the influence of the main unions.

In short, "membership" is a misnomer as applied to trade union affiliations to the Labour party. The party is run like a joint stock company in which unions are given voting powers according to the sums they are prepared to pay. In effect, unions use their political levy funds to purchase blocks of shares in the party, and their voting rights are determined by the number of shares ("members") they buy. When a union desires to increase its voting power, it may do so simply by paying for extra shares.

Were this system not so long established, it would be considered a scandal. It is a survival of the early period when the Labour Representation Committee—the precursor of the Labour party—was set up as a body consisting solely of the delegates of unions and socialist societies. Since that time, the Labour party has emerged as one of the two governing parties of the land. Yet its pattern of fund raising and its constitution have altered very little and are inappropriate for modern circumstances. Consequently, an excessive degree of power within the party remains in the hands of a few trade union chieftains. They possess financial clout and a control over huge blocks of votes at party conferences that would have made the legendary bosses of Tammany Hall pale with envy.

Changes in the method of financing the Labour party are much to be desired. The task of reform nevertheless presents thorny problems. Politically, it would be impossible for a Labour government to sponsor legislation to cut or loosen the ties between the party and its union patrons. It would be nearly as hard for a Conservative government to do so. The substitution of contracting in to the political levy in place of contracting out by Baldwin's Conservative government in 1927 was widely regarded as a spiteful and unjustified attack on the Labour movement. The system of contracting out was reintroduced as soon as a Labour government with a majority in the House of Commons

---

[62] Harrison, *Trade Unions and the Labour Party*, pp. 258-59. Occasionally the executive of a trade union has been dominated by a group of Communist activists. The best-documented example is that of the Electrical Trades Union in the 1940s and 1950s (see Harrison, *Trade Unions and the Labour Party*, p. 182). The block votes cast by the delegates of such unions have been cast in accordance with the mandates of their pro-Communist executive committees. As Harrison comments, the system of block voting means that "members of anti-Labour parties can have a say in Labour Party policy" (ibid., p. 170).

took office in 1945. Against this background, an attempt by a Conservative government to reverse the rules yet again would be likely to generate further industrial and political conflict.[63]

There is another difficulty. The problems of the existing system stem not only from the legislation concerning trade union political levy funds but also from the constitution of the Labour party. There has been a traditional reluctance in Britain to subject the internal affairs of political parties to legal controls. To use the law to enforce a change in the constitution of the Labour party would be seen as undesirable interference and as a use of legislative power for partisan, anti-Labour purposes.

A possible approach to the problem would be to ban companies and unions from making political contributions altogether. Were a measure to be enacted along these lines, the Labour party would need to alter its constitution. Trade unions could no longer pay affiliation fees to the party, and the rationale for union block votes would disappear. Nor could the unions continue to sponsor members of Parliament. These restrictions might prove acceptable to the Labour party if the ban on payments by unions were offset by a similar ban on company donations to the Tories.

If the Conservative and Labour parties were suddenly denied two of their main sources of funds, suitable alternatives would be demanded. The Liberal party leader Steel has proposed that, in return for an end to political payments by companies and unions, "it would be a healthy step if the next Parliament . . . substituted

---

[63] Some of the undesirable features of trade union political levy funds could be eliminated without reopening the controversy about contracting in versus contracting out. Legislation could be introduced to amend the rules for political levy funds and for political payments by companies. Under such a law: (1) Contracting out would be retained. (2) Each year union members liable to pay the political levy (that is, those who had not contracted out) would be given a ballot form on which they could name the party or organization to which they desired their portion of the political levy to be devoted. Union leaders would be committed to allocate money to different parties according to the proportion of votes cast in such a ballot. A share of political levy funds would go only to those organizations or parties receiving a minimum proportion of the total votes cast. (3) There could be a parallel system for companies. Under such a scheme, companies could make political contributions only if sanctioned to do so by an initial ballot of a majority of shareholders. Once this hurdle had been overcome, individual shareholders would be given each year the right to nominate the party or organization to which their proportion of a company's political giving was to be devoted. (The relevant form could be included with the notice sent to all shareholders of the annual general meeting.) It should be noted that a contracting out system is not being suggested for shareholders since it would present severe practical difficulties that do not exist for contracting out of trade union levies. These difficulties stem from the fact that different shareholders possess varying numbers of shares.

instead the American system of limited tax relief on the donations of individuals to parties of their choice."[64]

The idea of encouraging small donations in place of institutional contributions is superficially attractive. Closer examination reveals severe problems. Various forms of tax advantage for political payments have been introduced in the United States, Canada, and some West European countries. The only schemes that have succeeded in using the income tax machinery to raise substantial sums for political purposes are those providing for tax credits or tax checkoffs. Typically, taxpayers are permitted to earmark a small amount of their normal tax liability to a political party (or candidate) of their choice. These schemes do not normally involve any financial sacrifice on the part of individual taxpayers—the money allocated to the parties and to candidates comes from the general revenues of the state.[65] To all intents and purposes, the checkoff schemes are public subsidies and are hardly distinguishable from block payments to parties from the public Treasury. To introduce a system of tax checkoffs is, in effect, to introduce public subsidies by stealth.

It could be argued that a combination of (1) state aid and (2) a ban on institutional payments to parties would be an improvement on the existing system of political funding. I have already suggested that the damaging effects of public subsidies would probably outweigh the advantage accruing from a ban on trade union contributions to the Labour party. Moreover, the enactment of radical legislation would have disruptive, far-reaching, and largely uncertain consequences.

The recent experience of foreign countries, particularly the United States, provides a warning about the hazards of interfering with the laws relating to political money. The reforms passed in many countries in the 1960s and 1970s have frequently had unforeseen and unwelcome results. Some examples have been mentioned earlier in this chapter. In Paltiel's words, "too little thought has been given to the secondary consequences" of these new enactments.[66] Major developments have flowed, in some cases, from minor provisions in the new, hastily passed laws. The United States has been subjected to a rash of campaign finance laws. They have included the Federal Election Campaign Acts (FECA) of 1971, 1974, and 1976. Dozens of new laws have been passed at the state level during the

[64] *The Times*, August 24, 1978.

[65] Various forms of indirect subsidies are discussed by several contributors to Malbin, *Parties, Interest Groups.*

[66] Paltiel, "Public Financing Abroad," p. 370.

309

same period. Some of the new rules were designed to reduce the financial clout of special interests (an aim similar to that of a ban on institutional payments in Britain). Their actual effect has been to diminish the role of parties instead and to increase that of single-issue interest groups.

This experience has relevance for Britain. Although the financial links between the trade unions and the Labour party are, in my view, inconsistent with democratic principles, I do not feel that there is any simple legislative solution to the problem. The law is an uncertain, blunt, and dangerous instrument.

Students of political finance and committees set up to investigate the subject have usually been too ready to make recommendations for change. Certain alterations to existing laws and practices have been suggested in this book. No major proposal for legislative reform is being made. This is, quite simply, because legislative action might do more harm than good.

Appendix A

The Cost of Living, 1830-1980

TABLE 80

COST-OF-LIVING INDEX, 1830–1980

(1900 = 100)

1830	115.3	1907	107.1	1932	165.6
1831	127.1	1908	109.1	1933	161.1
1832	117.6	1909	109.1	1934	162.2
1835	103.5	1910	110.6	1935	164.3
1837	117.6	1911	111.6	1936	169.1
1841	127.1	1912	115.9	1937	176.5
1847	127.1	1913	115.9	1938	179.1
1852	98.8	1914	114.8	1939	184.7
1857	129.4	1915	141.2	1940	224.2
1859	122.3	1916	167.8	1941	250.0
1865	124.7	1917	201.7	1942	269.7
1868	130.6	1918	233.0	1943	278.9
1874	143.5	1919	247.4	1944	285.7
1880	118.8	1920	285.7	1945	292.8
1885	103.5	1921	260.9	1946	304.0
1886	94.1	1922	210.5	1947	324.1
1892	100.0	1923	200.0	1948	347.8
1895	97.6	1924	201.7	1949	358.2
1900	100.0	1925	201.7	1950	369.2
1901	101.3	1926	198.4	1951	400.0
1902	102.1	1927	192.0	1952	428.6
1903	103.5	1928	190.5	1953	428.6
1904	104.8	1929	189.0	1954	436.4
1905	103.5	1930	181.8	1955	452.8
1906	103.5	1931	169.1	1956	480.0

(Table continues)

TABLE 80 (continued)

1957	489.8	1965	585.3	1973	958.3
1958	500.0	1966	625.1	1974	1,121.8
1959	500.0	1967	645.9	1975	1,498.7
1960	510.6	1968	666.7	1976	1,745.9
1961	522.2	1969	708.4	1977	2,077.8
1962	545.6	1970	753.4	1978	2,229.3
1963	558.1	1971	833.6	1979	2,482.5
1964	571.4	1972	882.8	1980	2,828.2[a]

NOTE: The creation of a long-term index of the cost of living presents severe conceptual and practical problems. Different methods of indexation yield varying results. A revised cost-of-living index 1900-1979 is contained in David E. Butler and Anne Sloman, *British Political Facts, 1900-1979* (London: Macmillan, 1980), pp. 348-49. According to this index, the long-term increase in the cost of living during the twentieth century has been slightly smaller than shown in the index used for this study.

[a] February 1980.

SOURCES: For 1830-1900, William B. Gwyn, *Democracy and the Cost of Politics in Britain, 1832-1959* (London: Athlone Press, 1962) p. 247; for 1900-1967, David E. Butler and Jennie Freeman, *British Political Facts, 1900-1968* (London: Macmillan, 1969), pp. 222-24; and for 1968 onward, the retail price index (RPI) published in Central Statistical Office, *Annual Abstract of Statistics* (London: Her Majesty's Stationery Office).

Appendix B

The Foreign Exchange Value of the Pound Sterling

All statistics in this study are expressed in pounds sterling. The value of sterling in terms of other major currencies is as follows:
United States dollar:

> Between 1949 and 1967, £1 sterling was worth $2.80; between 1967 and 1971, $2.40. Since 1971 there has been a floating exchange rate. On August 1, 1980, £1 was worth $2.33.

Other exchange rates for August 1, 1980, for £1 sterling:

Australian dollar	2.02
Canadian dollar	2.70
French franc	9.96
Irish pound	1.11
Italian lira	1964.00
Japanese yen	530.00
Swiss franc	3.88
West German mark	4.18

SOURCE: *New York Times*, August 2, 1980.

Appendix C

Election Expenses of Parliamentary Candidates, by Party, 1885-1979

Since 1883 parliamentary candidates have been obliged to file returns setting out their campaign expenses. Regulations about filing had existed before 1883 but had frequently been unenforced. After every general election since 1885 except in 1918, the government has collected and published statistics about candidates' election expenses.

TABLE 81

AVERAGE EXPENSES OF CONSERVATIVE, LIBERAL, AND LABOUR CANDIDATES
IN GENERAL ELECTIONS, 1885–1979
(in pounds)

	At Constant 1980 Values			At Current Prices		
	Conservative	Liberal	Labour	Conservative	Liberal	Labour
1885	890	891	a	24,318	24,345	a
1886	752	659	a	22,600	19,805	a
1892	864	809	a	24,434	22,879	a
1895	863	748	a	25,006	21,674	a
1900	930	868	463	26,300	24,547	13,094
1906	n.a.	n.a.	627	n.a.	n.a.	7,268
1910	1,109	1,075	881	31,363	30,401	24,915
1910	918	882	736	25,961	24,943	20,814
1918	No published returns					
1922	n.a.	n.a.	541	n.a.	n.a.	7,268
1923	845	789	464	11,948	11,156	6,561
1924	n.a.	n.a.	433	n.a.	n.a.	6,071

TABLE 81 (continued)

	At Constant 1980 Values			At Current Prices		
	Conserv-ative	Liberal	Labour	Conserv-ative	Liberal	Labour
1929	905	782	452	13,541	11,701	6,763
1931	n.a.	n.a.	n.a.	n.a.	n.a.	n.a.
1935	777	495	365	13,374	8,520	6,283
1945	780	532	595	7,534	5,138	5,747
1950	777	459	694	5,952	3,516	5,316
1951	773	488	658	5,465	3,450	4,652
1955	692	423	611	4,322	2,642	3,816
1959	761	532	705	4,304	3,009	3,987
1964	790	579	751	3,910	2,866	3,717
1966	766	501	726	3,465	2,267	3,284
1970	949	667	828	3,562	2,504	3,108
1974	1,197	745	1,127	2,978	1,854	2,804
1974	1,275	725	1,163	2,842	1,616	2,592
1979	2,190	1,013	1,897	2,543	1,184	2,218

NOTES: For general elections since 1906, most statistics are based on David E. Butler and Anne Sloman, *British Political Facts, 1900-1979* (London: Macmillan, 1980), p. 229. For the analysis of candidates' expenditure in elections between 1885 and 1900, I am most grateful to Leslie Seidle for original work, as yet unpublished, which is quoted below with his kind permission. Average expenditures for 1885-1900 and for 1922 and 1924 are for opposed candidates only. According to Seidle, average expenditure by opposed Liberal Unionist candidates was: 1886, £840 (£25,245 at 1980 values); 1892, £944 (£26,696); 1895, £902 (£26,136); and 1900, £955 (£27,007). According to Seidle, average spending by unopposed candidates was as follows (number of unopposed candidates is given in parantheses): 1885, Conservative £324 (8), Liberal £218 (14); 1886, Conservative £184 (880), Liberal £141 (37), Liberal Unionist £187 (29); 1892, Conservative £178 (129), Liberal £148 (13), Liberal Unionist £235 (7); 1895, Conservative £214 (111), Liberal £196 (112), Liberal Unionist £305 (17); and 1900, Conservative £211 (135), Liberal £231 (124), Liberal Unionist £250 (24). Where figures are marked n.a., this is because an analysis of the published returns by party has not been made for the election concerned.

a The Labour Representation Committee (Labour party) was founded in 1900.

SOURCES: For 1885 and 1900, analysis by Seidle; Labour spending in 1900 and 1906, analysis by the author; Labour spending in 1922 and 1924, Ross McKibbin, *The Evolution of the Labour Party, 1910-1924* (Oxford: Oxford University Press, 1974), pp. 159, 161; other figures, Butler and Sloman, *British Political Facts 1900-1979*, p. 229.

As outlined in chapter 9, the official statistics do not in all cases show the amounts actually spent. Moreover, candidates' personal expenses are not included. For elections before 1918, the totals exclude each candidate's share of the returning officer's fee, and totals before 1950 may also exclude the election agent's fee (see table 68). For elections since 1918, the totals appear in most cases to exclude the cost of lost election deposits. All these sources of error or ambiguity do not seriously affect the overall pattern.

The long-term decline in parliamentary election expenses (all candidates) is shown in table 5, and the drastic fall in the cost per vote for Conservative candidates since 1880 is given in table 7. The relative equality of expenditure since 1945 by Conservative and Labour candidates is shown in table 74. The postwar pattern of spending by Liberal parliamentary candidates appears in table 56.

Table 81 gives (1) average spending by Conservative, Labour, and Liberal candidates in most general elections since 1885 and (2) average spending at constant 1980 values.

Appendix D

Financial Decentralization of British Parties in the Modern Era

National-level expenditure has become increasingly important for British political parties in comparison with constituency-level expenditure (see table 73). Nevertheless, the overall spending of local parties is still greater than that of the central organizations. Financial decentralization is greatest in the Liberal party and smallest in the Labour party, as shown in table 82.

This financial pattern affects the structure of power within the parties. For example, the fact that money for parliamentary campaigns is mostly raised by the local organizations partly accounts for their large influence on candidate selection.

TABLE 82

EXPENDITURE OF THE CONSERVATIVE, LABOUR, AND LIBERAL PARTIES
DEVOTED TO CENTRAL AND CONSTITUENCY EXPENSES IN THE MODERN ERA
(in percent)

	Conservative[a]	Labour[b]	Liberal[b]
Central			
Routine	30.8	39.2	22.2
Campaign	4.5	4.2	2.8
Total	35.3	43.4	25.0
Constituency			
Routine	60.6	47.2	60.7
Campaign	4.1	9.3	14.3
Total	64.7	56.5	75.0
Total	100.0	100.0	100.0

[a] Parliamentary cycle 1966-1970.
[b] Parliamentary cycle 1970-1974.
SOURCES: As for tables 36, 45, 57.

Appendix E

Scheme of State Subsidies Proposed by the Houghton Committee, 1976

We recommend the introduction of a system of state financial aid for political parties in the United Kingdom.

Such aid should take the form of:

(i) annual grants to be paid from Exchequer funds to the central organisations of the parties for their general purposes, the amounts being determined according to the extent of each party's electoral support;

(ii) at local level, a limited reimbursement of the election expenses of Parliamentary and local government candidates.

In order to qualify for a grant a party must at the previous general election have either:

(a) saved the deposits of its candidates in at least six constituencies; or

(b) had at least two of its candidates returned as Members; or

(c) had one of its candidates returned as a Member, and received as a party a total of not less than 150,000 votes.

The amount of the annual grant payable to each of the qualifying parties shall be calculated on the basis of 5p for each vote cast for its candidates at the previous general election.

The scheme for limited reimbursement of candidates' election expenses should apply to all Parliamentary elections, and to all elections for county and district councils in England and Wales, regional, island and district councils in Scotland, and the Greater London Council and the London borough councils.

Reimbursement should be restricted to those candidates who poll at least one eighth of the votes cast, and the amount to be reimbursed should be the candidate's actual election expenses up to a limit of half his legally permitted maximum expenditure. Payment shall be made directly to the candidate.

It is recommended that the first payment of the proposed annual grants payable to the parties should be on 1 April 1977, and that the scheme for the limited reimbursement of candidates' election expenses should operate for all Parliamentary and relevant local government elections held on or after 1 April 1977.

The total cost of state aid to the political parties under these proposals is estimated at, on average, about £2¼ million a year. Of this, the annual grants to the parties would comprise about £1,440,000 and the reimbursement of candidates' election expenses approximately £860,000 a year (including £360,000 in respect of Parliamentary candidates and £500,000 for local government candidates).

It is proposed that the reimbursement scheme should be extended to include elections to the European Parliament and to the Scottish and Welsh Assemblies as occasion arises.

Appendix F

A Guide to Published Central Party Accounts

The Conservatives started to publish annual accounts of their central income and expenditure in 1968. The Labour and Liberal parties had already done so for many years. The accounts of all three parties, however, are incomplete and potentially misleading. They cannot be compared with one another unless important adjustments are made and extra, normally unpublished information is obtained.

Routine Spending and Campaign Spending

None of the accounts have in the past distinguished clearly or consistently between routine and campaign income and expenditure.

Conservative. The published Conservative accounts make no distinction between "routine" and "campaign" items. Campaign spending is contained within the overall total spending for the relevant year. Estimates in this book of election expenditure in 1979 and in several earlier postwar elections are based on unpublished information supplied by the Conservative Central Office.

Labour. The national executive committee of the Labour party has since before the Second World War maintained a distinct general election fund. The total yearly income and expenditure from this fund are shown in the published accounts. These figures do not reliably show spending for election purposes, however. Money from the general election fund has sometimes been used for routine purposes, and at other times money from the general fund appears to have been used for campaign purposes. Moreover, the published figures do not regularly distinguish how much money has been paid into the general election fund by trade unions, constituency Labour

320

parties, and other sources (information that is given for the general fund). Nor has there been any published breakdown of categories of election expenditure (except for the 1979 election). Finally, when two elections have occurred in one year (as in 1974), there has been no distinction in the accounts between the spending for each campaign.

Liberal. For several elections before those of 1974, the accounts of the Liberal Party Organisation simply omitted election income and spending, a fact that seems curiously to have escaped the notice of some academic researchers and also of the Houghton Committee. The LPO annual report for 1974 included a brief account, separate from the routine income and expenditure account, for each of the elections of that year, but these election accounts excluded the activities of the Direct Aid Committee and did not give a breakdown of the main headings of expenditure. The fact that the Liberal party was later obliged, in the wake of the Norman Scott affair, to set up a special committee to examine important undisclosed aspects of election finance in the 1974 elections indicated how misleading the published accounts for these elections had been. A breakdown of LPO income and expenditure in the 1979 general election appears in the 1980 annual report.

What Is Included in the Central Party Accounts?

The central accounts of the three main parties differ in their definitions of what constitutes "central party organization." The checklist in table 83 gives a guide to what appears to be included and excluded by each party.

Some Special Features

Conservative. (1) The Conservative Central Office accounts do not include the costs of fund raising. The total received as donations is thus larger than shown. (2) Since the amount reportedly received from constituencies includes notional "quota credits," the sum actually paid to the center by the local parties is slightly less than published, and the amount received in the form of central donations is slightly larger. (3) The catchall category "donations" includes contributions from companies and professional partnerships, individual gifts, and bequests. As no distinction is made between these sources, it is not possible to tell from the accounts how much has been contributed by companies.

TABLE 83

Inclusiveness of the Central Published Accounts of the Conservative, Labour, and Liberal Parties

Unit of Organization	Whether Included in the Published Annual Central Accounts		
	Conservative	Labour	Liberal
Extraparliamentary headquarters	Yes	Yes	Yes
Scottish headquarters	Yes [a]	Partly [b]	No [c]
Welsh headquarters	Yes	Partly [b]	No [c]
Regional organizations	Yes	Partly [b]	No [c, d]
Parliamentary secretariat	Yes	Partly [b]	No [e]
Party leader's office	Yes	Partly [b]	No
Special units of national organization (women, youth, local government, etc.)	Yes	Yes	No [e]
State grant to opposition parties in the House of Commons	Yes	Yes	No [f]

[a] Only since 1977/1978.

[b] Funds paid by the NEC toward these units are included in the central accounts. Extra funds raised independently by the units concerned are not included.

[c] Ad hoc subsidies to these units by the LPO are included.

[d] In the late 1960s the costs of regional federations were largely included in the LPO accounts.

[e] These costs have normally been borne by a separate unit of national organization called the Liberal Central Association (LCA).

[f] The Liberal share of the grant is not included in the accounts of the LPO but in those of the LCA. The LCA accounts, previously secret, were first published, as a separate item, in the LPO's annual report of 1979.

Labour. (1) The national executive committee (NEC) accounts are divided into a number of separate funds. The most important of these is the general fund, but, for purposes of comparison with the other parties, it is also necessary to include the annual income and expenditure of the special funds. In 1978 the special funds were the development fund, general election fund, by-election fund, deposit insurance fund, and party headquarters fund. (2) The accounts show the payments into the general fund by trade unions, constituency Labour parties, and so on. But similar information is not regularly shown for the special funds; therefore, it is not possible to tell from the published figures the total annual contribution by trade unions to the NEC.

Bibliography

Private Papers

Asquith Papers, Bodleian Library, Oxford.
Neville Chamberlain Papers, Birmingham University Library, Birmingham.
Davidson Papers, House of Lords Records Office, London.
Lloyd George Papers, House of Lords Records Office, London.
Maclean Papers, Bodleian Library, Oxford.
Medlicott Papers, in the possession of Paul Medlicott, London.
Salisbury Papers, Hatfield House, Hatfield.
Sandars Papers, Bodleian Library, Oxford.
Woolton Papers, Bodleian Library, Oxford.

Party Publications and Official Publications

All England Law Reports.
British Broadcasting Corporation. *Handbook* (issued annually). London: British Broadcasting Corporation.
British Parliamentary Papers.
Central Statistical Office. *Annual Abstract of Statistics.* London: Her Majesty's Stationery Office.
Certification Officer for Trade Unions and Employers' Associations. Annual Reports. London: Her Majesty's Stationery Office.
Chief Registrar of Friendly Societies. Annual Reports. London: Her Majesty's Stationery Office.
Committee on Financial Aid to Political Parties. *Report.* Cmnd. 6601. London: Her Majesty's Stationery Office, 1976 (Houghton Report).
Conservative and Unionist Central Office. *Central Funds of the Conservative and Unionist Party: Income and Expenditure Accounts* (contained in press releases and annual reports).

Conservative and Unionist Central Office. *Parliamentary Election Manual.* 11th ed. London: Conservative and Unionist Central Office, 1963.

General Public Acts.

Houghton Report. *See* Committee on Financial Aid to Political Parties.

House of Commons Debates.

Labour Party. Annual Reports of the National Executive Committee.

Labour Party Commission of Enquiry. *Report of the Labour Party Commission of Enquiry, 1980.* London: Labour Party, 1980.

Labour Party Research Department. *Company Donations to the Tory Party and Other Political Organisations.* Information Paper No. 4a. London: Labour Party, November 1978.

————. *Company Donations to the Tory Party and Their Allies.* Information Paper No. 8. London: Labour Party, September 1977.

————. Information Paper No. 17. London: Labour Party, September 1979.

Liberal Magazine.

Liberal News.

Liberal Party Organisation. Annual Reports to the Assembly.

National Liberal Federation. Annual Reports.

National Society of Conservative and Unionist Agents. *Conservative Agents' Journal.*

Privy Council Office. *Referendum on United Kingdom Membership of the European Community: Accounts of Campaigning Organisations.* Cmnd. 6251. London: Her Majesty's Stationery Office, 1975.

Royal Commission on Standards of Conduct in Public Life. *Report.* Cmnd. 6524. London: Her Majesty's Stationery Office, 1976 (Salmon Report).

Salmon Report. *See* Royal Commission on Standards of Conduct in Public Life.

United States Library of Congress Law Library. *Government Financing of National Elections, Political Parties, and Campaign Spending in Various Foreign Countries.* Washington, D.C.: 1979.

Books and Articles

Adamany, David W. *Campaign Finance in America.* North Scituate, Mass.: Duxbury Press, 1972.

Adamany, David W., and Agree, George E. *Political Money: A Strategy for Campaign Financing in America.* Baltimore: Johns Hopkins University Press, 1975.

Alexander, Herbert E. "Links and Contrasts among American Parties and Party Subsystems." In *Comparative Political Finance: The Financing of Party Organizations and Election Campaigns,* edited by Arnold J. Heidenheimer. Lexington, Mass.: D.C. Heath, 1970.

————. *Money in Politics*. Washington, D.C.: Public Affairs Press, 1972.

————. *Financing Politics: Money, Elections, and Political Reform*. Washington, D.C.: Congressional Quarterly Press, 1976.

————. "Political Finance Regulation in International Perspective." In *Parties, Interest Groups, and Campaign Finance Laws*, edited by Michael J. Malbin. Washington, D.C.: American Enterprise Institute, 1980.

Alexander, Herbert E., ed. *Political Finance*. Beverly Hills, Calif.: Sage Publications, 1979.

Andrew, Christopher. "The British Secret Service and Anglo-Soviet Relations in the 1920s. Part 1: From the Trade Negotiations to the Zinoviev Letter." *Historical Journal* 20 (1977).

Astor, Michael. *Tribal Feeling*. London: John Murray, 1964.

Atkinson, Norman. "Priming the Pump." *Guardian*, August 10, 1978.

Bealey, Frank, and Pelling, Henry. *Labour and Politics, 1900–1906*. London: Macmillan, 1968.

Berkeley, Humphry. "Extra Money Should Go to MPs instead of the Party." *The Times*, April 21, 1975.

Blake, Robert. *The Conservative Party from Peel to Churchill*. London: Fontana, 1972.

————. *The Unknown Prime Minister: The Life and Times of Andrew Bonar Law, 1858–1923*. London: Eyre and Spottiswoode, 1955.

Blewett, Neal. *The Peers, the Parties, and the People: The General Elections of 1910*. London: Macmillan, 1972.

Bliss, Barbara. "The Lloyd George Fund." *New Outlook*, November 1966.

Bowles, T. Gibson. "The New Corruption: The Caucus and the Sale of Honours." *Candid Quarterly Review* 1 (1914).

Brainard, Alfred P. "The Law of Elections and Business Interest Groups in Britain." *Western Political Quarterly* 13 (1960).

Briggs, Asa. *The History of Broadcasting in the United Kingdom*, Vol. 2, *The Golden Age of Wireless*. Oxford: Oxford University Press, 1965.

"British Elections Are a Bargain." *Economist*, March 2, 1974.

Brockway, Fenner. *Lloyd George and the Traffic in Honours*. London: Independent Labour Party, 1922.

Butler, David E. *The British General Election of 1951*. London: Macmillan, 1952.

————. *The Electoral System in Britain since 1918*. 2d ed. Oxford: Oxford University Press, 1963.

Butler, David E., and Freeman, Jennie. *British Political Facts, 1900–1968*. London: Macmillan, 1969.

Butler, David E., and Kavanagh, Dennis. *The British General Election of February 1974*. London: Macmillan, 1974.

————. *The British General Election of October 1974*. London: Macmillan, 1975.

————. *The British General Election of 1979*. London: Macmillan, 1980.

Butler, David E., and King, Anthony. *The British General Election of 1964*. London: Macmillan, 1965.

————. *The British General Election of 1966*. London: Macmillan, 1966.

Butler, David E., and Kitzinger, Uwe. *The 1975 Referendum*. London: Macmillan, 1976.

Butler, David E., and Pinto-Duschinsky, Michael. *The British General Election of 1970*. London: Macmillan, 1971.

————. "The Conservative Elite, 1918–1978: Does Unrepresentativeness Matter?" In *Conservative Party Politics*, edited by Zig Layton-Henry. London: Macmillan, 1980.

Butler, David E., and Rose, Richard. *The British General Election of 1959*. London: Macmillan, 1960.

Butler, David E., and Sloman, Anne. *British Political Facts, 1900–1975*. London: Macmillan, 1975.

————. *British Political Facts, 1900–1979*. London: Macmillan, 1980.

Butler, David E., and Stokes, Donald. *Political Change in Britain: Forces Shaping Electoral Choice*. London: Macmillan, 1969.

Butt, Ronald. *The Power of Parliament*. London: Constable, 1969.

Cambray, Philip G. *The Game of Politics*. London: John Murray, 1932.

Cartland, Barbara. *Ronald Cartland*. London: Hutchinson, n.d.

Chamberlain, Sir Austen. *Politics from Inside: An Epistolary Chronicle, 1906–1914*. London: Cassell, 1936.

Chester, Lewis; Fay, Stephen; and Young, Hugo. *The Zinoviev Letter*. London: Heinemann, 1967.

Chester, Lewis; Linklater, Magnus; and May, David. *Jeremy Thorpe: A Secret Life*. London: Fontana, 1979.

Chilston, Lord. "Aretas Akers-Douglas: 1st Viscount Chilston (1851–1926): A Great Whip." *Parliamentary Affairs* 15 (1961–1962).

————. *Chief Whip: The Political Life and Times of Aretas Akers-Douglas, 1st Viscount Chilston*. London: Routledge and Kegan Paul, 1961.

Chippindale, Peter, and Leigh, David. *The Thorpe Committal: The Full Story of the Minehead Proceedings*. London: Arrow Books, 1979.

Clegg, Hugh A.; Fox, Alan; and Thompson, A. F. *A History of British Trade Unions since 1889*. Oxford: Oxford University Press, 1964.

Cole, G. Douglas H., and Postgate, Raymond. *The Common People, 1746–1946*. London: Methuen, 1968.

Cook, Chris. *The Age of Alignment: Electoral Politics in Britain, 1922–1929*. London: Macmillan, 1975.

Cook, Chris, and Keith, Brendan. *British Historical Facts 1830–1900*. London: Macmillan, 1975.

Crick, Bernard. "Paying for the Parties: A Review." *Political Quarterly* 46 (1975).

Cross, Colin, ed. *Life with Lloyd George: The Diary of A. J. Sylvester, 1931–45*. London: Macmillan, 1975.

Crossman, Richard H. S. "Financing Political Parties." *Political Quarterly* 45 (1974).

Cullen, Tom. *Maundy Gregory: Purveyor of Honours*. London: Bodley Head, 1974.

Doig, Alan. "Self-Discipline in the House of Commons: The Poulson Affair in a Parliamentary Perspective." *Parliamentary Affairs* 32 (1979).

Douglas, Roy. *The History of the Liberal Party, 1895–1970*. London: Sidgwick and Jackson, 1971.

Dowson, O. F., ed. *The Powers, Duties, and Liabilities of an Election Agent and of a Returning Officer at a Parliamentary Election in England and Wales*. London: Knight, 1920.

Drewry, Gavin. "The Price of a Vote." *New Society*, November 13, 1975.

Dunn, Delmar D. *Financing Presidential Elections*. Washington, D.C.: Brookings Institution, 1972.

Ensor, Sir Robert C. K. *England, 1870–1914*. Oxford: Oxford University Press, 1936.

Erskine May. See Lidderdale, Sir David, ed.

Feuchtwanger, Edgar J. *Disraeli, Democracy, and the Tory Party: Conservative Leadership and Organization after the Second Reform Bill*. Oxford: Oxford University Press, 1968.

Finer, Samuel E. *The Changing British Party System, 1945–1979*. Washington, D.C.: American Enterprise Institute, 1980.

————. "Patronage and the Public Service: Jeffersonian Bureaucracy and the British Tradition." *Public Administration* 30 (1952).

Finer, Samuel E., ed. *Adversary Politics and Electoral Reform*. London: Wigram, 1975.

Fothergill, Philip. "Political Party Funds. III—The Liberal View." *Parliamentary Affairs* 1 (1947–1948).

Gash, Norman. *Politics in the Age of Peel*. London: Longman, 1953; and Hassocks, Sussex: Harvester Press, 1977.

Geddes, Sir Reay. "The Finance of Political Parties." *Political Quarterly* 45 (1974).

Gilbert, Martin. *Winston S. Churchill.* Vol. 5, *1922–1939.* London: Heinemann, 1976.

Gillard, M., and Foot, Paul. *A Little Pot of Gold: The Story of Reginald Maudling and the Real Estate Fund of America.* London: Private Eye and André Deutsch, 1974.

Greenwood, Arthur. "Party Political Funds. I—The Labour View." *Parliamentary Affairs* 1 (1947–1948).

Gwyn, William B. *Democracy and the Cost of Politics in Britain, 1832–1959.* London: Athlone Press, 1962.

Hailsham, Lord, ed. *Halsbury's Laws of England.* 4th ed. Vols. 8 and 15. London: Butterworth's, 1974 and 1977.

Haines, Joe. *The Politics of Power.* London: Hodder and Stoughton, 1977.

Halévy, Elie. *A History of the English People in the Nineteenth Century.* Vol. 6, *The Rule of Democracy, 1905–1914.* 2d rev. ed. London: Ernest Benn, 1952.

Halsey, Albert H., ed. *Trends in British Society since 1900.* London: Macmillan, 1972.

Hanham, Harold J. "British Party Finance, 1868–1880." *Bulletin of the Institute of Historical Research* 127 (1954).

————. *Elections and Party Management: Politics in the Time of Disraeli and Gladstone.* London: Longman, 1959; and Hassocks, Sussex: Harvester Press, 1978.

————. *The Nineteenth-Century Constituton: Documents and Commentary.* Cambridge: Cambridge University Press, 1969.

————. "The Sale of Honours in Late Victorian England." *Victorian Studies* 3 (1960).

Harrison, Martin. "Britain." In "Comparative Political Finance: A Symposium," edited by Richard Rose and Arnold J. Heidenheimer. *Journal of Politics* 25 (1963).

————. *Trade Unions and the Labour Party since 1945.* London: Allen and Unwin, 1960.

Hartwell, Max. "Committees of the House of Commons, 1800–1850," unpublished article.

Heard, Alexander. *The Costs of Democracy.* Chapel Hill: University of North Carolina Press, 1960.

Heidenheimer, Arnold J. "Major Modes of Raising, Spending, and Controlling Political Funds during and between Election Campaigns." In *Comparative Political Finance: The Financing of Party Organizations and Election Campaigns,* edited by Arnold J. Heidenheimer. Lexington, Mass.: D.C. Heath, 1970.

Heidenheimer, Arnold J., ed. *Comparative Political Finance: The Financing of Party Organizations and Election Campaigns.* Lexington, Mass.: D.C. Heath, 1970.

Hill, A. P. "The Effect of Party Organisation: Election Expenses and the 1970 Election." *Political Studies* 22 (1974).

Hoffman, John D. *The Conservative Party in Opposition, 1945–51.* London: MacGibbon and Kee, 1964.

Howard, Anthony. "Political Parties and Public Funds." *New Statesman*, September 3, 1976.

Hughes, D., and Kogan, D. "Norman's Cheap Conquest." *New Statesman*, December 14, 1979.

Hurd, Douglas. "Don't Subsidise Politics." *Observer*, July 15, 1973.

————. "If Politics Goes on the Welfare." *Daily Telegraph*, August 27, 1976.

Jacobson, Gary C. *Money in Congressional Elections.* New Haven, Conn.: Yale University Press, 1980.

————. "Practical Consequences of Campaign Finance Reform: An Incumbent Protection Act?" *Public Policy* 24 (1976).

Jennings, Ivor. *Party Politics.* Vol. 1, *Appeal to the People.* Cambridge: Cambridge University Press, 1960.

Johnston, R. J. "Campaign Expenditure and the Efficacy of Advertising at the 1974 General Election in England." *Political Studies* 27 (1979).

King, Anthony. "Politics, Economics, and the Trade Unions, 1974–1979." In *Britain at the Polls, 1979: A Study of the General Election,* edited by Howard R. Penniman. Washington, D.C.: American Enterprise Institute, 1981.

Labour Research Department. *Labour Research.* London: Labour Research Department.

Laski, Harold. "The Prime Ministers' Honours Lists." *Nation*, July 15, 1922.

Layton-Henry, Zig. "The Young Conservatives, 1945–70." *Journal of Contemporary History* 8 (1973).

Leonard, Dick (R. L.). "Contrasts in Selected Western Democracies: Germany, Sweden, Britain." In *Political Finance,* edited by Herbert E. Alexander. Beverly Hills, Calif.: Sage Publications, 1979.

————. *Elections in Britain.* Princeton, N.J.: Van Nostrand, 1968.

————. "Paying for Our Politics." *Observer*, May 13, 1973.

————. *Paying for Party Politics: The Case for Public Subsidies.* Broadsheet no. 555, vol. 41. London: Political and Economic Planning, 1975.

Lidderdale, Sir David, ed. *Erskine May's Treatise on the Law, Privileges, Proceedings, and Usage of Parliament.* 19th ed. London: Butterworth's, 1976.

Lloyd, Trevor O. *The General Election of 1880.* Oxford: Oxford University Press, 1968.

————. "Uncontested Seats in British General Elections, 1852–1910." *Historical Journal* 8 (1965).

————. "The Whip as Paymaster: Herbert Gladstone and Party Organisation." *English Historical Review* 89 (1974).

Lowell, A. Lawrence. *The Government of England.* New York: Macmillan, 1908.

McCormick, Donald. *Murder by Perfection: Maundy Gregory, the Man behind Two Unsolved Mysteries?* London: Long John, 1970.

McGill, Barry. "Francis Schnadhorst and Liberal Party Organisation." *Journal of Modern History* 34 (1962).

McKenzie, Robert T. *British Political Parties: The Distribution of Power within the Conservative and Labour Parties.* London: Mercury Books, 1964.

McKibbin, Ross. *The Evolution of the Labour Party, 1910–1924.* Oxford: Oxford University Press, 1974.

Macmillan, Gerald. *Honours for Sale: The Strange Story of Maundy Gregory.* London: Richards Press, 1954.

Malbin, Michael J., ed. *Parties, Interest Groups, and Campaign Finance Laws.* Washington, D.C.: American Enterprise Institute, 1980.

Mallet, Sir Charles. *Herbert Gladstone: A Memoir.* London: Hutchinson, 1932.

————. *Mr. Lloyd George: A Study.* London: Ernest Benn, 1930.

Marquand, David. *Ramsay MacDonald.* London: Cape, 1977.

Marsh, P. T. *The Discipline of Popular Government: Lord Salisbury's Domestic Statecraft, 1881–1902.* Atlantic Highlands, N.J.: Humanities Press, 1978.

Marshall, Geoffrey. "The House of Commons and Its Privileges." In *The House of Commons in the Twentieth Century: Essays by Members of the Study of Parliament Group,* edited by S. A. Walkland. Oxford: Oxford University Press, 1979.

Matthew, H. Colin G. *The Liberal Imperialists.* Oxford: Oxford University Press, 1973.

May, Timothy. "Paying for Party Politics." *Political Quarterly* 48 (1977).

Medlicott, Sir Frank. "Finance Report: The Challenges Ahead." *Liberal News,* July 9, 1970.

Michels, Robert. *Political Parties: A Sociological Study of the Oligarchical Tendencies of Modern Democracy.* New York: Dover, 1959.

Milne, Edward J. *No Shining Armour: The Story of One Man's Fight against Corruption in Public Life.* London: John Calder, 1976.

Minkin, Lewis. *The Labour Party Conference: A Study of Intra-Party Democracy.* London: Allen Lane, 1978.

Muir, Ramsay. *How Britain Is Governed*. London: Constable, 1930.

Muller, William D. *The Kept Men? The First Century of Trade Union Representation in the British House of Commons*. Atlantic Highlands, N.J.: Humanities Press, 1977.

Newman, Frank C. "Money and Elections Law in Britain—Guide for America?" *Western Political Quarterly* 10 (1957).

————. "Reflections on Money and Politics in Britain." *Parliamentary Affairs* 10 (1956–1957).

Nicholas, Herbert G. *The British General Election of 1950*. London: Macmillan, 1951.

Noel-Baker, Francis. "'The Grey Zone': The Problems of Business Affiliations of Members of Parliament." *Parliamentary Affairs* 15 (1961–1962).

O'Leary, Cornelius. *The Elimination of Corrupt Practices in British Elections, 1868–1911*. Oxford: Oxford University Press, 1962.

Ostrogorski, Moisei. *Democracy and the Organization of Political Parties*. London: Macmillan, 1902.

Owen, Frank. *Tempestuous Journey: Lloyd George, His Life and Times*. London: Hutchinson, 1954.

Page Arnot, R. *The Miners: A History of the Miners' Federation of Great Britain, 1889–1910*. London: Allen and Unwin, 1949.

————. *The Miners: Years of Struggle, a History of the Miners' Federation of Great Britain (from 1910 Onwards)*. London: Allen and Unwin, 1953.

Paltiel, Khayyam Z. "Campaign Finance: Contrasting Practices and Reforms." In *Democracy at the Polls: A Comparative Study of Competitive National Elections*, edited by David E. Butler, Howard R. Penniman, and Austin Ranney. Washington, D.C.: American Enterprise Institute, 1981.

————. "The Impact of Election Expenses Legislation in Canada, Western Europe, and Israel." In *Political Finance*, edited by Herbert E. Alexander. Beverly Hills, Calif.: Sage Publications, 1979.

————. "Public Financing Abroad: Contrasts and Effects." In *Parties, Interest Groups, and Campaign Finance Laws*, edited by Michael J. Malbin. Washington, D.C.: American Enterprise Institute, 1980.

Pardoe, John. "The Penny-Pinching Which Hurts Democracy." *The Times*, October 13, 1969.

————. "A Voluntary Tax Plan to Finance Elections." *The Times*, October 14, 1969.

————. "Why a Fresh Injection of Cash Is Needed to Avoid Political Penny-Pinching." *The Times*, March 20, 1975.

"Paying for Politics." *Economist*, September 13, 1975.

Pelling, Henry. *The Origins of the Labour Party, 1880–1900*. Oxford: Oxford University Press, 1966.

"Pennies from Brussels." *Economist,* January 27, 1979.

Penniman, Howard R., and Winter, Ralph K., Jr. *Campaign Finances: Two Views of the Political and Constitutional Implications.* Washington, D.C.: American Enterprise Institute, 1971.

Penrose, Barrie, and Courtiour, Roger. *The Pencourt File.* London: Secker and Warburg, 1978.

Pierssené, S. H. "Political Party Funds. II—The Conservative View." *Parliamentary Affairs* 1 (1947-1948).

Pinto-Duschinsky, Michael. "Britain: The Problem of Non-Campaign Finance." Paper presented to the Conference on Political Money. Los Angeles: University of Southern California, 1977.

————. "Britain's General Election: Labour Funds Are Catching Up." *Economist,* November 11, 1978.

————. "Central Office and 'Power' in the Conservative Party." *Political Studies* 20 (1972).

————. "The Conservative Campaign: New Techniques versus Old." In *Britain at the Polls: The Parliamentary Elections of 1974,* edited by Howard R. Penniman. Washington, D.C.: American Enterprise Institute, 1975.

————. "Financing the British General Election of 1979." In *Britain at the Polls, 1979: A Study of the General Election,* edited by Howard R. Penniman. Washington, D.C.: American Enterprise Institute, 1981.

————. "The Limits of Professional Influence: A Study of Constituency Agents in the British Conservative Party." Paper presented to the colloquium on party professionals. Paris: Association Française de Science Politique, 1977.

————. "No Handouts Needed." *The Times,* November 9, 1978.

————. "The Role of Constituency Associations in the Conservative Party." D.Phil. thesis, Oxford University, 1972.

————. "These Bogus Arguments for Coming to the Aid of the Political Parties." *The Times,* September 7, 1976.

————. "What Should Be the Cost of a Vote?" *The Times,* March 10, 1980.

————. "Why Public Subsidies Have Become Major Sources of Party Funds in West Germany but Not in Great Britain." In *Comparative Political Finance: The Financing of Party Organizations and Election Campaigns,* edited by Arnold J. Heidenheimer. Lexington, Mass.: D.C. Heath, 1970.

Pollock, James K. *Money and Politics Abroad.* New York: Knopf, 1932.

Pulzer, Peter G. J. *Political Representation and Elections in Britain.* London: Allen and Unwin, 1967.   .

Punnett, R. Malcolm. *Front-Bench Opposition: The Role of the*

Leader of the Opposition, the Shadow Cabinet, and Shadow Government in British Politics. London: Heinemann, 1973.

Ramsden, John A. *The Age of Balfour and Baldwin, 1902–1940.* London: Longman, 1979.

————. "The Organisation of the Conservative and Unionist Party in Britain, 1910–1930." D.Phil. thesis, Oxford University, 1974.

Rasmussen, Jorgen. *Retrenchment and Revival: A Study of the Contemporary Liberal Party.* Tucson: University of Arizona Press, 1964.

Redlich, Josef. *The Procedure of the House of Commons.* London: Constable, 1908.

Rhodes James, Robert. *Memoirs of a Conservative: J. C. C. Davidson's Memoirs and Papers, 1910–37.* London: Weidenfeld and Nicolson, 1969.

Rose, Richard. *Influencing Voters: A Study of Campaign Rationality.* London: Faber, 1967.

————. "Money and Election Law." *Political Studies* 9 (1961).

————. "Pre-Election Public Relations and Advertising." In *The British General Election of 1964,* by David E. Butler and Anthony King. London: Macmillan, 1965.

————. *The Problem of Party Government.* New York: Free Press, 1975.

Rose, Richard, and Heidenheimer, Arnold J., eds. "Comparative Political Finance: A Symposium." *Journal of Politics* 25 (1963).

Roth, Andrew. *Sir Harold Wilson: Yorkshire Walter Mitty.* London: Macdonald and Jane's, 1977.

Seidle, F. Leslie D. "Electoral Law and the Limitation of Election Expenditure in Great Britain and Canada." B.Phil. thesis, Oxford University, 1978.

————. "State Aid for Political Parties." *Parliamentarian* 61 (1980).

Seymour-Ure, Colin. *The Political Impact of Mass Media.* London: Constable, 1974.

Sommer, R. M. "The Organization of the Liberal Party, 1936–1960." Ph.D. thesis, London School of Economics, 1962.

Spender, John A. *Sir Robert Hudson.* London: Cassell, 1930.

Steed, Michael. "Report on the Liberal Party of the United Kingdom of Great Britain and Northern Ireland." Paper presented to the colloquium on party professionals. Paris: Association Française de Science Politique, 1977.

Stewart, Robert. *The Foundation of the Conservative Party, 1830–1867.* London: Longman, 1978.

"A Stitch in Time—What Houghton Proposes." *Economist,* August 28, 1976.

Stokes, Donald E. "Parties and the Nationalization of Electoral

Forces." In *The American Party Systems: Stages of Development*, edited by William N. Chambers and Walter D. Burnham. Oxford: Oxford University Press, 1967.

Storer, Donald. *Conduct of Parliamentary Elections.* 8th ed. London: Labour Party, 1977.

Taylor, A. H. "The Effect of Party Organization: Correlation between Campaign Expenditure and Voting in the 1970 Election." *Political Studies* 20 (1972).

Taylor, A. J. P. *Beaverbrook.* London: Hamish Hamilton, 1972.

Vijay, K. I. "The Declaration of Interests by MPs: An Analysis of the Current Campaign for Reform." *Political Quarterly* 14 (1973).

Vincent, John R. *The Formation of the Liberal Party, 1857–1868.* London: Constable, 1966.

Vincent, John R., and Cooke, Alistair B. *The Governing Passion: Cabinet Government and Party Politics in Britain, 1885–1886.* Hassocks, Sussex: Harvester Press, 1974.

Walker, David. "Should the Political Parties Get a Subsidy from the Taxpayers' Pocket?" *The Times*, August 27, 1976.

Wallace, William. "The Liberal Revival: The Liberal Party in Britain, 1955–1966." Ph.D. dissertation, Cornell University, 1968.

Webb, Beatrice. *Our Partnership,* edited by Barbara Drake and Margaret I. Cole. London: Longman, 1948.

"Who's Going to Pay for the Parties?" *Economist*, April 27, 1974.

"Will the State Cough Up?" *Economist*, March 15, 1975.

Williams, Francis. *Dangerous Estate: The Anatomy of Newspapers.* London: Longman, 1957.

Wilson, David J., and Pinto-Duschinsky, Michael. "Conservative Party City Machines: The End of an Era." *British Journal of Political Science* 6 (1976).

Wilson, John. *CB: A Life of Sir Henry Campbell-Bannerman.* London: Constable, 1973.

Wilson, Trevor G. *The Downfall of the Liberal Party, 1914–1935.* London: Collins, 1966.

Winter, Ralph K., Jr. *Campaign Financing and Political Freedom.* Washington, D.C.: American Enterprise Institute, 1973.

Wintour, Patrick. "Bankrupt and Bruised." *New Statesman*, September 28, 1979.

Wollaston, H. W., ed. *Parker's Conduct of Parliamentary Elections.* London: Charles Knight, 1970.

Wood, David. "MPs' Pay and Growth of Expenses." *The Times*, July 31, 1978.

Woolton, Lord. *Memoirs.* London: Cassell, 1959.

Yates, Ivan. "Public Men, Private Interests." *Observer*, July 9, 1972.

Index

AEI's *At the Polls* Studies

Australia at the Polls: The National Elections of 1975, Howard R. Penniman, ed. Chapters by Leon D. Epstein, Patrick Weller, R. F. I. Smith, D. W. Rawson, Michelle Grattan, Margaret Bridson Cribb, Paul Reynolds, C. J. Lloyd, Terence W. Beed, Owen Harries, and Colin A. Hughes. Appendixes by David Butler and Richard M. Scammon. (373 pp.)

The Australian National Elections of 1977, Howard R. Penniman, ed. Chapters by David Butler, David A. Kemp, Patrick Weller, Jean Holmes, Paul Reynolds, Murray Goot, Terence W. Beed, C. J. Lloyd, Ainsley Jolley, Duncan Ironmonger, and Colin A. Hughes. Appendix by Richard M. Scammon. (367 pp.)

Britain at the Polls: The Parliamentary Elections of 1974, Howard R. Penniman, ed. Chapters by Anthony King, Austin Ranney, Dick Leonard, Michael Pinto-Duschinsky, Richard Rose, and Jay G. Blumler. Appendix by Richard M. Scammon. (256 pp.)

Britain Says Yes: The 1975 Referendum on the Common Market, Anthony King. (153 pp.)

Britain at the Polls, 1979: A Study of the General Election, Howard R. Penniman, ed. Chapters by Austin Ranney, Anthony King, Dick Leonard, William B. Livingston, Jorgen Rasmussen, Richard Rose, Michael Pinto-Duschinsky, Monica Charlot, and Ivor Crewe. Appendixes by Shelley Pinto-Duschinsky and Richard M. Scammon. (345 pp.)

Canada at the Polls: The General Election of 1974, Howard R. Penniman, ed. Chapters by John Meisel, William P. Irvine, Stephen Clarkson, George Perlin, Jo Surich, Michael B. Stein, Khayyam Z. Paltiel, Lawrence LeDuc, and Frederick J. Fletcher. Appendix by Richard M. Scammon. (310 pp.)

France at the Polls: The Presidential Election of 1974, Howard R. Penniman, ed. Chapters by Roy Pierce, J. Blondel, Jean Charlot, Serge Hurtig, Marie-Thérèse Lancelot, Alain Lancelot, Alfred Grosser, and Monica Charlot. Appendix by Richard M. Scammon. (324 pp.)

The French National Assembly Elections of 1978, Howard R. Penniman, ed. Chapters by Roy Pierce, Jérôme Jaffré, Jean Charlot, George Lavau, Roland Cayrol, Monica Charlot, and Jeane J. Kirkpatrick. Appendix by Richard M. Scammon. (255 pp.)

Germany at the Polls: The Bundestag Election of 1976, Karl H. Cerny, ed. Chapters by Gerhard Loewenberg, David P. Conradt, Kurt Sontheimer, Heino Kaack, Werner Kaltefleiter, Paul Noack, Klaus Schönbach, Rulolf Wildenmann, and Max Kaase. Appendix by Richard M. Scammon. (251 pp., $7.25)

Greece at the Polls: The National Elections of 1974 and 1977, Howard R. Penniman, ed. Chapters by Roy C. Macridis, Phaedo Vegleris, J. C. Loulis, Thanos Veremis, Angelos Elephantis, Michalis Papayannakis, and Theodore Couloumbis. Appendix by Richard M. Scammon. (220 pp., cloth $15.25, paper $7.25)

India at the Polls: The Parliamentary Elections of 1977, Myron Weiner. (150 pp., $6.25)

Ireland at the Polls: The Dáil Elections of 1977, Howard R. Penniman, ed. Chapters by Basil Chubb, Richard Sinnott, Maurice Manning, and Brian Farrell. Appendixes by Basil Chubb and Richard M. Scammon. (199 pp., $6.25)

Israel at the Polls: The Knesset Election of 1977, Howard R. Penniman, ed. Chapters by Daniel J. Elazar, Avraham Brichta, Asher Arian, Benjamin Akzin, Myron J. Aronoff, Efraim Torgovnik, Elyakim Rubinstein, Leon Boim, Judith Elizur, Elihu Katz, and Bernard Reich. Appendix by Richard M. Scammon. (333 pp., $8.25)

Italy at the Polls: The Parliamentary Elections of 1976, Howard R. Penniman, ed. Chapters by Joseph LaPalombara, Douglas Wertman, Giacomo Sani, Giuseppe Di Palma, Stephen Hellman, Gianfranco Pasquino, Robert Leonardi, William E. Porter, Robert D. Putnam, and Samuel H. Barnes. Appendix by Richard M. Scammon. (386 pp., $5.75)

Italy at the Polls, 1979: A Study of the Parliamentary Elections, Howard R. Penniman, ed. Chapters by Sidney Tarrow, Giacomo Sani, Douglas A. Wertman, Joseph LaPalombara, Gianfranco Pasquino, Robert Leonardi, Patrick McCarthy, Karen Beckwith, William E. Porter, and Samuel H. Barnes. Appendixes by Douglas A. Wertman and Richard M. Scammon. (335 pp., cloth $16.25, paper $8.25)

Japan at the Polls: The House of Councillors Election of 1974, Michael K. Blaker, ed. Chapters by Herbert Passin, Gerald L. Curtis, and Michael K. Blaker. (157 pp., $3)

A Season of Voting: The Japanese Elections of 1976 and 1977, Herbert Passin, ed. Chapters by Herbert Passin, Michael Blaker, Gerald L. Curtis, Nisihira Sigeki, and Kato Hirohisa. (199 pp.)

New Zealand at the Polls: The General Election of 1978, Howard R. Penniman, ed. Chapters by Stephen Levine, Keith Ovenden, Alan McRobie, Keith Jackson, Gilbert Antony Wood, Roderic Alley, Colin C. James, Brian Murphy, Les Cleveland, Judith Aitken, and Nigel S. Roberts. Appendix by Richard M. Scammon. (295 pp.)

Scandinavia at the Polls: Recent Political Trends in Denmark, Norway, and Sweden, Karl H. Cerny, ed. Chapters by Ole Borre, Henry Valen, Willy Martinussen, Bo Särlvik, Daniel Tarschys, Erik Allardt, Steen Sauerberg, Niels Thomsen, C. G. Uhr, Göran Ohlin, and Walter Galenson. (304 pp.)

Venezuela at the Polls: The National Elections of 1978, Howard R. Penniman, ed. Chapters by John D. Martz, Henry Wells, Robert E. O'Connor, David J. Myers, Donald L. Herman, and David Blank. Appendix by Richard M. Scammon. (287 pp.)

Democracy at the Polls: A Comparative Study of Competitive National Elections, David Butler, Howard R. Penniman, and Austin Ranney, eds. Chapters by David Butler, Arend Lijphart, Leon D. Epstein, Austin Ranney, Howard R. Penniman, Khayyam Zev Paltiel, Anthony Smith, Dennis Kavanagh, Ivor Crewe, Donald E. Stokes, Anthony King, and Jeane J. Kirkpatrick. (367 pp.)

Referendums: A Comparative Study of Practice and Theory, David Butler and Austin Ranney, eds. Chapters by Jean-François Aubert, Austin Ranney, Eugene C. Lee, Don Aitkin, Vincent Wright, Sten Sparre Nilson, Maurice Manning, and David Butler. (250 pp.)

At the Polls studies are forthcoming on the latest national elections in Australia, Belgium, Canada, Denmark, France, Germany, India, Ireland, Israel, Jamaica, Japan, the Netherlands, Norway, Portugal, Spain, Sweden, and Switzerland; and cross-national volumes on the first elections to the European Parliament, women in electoral politics, candidate selection, and the parties of the left are under way.

See also the first in a new series of studies of American elections edited by Austin Ranney:

The American Elections of 1980, Austin Ranney, ed. Chapters by Austin Ranney, Nelson W. Polsby, Charles O. Jones, Michael J. Malbin, Albert R. Hunt, Michael J. Robinson, William Schneider, Thomas E. Mann and Norman J. Ornstein, Anthony King, and Aaron Wildavsky. Statistical appendix. (391 pp.)

A Note on the Book

The typeface used for the text of this book is
Palatino, designed by Hermann Zapf.
The type was set by
Hendricks-Miller Typographic Company, of Washington, D.C.
Thomson-Shore, Inc., of Dexter, Michigan, printed
and bound the book, using
Warren's Olde Style paper.
The cover and format were designed by Pat Taylor,
and the figures were drawn by Hordür Karlsson.
The manuscript was edited by Jennifer Sparks and
by Gertrude Kaplan, of the AEI Publications staff.

SELECTED AEI PUBLICATIONS

Public Opinion, published bimonthly (one year, $18; two years, $34; single copy, $3.50)

A Conversation with Michael Novak and Richard Schifter: Human Rights and the United Nations (25 pp., $2.25)

Reconciliation and the Congressional Budget Process, Allen Schick (47 pp., $4.25)

Whom Do Judges Represent? John Charles Daly, mod. (31 pp., $3.75)

The Urban Crisis: Can Grass-Roots Groups Succeed Where Government Has Failed? John Charles Daly, mod. (25 pp., $3.75)

Italy at the Polls, 1979: A Study of the Parliamentary Elections, Howard R. Penniman, ed. (335 pp., paper $8.25, cloth $16.25)

Greece at the Polls: The National Elections of 1974 and 1977, Howard R. Penniman, ed. (220 pp., paper $7.25, cloth $15.25)

The American Elections of 1980, Austin Ranney, ed. (391 pp., paper $8.25, cloth $16.25)

The New Congress, Thomas E. Mann and Norman J. Ornstein, eds. (400 pp., paper $9.25, cloth $17.25)

Youth Crime and Urban Policy: A View from the Inner City, Robert L. Woodson, ed. (154 pp., paper $6.25, cloth $14.25)

Prices subject to change without notice.

AEI ASSOCIATES PROGRAM

The American Enterprise Institute invites your participation in the competition of ideas through its AEI Associates Program. This program has two objectives:

The first is to broaden the distribution of AEI studies, conferences, forums, and reviews, and thereby to extend public familiarity with the issues. AEI Associates receive regular information on AEI research and programs, and they can order publications and cassettes at a savings.

The second objective is to increase the research activity of the American Enterprise Institute and the dissemination of its published materials to policy makers, the academic community, journalists, and others who help shape public attitudes. Your contribution, which in most cases is partly tax deductible, will help ensure that decision makers have the benefit of scholarly research on the practical options to be considered before programs are formulated. The issues studied by AEI include:

- Defense Policy
- Economic Policy
- Energy Policy
- Foreign Policy
- Government Regulation
- Health Policy
- Legal Policy
- Political and Social Processes
- Social Security and Retirement Policy
- Tax Policy

For more information, write to:

AMERICAN ENTERPRISE INSTITUTE
1150 Seventeenth Street, N.W.
Washington, D.C. 20036